BLACK+DECKER™

THE BOOK OF
HOME HOW-TO

COMPLETE PHOTO GUIDE TO HOME REPAIR & IMPROVEMENT

COOL SPRINGS PRESS
Home and Garden Experts™

MINNEAPOLIS, MINNESOTA

COOL
SPRINGS
PRESS
Home and Garden Experts

First published in 2014 by Cool Springs Press, a member of the Quayside Publishing Group, 400 First Avenue North, Suite 400, Minneapolis, MN 55401

Cool Springs Press titles are also available at discounts in bulk quantity for industrial or sales-promotional use. For details write to Special Sales Manager at Cool Springs Press, 400 First Avenue North, Suite 400, Minneapolis, MN 55401 USA. To find out more about our books, visit us online at www.coolspringspress.com.

Library of Congress Cataloging-in-Publication Data

The book of home how-to : the complete photo guide to home repair & improvement / Black & Decker.
    pages cm
  Summary: " Clear, step-by-step instructions with full-color photography show how to accomplish the most common home repair, maintenance and improvement tasks. A complete homeowners manual for jobs that cover every part of the home, including electrical, plumbing, flooring, walls, windows and doors, kitchens, bathrooms, cabinetry, garages, basements, and exteriors." -- Provided by publisher.
  ISBN 978-1-59186-598-8 (hardback)
  1. Dwellings--Maintenance and repair--Amateurs' manuals. I. Black & Decker Corporation (Towson, Md.)

  TH4817.3.B64 2014
  643'.7--dc23

                                    2013047686

Acquisitions Editor: Mark Johanson
Design Manager: Brad Springer
Layout: Danielle Smith
Front Cover Design: Matthew Simmons

Printed in China
10 9 8 7 6 5 4 3 2 1

The Book of Home How-To
Created by: The Editors of Cool Springs Press, in cooperation with BLACK+DECKER.
BLACK+DECKER® is a trademark of The BLACK+DECKER Corporation and is used under license.

CONTENTS

▶ **In a Hurry? See the "Keywords" on pages 584 to 589** ▸

Cabinets & Countertops

Exterior

Floors

CONTENTS (CONT.)

Windows & Doors

Wiring

INTRODUCTION

The Book of Home How-To is not just another big book of home improvement and repair subjects. The world is full of these already and they are all more or less the same: You'll find a chapter on wiring, a chapter on plumbing, another chapter on flooring, one on trim carpentry, and on and on. And that's fine—it's the way these books have always been done. But we've realized that this approach no longer fits with the way we search for information today. So we have done away with the traditional "drop-down menu" way of searching and gotten back to basics: alphabetical listings.

Need to know how to replace a shingle? You'll find the information you need under "S" for "Shingles." Need to install a toilet? You can go the Table of Contents and look for the toilet listing among the Plumbing entries. Or, you can simply flip through to the "T" section of the book and there you'll find "Toilets," located right between "Tile" and "Trim." If you're not sure what to call your project (is it "Installing carpet" or "Carpet installation"?) you can find a direct page reference to either (and many more) in our handy list of Keywords starting on page 584.

We're very excited about this new way of organizing and presenting home improvement information. We believe you will find it to be intuitive and extremely easy to use, especially in those situations where you simply want to get to the point as quickly as possible. But here's the real reason you'll be glad to have this book in your home: once you find the material you're looking for, you will be amazed by the quality and depth of the information. We may have based our organization of the book on how most of us search for information online, but luckily we did not base our information on what you'll find online. With crystal-clear how-to photos and complete step-by-step instructions. *The Book of Home How-To* is as reliably instructive as it is heavy. From plumbing to wiring to home repair, every DIY project in this book has been produced by experts under the watchful eye of BLACK+DECKER, the most trusted name in home DIY. That's why, for over 25 years, BLACK+DECKER has been the most trusted name in DIY books, too.

BASEMENT FLOORS

Preparing a concrete floor for carpet, laminate, vinyl, or wood flooring has been simplified by the introduction of new subfloor products that have built-in vapor barriers and cleats that create a slight air gap between the subfloor and the concrete slab. This system allows air to circulate, protecting the finished flooring from any slab moisture. The new dry-floor subfloor systems are less than one inch thick and are very easy to install. There are several types of these dry-floor systems available, but the one most readily available and easiest to use is a product sold in 2 × 2 feet tongue-and-groove squares.

Although subfloor panels can be adjusted for slight irregularities in the concrete slab, they can't overcome problems with a floor that is badly cracked and heaved. Nor is the built-in air gap beneath the system a solution to a basement that has serious water problems. A badly heaved slab will need to be leveled with a cement-based leveling compound, and serious water problems will need to be rectified before you consider creating finished living space in a basement.

Allow the subfloor panel squares to acclimate in the basement for at least 24 hours with the plastic surfaces facing down before installing them. In humid summer months, the squares—as well as the finished wood flooring product, if that's what you'll be installing—should be allowed to acclimate for a full two weeks before installation.

The old way of installing subfloor (plywood over 2 × 4 sleepers) does make a sturdy floor and has the advantage of not requiring any special products—you can do it with materials found at any building center.

Instead of a subfloor and plywood underlayment, some flooring requires an isolation layer to separate it from the concrete basement floor. These are most often installed with ceramic floors.

If your concrete basement floor has cracks, holes, or other imperfections, address them before installing flooring.

Shown cutaway for clarity

Wood laminate flooring

Dry-floor subfloor square

Underlayment

Basement slab

Concrete basement floors have a high utility value, but whenever possible you'll want to cover them to improve livability in your new basement rooms. Some floor coverings can be installed directly over the concrete, but in most cases you should lay subfloor panels and underlayment before installing the floor covering. A system like the one above is ideal for basements because it can be removed readily: the laminate strip flooring snaps together and apart; the underlayment is unbonded and can be rolled up; and the subfloor panels also are snap-together for easy removal and re-laying.

Apply Floor Leveler ▸

Use floor leveler mix or a mortar mixture to fill in small dips in the concrete floor.

LEVELING BASEMENT FLOORS

Level line

Laser level

Test the floor to see how level it is. Use a laser level to project a level line on all walls. Mark the line and then measure down to the floor. Compare measurements to determine if floor is level. If you are installing a subfloor you can correct the unevenness by shimming under low areas. But if the floor height varies by more than an inch or two (not uncommon), you should pour floor leveler compound in the low areas. In more extreme examples you'll need to resurface the entire floor.

Break up and remove very high areas or eruptions, and patch the area with concrete that is leveled with the surrounding surfaces. Use a rental jack hammer to break up the concrete. A hand maul and cold chisel also may be used if the area is not too large: most concrete basement floors are only 3 to 4" thick.

Grind down high spots if they are small and far apart. A rented concrete grinder makes quick work of the job. Even larger areas can be ground down, if your ceiling height is already limited (less than 7 ft.).

HOW TO REPAIR FLOOR CRACKS

Prepare the crack for the repair materials by knocking away any loose or deteriorating material and beveling the edges down and outward with a cold chisel. Sweep or vacuum the debris and thoroughly dampen the repair area. Do not allow any water to pool, however.

Mix the repair product to fill the crack according to the manufacturer's instructions. Here, a fast-setting cement repair product with acrylic fortifier is being used. Trowel the product into the crack, overfilling slightly. With the edge of the trowel, trim the excess material and feather it so it is smooth and the texture matches the surrounding surface.

HOW TO PATCH A SMALL HOLE

Cut out around the damaged area with a masonry-grinding disc mounted on a portable drill (or use a hammer and stone chisel). The cuts should bevel about 15° away from the center of the damaged area. Chisel out any loose concrete within the repair area. Always wear gloves and eye protection.

Dampen the repair area with clean water and then fill it with vinyl concrete patcher. Pack the material in with a trowel, allowing it to crown slightly above the surrounding surface. Then, feather the edges so the repair is smooth and flat. Protect the repair from foot traffic for at least one day and from vehicle traffic for three days.

HOW TO PATCH A LARGE HOLE

Use a hammer and chisel or a heavy floor scraper to remove all material that is loose or shows any deterioration. Thoroughly clean the area with a hose and nozzle or a pressure washer.

OPTION: Make beveled cuts around the perimeter of the repair area with a circular saw and masonry-cutting blade. The bevels should slant down and away from the damage to create a "key" for the repair material.

Mix concrete patching compound according to the manufacturer's instructions, and then trowel it neatly into the damage area, which should be dampened before the patching material is placed. Overfill the damage area slightly.

Smooth and feather the repair with a steel trowel so it is even with the surrounding concrete surface. Finish the surface of the repair material to blend with the existing surface. For example, use a whisk broom to recreate a broomed finish. Protect the repair from foot traffic for at least one day and from vehicle traffic for three days.

BASEMENTS: INSULATING

Insulating basements is a tricky topic. In colder climates, insulation is necessary for the successful creation of a livable basement room. But the practice is fraught with pitfalls that can cause a host of problems. But here are two pieces of advice that are certain:

- The exterior wall is a far better location for new insulation than the interior foundation walls.
- Never insulate a wall that is not dry and well drained.

Almost all of the issues surrounding basement wall insulation have to do with moisture and water vapor. How these issues affect your plans will depend a great deal on your climate, as well as on the specific characteristics of your house, your building site, and whether or not your home was built with foundation drains and a pumping system.

Until recently, basements most often were insulated from the inside because it is easier, faster, and cheaper. A typical installation would be to attach furring strips (2 × 2, 2 × 3, or 2 × 4) to the foundation wall at standard wall stud spacing, and then fill in between the strips with fiberglass insulation batts. A sheet plastic vapor barrier would then be stapled over the insulated wall prior to hanging wallcoverings (usually wallboard or paneling). Experience has shown this model to be a poor method, very frequently leading to moisture buildup within the wall that encourages mold growth and has a negative impact on the indoor air quality. The building materials also tend to fail prematurely from the sustained moisture presence.

If your basement plans require that you insulate the foundation walls, make certain that the walls are dry and that any moisture problems are corrected (see pages 18 to 23). Then, look first at the exterior.

Install insulation on the exterior of the wall, not the interior, whenever possible. Exterior insulation results in a warm wall that will have less of a problem with condensation. The wall also can breathe and dry out more easily if the interior side has no vapor retarder.

Because it is often unnecessary to insulate the full height of the wall, you may find that an exterior apron insulating approach is easier than you imagined (see pages 14 to 15). If your circumstances absolutely require that you insulate inside, use insulating products such as extruded polystyrene or foil-faced isocyanurate that do not absorb water or provide food for mold. You should also keep the wall isolated from the insulation: attach the insulation first, seal it, and then construct a stud wall that has no direct contact with the concrete or concrete block wall (see pages 16 to 17).

High-Efficiency Upgrades ▶

Replace old gas water heaters with high-efficiency models. Not only will this save money on your utilities bill, it will also keep your basement warmer. The more efficient your heater is, the less air it will require for fuel combustion, which means less fresh cold air is drawn into the basement to replace the air consumed by the appliance.

HOW TO INSULATE BASEMENTS

Install rigid foam insulation in basements, both on the exterior and the interior. Extruded polystyrene (sometimes called beadboard) is an economical choice for larger areas, and it forms its own vapor retarding layer when properly installed and sealed. High-density polystyrene and isocyanruate are denser insulation boards with higher R-values. Isocyanurate usually has one or two foil faces. It is used to seal rim joists but is a good choice for any basement wall location.

Improve insulation and thermal seals in attics and other parts of your house to keep basements warmer in winter. By reducing the amount of warm air that escapes through the roof, you will reduce the amount of cold air that is drawn in through the basement walls to replace the air.

Seal furnace ducts to reduce air leakage. Use a combination of UL 181-rated duct tape (foil tape) and duct mastic. If cold-air return ducts leak, for example, they will draw air from the basement into the air supply system. As with heat loss through the attic, this will cause fresh cold air to enter the basement and lower the ambient temperature.

What is a Dry Wall ▸

When building experts warn never to insulate a wall that isn't dry, they have something very specific in mind. A wall that appears dry to the touch may not be classified as dry if it is constantly evaporating small amounts of moisture that will be blocked if you install any kind of vapor retarder (as is likely the case). A dry wall (suitable for interior insulation) is one that is superficially dry to the touch and also meets these criteria:

- Has a positive drainage system capable of removing water that accumulates from any source (this is typically in the form of a sump pump).
- The foundation wall and floor are structured to provide drainage of water away from the house, often through the use of drain tiles and footing drains.

WALLS & CEILINGS

INSULATION SOLUTION: EXTERIOR APRON INSULATION

Insulate foundation walls on the exterior side (and not the interior) whenever you can. The easiest way to accomplish this is by installing insulation in the apron area only, so you do not have to excavate all the way to the bottom of the wall. By adding a layer of horizontal insulation in the bottom of the trench, you can realize at least 70 percent of the energy savings of insulating the whole wall, while limiting your digging to 18 inches down and 24 inches out.

Because you will be adding width to the foundation wall by installing exterior insulation, you will need to install flashing to cover the top of the insulation layer and whatever protective wall surface you cover it with. For the project shown here, the insulation is covered with panelized veneer siding over 1-inch-thick rigid foam insulation boards. For extra protection, coat the cleaned walls with a layer of bituminous coating before installing the insulation boards.

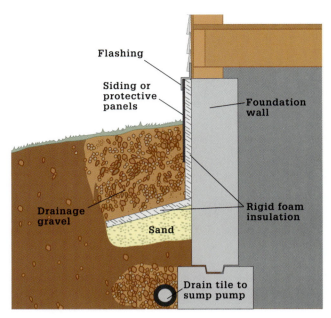

Apron insulation is an easy and effective way to enhance comfort in your basement without causing any major moisture issues.

HOW TO INSTALL APRON INSULATION

Dig an 18 × 24" wide trench next to the wall being insulated. Make sure to have your local utilities company flag any lines that may be in the area first.

Coat the wall with a layer of bituminous coating once you have cleaned it with a hose or pressure washer. The coating simply creates another layer of moisture protection for the basement and can be skipped if you wish.

3

Line the trench with a 2"-thick layer of coarse sand, and then strips of rigid foam insulation. The sand should slope away from the house slightly, and the insulation strips should butt up against the foundation wall.

4

Install drip edge flashing to protect the tops of the insulation board and new siding. Pry back the bottom edge of the siding slightly and slip the flashing flange up underneath the siding. The flashing should extend out far enough to cover both layers of new material (at least 1½ to 2").

5

Bond strips of rigid foam insulation board to the foundation wall using a panel adhesive that is compatible with foam. Press the tops of the boards up against the drip edge flashing. When all the boards are installed, tape over butted seams with insulation tape.

6

Install siding or another protective layer over the insulation. Here, 2 x 4 ft. faux stone panels are being used. Once the panels are in place, backfill the trench with dirt or gravel. Make sure to maintain minimum slopes for runoff at grade.

INSULATION SOLUTION FOR DRY WALLS: INTERIOR WALL INSULATION

As a general rule, avoid insulating the interior side of your basement walls. It is best to leave breathing space for the concrete or block so moisture that enters through the walls is not trapped. If your exterior basement walls meet the definition of a dry wall (see page 13) however, adding some interior insulation can increase the comfort level in your basement. If you are building a stud wall for hanging wallcovering materials, you can insulate between the studs with rigid foam—do not use fiberglass batts and do not install a vapor barrier. If you are building a stud wall, it's a good idea to keep the wall away from the basement wall so there is an air channel between the two.

Interior insulation can be installed if your foundation walls meet the conditions for dry walls (see page 13). It is important to keep the framed wall isolated from the basement wall with a seamless layer of rigid insulation board.

2" foil-faced isocyanurate

1½" foil-faced isocyanurate

Cap plate

½" drywall mounted to 2 × 2 frame

2" polystyrene

1½"-deep receptacle box

Sole plate

HOW TO INSULATE AN INTERIOR BASEMENT WALL

Begin on the exterior wall by digging a trench and installing a 2"-thick rigid foam insulation board up to the bottom of the siding and down at least 6" below grade. The main purpose of this insulation is to inhibit convection and air transfer in the wall above grade. See pages 14 to 15 for more information on how to use flashing and siding to conceal and protect the insulation board.

Insulate the rim joist with strips of 2"-thick isocyanurate rigid insulation with foil facing. Be sure the insulation you purchase is rated for interior exposure (exterior products can produce bad vapors). Use adhesive to bond the insulation to the rim joist, and then caulk around all the edges with acoustic sealant.

3

Seal and insulate the top of the foundation wall, if it is exposed, with strips of 1½"-thick, foil-faced isocyanurate insulation. Install the strips using the same type of adhesive and caulk you used for the rim joist insulation.

4

Attach sheets of 2"-thick extruded polystyrene insulation to the wall from the floor to the top of the wall. Make sure to clean the wall thoroughly and let it dry completely before installing the insulation.

5

Seal the gaps between the insulation boards with insulation vapor barrier tape. Do not caulk gaps between the insulation boards and the floor.

6

Install a stud wall by fastening the cap plate to the ceiling joists and the sole plate to the floor. If you have space, allow an air channel between the studs and the insulation. Do not install a vapor barrier.

BASEMENTS: WET WALLS

Basement moisture can destroy your efforts to create functional living space. Over time, even small amounts of moisture can rot framing, turn wallboard to mush, and promote the growth of mold and mildew. Before proceeding with your basement project, you must deal with any moisture issues. The good news is that moisture problems can be resolved, often very easily.

Basement moisture appears in two forms: condensation and seepage. Condensation comes from airborne water vapor that turns to water when it contacts cold surfaces. Vapor sources include humid outdoor air, poorly ventilated appliances, damp walls, and water released from concrete. Seepage is water that enters the basement by infiltrating cracks in the foundation or by leeching through masonry, which is naturally porous. Often caused by ineffective exterior drainage, seepage comes from rain or groundwater that collects around the foundation or from a rising water table.

If you have a wet basement, you'll see evidence of moisture problems. Typical signs include peeling paint, white residue on masonry (called efflorescence), mildew stains, sweaty windows and pipes, rusted appliance feet, rotted wood near the floor, buckled floor tile, and strong mildew odor.

To reduce condensation, run a high-capacity dehumidifier in the basement. Insulate cold-water pipes to prevent condensate drippage, and make sure your dryer and other appliances have vents running to the outside. Extending central air conditioning service to the basement can help reduce vapor during warm, humid months.

Crawlspaces can also promote condensation, as warm, moist air enters through vents and meets cooler interior air. Crawlspace ventilation is a source of ongoing debate, and there's no universal method that applies to all climates. It's best to ask the local building department for advice on this matter.

Solutions for preventing seepage range from simple do-it-yourself projects to expensive, professional jobs requiring excavation and foundation work. Since it's often difficult to determine the source of seeping water, it makes sense to try some common cures before calling in professional help. If the simple measures outlined here don't correct your moisture problems, you must consider more

Repairing cracks restores the integrity of concrete foundation walls that leak, but it is often only a temporary fix. Selecting an appropriate repair product and doing careful preparation will make the repair more long lasting. A hydraulic concrete repair product like the one seen here is perfect for basement wall repair because it actually hardens from contact with water.

extensive action. Serious water problems are typically handled by installing footing drains or sump pump systems. Footing drains are installed around the foundation's perimeter, near the footing, and they drain out to a distant area of the yard. These usually work in conjunction with waterproof coatings on the exterior side of the foundation walls. Sump systems use an interior underslab drainpipe to collect water in a pit, and water is ejected outside by an electric sump pump.

Installing a new drainage system is expensive and must be done properly. Adding a sump system involves breaking up the concrete floor along the basement's perimeter, digging a trench, and laying a perforated drainpipe in a bed of gravel. After the sump pit is installed, the floor is patched with new concrete. Installing a footing drain is far more complicated. This involves digging out the foundation, installing gravel and drainpipe, and waterproofing the foundation walls. A footing drain is considered a last-resort measure.

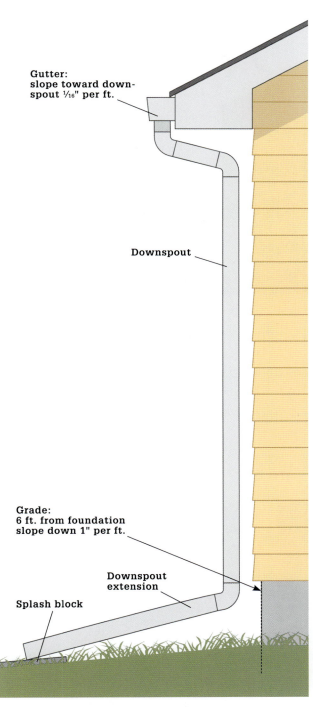

Gutter:
slope toward down-
spout 1/16" per ft.

Downspout

Grade:
6 ft. from foundation
slope down 1" per ft.

Downspout
extension

Splash block

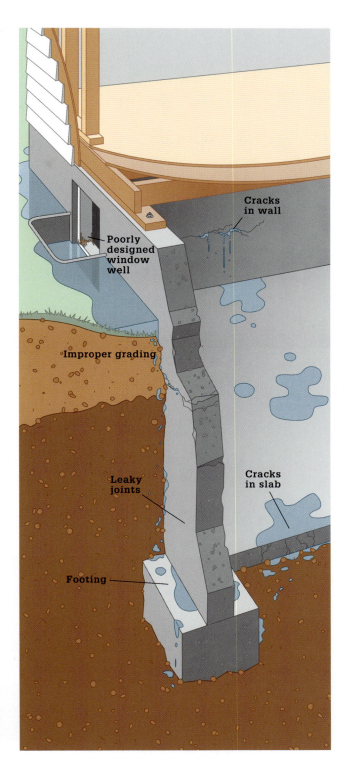

Cracks
in wall

Poorly
designed
window
well

Improper grading

Leaky
joints

Cracks
in slab

Footing

Improve your gutter system and foundation grade to prevent rainwater and snowmelt from flooding your basement. Keep gutters clean and straight. Make sure there's a downspout for every 50 ft. of roof eave, and extend downspouts at least 8 ft. from the foundation. Build up the grade around the foundation so that it carries water away from the house.

Common causes of basement moisture include improper grading around the foundation, inadequate or faulty gutter systems, condensation, cracks in foundation walls, leaky joints between structural elements, and poorly designed window wells. More extensive problems include large cracks in the foundation, damaged or missing drain tiles, a high water table, or the presence of underground streams. Often, a combination of factors is at fault.

HOW TO SEAL CRACKS IN A FOUNDATION WALL

To repair a stable crack, chisel cut a keyhole cut that's wider at the base then at the surface, and no more than ½" deep. Clean out the crack with a wire brush.

To help seal against moisture, fill the crack with expanding insulating foam, working from bottom to top.

Mix hydraulic cement according to the manufacturer's instructions, then trowel it into the crack, working from the bottom to top. Apply cement in layers no more than ¼" thick, until the patch is slightly higher than the surrounding area. Feather cement with the trowel until it's even with the surface. Allow to dry thoroughly.

HOW TO SKIM-COAT A FOUNDATION WALL

Resurface heavily cracked masonry walls with a water-resistant masonry coating such as surface bonding cement. Clean and dampen the walls according to the coating manufacturer's instructions, then fill large cracks and holes with the coating. Finally, plaster a ¼" layer of the coating on the walls using a square-end trowel. Specially formulated heavy-duty masonry coatings are available for very damp conditions.

Scratch the surface with a paintbrush cleaner or a homemade scratching tool after the coating has set up for several hours. After 24 hours, apply a second, smooth coat. Mist the wall twice a day for three days as the coating cures.

PREVENTING MOISTURE IN BASEMENTS

Waterproof Paint ▸

Masonry paints and sealers, especially those that are described as waterproof, are rather controversial products. Some manufacturers claim that applying a coat of their waterproof paint will create a seal that can hold back moisture, even under light hydrostatic pressure. Others suggest only that their product, when applied to a basement wall, will create a skin that inhibits water penetration from the interior side.

Masonry paints do hold up better on concrete surfaces than other types, largely because they are higher in alkali and therefore less reactive with cement-based materials. But they also can trap moisture in the concrete, which will cause the paint to fail prematurely and can cause the concrete to degrade, especially if the water freezes. Read the product label carefully before applying waterproof paint to your basement walls, and make sure to follow the preparation protocols carefully. If you have a foundation wall with an active water-seepage problem, address the problem with the other methods shown in this section, including grading and gutters. A coat of waterproof paint is not going to make your basement drier.

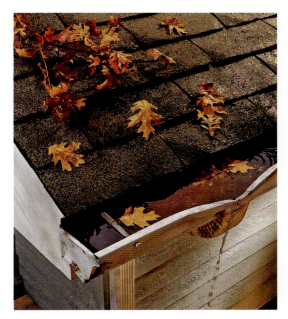

Clean your gutters and patch any holes. Make sure the gutters slope toward the downspouts at about ¹⁄₁₆" per ft. Add downspout extensions and splash blocks to keep roof runoff at least 8 ft. away from the foundation.

Cover window wells that will otherwise allow water into a basement. Covering them with removable plastic is the easiest way to keep them dry. Covers on egress window wells must be easily removed from inside (see pages 561 to 566). If you prefer to leave wells uncovered, add a gravel layer and a drain to the bottom of the well. Clean the well regularly to remove moisture-heavy debris.

DRAINAGE SOLUTION: HOW TO RE-GRADE

Establish the drainage slope. The yard around your house should slant away from the house at a minimum slope of ¾" per ft. for at least 10 ft. Till the soil or add new soil around the house perimeter. Drive a wood stake next to the house and another 10 ft. out. Tie a level mason's string between the stakes, and then move the string down at least 2½" at the end away from the house, establishing your minimum slope.

Redistribute the soil with a steel garden rake so the grade follows the slope line. Add topsoil at the high end if needed. Do not excavate near the end of the slope to accommodate the grade. The goal is to build up the yard to create runoff.

Use a grading rake to smooth out the soil so it slopes at an even rate. Drive additional stakes and tie off slope lines as necessary.

Tamp the soil with a hand tamper or plate compactor. Fill in any dips that occur with fresh dirt. Lay sod or plant grass or groundcover immediately.

Dry Wells for Drainage ▶

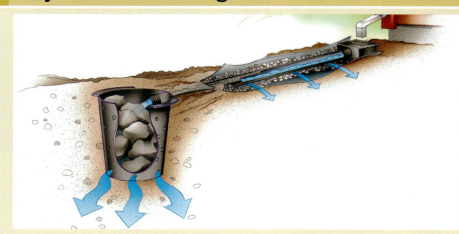

A dry well is installed to help give runoff water an escape route so it doesn't collect around the house foundation. See next page.

DRAINAGE SOLUTION: HOW TO INSTALL A DRY WELL

A dry well is a simple way to channel excess water out of low-lying or water-laden areas, such as the ground beneath a gutter downspout. A dry well system (see previous page) typically consists of a buried drain tile running from a catch basin positioned at the problem spot to a collection container some distance away.

A dry well system is easy to install and surprisingly inexpensive. In the project shown here, a perforated plastic drain tile carries water from a catch basin to a dry well fashioned from a plastic trash can that has been punctured, then filled with stone rubble. The runoff water percolates into the soil as it makes its way along the drainpipe and through the dry well.

The how-to steps of this project include digging the trench with a shovel. If the catch basin is a long distance from the problem area, you may want to rent a trencher to dig the trench quickly. Call local utility companies to mark the location of underground mechanicals before you start to dig.

Dig a trench (10" wide, 14" deep) from the area where the water collects to the catch basin location, sloping the trench 2" per 8 ft. Line the trench with landscape fabric and then add a 1" layer of gravel on top of the fabric.

Set a length of perforated drain tile on the gravel running the full length of the trench. If the trench starts at a downspout, position a grated catch basin directly beneath the downspout and attach the end of the drain tile to the outlet port.

Install the dry well by digging a hole that's big enough to hold a plastic trash can. Drill 1" holes through the sides and bottom of the can every 4 to 6". Also cut an access hole at the top of the can for the drain tile. Set the can in the hole and insert the free end of the tile. Backfill dirt over the tile and trench and plant grass or cover with sod.

BATHROOM VANITY: INSTALLING

Most bathroom countertops installed today are integral (one-piece) sink/countertop units made from cultured marble or other solid materials, like solid surfacing. Integral sink/countertops are convenient, and many are inexpensive, but style and color options are limited.

Some remodelers and designers still prefer the distinctive look of a custom-built countertop with a self-rimming sink basin, which gives you a much greater selection of styles and colors. Installing a self-rimming sink is very simple.

Tools & Materials ▸

Pencil	Stud finder
Carpenter's level	4-ft. level
Screwdriver	Shims
Cardboard	3" drywall screws
Masking tape	Drill
Plumber's putty	Protective
Tub & tile caulk	equipment

Integral sink/countertops are made in standard sizes to fit common vanity widths. Because the sink and countertop are cast from the same material, integral sink/countertops do not leak, and do not require extensive caulking and sealing.

HOW TO INSTALL A VANITY CABINET

Measure and mark the top edge of the vanity cabinet on the wall, then use a 4-ft. level to mark a level line at the cabinet height mark. Use an electronic stud finder to locate the framing members, then mark the stud locations along the line.

Slide the vanity into position so that the back rail of the cabinet can later be fastened to studs at both corners and in the center. The back of the cabinet should also be flush against the wall. (If the wall surface is uneven, position the vanity so it contacts the wall in at least one spot, and the back cabinet rail is parallel with the wall.)

Using a 4-ft. level as a guide, shim below the vanity cabinet until the unit is level.

Variation: To install two or more cabinets, set the cabinets in position against the wall, and align the cabinet fronts. If one cabinet is higher than the other, shim under the lower cabinet until the two are even. Clamp the cabinet faces together, then drill countersunk pilot holes spaced 12" apart through the face frames so they go at least halfway into the face frame of the second cabinet. Drive wood screws through the pilot holes to join the cabinets together.

At the stud locations marked on the wall, drive 3" drywall screws through the rail on the cabinet back and into the framing members. The screws should be driven at both corners and in the center of the back rail.

Run a bead of caulk along small gaps between the vanity and wall, and between the vanity and floor. For larger gaps, use quarter-round molding between the vanity and wall. Between the vanity and floor, install the same baseboard material used to cover the gap between the wall and floor.

HOW TO INSTALL AN INTEGRAL VANITY COUNTERTOP

Set the sink/countertop unit onto sawhorses. Attach the faucet and slip the drain lever through the faucet body. Place a ring of plumber's putty around the drain flange, then insert the flange in the drain opening.

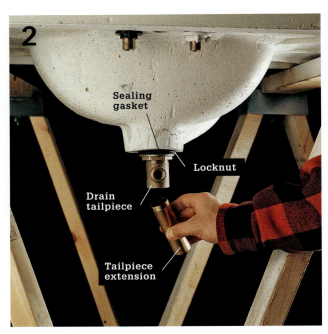

Thread the locknut and sealing gasket onto the drain tailpiece, then insert the tailpiece into the drain opening and screw it onto the drain flange. Tighten the locknut securely. Attach the tailpiece extension. Insert the pop-up stopper linkage.

Apply a layer of tub & tile caulk (or adhesive, if specified by the countertop manufacturer) to the top edges of the cabinet vanity, and to any corner braces.

Center the sink/countertop unit over the vanity, so the overhang is equal on both sides and the backsplash of the countertop is flush with the wall. Press the countertop evenly into the caulk.

5

Cabinets with corner braces: Secure the countertop to the cabinet by driving a mounting screw through each corner brace and up into the countertop. *Note: Cultured marble and other hard countertops require predrilling and a plastic screw sleeve.*

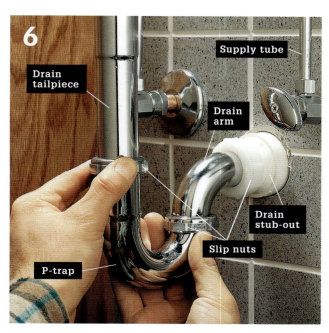

6

Supply tube

Drain tailpiece

Drain arm

Drain stub-out

Slip nuts

P-trap

Attach the drain arm to the drain stub-out in the wall using a slip nut. Attach one end of the P-trap to the drain arm, and the other to the tailpiece of the sink drain, using slip nuts. Connect supply tubes to the faucet tailpieces. Seal the gap between the backsplash and the wall with tub and tile caulk.

VARIATION: DROP-IN SINKS

An inexpensive alternative to an integral vanity countertop is to build your own countertop from postform laminate or another kitchen-style countertop material. Be sure to add buildup strips and caps to the exposed ends. Position the countertop on your vanity cabinet and trace a cutout for the drop-in lavatory.

Install the drop-in sink. Some sinks rely mostly on their own weight to stay put, requiring only a bead of plumber's putty for setting the sink flange. Lighter sinks are held in place with clips from below. It's usually recommended that you attach your faucet to the sink before installing it, and then make your hookups.

BATHTUBS: INSTALLING

Prepare for the new tub. Inspect and remove old or deteriorated wall surfaces or framing members in the tub area. With today's mold-resistant wallboard products, it makes extra sense to go ahead and strip off the old alcove wallcoverings and ceiling down to the studs so you can replace them. This also allows you to inspect for hidden damage in the wall and ceiling cavities.

Check the subfloor for level—if it is not level, use pour-on floor leveler compound to correct it (ask at your local flooring store). Make sure the supply and drain pipes and the shutoff valves are in good repair and correct any problems you encounter. If you have no bath fan in the alcove, now is the perfect time to add one.

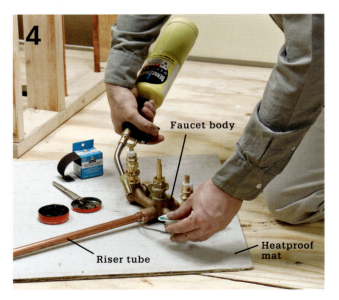

Faucet body

Riser tube

Heatproof mat

Check the height of the crossbraces for the faucet body and the showerhead. If your family members needed to stoop to use the old shower, consider raising the brace for the showerhead. Read the instructions for your new faucet/diverter and check to see that the brace for the faucet body will conform to the requirements (this includes distance from the surround wall as well as height). Adjust the brace locations as needed.

Begin by installing the new water supply plumbing. Measure to determine the required height of your shower riser tube and cut it to length. Attach the bottom of the riser to the faucet body and the top to the shower elbow.

Attach the faucet body to the cross brace with pipe hanger straps. Then, attach supply tubing from the stop valves to the faucet body, making sure to attach the hot water to the left port and cold to the right port. Also secure the shower elbow to its cross brace with a pipe strap. Do not attach the shower arm yet.

Slide the bathtub into the alcove. Make sure tub is flat on the floor and pressed flush against the back wall. If your tub did not come with a tub protector, cut a piece of cardboard to line the tub bottom, and tape pieces of cardboard around the rim to protect the finish from shoes and dropped tools.

Mark locations for ledger boards. To do this, trace the height of the top of the tub's nailing flange onto the wall studs in the alcove. Then remove the tub and measure the height of the nailing flange. Measure down this same amount from your flange lines and mark the new ledger board location.

Install 1 × 4 ledger boards. Drive two or three 3"-galvanized deck screws through the ledger board at each stud. All three walls should receive a ledger. Leave an open space in the wet wall to allow clearance for the DWO (drain-waste-overflow) kit. Measure to see whether the drain will line up with the tub's DWO. If not, you may need to cut and reassemble the drain.

(continued)

Install the drain-waste-overflow pipes before you install the tub. Make sure to get a good seal on the slip nuts at the pipe joints. Follow the manufacturer's instructions to make sure the pop-up drain linkage is connected properly. Make sure rubber gaskets are positioned correctly at the openings on the outside of the tub.

Drain strainer

Thread the male-threaded drain strainer into the female-threaded drain waste elbow. Wrap a coil of plumber's putty around the drain outlet underneath the plug rim first. Hand tighten only.

Attach the overflow coverplate, making sure the pop-up drain controls are in the correct position. Tighten the mounting screws that connect to the mounting plate to sandwich the rubber gasket snugly between the overflow pipe flange and the tub wall. Then, finish tightening the drain strainer against the waste elbow by inserting the handle of a pair of pliers into the strainer body and turning.

Working with a helper, place the tub in position, taking care not to bump the DWO assembly. If the DWO assembly does not line up with the drainpipe, remove the tub and adjust the drain location. Many acrylic, fiberglass, and steel tubs will have a much firmer feeling if they are set in a bed of sand-mix concrete. Check manufacturer's instructions, and pour concrete or mortar as needed. Set the tub carefully back in the alcove.

13

Attach the drain outlet from the DWO assembly to the drain P-trap. This is the part of the job where you will appreciate that you spent the time to create a roomy access panel for the tub plumbing. Test the drain and overflow to make sure they don't leak. Also test the water supply plumbing, temporarily attaching the handles, spout, and shower arm so you can operate the faucet and the diverter.

14

Drive a 1½" galvanized roofing nail at each stud location, just over the top of the tub's nailing flange. The nail head should pin the flange to the stud. Be careful here—an errant blow or overdriving can cause the enameled finish to crack or craze. *Option: You may choose to drill guide holes and nail through the flange instead.*

15

Install the wallcoverings and tub surround (see pages 386–390 for a 3-piece surround installation). You can also make a custom surround from tileboard or cementboard and tile.

16

Install fittings. First, thread the shower arm into the shower elbow and attach the spout nipple to the valve assembly. Also attach the shower head and escutcheon, the faucet handle/ diverter with escutcheon, and the tub spout. Use thread lubricant on all parts.

BATHTUBS: SLIDING TUB DOORS

Curtains on your bathtub shower are a hassle. If you forget to tuck them inside the tub, water flows freely onto your bathroom floor. If you forget to slide them closed, mildew sets up shop in the folds. And every time you brush against them, they stick to your skin. Shower curtains certainly don't add much elegance or charm to a dream bath. Neither does a deteriorated door. Clean up the look of your bathroom, and even give it an extra touch of elegance, with a new sliding tub door.

When shopping for a sliding tub door, you have a choice of framed or frameless. A framed door is edged in metal. The metal framing is typically aluminum but is available in many finishes, including those that resemble gold, brass, or chrome. Glass options are also plentiful. You can choose between frosted or pebbled glass, clear, mirrored, tinted, or patterned glass. Doors can be installed on ceramic tile walls or onto a fiberglass tub surround.

Tools & Materials ▶

Measuring tape	Marker
Pencil	Masonry bit for tile wall
Hacksaw	Phillips screwdriver
Miter box	Caulk gun
Level	Masking tape
Drill	Silicone sealant & remover
Center punch	Tub door kit
Razor blade	Protective equipment

A sliding tub door framed in aluminum gives the room a sleek, clean look and is just one of the available options. A model like this fits into a 60" alcove, so it can replace a standard tub, as long as you can provide access to the plumbing and an electrical connection.

HOW TO INSTALL SLIDING TUB DOORS

1

Remove the existing door and inspect the walls. Use a razor blade to cut sealant from tile and metal surfaces. Do not use a razor blade on fiberglass surfaces. Remove remaining sealant by scraping or pulling. Use a silicone sealant remover to remove all residue. Remove shower curtain rods, if present. Check the walls and tub ledge for plumb and level.

2

Measure the distance between the finished walls along the top of the tub ledge. Refer to the manufacturer's instructions for figuring the track dimensions. For the product seen here, ³⁄₁₆" is subtracted from the measurement to calculate the track dimensions.

3

Using a hacksaw and a miter box, carefully cut the track to the proper dimension. Center the track on the bathtub ledge with the taller side out and so the gaps are even at each end. Tape into position with masking tape.

4

Place a wall channel against the wall with the longer side out and slide into place over the track so they overlap. Use a level to check the channel for plumb, and then mark the locations of the mounting holes on the wall with a marker. Repeat for the other wall channel. Remove the track.

(continued)

5

Drill mounting holes for the wall channel at the marked locations. In ceramic tile, nick the surface of the tile with a center punch, use a ¼" masonry bit to drill the hole, and then insert the included wall anchors. For fiberglass surrounds, use a ⅛" drill bit; wall anchors are not necessary.

6

Apply a bead of silicone sealant along the joint between the tub and the wall at the ends of the track. Apply a minimum ¼" bead of sealant along the outside leg of the track underside.

7

Position the track on the tub ledge and against the wall. Attach the wall channels using the provided screws. Do not use caulk on the wall channels at this time.

8

Header

Wall channel

Cut and install the header. At a location above the tops of the wall channels, measure the distance between the walls. Refer to the manufacturer's instructions for calculating the header length. For the door seen here, the length is the distance between the walls minus ¹⁄₁₆". Measure the header and carefully cut it to length using a hacksaw and a miter box. Slide the header down on top of the wall channels until seated.

9

Mount the rollers in the roller mounting holes. To begin, use the second-from-the-top roller mounting holes. Follow the manufacturer's instructions for spacer or washer placement and orientation.

10

Roller

Carefully lift the inner panel by the sides and place the rollers on the inner roller track. Roll the door toward the shower end of the tub. The edge of the panel should touch both rubber bumpers. If it doesn't, remove the door and move the rollers to different holes. Drive the screws by hand to prevent overtightening.

11

Lift the outer panel by the sides with the towel bar facing out from the tub. Place the outer rollers over the outer roller track. Slide the door to the end opposite the shower end of the tub. If the door does not contact both bumpers, remove the door and move the rollers to different mounting holes.

12

Apply a bead of clear silicone sealant to the inside seam of the wall and wall channel at both ends and to the U-shaped joint of the track and wall channels. Smooth the sealant with a fingertip dipped in water.

CARPET: INSTALLING

Starting in a corner, nail tackless strips to the floor, keeping a gap between the strips and the walls that's about ⅔ the thickness of the carpet. Use plywood spacers to maintain the gap. Angled pins on the strip should point toward the wall.

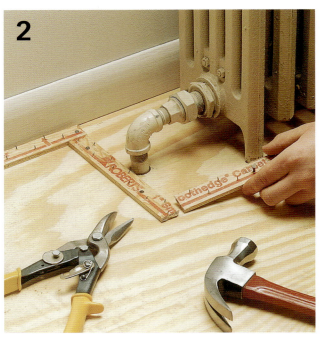

Use aviation snips to cut tackless strips to fit around radiators, door moldings, and other obstacles.

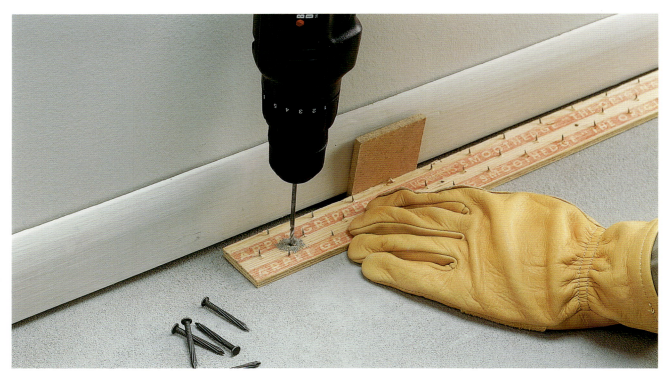

Variation: On concrete, use wider tackless strips. Using a masonry bit, drill pilot holes through the strips and into the floor. Then fasten the strips with 1½" fluted masonry nails.

HOW TO INSTALL CARPET PADDING

1

Roll out enough padding to cover the entire floor. Make sure the seams between the padding are tight. If one face of the padding has a slicker surface, keep the slick surface face up, making it easier to slide the carpet over the pad during installation.

2

Use a utility knife to cut away excess padding along the edges. The padding should touch, but not overlap, the tackless strips.

3

Tape the seams together with duct tape, then staple the padding to the floor every 12".

Variation: To fasten padding to a concrete floor, apply double-sided tape next to the tackless strips, along the seams, and in an "X" pattern across the floor.

HOW TO CUT & SEAM CARPET

Position the carpet roll against one wall, with its loose end extending up the wall about 6", then roll out the carpet until it reaches the opposite wall.

At the opposite wall, mark the back of the carpet at each edge about 6" beyond the point where the carpet touches the wall. Pull the carpet back away from the wall so the marks are visible.

Variation: When cutting loop-pile carpet, avoid severing the loops by cutting it from the top side using a row-running knife. Fold the carpet back along the cut line to part the pile (left) and make a crease along the part line. Lay the carpet flat and cut along the part in the pile (right). Cut slowly to ensure a smooth, straight cut.

3

Snap a chalk line across the back of the carpet between the marks. Place a scrap piece of plywood under the cutting area to protect the carpet and padding from the knife blade. Cut along the line using a straightedge and utility knife.

4

Next to walls, straddle the edge of the carpet and nudge it with your foot until it extends up the wall by about 6" and is parallel to the wall.

5

At the corners, relieve buckling by slitting the carpet with a utility knife, allowing the carpet to lie somewhat flat. Make sure that corner cuts do not cut into usable carpet.

6

Using your seaming plan as a guide, measure and cut fill-in pieces of carpet to complete the installation. Be sure to include a 6" surplus at each wall and a 3" surplus on each edge that will be seamed to another piece of carpet. Set the cut pieces in place, making sure the pile faces in the same direction on all pieces.

(continued)

7

Roll back the large piece of carpet on the side to be seamed, then use a chalk line to snap a straight seam edge about 2" from the factory edge. Keep the ends of the line about 18" from the sides of the carpet where the overlap onto the walls causes the carpet to buckle.

8

Using a straightedge and utility knife, carefully cut the carpet along the chalk line. To extend the cutting lines to the edges of the carpet, pull the corners back at an angle so they lie flat, then cut the line with the straightedge and utility knife. Place scrap wood under the cutting area to protect the carpet while cutting.

9

On smaller carpet pieces, cut straight seam edges where the small pieces will be joined to one another. Don't cut the edges that will be seamed to the large carpet piece until after the small pieces are joined together.

Option: Apply a continuous bead of seam glue along the cut edges of the backing at seams to ensure that the carpet will not fray.

Plug in the seam iron and set it aside to heat up, then measure and cut hot-glue seam tape for all seams. Begin by joining the small fill-in pieces to form one large piece. Center the tape under the seam with the adhesive side facing up.

Set the iron under the carpet at one end of the tape until the adhesive liquifies, usually about 30 seconds. Working in 12" sections, slowly move the iron along the tape, letting the carpet fall onto the hot adhesive behind it. Set weights at the end of the seam to hold the pieces in place.

(continued)

Press the edges of the carpet together into the melted adhesive behind the iron. Separate the pile with your fingers to make sure no fibers are stuck in the glue and the seam is tight, then place a weighted board over the seam to keep it flat while the glue sets.

Variation: To close any gaps in loop-pile carpet seams, use a knee kicker to gently push the seam edges together while the adhesive is still hot.

Continue seaming the fill-in pieces together. When the tape's adhesive has cooled, turn the seamed piece over and cut a fresh seam edge as done in steps 7 and 8. Reheat and remove about 1½" of tape from the end of each seam to keep it from overlapping the tape on the large piece.

14

Use hot-glue seam tape to join the seamed pieces to the large piece of carpet, repeating steps 10 through 12.

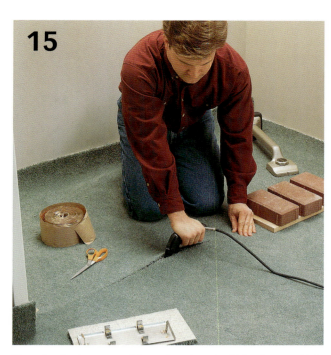

15

If you're laying carpet in a closet, cut a fill-in piece and join it to the main carpet with hot-glue seam tape.

16

At radiators, pipes, and other obstructions, cut slits in the carpet with a utility knife. Cut long slits from the edge of the carpet to the obstruction, then cut short cross-slits where the carpet will fit around the obstruction.

Partition Walls ▸

To fit carpet around partition walls where the edges of the wall or door jamb meet the floor, make diagonal cuts from the edge of the carpet at the center of the wall to the points where the edges of the wall meet the floor.

HOW TO STRETCH & SECURE CARPET

Before stretching the seamed carpet, read through this entire section and create a stretching sequence similar to the one shown here. Start by fastening the carpet at a doorway threshold using carpet transitions (see pages 50 to 51).

If the doorway is close to a corner, use the knee kicker to secure the carpet to the tackless strips between the door and the corner. Also secure a few feet of carpet along the adjacent wall, working toward the corner.

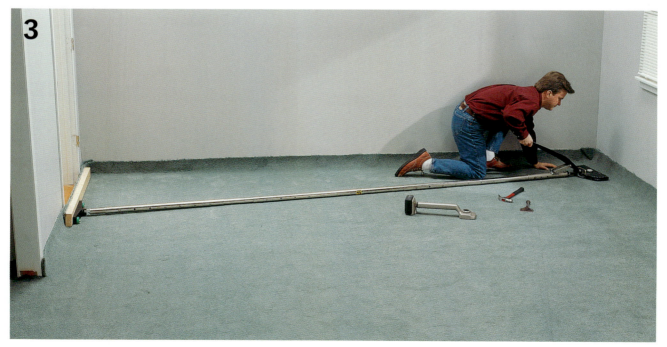

Use a power stretcher to stretch the carpet toward the wall opposite the door. Brace the tail with a length of 2 × 4 placed across the doorway. Leaving the tail in place and moving only the stretcher head, continue stretching and securing the carpet along the wall, working toward the nearest corner in 12 to 24" increments.

As you stretch the carpet, secure it onto the tackless strips with a stair tool and hammer.

With the power stretcher still extended from the doorway to the opposite side of the room, knee-kick the carpet onto the tackless strips along the closest wall, starting near the corner closest to the stretcher tail. Disengage and move the stretcher only if it's in the way.

Reposition the stretcher so its tail is against the center of the wall you just secured. Stretch and secure the carpet along the opposite wall, working from the center toward a corner. If there's a closet in an adjacent wall, work toward that wall, not the closet.

(continued)

7

Use the knee kicker to stretch and secure the carpet inside the closet (if necessary). Stretch and fasten the carpet against the back wall first, then do the side walls. After the carpet in the closet is stretched and secured, use the knee kicker to secure the carpet along the walls next to the closet. Disengage the power stretcher only if it's in the way.

8

Return the head of the power stretcher to the center of the wall. Finish securing carpet along this wall, working toward the other corner of the room.

9

Reposition the stretcher to secure the carpet along the last wall of the room, working from the center toward the corners. The tail block should be braced against the opposite wall.

10

Use a carpet edge trimmer to trim surplus carpet away from the walls. At corners, use a utility knife to finish the cuts.

Locate any floor vents under the stretched carpet, then use a utility knife to cut away the carpet, starting at the center. It's important that this be done only after the stretching is complete.

11

Tuck the trimmed edges of the carpet neatly into the gaps between the tackless strips and the walls using a stair tool and hammer.

CARPET: REPAIRING

Burns and stains are the most common carpeting problems. You can clip away the burned fibers of superficial burns using small scissors. Deeper burns and indelible stains require patching by cutting away and replacing the damaged area.

Another common problem, addressed on the opposite page, is carpet seams or edges that have come loose. You can rent the tools necessary for fixing this problem.

Tools & Materials ▶

Cookie-cutter tool	Replacement carpeting
Knee kicker	Double-face carpet tape
4" wallboard knife	Heat-activated seam tape
Utility knife	Weights
Seam iron	Boards
Seam adhesive	

Stained or damaged carpet can be replaced with specialized tools and DIY techniques.

HOW TO REPAIR SPOT DAMAGE

1

Use a cookie-cutter tool to cut a replacement patch from scrap carpeting. Press the cutter down over the damaged area and twist it to cut away the carpet.

2

Remove extensive damage or stains with the cookie-cutter tool (available at carpeting stores). Insert double-face carpet tape under the cutout, positioning the tape so it overlaps the patch seams.

3

Press the patch into place. Make sure the direction of the nap or pattern matches the existing carpet. To seal the seam and prevent unraveling, apply seam adhesive to the edges of the patch.

HOW TO RESTRETCH LOOSE CARPET

1

Adjust the knob on the head of the knee kicker so the prongs grab the carpet backing without penetrating through the padding. Starting from a corner or near a point where the carpet is firmly attached, press the knee kicker head into the carpet, about 2" from the wall.

2

Thrust your knee into the cushion of the knee kicker to force the carpet toward the wall. Tuck the carpet edge into the space between the wood strip and the baseboard using a 4" wallboard knife. If the carpet is still loose, trim the edge with a utility knife and stretch it again.

HOW TO GLUE LOOSE SEAMS

1

Remove the old tape from under the carpet seam. Cut a strip of new seam tape and place it under the carpet so it's centered along the seam with the adhesive facing up. Plug in the seam iron and let it heat up.

2

Pull up both edges of the carpet and set the hot iron squarely onto the tape. Wait about 30 seconds for the glue to melt. Move the iron about 12" farther along the seam. Quickly press the edges of the carpet together into the melted glue behind the iron. Separate the pile to make sure no fibers are stuck in the glue and the seam is tight. Place weighted boards over the seam to keep it flat while the glue sets. Remember, you have only 30 seconds to repeat the process.

CARPET: TRANSITION STRIPS

Doorways, entryways, and other transition areas require special treatment when installing carpet. Transition materials and techniques vary, depending on the level and type of the adjoining flooring.

For a transition to a floor that's the same height or lower than the bottom of the carpet, attach a metal carpet bar to the floor and secure the carpet inside the bar. This transition is often used where carpet meets a vinyl or tile floor. Carpet bars are sold in standard door-width lengths and in longer strips.

For a transition to a floor that's higher than the carpet bottom, use tackless strips, as if the adjoining floor surface was a wall. This transition is common where carpet meets a hardwood floor.

For a transition to another carpet of the same height, join the two carpet sections together with hot-glue seam tape.

For a transition in a doorway between carpets of different heights or textures, install tackless strips and a hardwood threshold (below). Thresholds are available predrilled and ready to install with screws.

Metal carpet bar

Tackless strip tuck-under

Hot-glue seam tape

Hardwood threshold

HOW TO MAKE TRANSITIONS WITH METAL CARPET BARS

Measure and cut a carpet bar to fit the threshold using a hacksaw. Nail the carpet bar in place. In doorways, the upturned metal flange should lie directly under the center of the door when it's closed.

Roll out, cut, and seam the carpet. Fold the carpet back in the transition area, then mark it for trimming. The edge of the carpet should fall ⅛ to ¼" short of the corner of the carpet bar so it can be stretched into the bar.

Use a knee kicker to stretch the carpet snugly into the corner of the carpet bar. Press the carpet down onto the pins with a stair tool. Bend the carpet bar flange down over the carpet by striking it with a hammer and a block of wood.

HOW TO MAKE TRANSITIONS WITH TACKLESS STRIPS

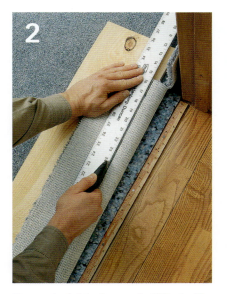

Install a tackless strip, leaving a gap equal to ⅔ the thickness of the carpet for trimming. Roll out, cut, and seam the carpet. Mark the edge of the carpet between the tackless strip and the adjoining floor surface about ⅛" past the point where it meets the adjacent floor.

Use a straightedge and utility knife to trim the excess carpet. Stretch the carpet toward the strip with a knee kicker, then press it onto the pins of the tackless strip.

Tuck the edge of the carpet into the gap between the tackless strip and the existing floor using a stair tool.

CARPET SQUARES: INSTALLING

Most carpeting has a single design and is stretched from wall to wall. It covers more square feet of American homes than any other material. You can install it yourself, following the instructions on pages 36 to 47. But if you want a soft floor covering that gives you more options, carpet squares are an excellent choice.

Manufacturers have found ways to create attractive new carpet using recycled fibers. This not only reuses material that would otherwise become landfill, it reduces waste in manufacturing as well. So, instead of adding to problems of resource consumption and pollution, carpet squares made from recycled materials help reduce them.

The squares are attached to each other and to the floor with adhesive dots. They can be installed on most clean, level, dry underlayment or onto an existing floor. If the surface underneath is waxed or varnished, check with the manufacturer before you use any adhesives on it.

Tools & Materials ▸

Adhesive	Marking pen or pencil
Carpenter's square	Straightedge
Chalk line	Carpet squares
Cleaning supplies	Scrap plywood
Craft/utility knife	Protective equipment
Measuring tape	

Carpet tiles combine the warmth and comfort of carpet with do-it-yourself installation, custom designs, and easy replacement. They can be laid wall-to-wall or in an area rug style, as shown above.

HOW TO INSTALL CARPET SQUARES

Take the squares out of the package. Usually, you want to keep new flooring out of the way until you're ready to install it. But some materials, such as carpet or sheet vinyl, should be at room temperature for at least 12 hours before you lay them down.

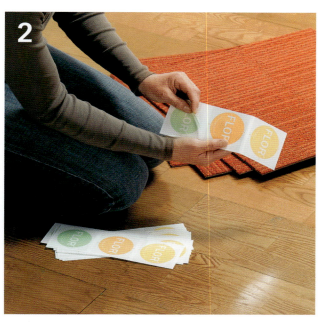

Check the requirements for the recommended adhesive. You can install carpet squares over many other flooring materials, including hardwood, laminates, and resilient sheets or tiles. The carpet squares shown here are fastened with adhesive dots, so almost any existing floor will provide a usable surface.

Make sure the existing floor is clean, smooth, stable, and dry. Use floor leveler if necessary to eliminate any hills or valleys. If any part of the floor is loose, secure it to the subfloor or underlayment before you install the carpet squares. Vacuum the surface and wipe it with a damp cloth.

Snap chalk lines between diagonally opposite corners to find the center point for the room. In rooms with unusual shapes, determine the visual center and mark it. Next, snap chalk lines across the center and perpendicular to the walls. This set of guidelines will show you where to start.

(continued)

FLOORS

5

Lay a base row of carpet squares on each side of the two guidelines. When you reach the walls, make note of how much you will need to cut. You should have the same amount to cut on each side. If not, adjust the center point and realign the squares.

6

Check the backs of the squares before you apply any adhesive. They should indicate a direction, using arrows or other marks, so that the finished pile has a consistent appearance. If you plan to mix colors, this is the time to establish your pattern.

7

Fasten the base rows in place using the manufacturer's recommended adhesive. This installation calls for two adhesive dots per square. As you place each square, make sure it is aligned with the guidelines and fits tightly against the next square.

8

When you reach a wall, flip the last square over. Push it against the wall until it is snug. If you are planning a continuous pattern, align the arrows with the existing squares. If you are creating a parquet pattern, turn the new square 90 degrees before marking it.

9

Mark notches or draw a line across the back where the new square overlaps the next-to-last one. Using a sharp utility knife, a carpenter's square, and a tough work surface, cut along this line. The cut square should fit neatly in the remaining space.

10

At a door jamb, place a square face up where it will go. Lean the square against the jamb and mark the point where they meet. Move the square to find the other cutline, and mark that as well. Flip the square over, mark the two lines using a carpenter's square, and cut out the corner.

11

Finish all four base rows before you fill in the rest of the room. As you work, check the alignment of each row. If you notice a row going out of line, find the point where the direction changed, then remove squares back to that point and start again.

12

Work outward from the center so that you have a known reference for keeping rows straight. Save the cut pieces from the ends. They may be useful for patching odd spaces around doorways, heat registers, radiator pipes, and when you reach the corners.

CEDAR SHAKES & SHINGLES: INSTALLING

Prepare the roof decking by installing valley flashing at all valleys (page 350). Apply felt paper underlayment to the first 36" of the roof deck. *Note: Depending on your climate and building codes, you may want to install ice and water shield for this step rather than felt paper.*

Install a starter shake so it overhangs the eaves and rake edge by 1½". Do the same on the opposite side of the roof. Run a taut string between the bottom edges of the two shakes. Install the remaining shakes in the starter row, aligning the bottoms with the string. Keep the manufacturer's recommended distance between shakes, usually ⅜ to ⅝".

Set the first course of shakes over the starter row, aligning the shakes along the rake ends and bottoms. Joints between shakes must overlap by at least 1½". Drive two nails in each shake, ¾ to 1" from the edges, and 1½ to 2" above the exposure line. Use the hatchet to rip shakes to fit. *Tip: Set the gauge on your roofer's hatchet to the exposure rate. You can then use the hatchet as a quick reference for checking the exposure.*

Snap a chalk line over the first course of shakes at the exposure line. Snap a second line at a distance that's twice the exposure rate. Staple an 18"-wide strip of felt paper at the second line. Overlap felt paper vertical seams by 4". Install the second course of shakes at the exposure line, offsetting joints by 1½" minimum. Install remaining courses the same way.

Set shakes in place along valleys, but don't nail them. Hold a 1 × 4 against the center of the valley flashing without nailing it. Place it over the shakes to use as a guide for marking the angle of the valley. Cut the shakes using a circular saw, then install.

Use the 1 × 4 to align the edge of the shakes along the valley. Keep the 1 × 4 butted against the valley center, and place the edge of the shake along the edge of the board. Avoid nailing through the valley flashing when installing the shakes.

Notch shakes to fit around a plumbing stack using a jigsaw, then install a course of shakes below the stack. Apply roofing cement to the underside of the stack flashing, then place it over the stack and over the shakes. Nail the flashing along the edges.

Overlap the exposed flashing with the next row of shakes. Cut notches in the shakes to fit around the stack, keeping a 1" gap between the stack and shakes.

(continued)

Install shakes under the bottom apron flashing beneath a skylight. Cut the shakes as necessary. Nail the shakes without driving nails through the flashing. Apply roofing cement to the underside of the flashing, then press to the shakes.

Flashing

Interweave skylight flashing along the skylight with rows of shakes. After each row of shakes, install a piece of flashing with the vertical plane placed under the edge lip of the skylight and the horizontal plane flush with the bottom edge of the shake. A row of shakes covers the top apron flashing.

Apply roofing cement along the underside of the roof louver flange, then set it over the vent cutout and over the shakes directly below it. Nail the louver in place. Install shakes over the sides and back of the louver, trimming to fit as needed.

As you approach the ridge, measure from the last installed row to the peak. Do this on each side of the roof. If the measurements are not equal, slightly adjust the exposure rate in successive rows until the measurements are the same. Make sure you're measuring to points that are aligned at the peak. The top of the sheathing is probably not level across the roof and cannot be a reference point.

Run shakes past the roof peak. Snap a chalk line across the shakes at the ridge. Set the circular saw blade to the depth of the shakes, then cut along the chalk line.

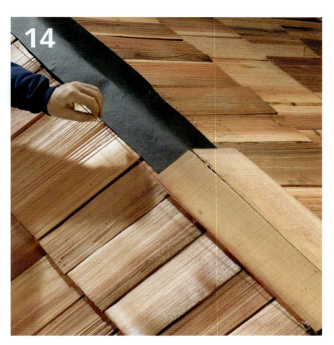

Cut 8" strips of felt paper and staple them over the hips and ridge. Set a factory-made hip and ridge cap at one end of the ridge, aligned with the roof peak. Do the same at the other end of the roof. Snap a chalk line between the outside edges of the caps.

Exposure rate

Set a ridge cap along the chalk line flush with the edge of the roof to serve as the starter. Install with two nails. Place a cap directly on top of the starter cap, and nail in place. Install caps along the remainder of the ridge, alternating the overlap pattern. The exposure rate should be the same as the roof shakes. Nails should penetrate the roof decking by ½".

Variation: If the ridge caps are not preassembled by the manufacturer, install the first cap along the chalk line, then place the second cap over the edge of the first. Alternate the overlap pattern across the ridge.

CEILING FANS: INSTALLING

Add a wood brace above the ceiling box if you have access from above (as in an attic). Cut a 24" brace to fit and nail it between the ceiling joists. Drive a couple of deck screws through the ceiling box and into the brace. If the box is not fan-rated, replace it with one that is.

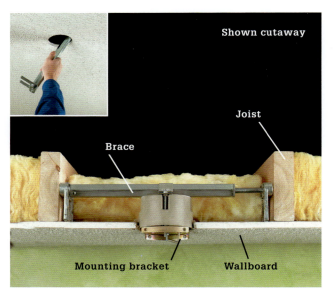

Install an adjustable fan brace if the ceiling is closed and you don't want to remove the wallcoverings. Remove the old light and the electrical box and then insert the fan brace into the box opening (inset photo). Twist the brace housing to cause it to telescope outward. The brace should be centered over the opening and at the right height so the ceiling box is flush with the ceiling surface once it is hung from the brace.

BRACKET-MOUNTED FANS

Direct-mount fan units have a motor housing with a mounting tab that fits directly into a slot on the mounting bracket. Fans with this mounting approach are secure and easy to install but difficult to adjust.

Ball-and-socket fan units have a downrod, but instead of threading into the mounting bracket, the downrod has an attached ball that fits into a hanger "socket" in the mounting bracket. This installation allows the fan to move in the socket and find its own level for quiet operation.

HOW TO INSTALL DOWNROD CEILING FANS

1

Shut off the power to the circuit at the service panel. Unscrew the existing fixture and carefully pull it away from the ceiling. Test for power by inserting the probes of a tester into the wire connectors on the black and the white wires. Disconnect and remove the old fixture.

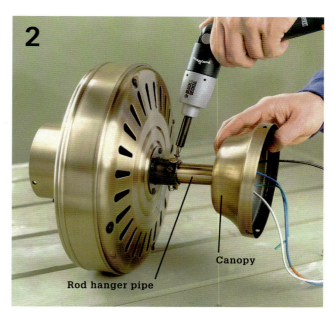

2

Canopy

Rod hanger pipe

Run the wires from the top of the fan motor through the canopy and then through the rod hanger pipe. Slide the rod hanger pipe through the canopy and attach the pipe to the motor collar using the included hanging pin. Tighten the mounting screws firmly.

3

Hanging pin

Hang the motor assembly by the hook on the mounting bracket. Connect the wires according to manufacturer's directions using wire connectors to join the fixture wires to the circuit wires in the box. Gather the wires together and tuck them inside the fan canopy. Lift the canopy and attach it to the mounting bracket.

4

Fan housing

Attach the fan blades with the included hardware. Connect the wiring for the fan's light fixture according to the manufacturer's directions. Tuck all wires into the switch housing and attach the fixture. Install light bulbs. Restore power and test the fan.

CEILING TILE: ACOUSTIC

Easy-to-install ceiling tile can lend character to a plain ceiling or help turn an unfinished basement or attic into beautiful living space. Made of pressed mineral and fiberboard, ceiling tiles are available in a variety of styles. They also provide moderate noise reduction.

Ceiling tiles typically can be attached directly to a drywall or plaster ceiling with adhesive. If your ceiling is damaged or uneven, or if you have an unfinished joist ceiling, install 1 × 2 furring strips as a base for the tiles, as shown in this project. Some systems include metal tracks for clip-on installation.

Unless your ceiling measures in even feet, you won't be able to install the 12-inch tiles without some cutting. To prevent an unattractive installation with small, irregular tiles along two sides, include a course of border tiles along the perimeter of the installation. Plan so that tiles at opposite ends of the room are cut to the same width and are at least half the width of a full tile.

Most ceiling tile comes prefinished, but it can be painted to match any decor. For best results, apply two coats of paint using a roller with a ¼-inch nap, and wait 24 hours between coats.

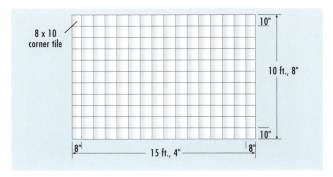

Measure the ceiling and devise a layout. If the length (or width) doesn't measure in even feet, use this formula to determine the width of the border tiles: add 12 to the number of inches remaining and divide by 2. The result is the width of the border tile. (For example, if the room length is 15 ft., 4", add 12 to the 4, then divide 16 by 2, which results in an 8" border tile.)

Acoustic tiles are attached to wood strips on the ceiling rather than suspended. They do not lower the ceiling height as much as a suspended ceiling, but they are also harder to remove for joist cavity access.

HOW TO INSTALL AN ACOUSTIC TILE CEILING

Install the first furring strip flush with the wall and perpendicular to the joists, fastening with two 8d nails or 2" screws at each joist. Measure out from the wall a distance equal to the border tile width minus ¾" and snap a chalk line. Install the second furring strip with its wall-side edge on the chalk line.

Install the remaining strips 12" on-center from the second strip. Measure from the second strip and mark the joist nearest the wall every 12". Repeat along the joist on the opposite side of the room, then snap chalk lines between the marks. Install the furring strips along the lines. Install the last furring strip flush against the opposite side wall.

Check the strips with a 4-ft. level. Insert wood shims between the strips and joists as necessary to bring the strips into a level plane.

Cut border tiles with a utility knife to fit (inset). Position the corner tile with the flange edges aligned with the two string lines and fasten it to the furring strips with four ½" staples. Cut and install two border tiles along each wall, making sure the tiles fit snugly together.

Fill in between the border tiles with full-size tiles. Continue working diagonally in this manner toward the opposite corner. For the border tiles along the far wall, trim off the flange edges and staple through the faces of the tiles close to the wall.

CIRCUIT BREAKERS & FUSES

The circuit breaker panel is the electrical distribution center for your home. It divides the current into branch circuits that are carried throughout the house. Each branch circuit is controlled by a circuit breaker that protects the wires from dangerous current overloads. When installing new circuits, the last step is to connect the wires to new circuit breakers at the panel. Working inside a circuit breaker panel is not dangerous if you follow basic safety procedures. Always shut off the main circuit breaker and test for power before touching any parts inside the panel, and never touch the service wire lugs. If unsure of your own skills, hire an electrician to make the final circuit connections. (If you have an older electrical service with fuses instead of circuit breakers, always have an electrician make these final hookups.)

If the main circuit breaker panel does not have enough open slots to hold new circuit breakers, install a subpanel. This job is well within the skill level of an

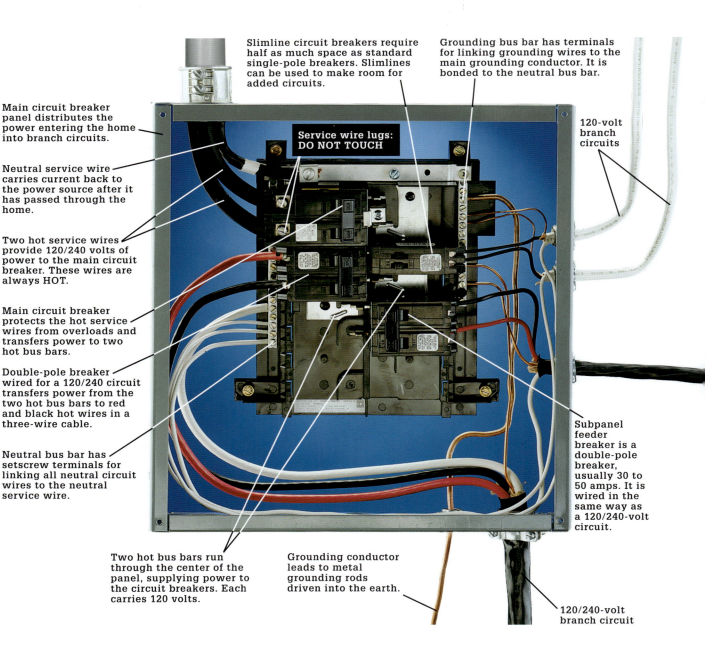

Main circuit breaker panel distributes the power entering the home into branch circuits.

Neutral service wire carries current back to the power source after it has passed through the home.

Two hot service wires provide 120/240 volts of power to the main circuit breaker. These wires are always HOT.

Main circuit breaker protects the hot service wires from overloads and transfers power to two hot bus bars.

Double-pole breaker wired for a 120/240 circuit transfers power from the two hot bus bars to red and black hot wires in a three-wire cable.

Neutral bus bar has setscrew terminals for linking all neutral circuit wires to the neutral service wire.

Slimline circuit breakers require half as much space as standard single-pole breakers. Slimlines can be used to make room for added circuits.

Service wire lugs: DO NOT TOUCH

Grounding bus bar has terminals for linking grounding wires to the main grounding conductor. It is bonded to the neutral bus bar.

120-volt branch circuits

Subpanel feeder breaker is a double-pole breaker, usually 30 to 50 amps. It is wired in the same way as a 120/240-volt circuit.

Two hot bus bars run through the center of the panel, supplying power to the circuit breakers. Each carries 120 volts.

Grounding conductor leads to metal grounding rods driven into the earth.

120/240-volt branch circuit

experienced do-it-yourselfer, although you can also hire an electrician to install the subpanel.

Before installing any new wiring, evaluate your electrical service to make sure it provides enough current to support both the existing wiring and any new circuits. If your service does not provide enough power, have an electrician upgrade it to a higher amp rating. During the upgrade, the electrician will install a new circuit breaker panel with enough extra breaker slots for the new circuits you want to install.

Safety Warning ▸

Never touch any parts inside a circuit breaker panel until you have checked for power (page 82). Circuit breaker panels differ in appearance, depending on the manufacturer. Never begin work in a circuit breaker panel until you understand its layout and can identify the parts.

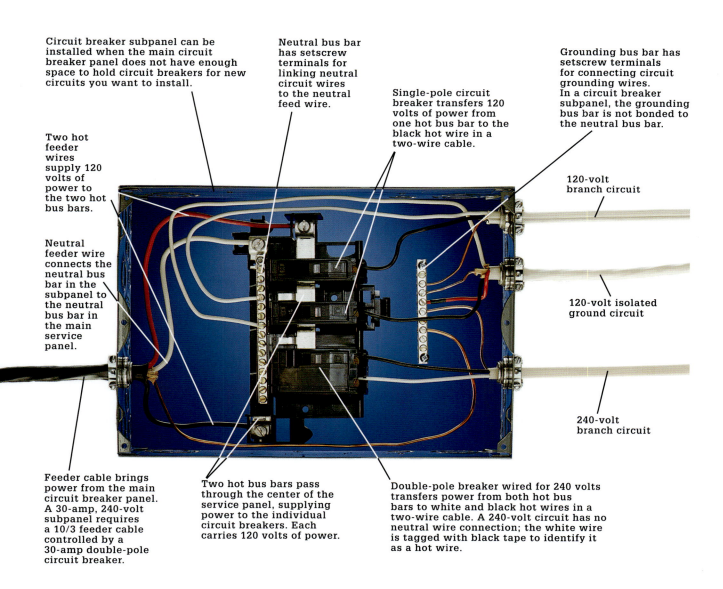

Circuit breaker subpanel can be installed when the main circuit breaker panel does not have enough space to hold circuit breakers for new circuits you want to install.

Neutral bus bar has setscrew terminals for linking neutral circuit wires to the neutral feed wire.

Single-pole circuit breaker transfers 120 volts of power from one hot bus bar to the black hot wire in a two-wire cable.

Grounding bus bar has setscrew terminals for connecting circuit grounding wires. In a circuit breaker subpanel, the grounding bus bar is not bonded to the neutral bus bar.

Two hot feeder wires supply 120 volts of power to the two hot bus bars.

Neutral feeder wire connects the neutral bus bar in the subpanel to the neutral bus bar in the main service panel.

120-volt branch circuit

120-volt isolated ground circuit

240-volt branch circuit

Feeder cable brings power from the main circuit breaker panel. A 30-amp, 240-volt subpanel requires a 10/3 feeder cable controlled by a 30-amp double-pole circuit breaker.

Two hot bus bars pass through the center of the service panel, supplying power to the individual circuit breakers. Each carries 120 volts of power.

Double-pole breaker wired for 240 volts transfers power from both hot bus bars to white and black hot wires in a two-wire cable. A 240-volt circuit has no neutral wire connection; the white wire is tagged with black tape to identify it as a hot wire.

FUSES & CIRCUIT BREAKERS

Fuses and circuit breakers are safety devices designed to protect the electrical system from short circuits and overloads. Fuses and circuit breakers are located in the main service panel.

Most service panels installed before 1965 rely on fuses to control and protect individual circuits. Screw-in plug fuses protect 120-volt circuits that power lights and receptacles. Cartridge fuses protect 240-volt appliance circuits and the main shutoff of the service panel.

Inside each fuse is a current-carrying metal alloy ribbon. If a circuit is overloaded, the metal ribbon melts and stops the flow of power. A fuse must match the amperage rating of the circuit. Never replace a fuse with one that has a larger amperage rating.

In most service panels installed after 1965, circuit breakers protect and control individual circuits. Single-pole circuit breakers protect 120-volt circuits, and double-pole circuit breakers protect 240-volt circuits. Amperage ratings for circuit breakers range from 15 to 100 amps.

Each circuit breaker has a permanent metal strip that heats up and bends when voltage passes through it. If a circuit is overloaded, the metal strip inside the breaker bends enough to "trip" the switch and stop the flow of power. Circuit breakers are listed to trip twice. After the second trip they weaken and tend to nuisance trip at lower currents. Replace breakers that have tripped more than twice—they may fail. Worn circuit breakers should be replaced by an electrician.

When a fuse blows or a circuit breaker trips, it is usually because there are too many light fixtures and plug-in appliances drawing power through the circuit. Move some of the plug-in appliances to another circuit, then replace the fuse or reset the breaker. If the fuse blows or the breaker trips again immediately, there may be a short circuit in the system. Call a licensed electrician if you suspect a short circuit.

Tools & Materials ▸

Fuse puller and continuity tester (for cartridge fuses only)
Replacement fuse

Circuit breakers are found in the majority of panels installed since the 1940s. Single-pole breakers control 120-volt circuits. Double-pole breakers rated for 20 to 60 amps control 240-volt circuits. Ground-fault circuit interrupter (GFCI) and arc-fault circuit interrupter (AFCI) breakers provide protection from shocks and fire-causing arcs for the entire circuit.

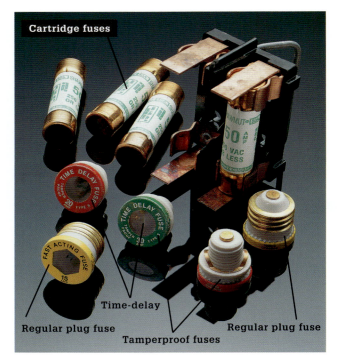

Fuses are used in older service panels. Plug fuses usually control 120-volt circuits rated for 15, 20, or 30 amps. Tamper-proof plug fuses have threads that fit only matching sockets, making it impossible to install a wrong-sized fuse. Time-delay fuses absorb temporary heavy power loads without blowing. Cartridge fuses control 240-volt circuits and range from 30 to 100 amps.

HOW TO IDENTIFY & REPLACE A BLOWN PLUG FUSE

Locate the blown fuse at the main service panel. If the metal ribbon inside is cleanly melted (right), the circuit was overloaded. If window is discolored (left), there was a short circuit.

Unscrew the fuse, being careful to touch only the insulated rim of the fuse. Replace it with a fuse that has the same amperage rating.

HOW TO REMOVE, TEST & REPLACE A CARTRIDGE FUSE

Remove cartridge fuses by gripping the handle of the fuse block and pulling sharply.

Remove the individual cartridge fuses from the block using a fuse puller.

Test each fuse using a continuity tester. If the tester glows, the fuse is good. If not, install a new fuse with the same amperage rating.

HOW TO RESET A CIRCUIT BREAKER

Open the service panel and locate the tripped breaker. The lever on the tripped breaker will be either in the OFF position, or in a position between ON and OFF.

Reset the tripped circuit breaker by pressing the circuit breaker lever all the way to the OFF position, then pressing it to the ON position.

Test AFCI and GFCI circuit breakers by pushing the TEST button. The breaker should trip to the OFF position. If not, the breaker is faulty and must be replaced by an electrician.

CONDUIT: INSTALLING

ELECTRICAL GROUNDING IN METAL CONDUIT

Electrical wiring that runs in exposed locations must be protected by rigid tubing called conduit. For example, conduit is used for wiring that runs across masonry walls in a basement laundry and for exposed outdoor wiring. THHN/THWN wire (opposite page) normally is installed inside conduit, although UF or NM cable can also be installed in conduit.

There are several types of conduit available, so check with your electrical inspector to find out which type meets code requirements in your area. Conduit installed outdoors must be rated for exterior use. Metal conduit should be used only with metal boxes, never with plastic boxes.

At one time, conduit could only be fitted by using elaborate bending techniques and special tools. Now, however, a variety of shaped fittings are available to let a homeowner join conduit easily.

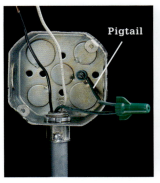
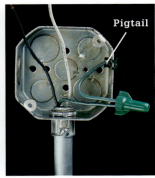

Pigtail

Pigtail

Install a green insulated grounding wire for any circuit that runs through metal conduit. Although code allows the metal conduit to serve as the grounding conductor, most electricians install a green insulated wire as a more dependable means of grounding the system. The grounding wires must be connected to metal boxes with a pigtail and grounding screw (left) or grounding clip (right).

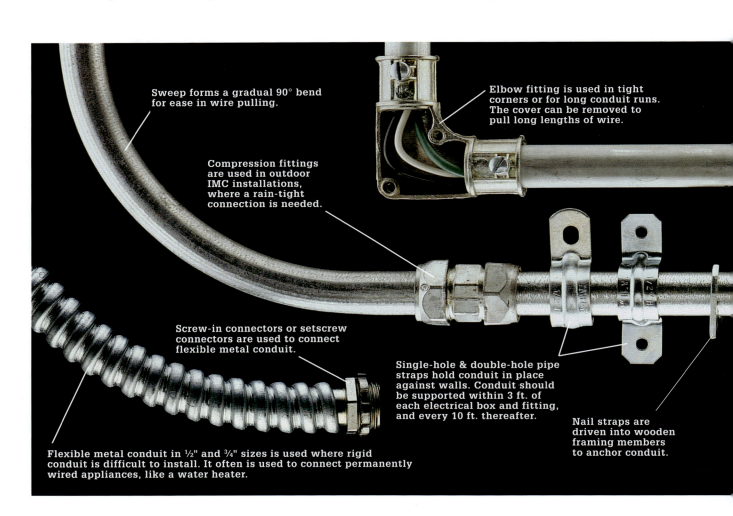

Sweep forms a gradual 90° bend for ease in wire pulling.

Elbow fitting is used in tight corners or for long conduit runs. The cover can be removed to pull long lengths of wire.

Compression fittings are used in outdoor IMC installations, where a rain-tight connection is needed.

Screw-in connectors or setscrew connectors are used to connect flexible metal conduit.

Single-hole & double-hole pipe straps hold conduit in place against walls. Conduit should be supported within 3 ft. of each electrical box and fitting, and every 10 ft. thereafter.

Nail straps are driven into wooden framing members to anchor conduit.

Flexible metal conduit in ½" and ¾" sizes is used where rigid conduit is difficult to install. It often is used to connect permanently wired appliances, like a water heater.

FILL CAPACITY

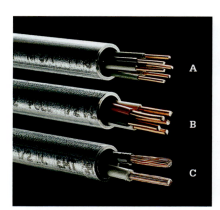

Conduit ½" in diameter can hold up to six 14-gauge or 12-gauge THHN/THWN wires (A), five 10-gauge wires (B), or two 8-gauge wires (C). Use ¾" conduit for greater capacity.

METAL CONDUIT

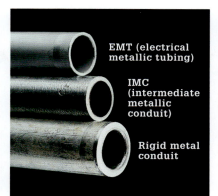

EMT (electrical metallic tubing)

IMC (intermediate metallic conduit)

Rigid metal conduit

EMT is lightweight and easy to install. IMC has thicker galvanized walls and is a good choice for exposed outdoor use. Rigid metal conduit provides the greatest protection for wires, but it is more expensive and requires threaded fittings. EMT is the preferred metal conduit for home use.

PLASTIC CONDUIT

Plastic PVC conduit is allowed by many local codes. It is assembled with solvent glue and PVC fittings that resemble those for metal conduit. When wiring with PVC conduit, always run a green grounding wire.

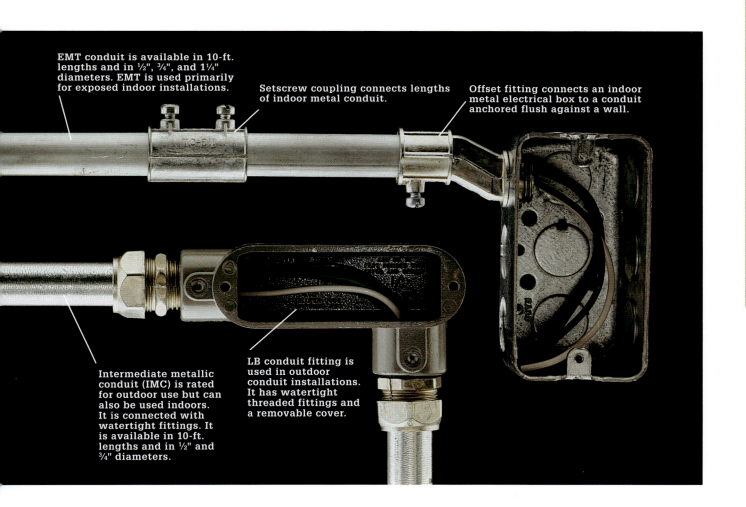

EMT conduit is available in 10-ft. lengths and in ½", ¾", and 1¼" diameters. EMT is used primarily for exposed indoor installations.

Setscrew coupling connects lengths of indoor metal conduit.

Offset fitting connects an indoor metal electrical box to a conduit anchored flush against a wall.

Intermediate metallic conduit (IMC) is rated for outdoor use but can also be used indoors. It is connected with watertight fittings. It is available in 10-ft. lengths and in ½" and ¾" diameters.

LB conduit fitting is used in outdoor conduit installations. It has watertight threaded fittings and a removable cover.

WORKING WITH CONDUIT

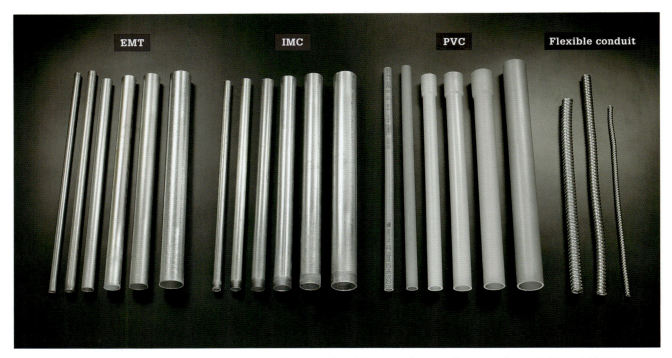

Conduit types used most in homes are EMT (electrical metallic tubing), IMC (intermediate metallic conduit), RNC (rigid nonmetallic conduit), and flexible metal conduit. The most common diameters by far are ½" and ¾", but larger sizes are stocked at most building centers.

Nonmetallic conduit fittings typically are solvent welded to nonmetallic conduit, as opposed to metal conduit, which can be threaded and screwed into threaded fittings or attached with setscrews or compression fittings.

A thin-wall conduit bender is used to bend sweeps into EMT or IMC conduit.

HOW TO MAKE NONMETALLIC CONDUIT CONNECTIONS

1

Cut the rigid nonmetallic conduit (RNC) to length with a fine-tooth saw, such as a hacksaw. For larger diameter (1½" and above), use a power miter box with a fine-tooth or plastic cutting blade.

2

Deburr the cut edges with a utility knife or fine sandpaper such as emery paper. Wipe the cut ends with a dry rag. Also wipe the coupling or fitting to clean it.

3

Apply a coat of PVC cement to the end of the conduit and to the inside walls of the coupling (inset). Wear latex gloves to protect your hands. The cement should be applied past the point on the conduit where it enters the fitting or coupling.

4

Insert the conduit into the fitting or coupling and spin it a quarter turn to help spread the cement. Allow the joint to set undisturbed for 10 minutes.

COUNTERTOPS: INSTALLING

Post-form laminate countertops are available in stock and custom colors. Pre-mitered sections are available for two- or three-piece countertops that continue around corners. If the countertop has an exposed end, you will need an endcap kit that contains a pre-shaped strip of matching laminate. Post-form countertops have either a waterfall edge or a no-drip edge. Stock colors are typically available in 4-, 6-, 8-, 10-, and 12-foot straight lengths and 6- and 8-foot mitered lengths.

Tools & Materials ▸

Tape measure
Framing square
Pencil
Straightedge
C-clamps
Hammer
Level
Caulking gun
Jigsaw
Compass
Adjustable wrench
Belt sander
Drill and spade bit
Cordless screwdriver

Post-form countertop
Wood shims
Take-up bolts
Drywall screws
Wire brads
Endcap laminate
Silicone caulk
Wood glue
Household iron
Fasteners
Sealer
File
Protective equipment

Post-form countertops are among the easiest and cheapest to install. They are a good choice for beginning DIYers, but the design and color options are fairly limited.

The following tools and materials will be used in this project: wood for shimming (A); take-up bolts for drawing miters together (B); household iron (C); endcap laminate to match countertop (D); endcap battens (E); file (F); adjustable wrench (G); buildup blocks (H); compass (I); fasteners (J); silicone caulk and sealer (K).

HOW TO INSTALL A POST-FORM COUNTERTOP

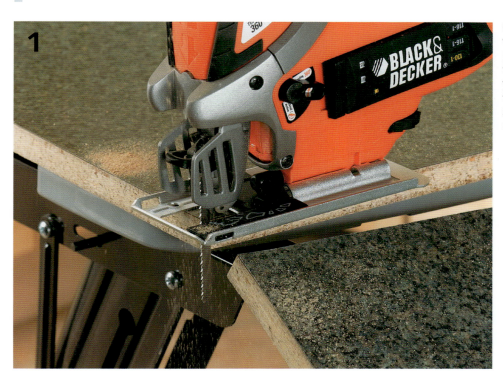

OPTION: Use a jigsaw fitted with a downstroke blade to cut post-form. If you are unable to locate a downstroke blade, you can try applying tape over the cutting lines, but you are still likely to get tear-out from a normal upstroke jigsaw blade.

Use a framing square to mark a cutting line on the bottom surface of the countertop. Cut off the countertop with a jigsaw using a clamped straightedge as a guide.

Attach the battens from the endcap kit to the edge of the countertop using carpenter's glue and small brads. Sand out any unevenness with a belt sander.

(continued)

4

Hold the endcap laminate against the end, slightly overlapping the edges. Activate adhesive by pressing an iron set at medium heat against the endcap. Cool with a wet cloth, then file the endcap laminate flush with the edges of the countertop.

5

Position the countertop on the base cabinets. Make sure the front edge of the countertop is parallel to the cabinet faces. Check the countertop for level. Make sure that drawers and doors open and close freely. If needed, adjust the countertop with shims.

6

Because walls are usually uneven, use a compass to trace the wall outline onto the backsplash. Set the compass arms to match the widest gap, then move the compass along the length of the wall to transfer the outline to the top of the backsplash. Apply painter's tape to the top edge of the backsplash, following the scribe line (inset).

7

Remove the countertop. Use a belt sander to grind the backsplash to the scribe line.

Mark cutout for self-rimming sink. Position the sink upside down on the countertop and trace its outline. Remove the sink and draw a cutting line ⅝" inside the sink outline.

Drill a starter hole just inside the cutting line. Make sink cutouts with a jigsaw. Support the cutout area from below so that the falling cutout does not damage the cabinet.

Apply a bead of silicone caulk to the edges of the mitered countertop sections. Force the countertop pieces tightly together.

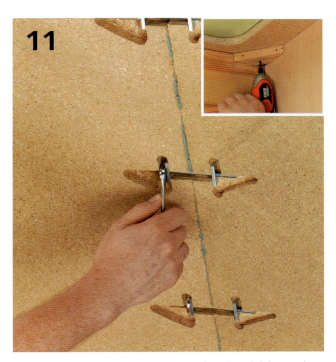

From underneath the countertop, install and tighten miter take-up bolts. Position the countertop tightly against the wall and fasten it to the cabinets by driving wallboard screws up through the corner brackets and into the countertop (inset). Screws should be long enough to provide maximum holding power, but not long enough to puncture the laminate surface.

Seal the seam between the backsplash and the wall with silicone caulk. Smooth the bead with a wet fingertip. Wipe away excess caulk.

DISHWASHER: INSTALLING

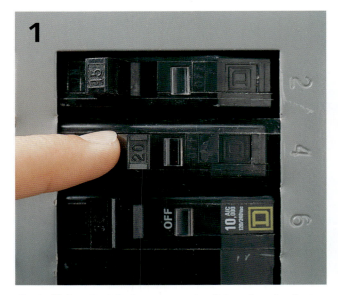

1

Shut off the electrical power to the dishwasher circuit at the service panel. Also, turn off the water supply at the shutoff valve, usually located directly under the floor.

2

Disconnect the old plumbing connections. First unscrew the front access panel. Once the access panel is removed, disconnect the water supply line from the L-fitting on the bottom of the unit. This is usually a brass compression fitting, so just turning the compression nut counterclockwise with an adjustable wrench should do the trick. Use a bowl to catch any water that might leak out when the nut is removed.

3

Disconnect the old wiring connections. The dishwasher has an integral electrical box at the front of the unit where the power cable is attached to the dishwasher's fixture wires. Take off the box cover and remove the wire connectors that join the wires together.

4

Disconnect the discharge hose, which is usually connected to the dishwasher port on the side of the garbage disposer. To remove it, loosen the screw on the hose clamp and pull it off. You may need to push this hose back through a hole in the cabinet wall and into the dishwasher compartment so it won't get caught when you pull the dishwasher out.

5

Detach the unit from the surrounding cabinets. Remove the screws that hold the brackets to the underside of the countertop. Then put a piece of cardboard or old carpet under the front legs to protect the floor from getting scratched, and pull the dishwasher out.

6

Prepare the new dishwasher. Tip it on its back and attach the new L-fitting into the threaded port on the solenoid. Apply some Teflon tape or pipe sealant to the fitting threads before tightening it in place to prevent possible leaks.

7

Attach a length of new automotive heater hose, usually ⅝" diameter, to the end of the dishwasher's discharge hose nipple with a hose clamp. The new hose you are adding should be long enough to reach from the discharge nipple to the port on the side of the kitchen sink garbage disposer.

8

Prepare for the wiring connections. Like the old dishwasher, the new one will have an integral electrical box for making the wiring connections. To gain access to the box, remove the box cover. Then install a cable connector on the back of the box and bring the power cable from the service panel through this connector. Power should be shut off at the main service panel at all times.

(continued)

9

Install a leveling leg at each of the four corners while the new dishwasher is still on its back. Just turn the legs into the threaded holes designed for them. Leave about ½" of each leg projecting from the bottom of the unit. These will have to be adjusted later to level the appliance. Tip the appliance up onto the feet and slide it into the opening. Check for level in both directions and adjust the feet as required.

10

Once the dishwasher is level, attach the brackets to the underside of the countertop to keep the appliance from moving. Then pull the discharge hose into the sink cabinet and install it so there's a loop that is attached with a bracket to the underside of the countertop. This loop prevents waste water from flowing from the disposer back into the dishwasher.

Lengthening a Discharge Hose ▶

1

If the discharge hose has to be modified to fit onto the disposer port, first insert a 4"-long piece of ½" copper tubing into the hose and hold it in place with a hose clamp. This provides a nipple for the rubber adapter that fits onto the disposer.

2

Clamp the rubber disposer adapter to the end of the copper tubing nipple. Then tighten the hose clamp securely.

Push the adapter over the disposer's discharge nipple and tighten it in place with a hose clamp. If you don't have a disposer, this discharge hose can be clamped directly to a modified sink tailpiece that's installed below a standard sink strainer.

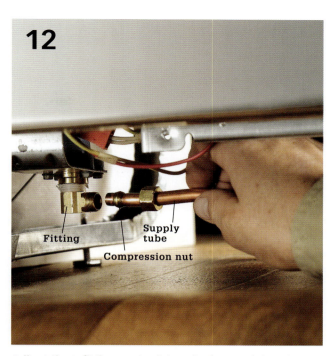

Adjust the L-fitting on the dishwasher's water inlet valve until it points directly toward the water supply tubing. Lubricate the threads slightly with a drop of dishwashing liquid and tighten the tubing's compression nut onto the fitting. Use an adjustable wrench and turn the nut clockwise.

Complete the electrical connections by tightening the connector's clamp on the cable and then joining the power wires to the fixture wires with wire connectors. Attach the ground wire (or wires) to the grounding screw on the box, and replace the cover.

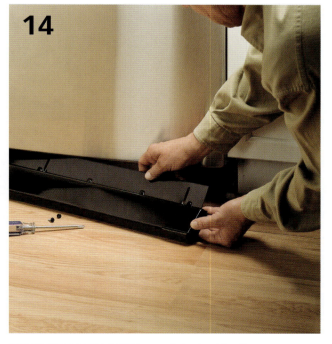

Install the access panel, usually by hooking it on a couple of prongs just below the dishwasher's door. Install the screws (if any) that hold it in place, and turn on the water and power supplies. Replace the toe-kick panel at the bottom of the dishwasher.

DOOR: LOCKS: DEADBOLT

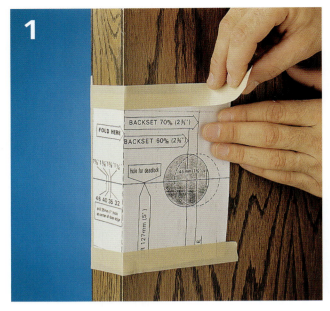

Measure up from the floor or existing lockset to locate the lock. Its center should be at least 3½" from the lockset center. Tape the template (supplied with lock) to the door. Use an awl to mark the center-points of the cylinder and deadbolt holes on the door. Close the door and use the template to mark the centerline for the deadbolt hole in the door jamb.

Bore the cylinder hole with a hole saw and drill. To avoid splintering the door, drill through one side until the hole saw pilot (mandrel) just comes out the other side. Remove the hole saw, then complete the hole from the opposite side of the door.

Use a spade bit to bore the deadbolt hole from the edge of the door into the cylinder hole. Be sure to keep the drill perpendicular to the door edge while drilling.

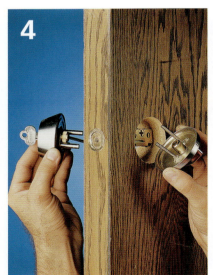

Insert the deadbolt into the edge hole. Fit the two halves of the lock into the door, aligning the cylinder tailpiece and connecting screw fittings with the proper holes in the deadbolt. Secure the two halves together with the connecting screws.

Use the centerline mark on the jamb to locate the hole for the deadbolt. Bore the hole, then chisel a mortise for the strike plate. Install the strike plate. Or, for greater security, install a security box strike, instead of the standard strike plate.

DOORBELLS: INSTALLING

Most doorbell problems are caused by loose wire connections or worn-out switches. Reconnecting loose wires or replacing a switch requires only a few minutes. Doorbell problems also can occur if the chime unit becomes dirty or worn, or if the low-voltage transformer burns out. Both parts are easy to replace. Because doorbells operate at low voltage, the switches and the chime unit can be serviced without turning off power to the system. However, when replacing a transformer, always turn off the power at the main service panel.

Most houses have other low-voltage transformers in addition to the doorbell transformer. These transformers control heating and air-conditioning thermostats (page 459 to 462), or other low-voltage systems. When testing and repairing a doorbell system, it is important to identify the correct transformer. A doorbell transformer has a voltage rating of 24 volts or less. This rating is printed on the face of the transformer. A doorbell transformer often is located near the main service panel and in some homes is attached directly to the service panel. The transformer that controls a heating/air-conditioning thermostat system is located near the furnace and has a voltage rating of 24 volts or more.

Occasionally, a doorbell problem is caused by a broken low-voltage wire somewhere in the system. You can test for wire breaks with a battery-operated multitester. If the test indicates a break, new low-voltage wires must be installed between the transformer and the switches, or between the switches and chime unit. Replacing low-voltage wires is not a difficult job, but it can be time-consuming. You may choose to have an electrician do this work.

Tools & Materials ▸

Continuity tester	Replacement doorbell
Screwdriver	switch (if needed)
Multimeter	Masking tape
Needlenose pliers	Replacement chime
Cotton swab	unit (if needed)
Rubbing alcohol	Protective equipment

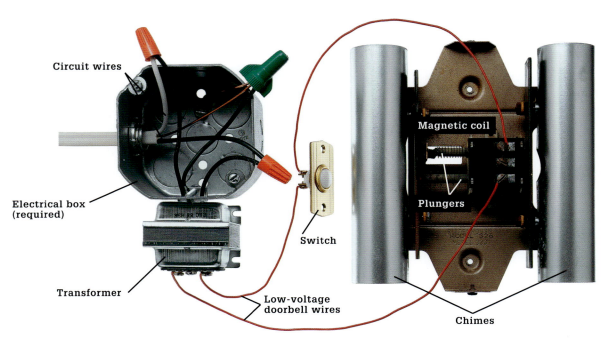

Circuit wires

Electrical box (required)

Transformer

Switch

Low-voltage doorbell wires

Magnetic coil

Plungers

Chimes

A home doorbell system is powered by a transformer that reduces 120-volt current to low-voltage current of 24 volts or less. Current flows from the transformer to one or more push-button switches. When pushed, the switch activates a magnetic coil inside the chime unit, causing a plunger to strike a musical tuning bar.

HOW TO TEST A NONFUNCTIONAL DOORBELL SYSTEM

1

Remove the mounting screws holding the doorbell switch to the siding.

2

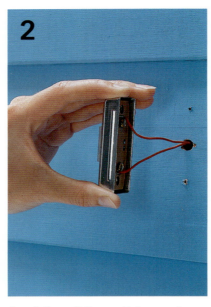

Carefully pull the switch away from the wall.

3

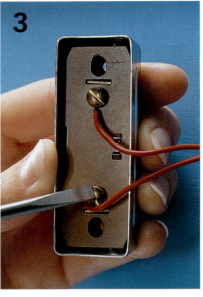

Inspect wire connections on the switch. If wires are loose, reconnect them to the screw terminals. Test the doorbell by pressing the button. If the doorbell still does not work, disconnect the switch and test it with a continuity tester.

4

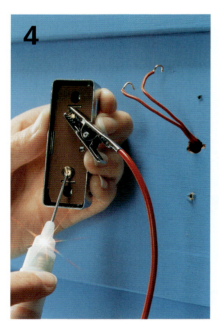

Attach the clip of a continuity tester to one screw terminal and touch the probe to the other screw terminal. Press the switch button. Tester should glow. If not, then the switch is faulty and must be replaced.

5

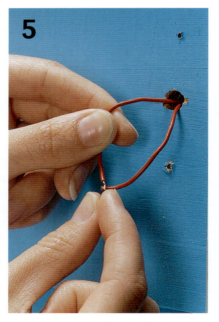

Twist the doorbell switch wires together temporarily to test the other parts of the doorbell system.

6

Transformer

Locate the doorbell transformer, often found near the main service panel. Transformer may be attached to an electrical box, or may be attached directly to the side of the service panel.

WIRING

D

Identify the doorbell transformer by reading its voltage rating. Doorbell transformers have a voltage rating of 24 volts or less. Turn off power to the transformer at main service panel. Remove cover on electrical box, and test wires for power. Reconnect any loose wires. Replace taped connections with wire connectors.

Reattach cover plate. Inspect the low-voltage wire connections, and reconnect any loose wires using needlenose pliers or a screwdriver. Turn on power to the transformer at the main service panel.

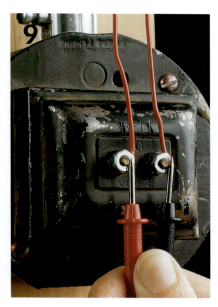

Touch the probes of the multitester to the low-voltage screw terminals on the transformer. If transformer is operating properly, the meter will detect power within 2 volts of transformer's rating. If not, the transformer is faulty and must be replaced.

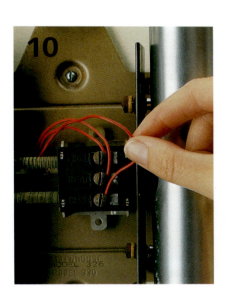

Test the chime unit. Remove the cover plate on the doorbell chime unit. Inspect the low-voltage wire connections, and reconnect any loose wires.

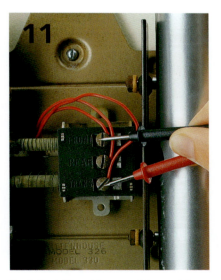

Test that the chime unit is receiving current. Touch probes of a multimeter to screw terminals. If the multimeter detects power within 2 volts of the transformer rating, then the unit is receiving proper current. If it detects no power or very low power, there is a break in the low-voltage wiring and new wires must be installed.

Clean the chime plungers (some models) with a cotton swab dipped in rubbing alcohol. Reassemble doorbell switches, then test the system by pushing one of the switches. If doorbell still does not work, then the chime unit is faulty and must be replaced (page 84).

HOW TO REPLACE A DOORBELL SWITCH

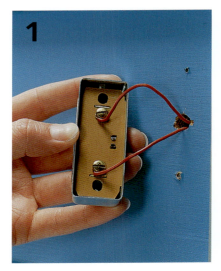

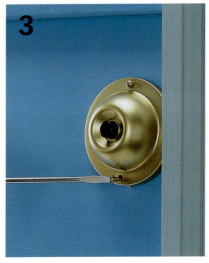

Remove the doorbell switch mounting screws, and carefully pull the switch away from the wall.

Disconnect wires from the switch. Tape wires to the wall to prevent them from slipping into the wall cavity.

Purchase a new doorbell switch, and connect wires to screw terminals on new switch. (Wires are interchangeable and can be connected to either terminal.) Anchor the switch to the wall.

HOW TO REPLACE A DOORBELL CHIME UNIT

Turn off power to the doorbell at the main panel. Remove the cover plate from the old chime. Label the low-voltage wires FRONT, REAR, or TRANS to identify their screw terminal locations. Disconnect the wires. Remove the old chime unit.

Purchase a new chime unit that matches the voltage rating of the old unit. Thread the low-voltage wires through the base of the new chime unit. Attach the chime unit to the wall using the mounting screws included with the installation kit.

Connect the low-voltage wires to the screw terminals on the new chime unit. Attach the cover plate and turn on the power at the main service panel.

DOORS: BIFOLD

Bifold doors provide easy access to a closet without requiring much clearance for opening. Most home centers stock kits that include two pairs of prehinged doors, a head track, and all the necessary hardware and fasteners. Typically, the doors in these kits have predrilled holes for the pivot and guide posts. Hardware kits are also sold separately for custom projects. There are many types of bifold door styles, so be sure to read and follow the manufacturer's instructions for the product you use.

Tools & Materials ▸

Tape measure
Level
Straightedge
 (optional)
Drill
Screwdriver
Prehinged bifold doors

Head track
Mounting hardware
Panhead screws
Flathead screws
Protective
 equipment

HOW TO INSTALL BIFOLD DOORS

Cut the head track to the width of the opening using a hacksaw. Insert the roller mounts into the track, then position the track in the opening. Fasten it to the header using panhead screws.

Measure and mark each side jamb at the floor for the anchor bracket so the center of the bracket aligns exactly with the center of the head track. Fasten the brackets in place with flathead screws.

Check the height of the doors in the opening, and trim if necessary. Insert pivot posts into predrilled holes at the bottoms and tops of the doors. Insert guide posts at the tops of the leading doors. Make sure all posts fit snugly.

Fold one pair of doors closed and lift into position, inserting the pivot and guide posts into the head track. Slip the bottom pivot post into the anchor bracket. Repeat for the other pair of doors. Close the doors and check alignment along the side jambs and down the center. If necessary, adjust the top and bottom pivots following the manufacturer's instructions.

DOORS: ENTRY

A new entry door will provide you with a fine opportunity to dress up the house. Your choice of exterior door design should be driven by the style of other exterior doors on the house. In addition to the number of panels or other design elements, you'll need to determine whether you want an "inswing" or "outswing" door, and what "hand" it should be. This is a matter of space and precedent. Most exterior doors swing in, but if your space is small and cluttered, you may want to opt for an outswing door. The "hand" of the door is simply the location of the handle on the side the door swings toward. For example, a left handed inswing door will have the handle on the left side as you face it from inside the space. The hand of the door should be determined by practicality; if there is a perpendicular wall right next to the door, the door should open on the side away from the wall so that visitors don't feel crowded upon entering.

If you are adding a door at the rear of the house, it may contain an entry door that is less of a design statement than simply a serviceable way to get in and out. The following service door installation includes a fairly plain steel door leading to a workshop addition. If you are installing a fancier front door, the techniques are fundamentally the same.

Tools & Materials ▸

Handsaw	Exterior-grade
Hammer	silicone caulk
Caulk gun	Galvanized
Prehung	casing nails
exterior door	Self-adhesive
Brickmold	flashing tape
Shims	Protective equipment

▌ HOW TO INSTALL A PREHUNG ENTRY DOOR

Flash the bottom and sides. Apply two strips of self-adhesive flashing tape to cover the jack studs in the door's rough opening. Cut a slit in the tape and extend the outer ear 4 to 6" past the bottom edge of the header. Fold the tape over the housewrap to create a 3" overlap. Peel off the backing and press the tape firmly in place.

Flash the header. Cover the header with a third piece of self-adhesive flashing tape, extending the ends of the tape 6" beyond the side flashing. Fold the extra tape over the housewrap to form a 3" overlap.

Seal the opening. Apply a ½"-wide bead of caulk up the outside edges of the jack stud area and around the header to seal the brickmold casing.

Position the door in the opening. Set the bottoms of the side jambs inside the rough opening, and tip the door into place. Adjust the door so it's level, plumb, and centered in the opening.

Attach the door. Drive 2½" galvanized casing nails through the brickmold to fasten the door to the jack studs and header. Space the nails every 12".

Shim at the dead bolt and behind the hinges. Insert pairs of shims with the door closed, adjusting the shims in or out until there's a consistent ⅛" gap between the door and the jamb. If your door came with them, insert one long screw at each hinge into the framing. Then fill the gap with non-expanding foam.

DOORS: NON-PREHUNG: INSTALLING

Have a helper hold the new door in place against the jamb from inside the room. Slide a pair of thick shims under the door to raise it up slightly off the floor or threshold. Move the shims in or out until the door's top and side rails are roughly even with the jamb so it looks balanced in the opening, then make a mark along the top edge of the door.

Use pieces of colored masking tape to mark the outside of the door along the hinge edge. This will help keep the door's orientation clear throughout the installation process.

Use a pencil compass, set to an opening of ³⁄₁₆", to scribe layout lines along both long edges of the door and across the top. These lines will create a clear space for the hinges and door swing. If the bottom of the door will close over carpet, set the dividers for ½" and scribe the bottom edge. Remove the door and transfer these scribe lines to the other door face.

Lay the door on a sturdy bench or across a pair of sawhorses with the tape side facing up. Score the top and bottom scribe lines with a utility knife to keep the wood fibers from splintering when you cut across the ends.

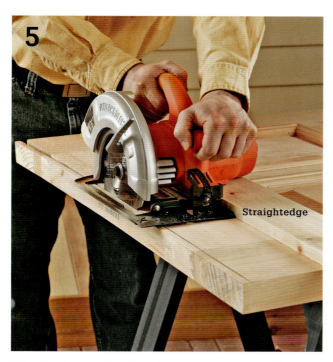

Trim the door ends with a circular saw equipped with a fine-cutting blade. Run the saw base along a clamped straightedge with the blade cutting 1/16" on the waste side of the layout lines. Check to make sure the blade is set square to the saw base before cutting. Use a power planer or hand plane to plane the door ends to the layout lines.

Stand the door on edge and use a power planer or hand plane to plane down to the edge of the scribe lines. Set the tool for a fine cut; use a 1/16" cutting depth for power planing and a shallower cutting depth for a hand plane. Try to make each planing pass in long strokes from one end of the door to the other.

Shim the door back into position in the jamb with a helper supporting it from behind. Set the door slightly out from the doorstop moldings so you can mark the hinge locations on the door face.

Use a combination square or one of the hinge leaves to draw hinge mortise layout lines on the door edge. Score the layout lines with a utility knife.

(continued)

Cut shallow hinge leaf mortises in the door edge with a sharp chisel and hammer. First score the mortise shape with a straightedge and utility knife or a chisel, then make a series of shallow chisel cuts inside the hinge leaf area. Pare away this waste so the mortise depth is slightly deeper than the hinge leaf thickness.

Set the hinges in the door mortises, and drill pilot holes for the hinge screws. Attach the hinges to the door.

Hang the door in the jamb by tipping it into place so the top hinge leaf rests in the top mortise of the jamb. Drive one screw into this mortise. Then set the other leaves into their mortises and install the remaining hinge screws.

Bore holes for the lockset and bolt using a hole saw and spade bit. If you're reusing the original hardware, measure the old door hole sizes and cut matching holes in the new door, starting with the large lockset hole. For new locksets, use the manufacturer's template and hole sizing recommendations to bore the holes. Install the hardware.

DOORS: POCKET

Pocket doors are a space-saving alternative to traditional hinged interior doors. Swinging doors can monopolize up to 16 square feet of floor space in a room, which is why pocket doors are a perfect choice for tight spaces, like small bathrooms. Installed in pairs, pocket doors can divide large rooms into more intimate spaces and can still be opened to use the entire area.

Pocket door hardware kits generally are universal and can be adapted for almost any interior door. In this project, the frame kit includes an adjustable track, steel-clad split studs, and all the required hanging hardware. The latch hardware, jambs, and the door itself are all sold separately. Pocket door frames can also be purchased as preassembled units that can be easily installed into a rough opening.

Framing and installing a pocket door is not difficult in new construction or a major remodel. But retrofitting a pocket door in place of a standard door or installing one in a wall without an existing door, is a major project that involves removing the wall material, framing the new opening, installing and hanging the door, and refinishing the wall. Hidden utilities, such as wiring, plumbing, and heating ducts, must be rerouted if encountered.

The rough opening for a pocket door is at least twice the width of a standard door opening. If the wall is load bearing, you will need to install an appropriately sized header.

Because pocket doors are easy to open and close and require no threshold, they offer increased accessibility for wheelchair or walker users, provided the handles are easy to use. If you are installing a pocket door for this purpose, be aware that standard latch hardware may be difficult to use for some individuals.

Tools & Materials ▶

Tape measure
Hammer
Nail set
Screwdriver
Level
Drill
Hacksaw
Wallboard tools
8d common nails
Pocket door frame kit
Door
1¼" wallboard screws
Wallboard materials
Manufactured pocket door
    jambs (or cut jambs
    from 1× lumber)
8d and 6d finish nails
1½" wood screws
Door casing
Wood finishing materials
Protective equipment

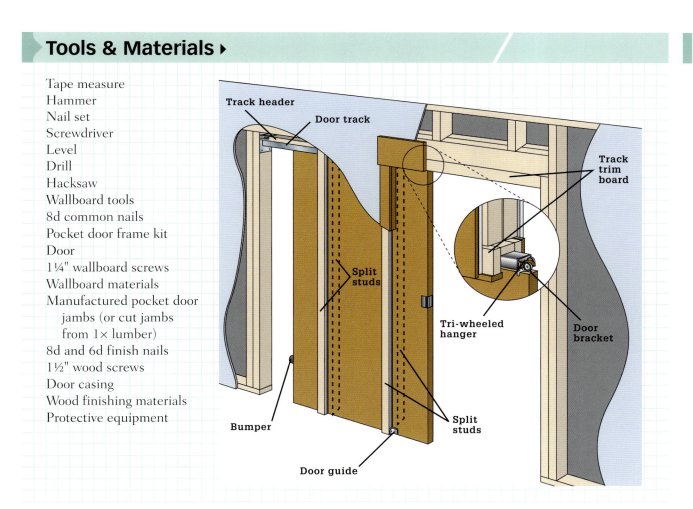

Track header
Door track
Track trim board
Split studs
Tri-wheeled hanger
Door bracket
Bumper
Split studs
Door guide

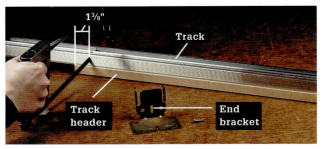

Frame the rough opening for the pocket door according to the manufacturer's sizing instructions. Determine the proper height for the overhead track and drive a nail at each side of the door opening. Leave the nailheads protruding slightly so you can support the track on them temporarily.

Cut the overhead track to length according to the width of the pocket door. The wooden portion of the track should be premarked with cutting lines for standard door sizes (top). The metal part of the track is cut shorter than the wood part (here, by 1⅜"). Attach the end brackets to the track after the trim cuts are made.

Position the overhead track in the framed opening, resting the end bracket on the nails driven in step 1 for temporary support. Center the assembly and secure it by driving 8d common nails through the nailing holes in the brackets.

Attach the split studs in the framed opening. Split studs are the secret to pocket doors. They have an open center that allows the door to pass through. Because they are reinforced with steel they can perform structural bearing comparable to a solid wood stud. Nail the split studs to the wooden part of the overhead track.

Fasten split studs to the floor by nailing through the bottom plate into the subfloor. Snap chalk lines aligned with the front and back of the sole plate in the framed opening as guidance.

WINDOWS & DOORS

6

Fasten rolling brackets to the top of the door following the spacing recommended by the door manufacturer (usually a couple of inches in from each end). Attach wall coverings around the framed opening, making sure your fasteners are not long enough to protrude into the pocket. *Tip: Paint or stain the door before hanging it.*

7

Tri-wheeled hanger

Lock arm

Hang the door by pressing the bracket up into the tri-wheeled hangers in the overhead track and then snapping the lock arm over the hanger. If you have not installed floor covering yet, do so before proceeding to the trim installation.

8

Attach a full-width door jamb for the door to close against. Nail the jamb to the framed opening stud with 8d casing nails.

9

3/16"

Attach split jambs to the side of the framed opening housing the door. Maintain a gap of 3/16" between the door and the inside edges of the split jambs.

10

Install split head jambs with countersunk wood screws. This allows you to easily remove the head jamb if the door needs to be replaced or removed for repair.

11

Attach the latch and pull hardware, which is usually supplied with the door. Also attach door guide hardware at the wall opening to help track the door. Fill nail holes and finish the jambs and walls.

DRAIN-WASTE-VENT LINES

Cut rigid ABS, PVC, or CPVC plastic pipes with a tubing cutter or with any saw. Cuts must be straight to ensure watertight joints.

Rigid plastics are joined with plastic fittings and solvent glue. Use a solvent glue that is made for the type of plastic pipe you are installing. For example, do not use ABS solvent on PVC pipe. Some solvent glues, called "all-purpose" or "universal" solvents, may be used on all types of plastic pipe.

Solvent glue hardens in about 30 seconds, so test-fit all plastic pipes and fittings before gluing the first joint. For best results, the surfaces of plastic pipes and fittings should be dulled with emery cloth and liquid primer before they are joined.

Liquid solvent glues and primers are toxic and flammable. Provide adequate ventilation when fitting plastics, and store the products away from any source of heat.

Plastic grip fittings can be used to join rigid or flexible plastic pipes to copper plumbing pipes.

Tools & Materials ▸

Tape measure	Plastic pipe
Felt-tipped pen	Fittings
Tubing cutter	Emery cloth
(or miter box	Plastic pipe primer
or hacksaw)	Solvent glue
Utility knife	Rag
Channel-type pliers	Protective
Vinyl or latex gloves	equipment

Solvent welding is a chemical bonding process used to permanently join PVC pipes and fittings.

Primer and solvent glue are specific to the plumbing material being used. Do not use all-purpose or multipurpose products. Light to medium body glues are appropriate for DIYers as they allow the longest working time and are easiest to use. When working with large pipe, 3 or 4 inches in diameter, buy a large-size can of cement, which has a larger dauber. If you use the small dauber (which comes with the small can), you may need to apply twice, which will slow you down and make connections difficult. (The smaller can of primer is fine for any other size pipe, since there's no rush in applying primer.) Cement (though not primer) goes bad in the can within a month or two after opening, so you may need to buy a new can for a new project.

HOW TO CUT RIGID PLASTIC PIPE

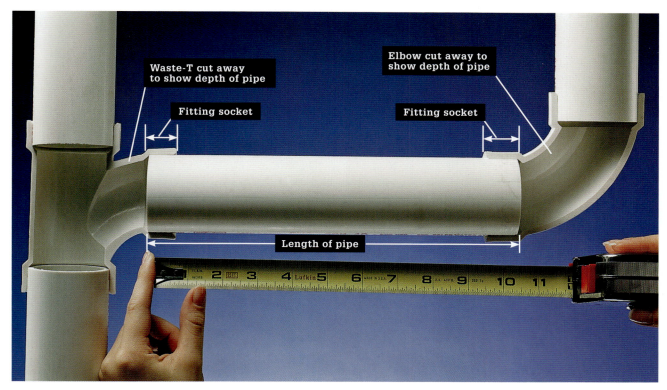

Find the length of plastic pipe needed by measuring between the bottoms of the fitting sockets (fittings shown in cutaway). Mark the length on the pipe with a felt-tipped pen.

Plastic tubing cutters do a fast, neat job of cutting. You'll probably have to go to a professional plumbing supply store to find one, however. They are not interchangeable with metal tubing cutters.

The best cutting tool for plastic pipe is a power miter saw with a fine tooth woodworking blade or a plastic-specific blade.

A ratcheting plastic-pipe cutter can cut smaller diameter PVC and CPVC pipe in a real hurry. If you are plumbing a whole house you may want to consider investing in one. They also are sold only at plumbing supply stores.

HOW TO SOLVENT-GLUE RIGID PLASTIC PIPE

Remove rough burrs on cut ends of plastic pipe, using a utility knife or deburring tool (inset).

Fitting sockets

Test-fit all pipes and fittings. Pipes should fit tightly against the bottom of the fitting sockets.

Mark the depth of the fitting sockets on the pipes. Take pipes apart. Clean the ends of the pipes and fitting sockets with emery cloth.

Apply a light coat of plastic pipe primer to the ends of the pipes and to the insides of the fitting sockets. Primer dulls glossy surfaces and ensures a good seal.

5

Solvent-glue each joint by applying a thick coat of solvent glue to the end of the pipe. Apply a thin coat of solvent glue to the inside surface of the fitting socket. Work quickly: solvent glue hardens in about 30 seconds.

6

Quickly position the pipe and fitting so that the alignment marks are offset by about 2". Force the pipe into the fitting until the end fits flush against the bottom of the socket.

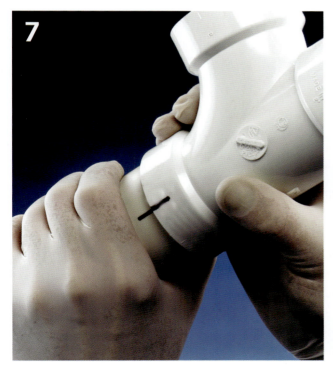

7

Spread solvent by twisting the pipe until the marks are aligned. Hold the pipe in place for about 20 seconds to prevent the joint from slipping.

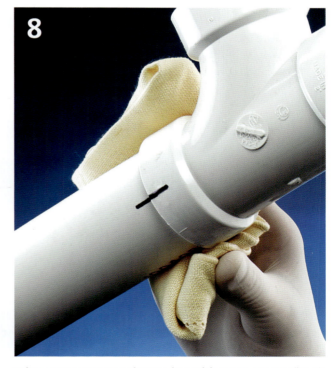

8

Wipe away excess solvent glue with a rag. Do not disturb the joint for 30 minutes after gluing.

DRYWALL: CORNER BEAD: INSTALLING

After the drywall is hung, the next step is to install corner bead to protect outside corners, soffits, drywall-finished openings, and any other outside angles. Corner bead provides a clean, solid-edge wall corner that can withstand moderate abuse. It is available in a variety of styles for a variety of applications (see page 101). The three most common types are metal, vinyl, and paper-faced beads.

Metal beads can be fastened with nails, screws, or a crimper tool. Vinyl beads are easily installed with spray adhesive and staples, or can be embedded in compound, similar to paper-faced beads.

A number of specialty beads are also available, including flexible archway beads for curved corners and J-bead for covering panel ends that meet finished surfaces. Decorative bullnose beads and caps for 2- and 3-way corners are easy ways to add interesting detail to a room.

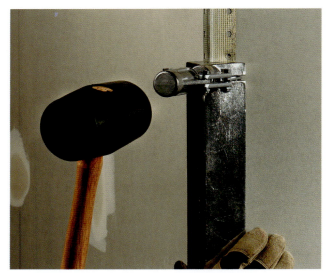

Metal corner bead installed over steel framing can be fastened using a crimper tool. Cut the bead to size and position in the corner (see step 1 below), then crimp every 4 to 6".

Tools & Materials ▸

Work gloves	Stapler	1¼" drywall screws	½" staples
Eye and ear protection	Hammer	1½" ring-shank drywall nails	Archway bead
Aviation snips	Corner bead	Spray adhesive	Metal file
Screwgun or drill			

HOW TO INSTALL METAL CORNER BEAD

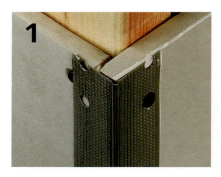

1

Cut metal corner bead to length using aviation snips, leaving a ½" gap at the floor. Position the bead so the raised spine is centered over the corner and the flanges are flat against both walls.

2

Starting at the top, fasten the bead flanges with drywall nails, driven every 9" and about ¼" from the edge. Alternate sides with each screw to keep the bead centered. The screws must not project beyond the raised spine.

3

Use full lengths of corner bead where possible. If you must join two lengths, cut the two pieces to size, then butt together the finished ends. Make sure the ends are perfectly aligned and the spine is straight along the length of the corner. File ends, if necessary.

HOW TO INSTALL VINYL CORNER BEAD

1

2

Cut vinyl bead to length and test fit over corner. Spray vinyl adhesive evenly along the entire length of the corner, then along the bead.

Quickly install the bead, pressing the flanges into the adhesive. Fasten the bead in place with ½" staples every 8".

HOW TO INSTALL CORNER BEAD AT THREE-WAY CORNERS

1

2

File Edges ▶

Where two or more outside corners meet, trim back the overlapping flanges of each bead to 45° mitered ends using aviation snips. The ends don't have to match perfectly, but they should not overlap.

Fasten the first bead in place, then test fit each subsequent piece, trimming any overlapping flanges. Align the tips of the two pieces and fasten in place. Install additional beads in the same way.

Blunt any sharp edges or points created by metal bead at three-way corners using a metal file.

HOW TO INSTALL FLEXIBLE BEAD FOR AN ARCHWAY

1

Install standard corner bead on the straight lengths of the corners (see pages 98 to 99) so it is ½" from the floor and 2" from the start of the arch.

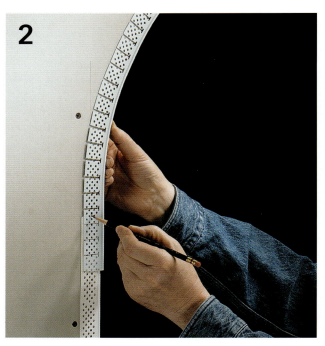

2

Flatten flexible vinyl bead along the archway to determine the length needed, then add 3". Cut two pieces of bead to this length, one for each side of the archway.

3

Spray one side of the archway with vinyl adhesive, then spray the bead. Immediately install the bead—work from one end, pushing the bead tight into the corner along the arch. Secure with ½" staples every 2". Trim the overlapping end so it meets the end of the straight length of corner bead.

Variation: To substitute for flexible bead, snip one flange of standard vinyl bead at 1" intervals. Be careful not to cut into or through the spine.

HOW TO INSTALL L-BEAD

L-bead caps the ends of drywall panels that abut finished surfaces such as paneling or wood trim, providing a finished edge. The drywall is installed ⅛" from the finished surface, then the L-bead is positioned tight against the panel, so its finished edge covers the edge of the adjacent surface.

Fasten L-bead to the drywall with ½" staples or drywall screws every 6", then finish with a minimum of three coats of compound (see pages 126 to 129). After final sanding, peel back the protective strip to expose the finished edge of the L-bead.

Installing Vinyl Bullnose Corner Bead ▸

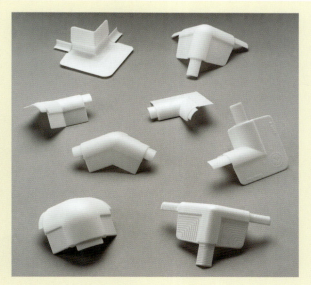

Vinyl bullnose corner bead is installed with vinyl adhesive and ½" staples, just like standard vinyl bead (see page 99). However, bullnose beads that have shallow curves may require that the ends of drywall panels be cut back (inset).

Drywall manufacturers offer a variety of corner caps to ease the process of finishing soffits and other openings trimmed out with bullnose corner bead.

DRYWALL: CURVED WALLS: INSTALLING

Curved walls have obvious appeal and are surprisingly easy to build. Structurally, a curved wall is very similar to a standard nonload-bearing partition wall, with two key differences: the stud spacing and the materials used for the top and bottom wall plates.

Traditionally, plates for curved walls were cut from ¾-inch plywood—a somewhat time-consuming and wasteful process—but now a flexible track product made of light-gauge steel has made the construction much easier. Using the steel track, frame the wall based on a layout drawn onto the floor. Shape the track to follow the layout, screw together the track pieces to lock-in the shape, then add the studs.

The ideal stud spacing for your project depends upon the type of finish material you plan to use. If it's drywall, ¼-inch flexible panels (usually installed in double layers) require studs spaced a maximum of 9-inch O.C. for curves with a minimum radius of 32 inches. For radii less than 32 inches, you may have to wet the panels.

By virtue of their shape, curved walls provide some of their own stability. Half-walls with pronounced curves may not need additional support if they're secured at one end. If your wall needs additional support, look for ways to tie it into the existing framing, or install cabinets or other permanent fixtures for stability.

If you are planning a curved wall of full height, use a plumb bob to transfer the layout of the bottom track up to the ceiling for the layout of the top track. Check the alignment by placing a few studs at the ends and middle, and then fasten the top track to the ceiling joists with drywall screws.

When hanging drywall on curved walls, it's best to install the panels perpendicular to the framing. Try to avoid joints, but if they are unavoidable, note that vertical seams are much easier to hide in the curve than horizontal seams. If panels have been wetted for the installation, allow them to dry thoroughly before taping seams.

Cutting Standard Steel Tracks ▸

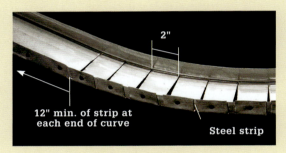

12" min. of strip at each end of curve

2"

Steel strip

As a substitute for flexible track, use standard 20- or 25-gauge steel track. Along the curved portion of the wall, cut the web and flange along the outside of the curve at 2" intervals. From the web of a scrap piece, cut a 1"-wide strip that runs the length of the curve, plus 8". Bend the track to follow the curve, then screw the strip to the inside of the outer flange, using ⁷⁄₁₆" Type S screws. This construction requires 12" of straight (uncut) track at both ends of the curve.

A curved wall can be created in several ways using traditional framing and drywall methods or modern products that eliminate much of the work.

HOW TO FRAME A CURVED WALL

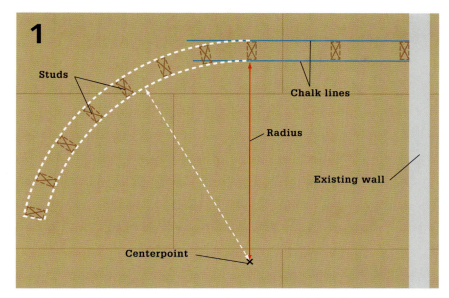

Draw the wall layout. Mark straight portions with parallel chalk lines representing the outside edges of the wall track. Use a framing square to make sure the lines are perpendicular to the adjoining wall. At the start of the curve, square off from the chalk line and measure out the distance of the radius to mark the curve's centerpoint. For small curves (4 ft. or so), drive a nail at the centerpoint, hook the end of a tape measure on the nail, and draw the curve using the tape and a pencil as a compass; for larger curves, use a straight board nailed at the centerpoint.

Position the track along the layout lines, following the curve exactly. Mark the end of the wall onto the track using a marker, then cut the track to length with aviation snips. Cut the top track to the same length.

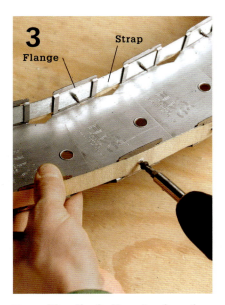

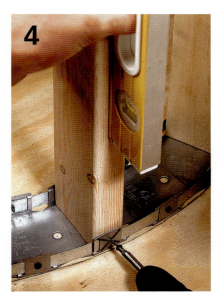

Reposition the bottom track on the layout, then apply masking tape along the outside flanges. Secure the track by driving a Type S screw through each flange and into the strap. Screw both sides of the track. Turn over the bottom track, then set the top track on top and match its shape. Tape and screw the top track.

Fasten the bottom track to the floor, using 1¼" drywall screws. Mark the stud layout onto both tracks. Cut the studs to length. Install the studs one at a time, using a level to plumb each along its narrow edge, then driving a 1¼" screw through the flange or strap and into the stud on both sides.

Fit the top track over the studs and align them with the layout marks. Fasten the studs to the top track with one screw on each side, checking the wall for level and height as you work. Set the level on top of the track, both parallel and perpendicular to the track, before fastening each stud.

INSTALLING DRYWALL ON CURVES

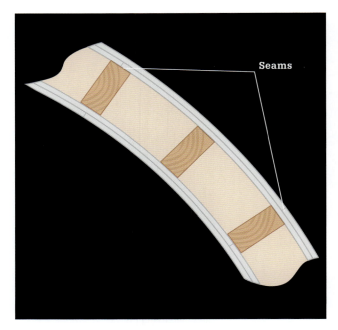

Use two layers of ¼" flexible drywall for curved walls and arches. If there are butted seams, stagger the seams between layers.

Install corner bead with adhesive and staples or drywall nails. Do not use screws to attach corner bead—they will cause the bead material to kink and distort.

HANGING FLEXIBLE DRYWALL

Start at the center for concave curves. Cut the first panel a little long and position it lengthwise along the wall. Carefully bend the panel toward the midpoint of the curve and fasten it to the center stud. Work toward the ends to fasten the rest of the panel. Install the second panel over the first, then trim along the top of the wall with a drywall saw.

Start at one end for convex curves. Cut the panel long and fasten it lengthwise along the wall, bending the panel as you work. Add the second layer, then trim both to the framing. To cover the top of a curved wall, set a ½" panel on the wall and scribe it from below.

HANGING DRYWALL IN ARCHWAYS

Cut ¼" flexible drywall to width and a few inches longer than needed. Fasten to the arch with 1¼" drywall screws, working from the center out to the ends. Trim the ends of the piece and install a second to match the thickness of the surrounding drywall.

Variation: Score the backside of ½" drywall every inch (or more for tighter curves) along the length of the piece. Starting at one end, fasten the piece along the arch; the scored drywall will conform to the arch.

Wet-bending ▸

Drywall is relatively easy to conform to surfaces that curve in just one direction, as long as you wet the tensioned surface of the drywall and don't try to bend it farther than it will go. When wetted and rested for an hour, ½" drywall will bend to a 4 ft. radius, ⅜" to a 3 ft. radius, and ¼" to a 2 ft. radius. Special flexible ¼" drywall does not require wetting for radii greater than 32".

Set framing members closer together for curved surfaces to avoid flat spots. Radii less than 5 ft. require 12" frame spacing, less than 4 ft. require 8" spacing, and less than 3 ft. require 6" spacing. Hang the factory edge of panels perpendicular to the framing so the panels bend longwise. ¼" panels should be doubled up; stagger the panels so no joints line up.

Wet the side of the panel that will be stretched by the bend with about 1 quart of water using a paint roller. Cover the panel with plastic or face the wet sides of two sheets of drywall toward each other and let sit for 1 hour before application.

DRYWALL FINISHING: TEXTURING

Textures may be applied with spray equipment, rollers, or trowels. These application methods create different looks. Spray equipment is expensive and requires some practice and skill to master. Still, spraying is the quickest application method, and equipment may be rented. Rolling is easy and safe and creates less mess, but is slower, does not work well with aggregated textures, and can be tricky on inside corners. Troweling is slower still, but works well for applying thick, smooth compound for deep texture effects.

When spraying or rolling, appropriate texturing compound is thinned to the consistency of pancake batter or thick paint. The best consistency is one that goes on smooth and doesn't run. Use trial and error on scrap drywall to find this point. Carefully record the water-to-compound ratio that produces the best results, and do not vary this during a job. Set spray equipment air pressure and use nozzle heads according to recommendations from the manufacturer or rental agency. Always test spray on scrap drywall to fine tune the pressure, and then keep the settings consistent throughout the job.

Apply compound or texture evenly. Before tooling rolled or sprayed surfaces, let the material dry for 10 to 15 minutes to a dull sheen. At this point, the surface can be textured with a dry roller, lightly knocked down with a large knife or trowel, or twisted, swirled, and stippled into any number of patterns with any number of instruments. Repeat a pattern in a meticulously measured and regular way or make completely random patterns. Avoid patterns that start off regular and then disintegrate.

Use a spray shield to protect surfaces you don't want to receive texture during the texture application process.

Mix texture compound in a bucket using a joint-compound-mixing paddle mounted in a ½" drill. Follow the directions on the bag. Powdered compounds usually have a rest time that follows mixing before application may occur.

APPLYING A POPCORN CEILING TEXTURE

Popcorn texture is a popular treatment for ceilings. Its bumpy surface is created by tiny particles of vermiculite or polystyrene that give it sound-deadening properties. Mixtures are available in fine, medium, and coarse grades.

Mix the dry texture following the manufacturer's directions, then load the hopper of the texture gun. Apply the texture, holding the gun 2 to 4 ft. below the ceiling. Spray in a side-to-side motion (not arching), leaving a thin, even layer over the entire ceiling. Immediately following the first layer, spray on a second thin layer, working in a direction perpendicular to the first. Allow the texture to dry. For a heavy texture, the manufacturer may recommend applying an additional coat.

APPLYING AN ORANGE PEEL TEXTURE

Orange peel textures are most commonly applied to walls. They have a distinctive, spattered look created by spraying a thin texturing product or water-thinned all-purpose drywall compound through a texturing gun. For a heavier spattered texture, repeat the step at right using less air pressure at the gun (atomizing air) and the compressor (feed pressure).

Mix the texture product or compound to the consistency of latex paint. Spray the surface with long, side-to-side strokes, keeping the gun perpendicular to the surface and about 18" away from it. To apply a heavy spatter-coat, let the surface dry for 10 to 15 minutes, then spray with random motions from about 6 ft. away.

CREATING A KNOCK-DOWN TEXTURE

A knock-down texture is an orange peel texture that is partially smoothed with a drywall knife. Its relative flatness creates a subtle effect, and it's easier to paint and maintain than the heavier textures, making it a good choice for walls. Because of the light troweling required, this texture works best on smooth, flat surfaces.

Mix the texture product or all-purpose drywall compound to pancake batter consistency. Spray-texture the entire surface following the orange peel procedure on page 107. Let the texture dry for 10 to 15 minutes, then lightly trowel the surface with a 12" or larger drywall knife. Hold the knife almost flat, and work perpendicularly to the drywall seams.

APPLYING A STIPPLE TEXTURE

Stipple textures are made with a paint roller and texture paint or all-purpose drywall compound. Randomly shaped ridges have a noticeable grain orientation. The amount of texture is affected by the nap of the roller, which can vary from ¼" to 1". Stippling can be knocked down for a flatter finish.

Mix paint or compound to a heavy latex-paint consistency. Coat the roller and roll the surface, recoating the roller as needed to create an even layer over the entire work area. Let the texture dry to a dull-wet sheen, then roll the surface again—without loading the roller—to create the finished texture.

Variation: Knock down the stipple finish for a smoother texture. Apply the stipple texture with a roller, and let it dry for about 10 minutes. Smooth the surface with a 12" or larger drywall knife, holding the knife almost flat and applying very light pressure.

CREATING A SWIRL TEXTURE

Swirl textures and other freehand designs can have the look of traditionally applied plaster. Swirls can be made with a wallpaper brush, whisk broom, or any type of raking or combing tool.

Mix the texture product or all-purpose drywall compound to a heavy latex-paint consistency. For a shallow texture, use a paint roller with a ½" nap to apply an even coat over the entire surface; for a deeper texture, apply an even, ⅛"-thick coat with a drywall knife. Let the surface dry to a dull-wet appearance. Brush the pattern into the material using arching or circular motions. Start at one end of the area and work backward, overlapping the starting and end points of previous swirls with each new row.

APPLYING A TROWELED TEXTURE

A troweled texture can have almost any design but should be applied with varied motions to create a random appearance. Premixed all-purpose drywall compound works well for most troweled textures, and it's usually best to work in small sections.

Apply the compound to the surface using a 6" or 8" drywall knife. Vary the direction of the strokes and the thickness of compound. If desired, stipple the surface by stamping the knife into the compound and pulling it away sharply.

Partially smooth the surface using a 6", 8" or 12" knife. Flatten the tops of ridges and stipples without smoothing lower areas. When you're satisfied with the design, repeat step 1 in an adjacent section, overlapping the edges of the textured area by a few inches.

DRYWALL: HANGING

Hanging drywall is a project that can be completed quickly and easily with a little preplanning and a helping hand.

If you're installing drywall on both the ceilings and the walls, do the ceilings first so the wall panels add extra support for the ceiling panels. When it comes time to install the walls, hang all full panels first, then measure and cut the remaining pieces about ⅛" too small to allow for easy fit.

In nearly every installation, you'll deal with corners. For standard 90° corners, panels most often can butt against one another. But other corners, such as those lacking adequate nailing surfaces or ones that are prone to cracking, may require the use of drywall clips or specialty beads.

Drywall is heavy. While it's possible to hang drywall by yourself, work with a helper whenever possible. A panel lift is also a time and back saver, simplifying installation to ceilings and the upper portion of walls. If you don't want to rent a panel lift, you can make a pair of T-braces, called "deadmen" (see page 112) to hold ceiling panels tight against framing for fastening.

Use a panel lifter to position drywall for fastening. Slide the front end of the lifter beneath the panel edge, then rock backward with your foot to raise the panel into place.

Tip ▶

Where untapered panel ends will be butted together, bevel-cut the outside edges of each panel at 45°, removing about ⅛" of material. This helps prevent the paper from creating a ridge along the seam. Peel off any loose paper from the edge.

Tools & Materials ▶

Work gloves	Drywall panels
Eye and ear	Drywall screws
protection	Deadmen
T-square	Ladders
Utility knife	Metal flashing
Screwgun or drill	Self-tapping
Panel lift	steel screws
Chalk line	Drywall clips

HOW TO INSTALL DRYWALL ON FLAT CEILINGS

1

2

Snap a chalk line perpendicular to the joists, 48⅛" from the starting wall.

Measure to make sure the first panel will break on the center of a joist. If necessary, cut the panel on the end that abuts the side wall so the panel breaks on the next farthest joist. Load the panel onto a rented panel lift, or use a helper, and lift the panel flat against the joists.

3

4

Position the panel with the leading edge on the chalk line and the end centered on a joist. Fasten the panel with appropriately sized screws.

After the first row of panels is installed, begin the next row with a half-panel. This ensures that the butted end joints will be staggered between rows.

HOW TO INSTALL CEILING PANELS USING DEADMEN

Construct two 2 × 4 deadmen. Lean one against the wall where the panel will be installed, with the top arm a couple inches below the joists. Have a helper assist in lifting the panel and placing the lead edge on the arm. Angle the deadman to pin the panel flush against the joists, but don't use so much pressure you risk damage to the panel.

As the helper supports the panel, use the other deadman to hoist the panel against the joists 24" from the back end. Place ladders at each deadman location and adjust the panel's position by loosening the braces with one hand and moving the panel with the other. Replace the braces and fasten the panel to the framing.

Setting Your Clutch ▸

Professional drywallers drive hundreds, even thousands, of screws per day. Consequently, they invest in pro-quality screwdriving equipment, often with self-feeding coils of screws for rapid-fire work. For DIYers, this equipment can be rented—and may be worth the investment for a very large project. But in most cases a decent quality cordless drill/driver will do nicely. If the drill/driver has a clutch (and most do these days), so much the better. Essentially, a clutch stops the drill's chuck from spinning when the screw encounters a specific amount of resistance. This prevents overdriving of the screw, which is especially important when drywalling (you want to avoid driving the screw far enough into the drywall to break the surface paper). But for the clutch to work properly you need to make sure it is set to the appropriate level of sensitivity. A drill/driver normally has several settings indicated on a shroud or ring near the drill chuck. The highest setting is used for drilling. Basically, the clutch won't disengage the chuck unless it encounters so much resistance that the drill could be damaged. On the lowest setting, the drill will disengage when it encounters only very slight resistance,

as when completing driving a screw into drywall. Before you start driving any drywall screws, test your clutch setting by driving a screw into a piece of scrap drywall and a 2 × 4. Reset the clutch as needed until it stops driving the moment the screwhead becomes countersunk, creating a very slight dimple. Having the clutch set correctly ensures that your fasteners will have maximum holding power with just enough of a surrounding dimple to give the joint compound a place to go.

WALLS & CEILINGS

INSTALLING FLOATING CEILING JOINTS

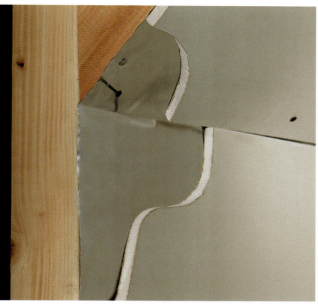

Use metal flashing to prevent cracks along the peak of pitched and cathedral ceilings (left) and the angle between pitched ceilings and sidewalls (right). For both applications, cut metal flashing 16" wide and to the length of the joint, then bend it lengthwise to match the angle of the peak or corner. Fasten flashing to the framing on one side only, then fasten the panels on that side to the framing. However, fasten the panels at the unfastened side to the flashing only, using self-tapping steel screws. Drive the first row of screws into the framing not less than 12" from the "floating" edge of the panels. *Note: Flexible vinyl bead can also be used for corners prone to cracking.*

Bending Flashing ▸

To bend flashing, make a bending jig by driving screws into a piece of wood, creating a space one-half the width of the flashing when measured from the edge of the board. Clamp the bending jig to a work surface. Lay a piece of flashing flat on the board and bend it over the edge.

For a ceiling with trusses, use drywall clips to eliminate cracks caused by "truss uplift," the seasonal shifting caused by weather changes. Slip clips on the edge of the panel prior to installation, then fasten the clips to the top plate. Fasten the panel to the trusses not less than 18" from the edge of the panel.

HOW TO INSTALL DRYWALL ON WOOD-FRAMED WALLS

Measure from the wall end or corner to make sure the first panel will break on the center of the stud. If necessary, trim the sheet on the side or end that will be placed in the corner. Mark the stud centers on the panel face and pre-drive screws at each location along the top edge to facilitate fastening. Apply adhesive to the studs, if necessary.

With a helper or a drywall lifter, hoist the first panel tight against the ceiling, making sure the side edge is centered on a stud. Push the panel flat against the framing and drive the starter screws to secure the panel. Make any cutouts, then fasten the field of the panel.

Measure, cut, and install the remaining panels along the upper wall. Bevel panel ends slightly, leaving a ⅛" gap between them at the joint. Butt joints can also be installed using back blocking to create a recess (see page 119).

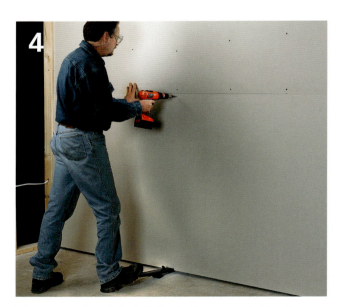

Measure, cut, and install the bottom row, butting the panels tight to the upper row and leaving a ½" gap at the floor. Secure to the framing along the top edge using the starter screws, then make all cutouts before fastening the rest of the panel.

Variation: When installing drywall vertically, cut each panel so it's ½" shorter than the ceiling height to allow for expansion. (The gap will be covered by base molding.) Avoid placing tapered edges at outside corners, which makes them difficult to finish.

INSTALLING DRYWALL AT INSIDE CORNERS

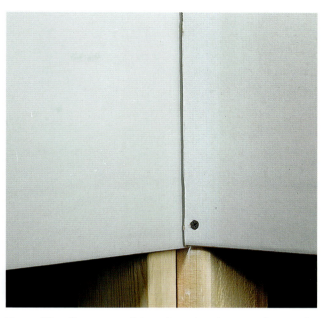

Standard 90° inside corners are installed with the first panel butted against the framing and the adjacent panel butted against the first. The screw spacing remains the same as on a flat wall.

Use a "floating corner" to reduce the chances of popped fasteners and cracks. Install the first panel, fastening only to within one stud bay of the corner. Push the leading edge of the adjacent panel against the first to support the unfastened edge. Fasten the second panel normally, including the corner.

Drywall clips can be used at corners that lack an adequate nailing surface, allowing two panels to be secured to the same stud. Slide clips onto the leading edge of the first panel, with the metal nailing flange outward. Install the panel, fastening the flange to the stud on the adjacent wall with drywall screws. Install the adjacent panel normally.

For off-angle corners, do not overlap panel ends. Install so the panel ends meet at the corner with a ⅛" gap between them.

INSTALLING DRYWALL AT OUTSIDE CORNERS

At outside corners, run panels long so they extend past the corner framing. Fasten the panel in place, then score the backside and snap cut to remove the waste piece.

For standard 90° outside corners, install the first panel so the outside edge is flush with the framing, then install the adjacent panel so it overlaps the end of the first panel.

For off-angle corners or corners where bullnose bead will be installed, do not overlap panel ends. Install each panel so it's leading edge breaks ⅛" from the outside edge of the framing. *Note: Bullnose beads with a slight radius may require a larger reveal.*

For drywall that abuts a finished edge, such as paneling or wood trim, install panels ⅛" from the finished surface, then install a an L-bead to cover the exposed edge (see page 101).

HOW TO INSTALL DRYWALL ABUTTING A FINISHED SURFACE

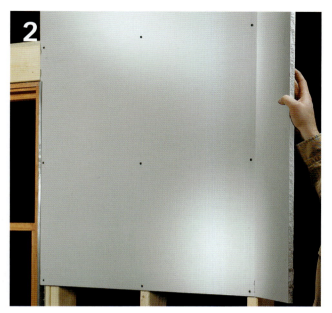

Cut the J-bead (see page 124) to size, then position it flush against the finished surface. Fasten it to the adjacent framing with drywall screws. *Note: Make sure to install J-bead that matches the thickness of your drywall.*

Cut a piece of drywall to size, but let the end run long for final trimming. Slide the end of the drywall into the J-bead until it fits snugly, then fasten the panel to the framing. Score the backside flush with the face of the wall, then snap cut to remove the waste.

INSTALLING DRYWALL ON GABLE WALLS

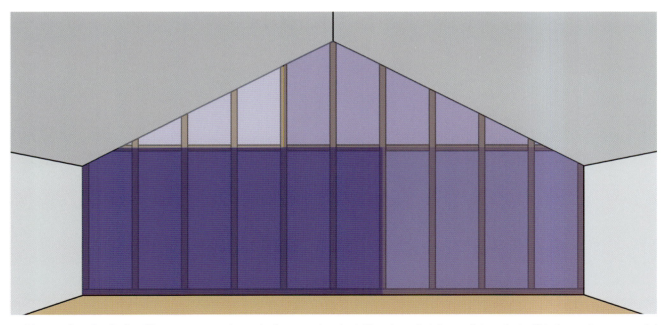

Gables and cathedral ceilings present unique challenges when installing drywall. A few pointers that will help you be successful include: use as many of the panel's factory edges as possible; test-fit each piece directly on the wall; do not force pieces into place, but trim edges as needed instead; install pieces horizontally, with 2 × 4 blocking between the framing member; align horizontal seams, but not vertical seams—stagger these to minimize any twisting in the framing members.

HOW TO INSTALL DRYWALL ON METAL STUD WALLS

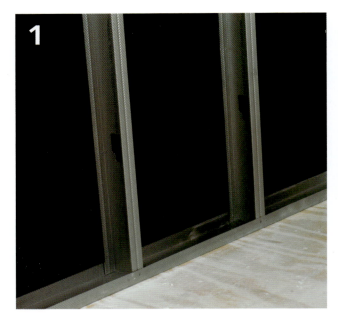

Metal stud walls in residential construction are generally created with C-shaped 20- to 25-gauge steel studs that are secured at the top and bottom with flanged tracks. If the wall is built correctly, all of the open sides of the C-shaped studs will face in the same direction. Before you begin installing drywall, note which direction the open sides are on.

Begin installing drywall panels in the corner of the room that's closer to the open sides of the metal studs. The first panel should fall midway across a stud, coming from the direction of the open side. Attaching the panel this way will stabilize it; if you install the panel so the free end of the stud flange is loose, it may flex when you attach the drywall screws.

Screw the first panel at each corner using Type S drywall screws (1" is recommended for ½" drywall). These screws have a fairly sharp point that can penetrate the light-gauge metal flanges of the steel studs. As when attaching drywall to wood framing, take care not to overdrive the screws—they tend to take off rather aggressively once they engage in the metal.

Install the second drywall panel, leaving a slight gap at the joint. The new panel should be crossing the closed side of the C-shaped stud. Continue working in this direction until the wall is covered. Taping and seaming are done the same way as for wood framing.

INSTALLING BACK BLOCKERS

No matter how good a job you do installing and finishing a butt joint, there's always a chance it'll be visible, even after a coat of paint or layer of wallcovering. Drywall panels can expand and contract as the temperature and humidity in your home changes, causing butted panel ends to push outward and create ridges. While ridging eventually stops (up to a year after installation), you can install back blocking to help prevent the problem before it even starts.

Back blocking creates a recessed butt joint by slightly bending panel ends into the bay between framing members, where they are secured to a floating blocking device with drywall screws. The result is a recessed joint that approximates a tapered joint and can be finished just as easily using standard techniques. And because the joint floats between framing members, it's unlikely to crack or ridge. Back blocking can be used for both walls and ceilings.

Although commercial back blockers are available, you can easily make your own back blocker by attaching narrow strips of ¼" hardboard to the edges of a 6 to 10" wide strip of ¾" plywood. When placed behind a drywall butt joint, the hardboard strips will create a thin space, into which the edges of the drywall will be deflected when it's screwed to the back blocker. The instructions below show a homemade back blocker in use.

Tools & Materials ▶

Work gloves	Tape measure
Eye and ear	Drywall screws
protection	¾ × 10 × 48" plywood
Screwgun	¼ × ¾ × 48"
or ⅜" drill	hardboard

HOW TO INSTALL A BACK BLOCKER

Hang the first drywall panel so the end breaks midway between the framing members. Position the back blocker behind the panel so the end covers half of the wood center strip, then fasten every 6" along the end.

Install the second panel so it butts against the first panel. Fasten the end of the second panel to the back blocker with drywall screws every 6". The screws will pull the end of the panel into the blocker, creating the recessed joint.

DRYWALL: REPAIRING

Patching holes and concealing popped nails are common drywall repairs. Small holes can be filled directly, but larger patches must be supported with some kind of backing, such as plywood. To repair holes left by nails or screws, dimple the hole slightly with the handle of a utility knife or taping knife and fill it with spackle or joint compound.

Use joint tape anywhere the drywall's face paper or joint tape has torn or peeled away. Always cut away any loose drywall material, face paper or joint tape from the damaged area, trimming back to solid drywall material.

All drywall repairs require three coats of joint compound, just as in new installations. Lightly sand your repairs before painting or adding texture.

Tools & Materials ▸

Drill or screwgun	Wood scraps
Hammer	Paper joint tape
Utility knife	Self-adhesive
Taping knives	fiberglass mesh
Framing square	joint tape
Drywall saw	Drywall repair patch
Hacksaw	Drywall repair clips
Fine metal file	Corner bead
1¼" drywall screws	Paintable latex
Lightweight spackle	or silicone caulk
All-purpose	Drywall wet sander
joint compound	Drywall scraps
150-grit sandpaper	Protective equipment

Most drywall problems can be remedied with basic dry wall materials and specialty materials: drywall screws (A); paper joint tape (B); self-adhesive fiberglass mesh tape (C); corner bead (D); paintable latex or silicone caulk (E); all-purpose joint compound (F); lightweight spackling compound (G); drywall repair patches (H); scraps of drywall (I); and drywall repair clips (J).

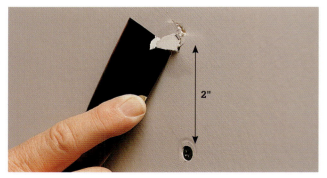

To repair a popped nail, drive a drywall screw 2" above or below the nail, so it pulls the panel tight to the framing. Scrape away loose paint or compound, then drive the popped nail ¹⁄₁₆" below the surface. Apply three coats of joint compound to cover the holes.

If drywall is dented, without cracks or tears in the face paper, just fill the hole with lightweight spackling or all-purpose joint compound, let it dry, and sand it smooth.

HOW TO REPAIR CRACKS & GASHES

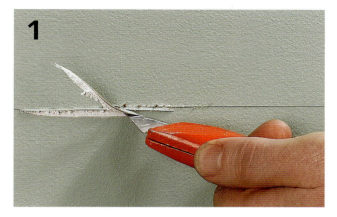

1

Use a utility knife to cut away loose drywall or face paper and widen the crack into a "V"; the notch will help hold the joint compound.

2

Push along the sides of the crack with your hand. If the drywall moves, secure the panel with 1¼" drywall screws driven into the nearest framing members. Cover the crack and screws with self-adhesive mesh tape.

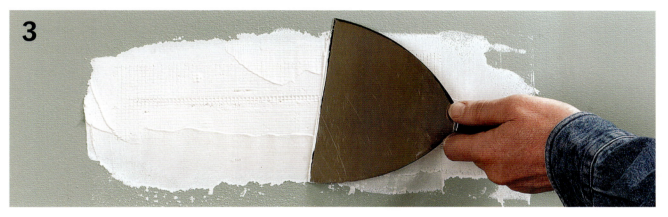

3

Cover the tape with compound, lightly forcing it into the mesh, then smooth it off, leaving just enough to conceal the tape. Add two more coats, in successively broader and thinner coats to blend the patch into the surrounding area.

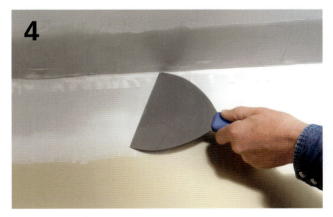

4

For cracks at corners or ceilings, cut through the existing seam and cut away any loose drywall material or tape, then apply a new length of tape or inside-corner bead and two coats of joint compound.

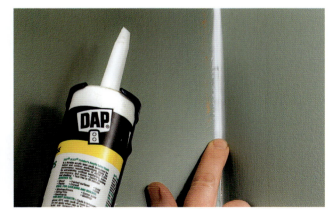

Variation: For small cracks at corners, apply a thin bead of paintable latex or silicone caulk over the crack, then use your finger to smooth the caulk into the corner.

HOW TO PATCH SMALL HOLES IN DRYWALL

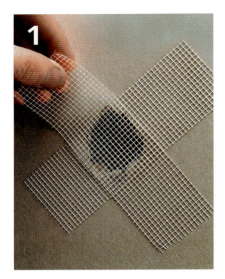

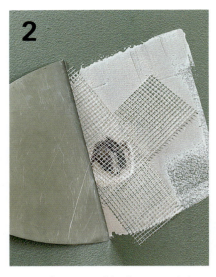

Trim away any broken drywall, face paper, or joint tape around the hole using a utility knife. Cover the hole with crossed strips of self-adhesive mesh tape.

Cover the tape with all-purpose joint compound, lightly forcing it into the mesh, then smooth it off, leaving just enough to conceal the tape.

Add two more coats of compound in successively broader and thinner coats to blend the patch into the surrounding area. Use a drywall wet sander to smooth the repair area.

OTHER OPTIONS FOR PATCHING SMALL HOLES IN DRYWALL

Drywall repair patches: Cover the damaged area with the self-adhesive patch; the thin metal plate provides support and the fiberglass mesh helps hold the joint compound.

Beveled drywall patch: Bevel the edges of the hole with a drywall saw, then cut a drywall patch to fit. Trim the beveled patch until it fits tight and flush with the panel surface. Apply plenty of compound to the beveled edges, then push the patch into the hole. Finish with paper tape and three coats of compound.

Drywall paper-flange patch: Cut a drywall patch a couple inches larger than the hole. Mark the hole on the backside of the patch, then score and snap along the lines. Remove the waste material, keeping the face paper "flange" intact. Apply compound around the hole, insert the patch, and embed the flange into the compound. Finish with two additional coats.

HOW TO PATCH LARGE HOLES IN DRYWALL

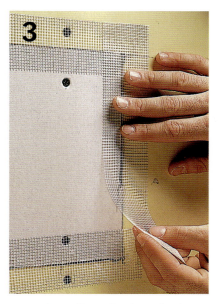

Outline the damaged area using a framing square. (Cutting four right angles makes it easier to measure and cut the patch.) Use a drywall saw to cut along the outline.

Cut plywood or lumber backer strips a few inches longer than the height of the cutout. Fasten the strips to the back side of the drywall using 1¼" drywall screws.

Cut a drywall patch ⅛" smaller than the cutout dimensions and fasten it to the backer strips with screws. Apply mesh joint tape over the seams. Finish the seams with three coats of compound.

HOW TO PATCH LARGE HOLES WITH REPAIR CLIPS

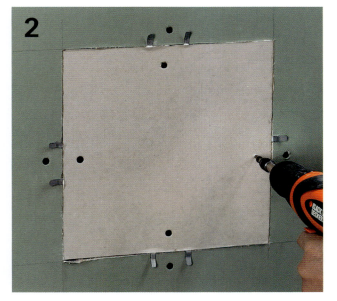

Cut out the damaged area using a drywall saw. Center one repair clip on each edge of the hole. Using the provided drywall screws, drive one screw through the wall and into the clips; position the screws ¾" from the edge and centered between the clip's tabs.

Cut a new drywall patch to fit in the hole. Fasten the patch to the clips, placing drywall screws adjacent to the previous screw locations and ¾" from the edge. Remove the tabs from the clips, then finish the joints with tape and three coats of compound.

DRYWALL: TAPING

Finishing drywall is the more difficult phase of surfacing walls and ceilings, but it's a project well within the ability of any homeowner. Armed with a basic understanding of the variety of finish materials available, you'll be able to walk out of your local home center with the exact supplies you need to cover all joints, corners, and fasteners for a successful wallboard finish project.

Corner bead is the angle strip, usually made of metal or vinyl, that covers a wallboard corner, creating a straight, durable edge where walls intersect. Most corner beads are installed over the wallboard and are finished with compound. In addition to standard 90° outside-corner bead, there's an ever-growing variety of bead types designed for specific situations and easy application. There are beads for inside corners, flexible beads for off-angles and curves, J-beads and L-beads for flat panel edges, and bullnose beads for creating rounded inside and outside corners. While metal beads are installed with fasteners, vinyl beads can be installed with vinyl adhesive and staples, or be embedded in joint compound using the same techniques for installing paper-faced beads.

A selection of taping knives is required to handle different parts of the process of applying joint tape and compound. A 6" knife is used for the initial compound application of tape beds and to set tape into the beds. A 12" knife is used for the final coat, and a knife with an L-shaped blade gets into corners.

Joint tape is combined with joint compound to create a permanent layer that covers the wallboard seams, as well as small holes and gaps. Without tape, thick applications of compound are highly prone to cracking. There are two types of joint tape—paper and self-adhesive fiberglass mesh.

Joint compound, commonly called mud, seals and levels all seams, corners, and depressions in a wallboard installation. It's also used for skim-coating and some texturing treatments. There are several types of compounds with important differences among them, but the two main forms are setting-type and drying-type.

Setting-type compound is sold in dry powder form that is mixed with water before application. Because it dries through chemical reaction, setting compound dries quickly and is virtually unaffected by humidity and temperature. Setting compounds generally shrink less, bond better, and become harder than drying types, but they're more difficult to sand, a characteristic that makes them a better choice for the taping coat than for the filler and final coats. Drying-type compounds dry through evaporation and usually take about 24 hours to dry completely. Available in dry powder and convenient premixed forms in resealable one- and five-gallon buckets, drying compounds are highly workable and consistent.

Achieving a smooth wall surface depends completely on how well you manage the taping, "mudding," and sanding tasks in your project.

HOW TO INSTALL METAL CORNER BEAD

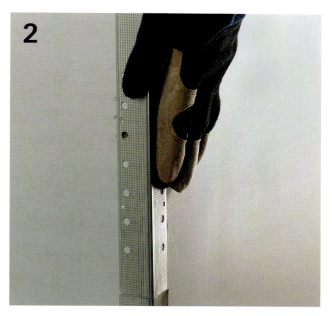

Starting at the top, fasten the bead flanges with 1¼" drywall screws driven every 9" and about ¼" from the edge. Alternate sides with each screw to keep the bead centered. The screws must not project beyond the raised spine.

Use full lengths of corner bead where possible. If you must join two lengths, cut the two pieces to size, then butt together the finished ends. Make sure the ends are perfectly aligned and the spine is straight along the length of the corner. File ends, if necessary.

HOW TO INSTALL VINYL CORNER BEAD

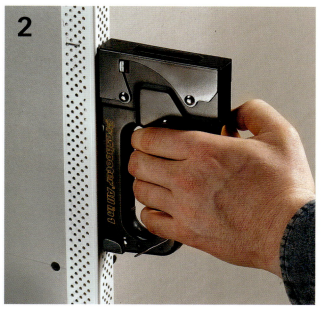

Cut vinyl bead to length and test fit over corner. Spray vinyl adhesive evenly along the entire length of the corner, then along the bead.

Quickly install the bead, pressing the flanges into the adhesive. Fasten the bead in place with ½" staples every 8".

The Finishing Sequence ▶

Finishing newly installed drywall is satisfying work that requires patience and some basic skill, but it's easier than most people think. Beginners make their biggest, and most lasting, mistakes by rushing the job and applying too much compound in an attempt to eliminate coats. But even for professionals, drywall finishing involves three steps, and sometimes more, plus the final sanding. The first step is the taping coat, when you tape the seams between the drywall panels. If you're using standard metal corner bead on the outside corners, install it before starting the taping coat; paper-faced beads go on after the tape. The screw heads get covered with compound at the beginning of each coat. After the taping comes the second, or filler, coat. This is when you leave the most compound on the wall, filling in the majority of each depression. With the filler coat, the walls start to look pretty good, but they don't have to be perfect; the third coat will take care of minor imperfections. Lightly sand the second coat, then apply the final coat.

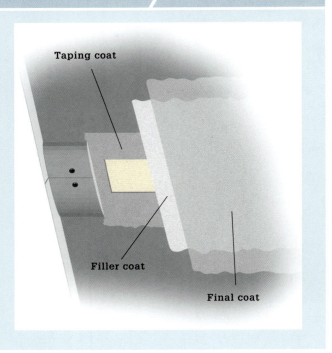

Taping coat

Filler coat

Final coat

HOW TO MIX JOINT COMPOUND

Mix powdered setting-type compound with cool, potable water in a clean 5-gal. bucket, following the manufacturer's directions. All tools and materials must be clean—dirty water, old compound, and other contaminants will affect compound set time and quality.

Use a heavy-duty drill with a mixing paddle to thoroughly mix the compound to a stiff yet workable consistency. Use a low speed to avoid whipping air into the compound. Do not overwork setting-type compound, as it will begin setup. For powdered drying-type compound, remix after 15 minutes. Clean tools thoroughly immediately after use.

Use a hand masher to loosen premixed compound. If the compound has been around a while and is stiff, add a little water and mix to an even consistency.

HOW TO TAPE & MUD

1

Using a 4 or 6" taping knife, apply compound over each screw head, forcing it into the depression. Firmly drag the knife in the opposite direction, removing excess compound from the panel surface.

2

Apply an even bed layer of setting-type compound about ⅛" thick and 6" wide over tapered seams using a 6" taping knife. *Note: With paper tape, you can also use premixed taping or all-purpose compound.*

3

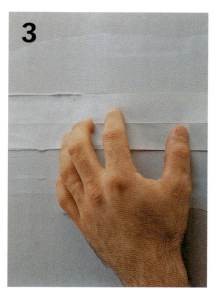

Center the tape over the seam and lightly embed it in the compound, making sure the tape is smooth and straight. At the end of the seam, tear off the tape so it extends all the way into the inside corners and up to the corner bead at outside corners.

4

Smooth the tape with the taping knife, working out from the center. Apply enough pressure to force compound from underneath the tape, so the tape is flat and has a thin layer beneath it.

5

At inside corners, smooth the final bit of tape by reversing the knife and carefully pushing it toward the corner. Carefully remove excess compound along the edges of the bed layer with the taping knife.

6

Cover vertical butt seams with a ⅛"-thick layer of joint compound. You should try and avoid this kind of joint, but in some cases there is no way around it. Cover the compound with seam tape and more compound. Make the taped area extrawide so you can feather it back gradually.

(continued)

WALLS & CEILINGS

D

127

7

Fold precreased paper tape in half to create a 90° angle to tape inside corners.

8

Apply an even layer of setting-type compound about ⅛" thick and 3" wide, to both sides of the corner, using a 4" taping knife. Embed the tape into the compound using your fingers and a taping knife.

9

Carefully smooth and flatten both sides of the tape, removing excess compound to leave only a thin layer beneath. Make sure the center of the tape is aligned straight with the corner.

Tip ▶

An inside corner knife can embed both sides of the tape in one pass—draw the knife along the tape, applying enough pressure to leave a thin layer of compound beneath. Feather each side using a straight 6" taping knife, if necessary.

10

Finish outside corner bead with a 6" knife. Apply the compound while dragging the knife along the raised spine of the bead. Make a second pass to feather the outside edge of the compound, then a third dragging along the bead again. Smooth any areas where the corner bead meets taped corners or seams.

11

Scrape off any remaining ridges and chunks after the taping coat has dried completely, then second-coat the screw heads, using a 6" taping knife and all-purpose compound. *Note: Setting-type compound and drying-type topping compound are also acceptable.*

12

Apply an even layer of compound to both sides of each inside corner using a 6" taping knife. Smooth one side at a time, holding the blade about 15° from horizontal and lightly dragging the point along the corner. Make a second pass to remove excess compound along the outer edges. Repeat, if necessary.

13

Coat tapered seams with an even layer of all-purpose compound using a 12" taping knife. Whenever possible, apply the coat in one direction and smooth it in the opposite. Feather the sides of the compound first, holding the blade almost flat and applying pressure to the outside of the blade so the blade just skims over the center of the seam.

14

After feathering both side edges of the compound, make a pass down the center of the seam, applying even pressure to the blade. This pass should leave the seam smooth and even, with the edges feathered out to nothing. The joint tape should be completely covered.

15

Second-coat the outside corners, one side at a time, using a 12" knife. Apply an even layer of compound, then feather the outside edge by applying pressure to the outside of the knife— enough so that the blade flexes and removes most of the compound along the edge but leaves the corner intact. Make a second pass with the blade riding along the raised spine, applying even pressure.

16

After the filler coat has dried, lightly sand all of the joints, then third-coat the screws. Apply the final coat, following the same steps used for the filler coat but do the seams first, then the outside corners, followed by the inside corners. Use a 12" knife and spread the compound a few inches wider than the joints in the filler coat. Remove most of the compound, filling scratches and low spots but leaving only traces elsewhere. Make several passes, if necessary, until the surface is smooth and there are no knife tracks or other imperfections. Carefully blend intersecting joints so there's no visible transition.

HOW TO SAND JOINT COMPOUND

1

2

Tip ▶

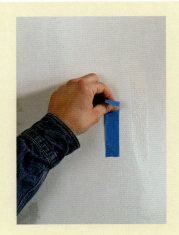

As you work, if you oversand or discover low spots that require another coat of compound, mark the area with a piece of tape for repair after you finish sanding. Make sure to wipe away dust so the tape sticks to the surface.

Use sheet plastic and 2" masking tape to help confine dust to the work area. Cover all doorways, cabinets, built-ins, and any gaps or other openings with plastic, sealing all four edges with tape; otherwise the fine dust produced by sanding can find its way through.

Knock down any ridges, chunks, or tool marks prior to sanding, using a 6" taping knife. Do not apply too much pressure—you don't want to dig into the compound, only remove the excess.

3

4

Lightly sand all seams and outside corners using a pole sander with 220-grit sanding screen or 150-grit sandpaper. Work in the direction of the joints, applying even pressure to smooth transitions and high areas. Don't sand out depressions; fill them with compound and resand. Be careful not to oversand or expose joint tape.

Inside corners often are finished with only one or two thin coats of compound over the tape. Sand the inside edge of joints only lightly and smooth the outside edge carefully; inside corners will be sanded by hand later.

Fine-sand the seams, outside corners, and fastener heads using a sanding block with 150- to 220-grit sanding screen or sandpaper. As you work, use your hand to feel for defects along the compound. A bright work light angled to highlight seams can help reveal problem areas.

To avoid damage from oversanding, use a 150-grit dry sanding sponge to sand inside corners. The sides of sanding sponges also contain grit, allowing you to sand both sides of a corner at once to help prevent oversanding.

For tight or hard-to-reach corners, fold a piece of sanding screen or sandpaper in thirds and sand the area carefully. Rather than using just your fingertips, try to flatten your hand as much as possible to spread out the pressure to avoid sanding too deep.

Repair depressions, scratches or exposed tape due to oversanding after final sanding is complete. Wipe the area with a dry cloth to remove dust, then apply a thin coat of all-purpose compound. Allow to dry thoroughly, then resand.

With sanding complete, remove dust from the panels with a dry towel or soft broom. Use a wet-dry vacuum to clean out all electrical boxes and around floors, windows, and doors, then carefully roll up sheet plastic and discard. Finally, damp mop the floor to remove any remaining dust.

DRYWALL: TYPES

Up until the 1930s, interior walls were created by troweling wet plaster onto wood or metal lath that had been nailed to the wall framing members. The finished wall required three coats of plaster, each of which had to be permitted to dry or set. The first generation of drywall panels replaced the lath and the heavy "scratch" coat of plaster. Today, even when a traditional plaster wall finish is desired, special blue-papered drywall panels are anchored to the framing to form the base of the wall instead of a hand-troweled scratch coat. This reduces labor and drying time greatly. Since the end of World War II, the typical drywall panel wall requires no finish layer of plaster. Only minor surface corrections are required, including the filling of seams and covering of fastener dimples with joint compound. Eliminating hand-troweled finishes saves time, labor, and money.

Drywall usually consists of a strong paper skin adhered to a gypsum core. The finish-ready face paper wraps around to the back of the panel at the sides, where it overlaps the coarser, more rigid paper used on the back. For handling purposes, sheets of drywall are joined at the ends by removable strips of tape. To facilitate finishing, panels are typically tapered at the long edges. The shallow depression formed where panels meet is easily covered with tape and filled with joint compound for a flat surface that appears continuous. The short, butt-end joints are not recessed and are more challenging to finish.

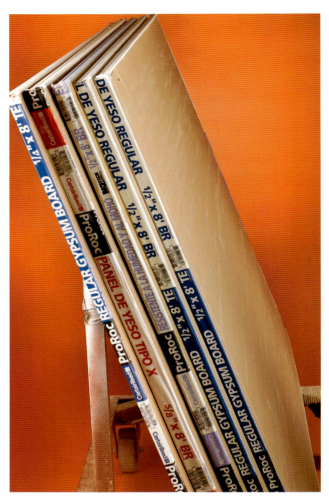

Drywall is a broad category of building materials that covers many types of panels with various purposes, including common gypsum-based wallcovering panels as well as specialty wallcoverings and tile backers.

Gypsum ▸

Gypsum is a naturally occurring crystal mined from the earth. It is formed when calcium sulfate chemically combines with water. The scrubbers that neutralize sulfuric acid emitted from power plants also create gypsum synthetically. Today much of our gypsum drywall is a byproduct of this effort to protect the environment from acid rain. When buildings burn, the water is driven out of gypsum crystals in drywall, producing steam. This characteristic makes gypsum a fire suppressant, though eventually the dehydrated gypsum will collapse.

Piles of mined gypsum await processing into the basic constituent material used to make drywall.

TYPES OF PANELS

Standard drywall is used for most walls and ceilings in dry, interior areas. It comes in 4-ft.-wide panels in lengths ranging from 8 ft. to 16 ft. and in thicknesses of ¼", ⅜", ½", and ⅝". There are also 54"-wide panels for horizontal installations on walls with 9-ft. ceilings.

Flexible drywall, specially made for curved walls, is a bendable version of standard ¼"-thick drywall. It can be installed dry or dampened with water to increase its flexibility.

Fire-resistant drywall has a dense, fiber-reinforced core that helps contain fire. Thicknesses are ½", ⅝", and ¾". Most fire-resistant drywall is called "Type X." Fire-resistant panels are generally required in attached garages, on walls adjacent to garages, and in furnace and utility rooms.

Moisture-resistant drywall, commonly called "greenboard" for the color of its face paper, is designed for areas of high humidity and is used most often in bathrooms, behind kitchen sinks, and in laundry rooms.

Abuse-resistant drywall withstands surface impacts and resists penetrations better than standard drywall. It's available in ½" regular and ⅝" fire-resistant types.

Decorative drywall products include prefinished vinyl-coated panel systems, decorative corner treatments, prefabricated arches, and drywall panels that look like traditional raised-panel paneling.

Sound-resistant drywall products have up to eight times as much sound-deadening capability as standard drywall. These products are good for home theaters.

Plaster-base drywall, sometimes called "blueboard," is used with veneer plaster systems instead of a traditional hand-troweled scratch coat. Panels have two layers of paper—a blue-colored face paper that's highly absorptive over a moisture-resistant paper to protect the gypsum core.

Mold-resistant drywall is a specialty board designed for areas that are regularly damp, have high humidity, or that are otherwise susceptible to mold and mildew growth.

ELECTRICAL BOXES

The National Electrical Code requires that wire connections and cable splices be contained inside an approved metal or plastic box. This shields framing members and other flammable materials from electrical sparks.

Electrical boxes come in several shapes. Rectangular and square boxes are used for switches and receptacles. Rectangular (2 × 3-inch) boxes are used for single switches or duplex receptacles. Square (4 × 4-inch) boxes are used any time it is convenient for two switches or receptacles to be wired, or "ganged," in one box, an arrangement common in kitchens or entry hallways. Octagonal electrical boxes contain wire connections for ceiling fixtures.

All electrical boxes are available in different depths. A box must be deep enough so a switch or receptacle can be removed or installed easily without crimping and damaging the circuit wires. Replace an undersized box with a larger box using the Electrical Box Fill Chart (right) as a guide. The NEC also says that all electrical boxes must remain accessible. Never cover an electrical box with drywall, paneling, or wallcoverings.

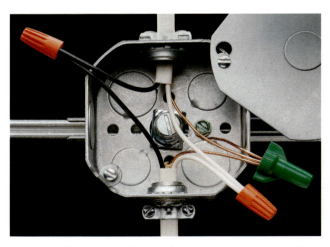

Octagonal boxes usually contain wire connections for ceiling fixtures. Cables are inserted into the box through knockout openings and are held with cable clamps. Because the ceiling fixture attaches directly to the box, the box should be anchored firmly to a framing member. Often, it is nailed directly to a ceiling joist. However, metal braces are available that allow a box to be mounted between joists or studs. A properly installed octagonal box can support a ceiling fixture weighing up to 35 pounds. Any box must be covered with a tightly fitting cover plate, and the box must not have open knockouts.

Electrical Box Fill Chart ▸

Box size and shape	Maximum number of conductors permitted (see Notes below)			
	18 AWG	16 AWG	14 AWG	12 AWG
Junction Boxes				
4 × 1¼" R or O	8	7	6	5
4 × 1½" R or O	10	8	7	6
4 × 2⅛" R or O	14	12	10	9
4 × 1¼" S	12	10	9	8
4 × 1½" S	14	12	10	9
4 × 2⅛" S	20	17	15	13
4¹¹⁄₁₆ × 1¼" S	17	14	12	11
4¹¹⁄₁₆ × 1½" S	19	16	14	13
4¹¹⁄₁₆ × 2⅛" S	28	24	21	18
Device Boxes				
3 × 2 × 1½"	5	4	3	3
3 × 2 × 2"	6	5	5	4
3 × 2 × 2¼"	7	6	5	4
3 × 2 × 2½"	8	7	6	5
3 × 2 × 2¾"	9	8	7	6
3 × 2 × 3½"	12	10	9	8
4 × 2⅛ × 1½"	6	5	5	4
4 × 2⅛ × 1⅞"	8	7	6	5
4 × 2⅛ × 2⅛"	9	8	7	6

Notes:

- *R = Round; O = Octagonal; S = Square or rectangular*
- *Each hot or neutral wire entering the box is counted as one conductor.*
- *Grounding wires are counted as one conductor in total—do not count each one individually.*
- *Raceway fittings and external cable clamps do not count. Internal cable connectors and straps count as either half or one conductor, depending on type.*
- *Devices (switches and receptacles mainly) each count as two conductors.*
- *When calculating total conductors, any nonwire components should be assigned the gauge of the largest wire in the box.*
- *For wire gauges not shown here, contact your local electrical inspections office.*

COMMON ELECTRICAL BOXES

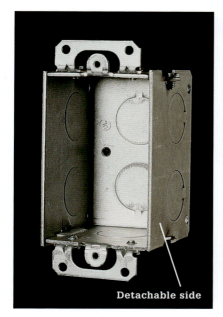

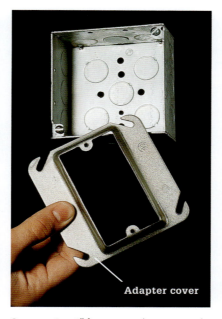

Detachable side

Adapter cover

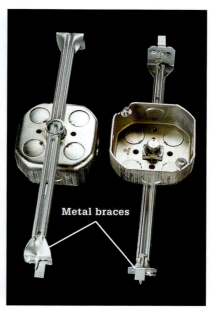

Metal braces

Rectangular boxes are used with wall switches and duplex receptacles. Single-size rectangular boxes (shown above) may have detachable sides that allow them to be ganged together to form double-size boxes.

Square 4 × 4" boxes are large enough for most wiring applications. They are used for cable splices and ganged receptacles or switches. To install one switch or receptacle in a square box, use an adapter cover.

Braced octagonal boxes fit between ceiling joists. The metal braces extend to fit any joist spacing and are nailed or screwed to framing members.

Foam gasket

Outdoor boxes have sealed seams and foam gaskets to guard a switch or receptacle against moisture. Corrosion-resistant coatings protect all metal parts. Code compliant models include a watertight hood.

Retrofit boxes can be installed to upgrade older boxes or to allow you to add new additional receptacles and switches. One type (above) has built-in clamps that tighten against the inside of a wall and hold the box in place.

Plastic boxes are common in new construction. They can be used only with NM (nonmetallic) cable. The box may include preattached nails for anchoring it to framing members. Wall switches must have grounding screws if installed in plastic boxes.

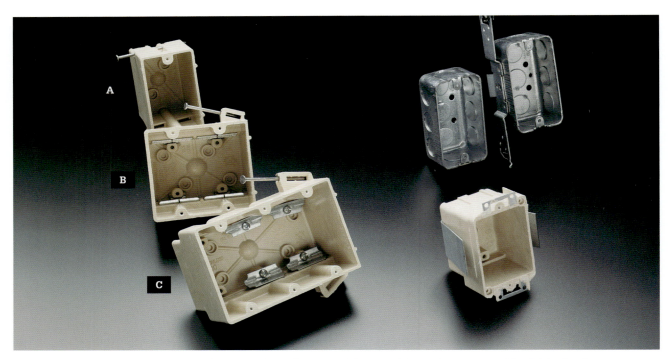

3½"-deep plastic boxes with preattached mounting nails are used for any wiring project protected by finished walls. Common styles include single-gang (A), double-gang (B), and triple-gang (C). Double-gang and triple-gang boxes require internal cable clamps. Metal boxes should be used for exposed indoor wiring, such as conduit installations in an unfinished basement. Metal boxes also can be used for wiring that will be covered by finished walls. Plastic retrofit boxes are used when a new switch or receptacle must fit inside a finished wall. Use internal cable clamps.

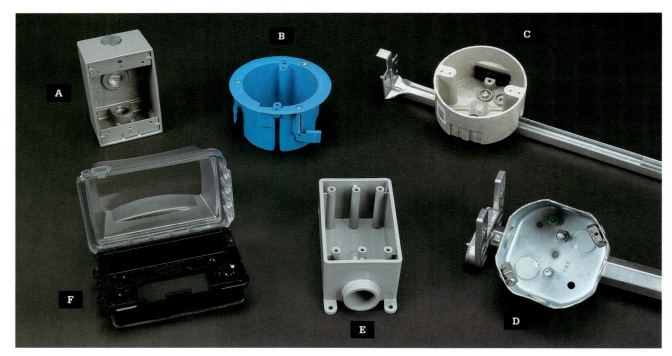

Additional electrical boxes include: Cast aluminum box (A) for use with outdoor fixtures, including receptacles that are wired through metal conduit. These must have in-use covers if they house receptacles; retrofit ceiling box (B) used for light fixtures; light-duty ceiling fan box (C) with brace that spans ceiling joists; heavy-duty retrofit ceiling fan box (D) designed for retrofit; PVC box (E) for use with PVC conduit in indoor or outdoor setting; wall-mounted in-use cover (F) for exterior receptacle.

Box Specifications ▶

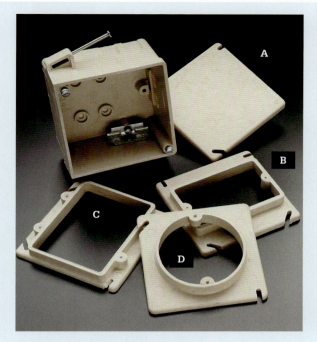

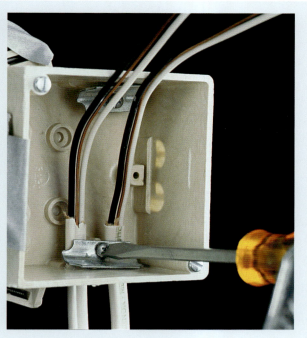

High-quality nonmetallic boxes are rigid and don't contort easily. A variety of adapter plates are available, including junction box cover plate (A), single-gang (B), double-gang (C), and light fixture (D). Adapter plates come in several thicknesses to match different wall constructions.

Boxes larger than 2 × 4" and all retrofit boxes must have internal cable clamps. After installing cables in the box, tighten the cable clamps over the cables so they are gripped firmly, but not so tightly that the cable sheathing is crushed.

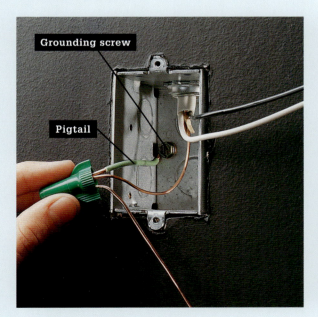

Metal boxes must be grounded to the circuit grounding system. Connect the circuit grounding wires to the box with a green insulated pigtail wire and wire connector (as shown) or with a grounding clip (page 68).

Cables entering a metal box must be clamped. A variety of clamps are available, including plastic clamps (A, C) and threaded metal clamps (B).

ELECTRICAL CIRCUITS

An electrical circuit is a continuous loop. Household circuits carry eletricity from the main service panel, throughout the house, and back to the main service panel. Several switches, receptacles, light fixtures, or appliances may be connected to a single circuit.

Current enters a circuit loop on hot wires and returns along neutral wires. These wires are color coded for easy identification. Hot wires are black or red, and neutral wires are white or light gray. For safety, all modern circuits include a bare copper or green insulated grounding wire. The grounding wire conducts current in the event of a ground fault, and helps reduce the chance of severe electrical shock. The service panel also has a bonding wire connected to a metal water pipe and a grounding wire connected to a metal grounding rod buried underground or to another type of grounding electrode.

If a circuit carries too much current, it can overload. A fuse or a circuit breaker protects each circuit in case of overloads.

Current returns to the service panel along a neutral circuit wire. Current then leaves the house on a large neutral service wire that returns it to the utility transformer.

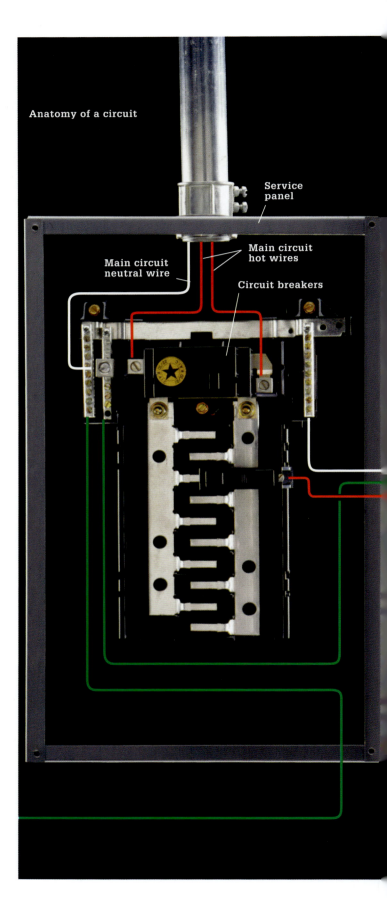

Anatomy of a circuit

Service panel

Main circuit hot wires

Main circuit neutral wire

Circuit breakers

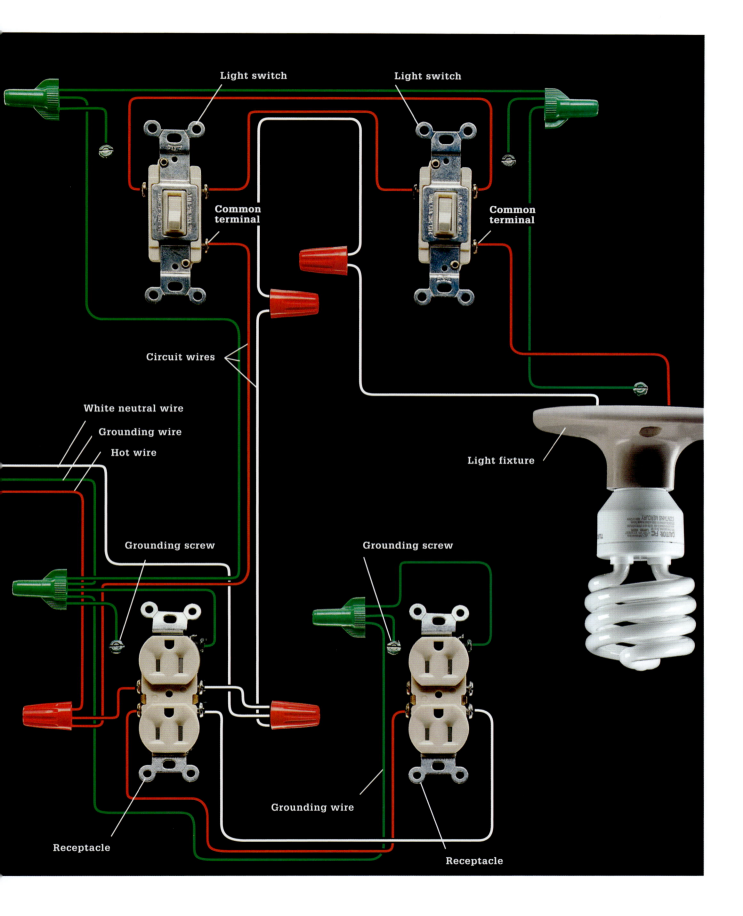

Light switch

Light switch

Common
terminal

Common
terminal

Circuit wires

White neutral wire

Grounding wire

Hot wire

Light fixture

Grounding screw

Grounding screw

Receptacle

Grounding wire

Receptacle

ELECTRICITY: BASICS

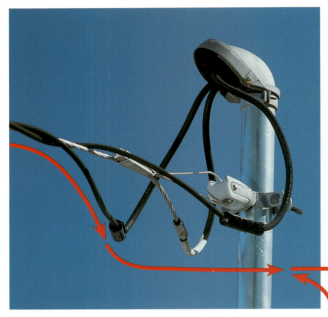

The service mast (metal pole) and the weatherhead create the entry point for electricity into your home. The mast is supplied with three wires two of which (the insulated wires) each carry 120 volts and originate at the nearest transformer. In some areas electricity enters from below ground as a lateral, instead of the overhead drop shown above.

The meter measures the amount of electricity consumed. It is usually attached to the side of the house, and connects to the service mast. A thin metal disc inside the meter rotates when power is used. The electric meter belongs to your local power utility company. If you suspect the meter is not functioning properly, contact the power company.

Surges in current flow to grounding rod

A grounding wire connects the electrical system to the earth through a metal grounding rod driven next to the house.

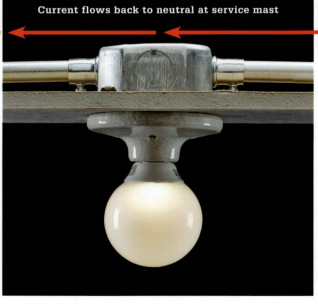

Current flows back to neutral at service mast

Light fixtures attach directly to a household electrical system. They are usually controlled with wall switches. The two common types of light fixtures are incandescent and fluorescent.

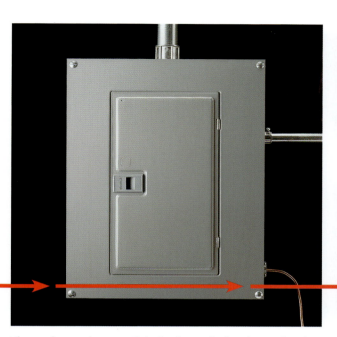

The main service panel, in the form of a fuse box or breaker box, distributes power to individual circuits. Fuses or circuit breakers protect each circuit from short circuits and overloads. Fuses and circuit breakers also are used to shut off power to individual circuits while repairs are made.

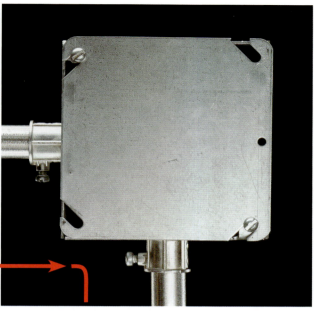

Electrical boxes enclose wire connections. According to the National Electrical Code, all wire splices and connections must be contained entirely in a covered plastic or metal electrical box.

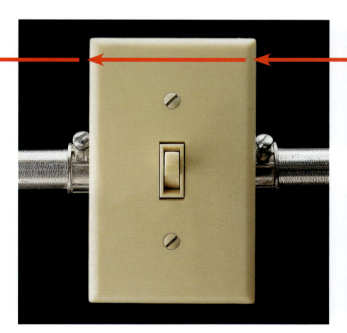

Switches control electricity passing through hot circuit wires. Switches can be wired to control light fixtures, ceiling fans, appliances, and receptacles.

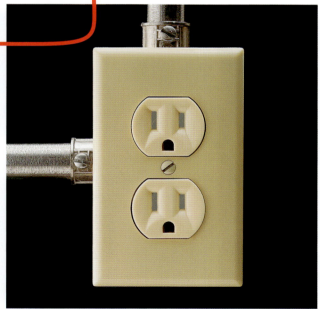

Receptacles, sometimes called outlets, provide plug-in access to electricity. A 120-volt, 15-amp receptacle with a grounding hole is the most typical receptacle in wiring systems installed after 1965. Most receptacles have two plug-in locations and are called duplex receptacles.

Glossary of Electrical Terms ▶

Ampere (or amp): Refers to the rate at which electrical power flows to a light, tool, or appliance.

Armored cable: Two or more wires that are grouped together and protected by a flexible metal covering.

Box: A device used to contain wiring connections.

BX: See armored cable (Bx is the older term).

Cable: Two or more wires that are grouped together and protected by a covering or sheath.

Circuit: A continuous loop of electrical current flowing along wires or cables.

Circuit breaker: A safety device that interrupts an electrical circuit in the event of an overload or short circuit.

Conductor: Any material that allows electrical current to flow through it. Copper wire is an especially good conductor.

Conduit: A metal or plastic pipe used to protect wires.

Continuity: An uninterrupted electrical pathway through a circuit or electrical fixture.

Current: The movement of electrons along a conductor.

Duplex receptacle: A receptacle that provides connections for two plugs.

Feed wire: A conductor that carries 120-volt current uninterrupted from the service panel.

Fuse: A safety device, usually found in older homes, that interrupts electrical circuits during an overload or short circuit.

Greenfield: Materials used in flexible metal conduit. See armored cable.

Grounded wire: See neutral wire.

Grounding wire: A wire used in an electrical circuit to conduct current to the earth in the event of a short circuit. The grounding wire often is a bare copper wire.

Hot wire: Any wire that carries voltage. In an electrical circuit, the hot wire usually is covered with black or red insulation.

Insulator: Any material, such as plastic or rubber, that resists the flow of electrical current. Insulating materials protect wires and cables.

Junction box: See box.

Meter: A device used to measure the amount of electrical power being used.

Neutral wire: A wire that returns current at zero voltage to the source of electrical power. Usually covered with white or light gray insulation. Also called the grounded wire.

Nonmetallic sheathed cable: NM cable consists of two or more insulated conductors and, in most cases, a bare ground wire housed in a durable PVC casing.

Outlet: See receptacle.

Overload: A demand for more current than the circuit wires or electrical device was designed to carry. Usually causes a fuse to blow or a circuit breaker to trip.

Pigtail: A short wire used to connect two or more circuit wires to a single screw terminal.

Polarized receptacle: A receptacle designed to keep hot current flowing along black or red wires, and neutral current flowing along white or gray wires.

Power: The result of hot current flowing for a period of time. Use of power makes heat, motion, or light.

Receptacle: A device that provides plug-in access to electrical power.

Romex: A brand name of plastic-sheathed electrical cable that is commonly used for indoor wiring. Commonly known as NM cable.

Screw terminal: A place where a wire connects to a receptacle, switch, or fixture.

Service panel: A metal box usually near the site where electrical power enters the house. In the service panel, electrical current is split into individual circuits. The service panel has circuit breakers or fuses to protect each circuit.

Short circuit: An accidental and improper contact between two current-carrying wires, or between a current-carrying wire and a grounding conductor.

Switch: A device that controls electrical current passing through hot circuit wires. Used to turn lights and appliances on and off.

UL: An abbreviation for Underwriters Laboratories, an organization that tests electrical devices and manufactured products for safety.

Voltage (or volts): A measurement of electricity in terms of pressure.

Wattage (or watt): A measurement of electrical power in terms of total energy consumed. Watts can be calculated by multiplying the voltage times the amps.

Wire connector: A device used to connect two or more wires together. Also called a wire nut.

Best Practices for Home Wiring ▸

BY MATERIAL

Service Panel

- Maintain a minimum 30" wide by 36" deep of clearance in front of the service panel.
- Ground all 120-volt and 240-volt circuits.
- Match the amperage rating of the circuit when replacing fuses.
- Use handle-tie breakers for 240-volt loads (line to line).
- Close all unused service panel openings.
- Label each fuse and breaker clearly on the panel.

Electrical Boxes

- Use boxes that are large enough to accommodate the number of wires entering the box.
- Locate all receptacle boxes 12 to 18" above the finished floor (standard).
- Locate all switch boxes 48" above the finished floor (standard). For special circumstances, inspectors will allow switch and location measurements to be altered, such as a switch at 36" above the floor in a child's bedroom or receptacles at 24" above the floor to make them more accessible for someone using a wheelchair.
- Install all boxes so they remain accessible.
- Leave no gaps greater than ⅛" between wallboard and front of electrical boxes.
- Place receptacle boxes flush with combustible surfaces.
- Leave a minimum of 6" of usable cable or wire extending past the front of the electrical box.

Wires & Cables

- Use wires that are large enough for the amperage rating of the circuit (see Wire Size Chart, page 571).
- Drill holes at least 2" back from the exposed edge of joists to run cables through. Do not attach cables to the bottom edge of joists.
- Do not run cables diagonally between framing members.
- Run cable between receptacles 20" above the floor.
- Use nail plates to protect cable that is run through holes drilled or cut into studs less than 1¼" from front edge of stud.
- Do not crimp cables sharply.
- Contain spliced wires or connections entirely in a plastic or metal electrical box.
- Use wire connectors to join wires.
- Use staples to fasten cables within 8" of an electrical box and every 48" along its run.
- Leave a minimum ¼" (maximum 1") of sheathing where cables enter an electrical box.

- Clamp cables and wires to electrical boxes with approved NM clamp. No clamp is necessary for one-gang plastic boxes if cables are stapled within 8".
- Label all cables and wires at each electrical box to show which circuits they serve for the rough-in inspection.
- Connect only a single wire to a single screw terminal. Use pigtails to join more than one wire to a screw terminal.

Switches

- Use a switch-controlled receptacle in rooms without a built-in light fixture operated by a wall switch.
- Use three-way switches at the top and bottom on stairways with six steps or more.
- Use switches with grounding screw with plastic electrical boxes.
- Locate all wall switches within easy reach of the room entrance.

Receptacles

- Match the amp rating of a receptacle with the size of the circuit.
- Install receptacles on all walls 24" wide or greater.
- Install receptacles so a 6-ft. cord can be plugged in from any point along a wall or every 12 ft. along a wall.
- Include receptacles in any hallway that is 10 ft. long or more.
- Use three-prong, grounded receptacles for all 15- or 20-amp, 120-volt branch circuits.
- Include a switch-controlled receptacle in rooms without a built-in light fixture operated by a wall switch.
- Install GFCI-protected receptacles in bathrooms, kitchens, garages, crawl spaces, unfinished basements, and outdoor receptacle locations.
- Install an isolated-ground circuit to protect sensitive equipment, like a computer, against tiny power fluctuations. Computers should also be protected by a standard surge protector.

Light Fixtures

- Use mounting straps that are anchored to the electrical boxes to mount ceiling fixtures.
- Keep non-IC-rated recessed light fixtures 3" from insulation and ½" from combustibles.
- Include at least one switch-operated lighting fixture in every room.

(continued)

(continued from previous page) ▶

Grounding

- Ground all receptacles by connecting receptacle grounding screws to the circuit grounding wires.
- Use switches with grounding screws whenever possible. Always ground switches installed in plastic electrical boxes and all switches in kitchens, bathrooms, and basements.

BY ROOM
Kitchens/Dining Rooms

- Install a dedicated 40- or 50-amp, 120/240-volt circuit for a range (or two circuits for separate oven and countertop units).
- Install two 20-amp small appliance circuits.
- Install dedicated 15-amp, 120-volt circuits for dishwashers and food disposals (required by many local codes).
- Use GFCI receptacles for all accessible countertop receptacles; receptacles behind fixed appliances do not need to be GFCIs.
- Position receptacles for appliances that will be installed within cabinets, such as microwaves or food disposals, according to the manufacturer's instructions.
- Include receptacles on all counters wider than 12".
- Space receptacles a maximum of 48" apart above countertops and closer together in areas where many appliances will be used.
- Locate receptacles 4" above the top of the backsplash. If backsplash is more than the standard 4" or the bottom of cabinet is less than 18" from countertop, center the box in space between countertop and bottom of wall cabinet.
- Mount one receptacle within 12" of the countertop on islands and peninsulas that are 12 × 24" or greater.
- Do not put lights on small appliance circuits.
- Install additional lighting in work areas at a sink or range for convenience and safety.

Bathrooms

- Install a separate 20-amp circuit.
- Ground switches in bathrooms.
- Use GFCI-protected receptacles.
- Install at least one ceiling-mounted light fixture.
- Place blower heaters in bathrooms well away from the sink and tub.

Utility/Laundry Rooms

- Install a separate 20-amp circuit for a washing machine.
- Install a minimum feed 30-amp #10 THHN wire for the dryer powered by a separate 120/240-volt major appliance circuit.
- Install metal conduit for cable runs in unfinished rooms.
- Use GFCI-protected receptacles.

Living, Entertainment, Bedrooms

- Install a minimum of two 15-amp circuits in living rooms.
- Install a minimum of one 15- or 20-amp basic lighting/receptacle circuit for each 600 sq. ft. of living space.
- Install a dedicated circuit for each permanent appliance, like an air conditioner, computer, or group of electric baseboard heaters.
- Do not use standard electrical boxes to support ceiling fans.
- Include receptacles on walls 24" wide or more.
- Space receptacles on basic lighting/receptacle circuits a maximum of 12 ft. apart. For convenience you can space them as close as 6 ft.
- Position permanent light fixtures in the center of the room's ceiling.
- Install permanently wired smoke alarms in room additions that include sleeping areas and hallways.

Outdoors

- Check for underground utilities before digging.
- Use UF cable for outdoor wiring needs.
- Run cable in schedule 80 PVC plastic, as required by local code.
- Most local codes now require in-use rated weatherproof box covers.
- Bury cables housed in conduit at least 18" deep; cable not in conduit must be buried at least 24" deep.
- Use weatherproof electrical boxes with watertight covers.
- Use GFCI-protected receptacles.
- Install receptacles a minimum of 12" above ground level.
- Anchor freestanding receptacles not attached to a structure by embedding the schedule 80 PVC plastic conduit in a concrete footing, so that it is at least 12" but no more than 18" above ground level.
- Plan on installing a 20-amp, 120-volt circuit if the circuit contains more than one light fixture rated for 300 watts, or more than four receptacles.

Stairs/Hallways

- Use three-way switches at the top and bottom on stairways with six steps or more.
- Include receptacles in any hallway that is 10 ft. long or more.
- Position stairway lights so each step is illuminated.

ELECTRICITY: BASICS: SAFETY

Safety should be the primary concern of anyone working with electricity. Although most household electrical repairs are simple and straightforward, always use caution and good judgment when working with electrical wiring or devices. Common sense can prevent accidents.

The basic rule of electrical safety is: Always turn off power to the area or device you are working on. At the main service panel, remove the fuse or shut off the circuit breaker that controls the circuit you are servicing. Then check to make sure the power is off by testing for power with a voltage tester. *Tip: Test a live circuit with the voltage tester to verify that it is working before you rely on it.* Restore power only when the repair or replacement project is complete.

Follow the safety tips shown on these pages. Never attempt an electrical project beyond your skill or confidence level. Never attempt to repair or replace your main service panel or service entrance head. These are jobs for a qualified electrician and require that the power company shut off power to your house.

Shut power OFF at the main service panel or the main fuse box before beginning any work.

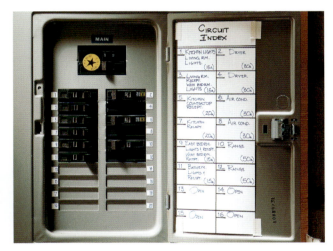

Create a circuit index and affix it to the inside of the door to your main service panel. Update it as needed.

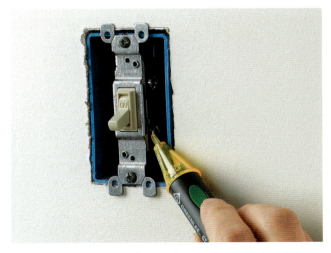

Confirm power is OFF by testing at the outlet, switch, or fixture with a voltage tester.

Use only UL-approved electrical parts or devices. These devices have been tested for safety by Underwriters Laboratories.

Wear rubber-soled shoes while working on electrical projects. On damp floors, stand on a rubber mat or dry wooden boards.

Use fiberglass or wood ladders when making routine household repairs near the service mast.

Extension cords are for temporary use only. Cords must be rated for the intended usage.

Breakers and fuses must be compatible with the panel manufacturer and match the circuit capacity.

Never alter the prongs of a plug to fit a receptacle. If possible, install a new grounded receptacle.

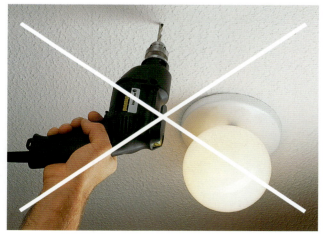

Do not penetrate walls or ceilings without first shutting off electrical power to the circuits that may be hidden.

FASCIA: ALUMINUM: INSTALLING

Fascia fits under the drip edge and against the subfascia to provide a smooth transition from the roof to the eaves. You may need to temporarily remove any nails in the face of the drip edge so the fascia can slide in behind it. If your roof does not have drip edge, install a finish trim, such as undersill, at the top of the subfascia to receive the fascia.

If you're also replacing your gutters, take down the gutters first, then install the fascia. If you don't want to remove the gutters, you can slip the fascia behind them while they're in place.

Fascia is nailed along the lip covering the soffits, and the top is held in place by the drip edge, so it doesn't require any face nailing.

Tools & Materials ▸

Hammer	Fascia
Aviation snips	Aluminum trim nails
Tape measure	Protective
Chalk line	equipment

The fascia is installed over the subfascia to cover the exposed edges of the soffits and enhance the appearance of your home. The fascia is usually the same color and material as your soffits.

HOW TO INSTALL ALUMINUM FASCIA

Remove the old fascia, if necessary. Measure from the top of the drip edge to the bottom of the soffits, and subtract ¼". Cut the fascia to this measurement by snapping a chalk line across the face and cutting with aviation snips. (This cut edge will be covered by the drip edge.) *Tip: If your old fascia is wood and still in good shape, you can install aluminum fascia over it without removing it.*

Slide the cut edge of the fascia behind the drip edge. Place the bottom lip over the soffits. Make sure the fascia is tight against the soffits and against the subfascia, then nail through the lip into the subfascia. Nail approximately every 16" at a V-groove location in the soffits.

(continued)

3

To overlap fascia panels, cut the ridge on the lip of the first panel 1" from the end using aviation snips. Place the second panel over the first, overlapping the seam by 1". Nail the fascia in place.

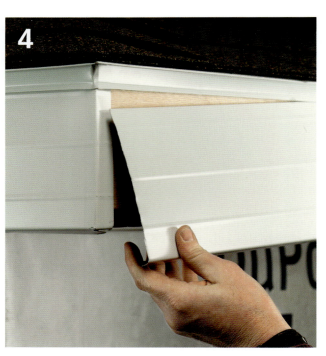

4

At outside corners, cut the lip and top edge of the first panel 1" from the end. Place a piece of wood 1" from the end, and bend the panel to form a 90° angle. Install the panel at the corner. Cut a 45° angle in the lip of the second panel. Align the end of this panel with the corner, overlapping the first panel.

5

For inside corners, cut and bend the first panel back 1" from the end to make a tab. Install the panel. On the second panel, cut a 45° angle in the lip. Slide the panel over the first panel, butting the end against the adjacent fascia. Nail the panel in place.

6

Install soffit panels to close off the area between the fascia cover and the exterior wall (see pages 423 to 425).

FAUCETS: BATHROOM: INSTALLING

1
- Spout shank
- Plumber's putty

Insert the shank of the faucet spout through one of the holes in the sink deck (usually the center hole, but you can offset it in one of the end holes if you prefer). If the faucet is not equipped with seals or O-rings for the spout and handles, pack plumber's putty on the undersides before inserting the valves into the deck. *Note: If you are installing the widespread faucet in a new sink deck, drill three holes of the size suggested by the faucet manufacturer.*

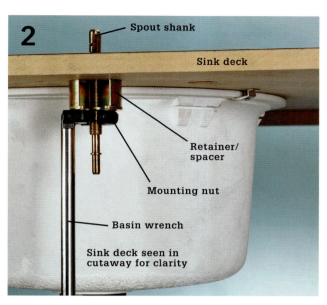

2
- Spout shank
- Sink deck
- Retainer/ spacer
- Mounting nut
- Basin wrench
- Sink deck seen in cutaway for clarity

In addition to mounting nuts, many spout valves for widespread faucets have an open-retainer fitting that goes between the underside of the deck and the mounting nut. Others have only a mounting nut. In either case, tighten the mounting nut with pliers or a basin wrench to secure the spout valve. You may need a helper to keep the spout centered and facing forward.

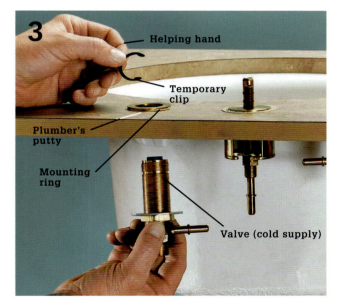

3
- Helping hand
- Temporary clip
- Plumber's putty
- Mounting ring
- Valve (cold supply)

Mount the valves to the deck using whichever method the manufacturer specifies (it varies quite a bit). In the model seen here, a mounting ring is positioned over the deck hole (with plumber's putty seal) and the valve is inserted from below. A clip snaps onto the valve from above to hold it in place temporarily (you'll want a helper for this).

4
- Valve
- Spout shank

From below, thread the mounting nuts that secure the valves to the sink deck. Make sure the cold water valve (usually has a blue cartridge inside) is in the right-side hole (from the front) and the hot water valve (red cartridge) is in the left hole. Install both valves.

(continued)

5

Water outlet (cold)

Water outlet (hot)

Water inlet (spout)

Once you've started the nut on the threaded valve shank, secure the valve with a basin wrench, squeezing the lugs where the valve fits against the deck. Use an adjustable wrench to finish tightening the lock nut onto the valve. The valves should be oriented so the water outlets are aimed at the inlet on the spout shank.

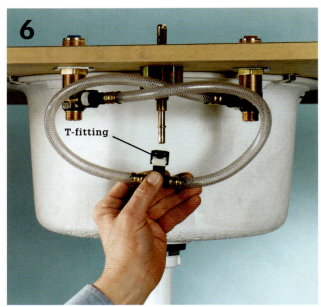

6

T-fitting

Attach the flexible supply tubes (supplied with the faucet) to the water outlets on the valves. Some twist onto the outlets, but others (like the ones above) click into place. The supply hoses meet in a T-fitting that is attached to the water inlet on the spout.

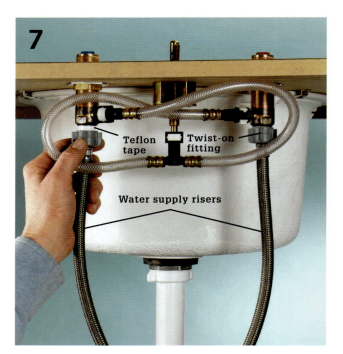

7

Teflon tape

Twist-on fitting

Water supply risers

Attach flexible braided-metal supply risers to the water stop valves and then attach the tubes to the inlet port on each valve (usually with Teflon tape and a twist-on fitting at the valve end of the supply riser).

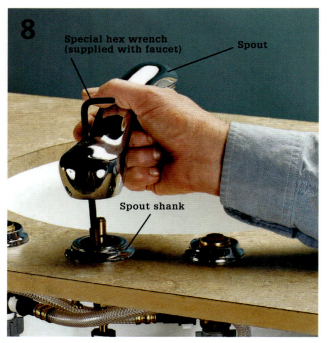

8

Special hex wrench (supplied with faucet)

Spout

Spout shank

Attach the spout. The model shown here comes with a special hex wrench that is threaded through the hole in the spout where the lift rod for the pop-up drain will be located. Once the spout is seated cleanly on the spout shank, you tighten the hex wrench to secure the spout. Different faucets will use other methods to secure the spout to the shank.

9

Lift rod

Clevis screw housing

Clevis strap

If your sink did not have a pop-up stopper, you'll need to replace the sink drain tailpiece with a pop-up stopper body (often supplied with the faucet). See page 404. Insert the lift rod through the hole in the back of the spout and, from below, thread the pivot rod through the housing for the clevis screw.

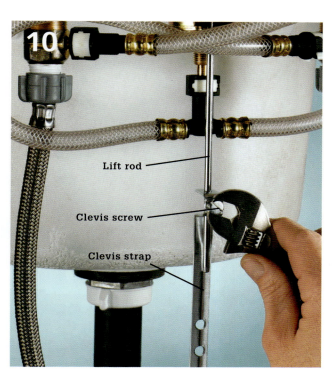

10

Lift rod

Clevis screw

Clevis strap

Attach the clevis strap to the pivot rod that enters the pop-up drain body, and adjust the position of the strap so it raises and lowers properly when the lift rod is pulled up. Tighten the clevis screw at this point. It's hard to fit a screwdriver in here, so you may need to use a wrench or pliers.

11

Attach the faucet handles to the valves using whichever method is required by the faucet manufacturer. Most faucets are designed with registration methods to ensure that the handles are symmetrical and oriented in an ergonomic way once you secure them to the valves.

12

Aerator

Turn on the water supply and test the faucet. Remove the faucet aerator and run the water for 10 to 20 seconds so any debris in the lines can clear the spout. Replace the aerator.

Variation: How to Install a Single-body Faucet ▶

High-quality faucets come with flexible plastic gaskets that create a durable watertight seal at the bottom of the faucet, where it meets the sink deck. However, an inexpensive faucet may have a flimsy-looking foam seal that doesn't do a good job of sealing and disintegrates after a few years. If that is the case with your faucet, discard the seal and press a ring of plumber's putty into the sealant groove on the underside of the faucet body.

Insert the faucet tailpieces through the holes in the sink. From below, thread washers and mounting nuts over the tailpieces, then tighten the mounting nuts with a basin wrench until snug. Put a dab of pipe joint compound on the threads of the stop valves and thread the metal nuts of the flexible supply risers to these. Wrench tighten about a half-turn past hand tight. Overtightening these nuts will strip the threads. Now tighten the coupling nuts to the faucet tailpieces with a basin wrench.

Slide the lift rod of the new faucet into its hole behind the spout. Thread it into the clevis past the clevis screw. Push the pivot rod all the way down so the stopper is open. With the lift rod also all the way down, tighten the clevis to the lift rod.

Grease the fluted valve stems with faucet grease, then put the handles in place. Tighten the handle screws firmly, so they won't come loose during operation. Cover each handle screw with the appropriate index cap—Hot or Cold.

Unscrew the aerator from the end of the spout. Turn the hot and cold water taps on full. Turn the water back on at the stop valves and flush out the faucet for a couple of minutes before turning off the water at the faucet. Check the riser connections for drips. Tighten a compression nut only until the drip stops.

FAUCETS: KITCHEN: INSTALLING

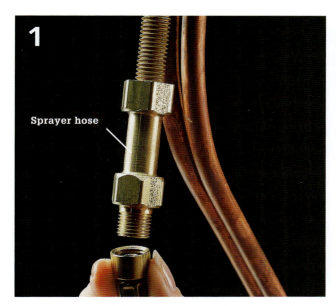

1

Sprayer hose

To remove the old faucet, start by clearing out the cabinet under the sink and laying down towels. Turn off the hot and cold stop valves and open the faucet to make sure the water is off. Detach the sprayer hose from the faucet sprayer nipple and unscrew the retaining nut that secures the sprayer base to the sink deck. Pull the sprayer hose out through the sink deck opening.

2

Mounting nut

Spray the mounting nuts that hold the faucet or faucet handles (on the underside of the sink deck) with penetrating oil for easier removal. Let the oil soak in for a few minutes. If the nut is rusted and stubbornly stuck, you may need to drill a hole in its side, then tap the hole with a hammer and screwdriver to loosen it.

3

Unhook the supply tubes at the stop valves. Don't reuse old chrome supply tubes. If the stops are missing or unworkable, replace them. Then remove the coupling nuts and the mounting nuts on the tailpieces of the faucet with a basin wrench or channel-type pliers.

4

Pull the faucet body from the sink. Remove the sprayer base if you wish to replace it. Scrape off old putty or caulk with a putty knife and clean off the sink with a scouring pad and an acidic scouring cleaner. *Tip: Scour stainless steel with a back and forth motion to avoid leaving unsightly circular markings.*

HOW TO INSTALL A PULLOUT KITCHEN SINK FAUCET

1

Install the base plate (if your faucet has one) onto the sink flange so it is centered. Have a helper hold it straight from above as you tighten the mounting nuts that secure the base plate from below. Make sure the plastic gasket is centered under the base plate. These nuts can be adequately tightened by hand.

2
Pullout hose
Threaded shank
Hose end

Retract the pullout hose by drawing it out through the faucet body until the fitting at the end of the hose is flush with the bottom of the threaded faucet shank. Insert the shank and the supply tubes down through the top of the deck plate.

3
Cabinet back removed for clarity
Mounting nut
Washer
Retainer screw

Slip the mounting nut and washer over the free ends of the supply tubes and pullout hose, then thread the nut onto the threaded faucet shank. Hand tighten. Tighten the retainer screws with a screwdriver to secure the faucet.

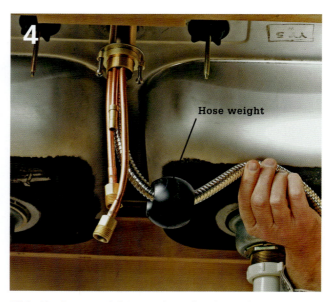

4
Hose weight

Slide the hose weight onto the pullout hose (the weight helps keep the hose from tangling and it makes it easier to retract).

Connect the end of the pullout hose to the outlet port on the faucet body using a quick connector fitting.

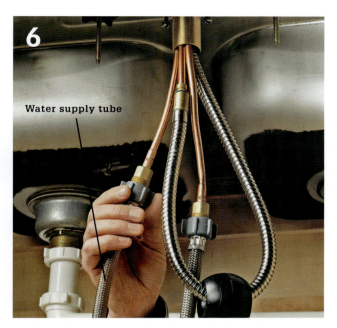

Hook up the water supply tubes to the faucet inlets. Make sure the tubes are long enough to reach the supply risers without stretching or kinking.

Connect the supply tubes to the supply risers at the stop valves. Make sure to get the hot lines and cold lines attached correctly.

Attach the spray head to the end of the pullout hose and turn the fitting to secure the connection. Turn on water supply and test. *Tip: Remove the aerator in the tip of the spray head and run hot and cold water to flush out any debris.*

Variation: One-Piece Faucet with Sprayer ▶

1

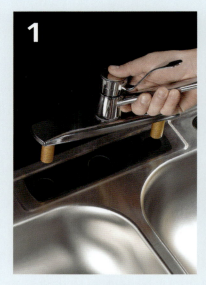

Thoroughly clean the area around the sink's holes. Slip the faucet's plastic washer onto the underside of the base plate. Press the faucet in place, and have a helper hold it in place while you work from below.

2

Friction washer

Mounting nut

Slip a friction washer onto each tailpiece and then hand tighten a mounting nut. Tighten the mounting nut with channel-type pliers or a basin wrench. Wipe up any silicone squeeze-out on the sink deck with a wet rag before it sets up.

3

Tailpiece

Supply tube

Coupling nut

Connect supply tubes to the faucet tailpieces. Make sure the tubes you buy are long enough to reach the stop valves and that the coupling nuts will fit the tubes and tailpieces.

4

Sprayer tailpiece

Apply a ¼" bead of plumber's putty to the underside of the sprayer base. With the base threaded onto the sprayer hose, insert the tailpiece of the sprayer through the opening in the sink deck.

5

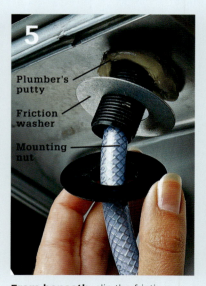

Plumber's putty

Friction washer

Mounting nut

From beneath, slip the friction washer over the sprayer tailpiece and then screw the mounting nut onto the tailpiece. Tighten with channel-type pliers or a basin wrench. Clean up any excess putty or caulk.

6

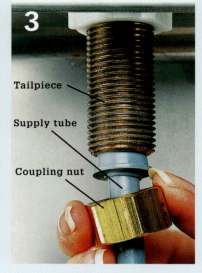

Screw the sprayer hose onto the hose nipple on the bottom of the faucet. Hand tighten and then give the nut one quarter turn with channel-type pliers or a basin wrench. Turn on the water supply at the shutoff, remove the aerator, and flush debris from the faucet.

FAUCETS: KITCHEN SPRAYER: REPAIRING

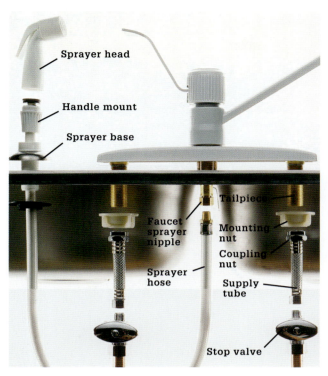

The standard sprayer hose attachment is connected to a nipple at the bottom of the faucet valve. When the lever of the sprayer is depressed, water flows from a diverter valve in the faucet body out to the sprayer. If your sprayer stream is weak or doesn't work at all, the chances are good that the problem lies in the diverter valve.

Sprayer heads can be removed from the sprayer hose, usually by loosening a retaining nut. A sprayer's head can get clogged with minerals. Unscrew the sprayer from the hose and remove any parts at its tip. Soak it in mineral cleaner, and use a small brush to open any clogged orifices.

HOW TO REPAIR A SPRAYER

Shut off the water at the stop valves and remove the faucet handle to gain access to the faucet parts. Disassemble the faucet handle and body to expose the diverter valve. Ball-type faucets like the one shown here require that you also remove the spout to get at the diverter.

Locate the diverter valve, seen here at the base of the valve body. Because different types and brands of faucets have differently configured diverters, do a little investigating beforehand to try and locate information about your faucet. The above faucet is a ball type.

(continued)

3

Pull the diverter valve from the faucet body with needlenose pliers. Use a toothbrush dipped in white vinegar to clean any lime buildup from the valve. If the valve is in poor condition, bring it to the hardware store and purchase a replacement.

4

Diverter valve washer

Diverter valve

Coat the washer or O-ring on the new or cleaned diverter valve with faucet grease. Insert the diverter valve back into the faucet body. Reassemble the faucet. Turn on the water and test the sprayer. If it still isn't functioning to your satisfaction, remove the sprayer tip and run the sprayer without the filter and aerator in case any debris has made its way into the sprayer line during repairs.

Finding the Diverter on a Two-Handle Faucet ▸

On a two-handle faucet, the diverter is usually located in a vertical position just under the spout. Remove the spout. You may need to use longnose pliers to pull out the diverter. Try cleaning out any debris. If that does not restore operation, replace the valve.

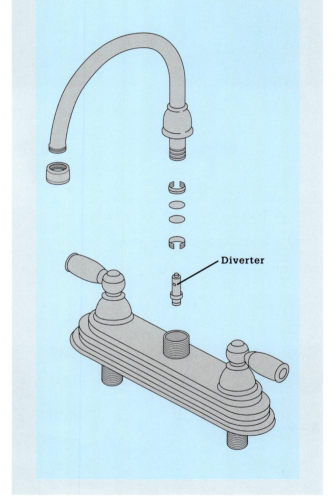

Diverter

FAUCETS: SINK: REPAIRING

It's not surprising that sink faucets leak and drip. Any fitting that contains moving mechanical parts is susceptible to failure. But add to the equation the persistent force of water pressure working against the parts, and the real surprise is that faucets don't fail more quickly or often. It would be a bit unfair to say that the inner workings of a faucet are regarded as disposable by manufacturers, but it is safe to say that these parts have become more easy to remove and replace.

The older your faucet, the more likely you can repair it by replacing small parts like washers and O-rings. Many newer faucets can be repaired only by replacing the major inner components, like a ceramic disk or a cartridge that encapsulates all the washers and O-rings that could possibly wear out.

The most important aspect of sink faucet repair is identifying which type of faucet you own. In this chapter we show all of the common types and provide instructions on repairing them. In every case, the easiest and most reliable repair method is to purchase a replacement kit with brand-new internal working parts for the model and brand of faucet you own.

Tools & Materials ▶

Pliers	Repair kit
Needlenose pliers	(exact type varies)
Heatproof grease	Teflon tape
Channel-type pliers	Screwdrivers
Utility knife	Pipe joint compound
White Vinager	Plumber's putty
Old toothbrush	Rag
Tape measure	Protective equipment

Eventually, just about every faucet develops leaks and drips. Repairs can usually be accomplished simply by replacing the mechanical parts inside the faucet body (the main trick is figuring out which kind of parts your faucet has).

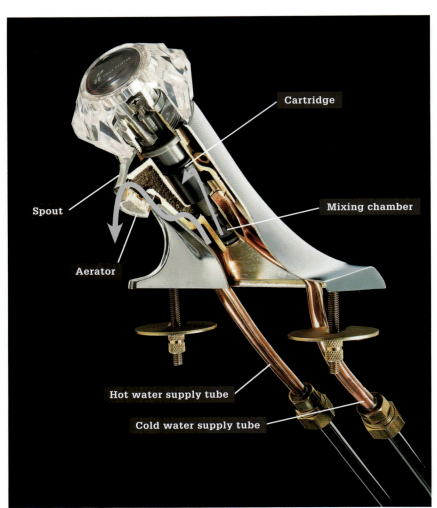

Cartridge

Spout

Mixing chamber

Aerator

Hot water supply tube

Cold water supply tube

All faucets, no matter the type, have valves that move many thousands of times to open and close hot- and cold-water ports. These valves—or the rubber or plastic parts that rub against other parts when the faucet is being adjusted—wear out in time. Depending on the faucet, you may be able to fix the leak by cleaning or replacing small parts, such as washers or O-rings; or you may need to buy a repair kit and replace a number of parts; or the only solution may be to replace a self-enclosed "cartridge" that contains all the moving parts.

Common Problems and Repairs ▸

Problems	Repairs
Faucet drips from the end of the spout or leaks around the base.	1. Identify the faucet design (page 161), then install replacement parts, using directions on the following pages.
Old worn-out faucet continues to leak after repairs are made.	1. Replace the old faucet (pages 153 to 156).
Water pressure at spout seems low, or water flow is partially blocked.	1. Clean faucet aerator. 2. Replace corroded galvanized pipes with copper.
Water pressure from sprayer seems low, or sprayer leaks from handle.	1. Clean sprayer head (page 157). 2. Fix diverter valve (pages 157 to 158).
Water leaks onto floor underneath faucet.	1. Replace cracked sprayer hose (page 262). 2. Tighten water connections, or replace supply tubes and shutoff valves (pages 186 to 187). 3. Replace leaky sink strainer (page 410).
Hose bib or valve drips from spout or leaks around handle.	1. Take valve apart and replace washers and O-rings (pages 162 to 167).

IDENTIFYING YOUR FAUCET AND THE PARTS YOU NEED

A leaky faucet is the most common home plumbing problem. Fortunately, repair parts are available for almost every type of faucet, from the oldest to the newest, and installing these parts is usually easy. But if you don't know your make and model, the hardest part of fixing a leak may be identifying your faucet and finding the right parts. Don't make the common mistake of thinking that any similar-looking parts will do the job; you've got to get exact replacements.

There are so many faucet types that even experts have trouble classifying them into neat categories. Two-handle faucets are either compression (stem) or washerless two-handle. Single-handle faucets are classified as mixing cartridge; ball; disc; or disc/cartridge.

A single-handle faucet with a rounded, dome-shaped cap is often a ball type. If a single-handle faucet has a flat top, it is likely a cartridge or a ceramic disc type. An older two-handle faucet is likely of the compression type; newer two-handle models use washerless cartridges. Shut off the water, and test to verify that the water is off. Dismantle the faucet carefully. Look for a brand name: it may be clearly visible on the baseplate, or may be printed on an inner part, or it may not be printed anywhere. Put all the parts into a reliable plastic bag and take them to your home center or plumbing supply store. A knowledgeable salesperson can help you identify the parts you need.

If you cannot find what you are looking for at a local store, check online faucet sites or the manufacturers' sites; they often have step-by-step instruction for identifying what you need. Note that manufacturers' terminology may not match the terms we use here. For example, the word "cartridge" may refer to a ceramic-disc unit.

Most faucets have repair kits, which include all the parts you need, and sometimes a small tool as well. Even if some of the parts in your faucet look fine, it's a good idea to install the parts provided by the kit, to ensure against future wear.

Repair Tips ▸

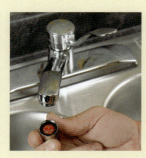

If water flow is weak, unscrew the aerator at the tip of the spout. If there is sediment, then dirty water is entering the faucet, which could damage the faucet's inner workings.

To remove handles and spouts, work carefully and look for small screw heads. You often need to first pry off a cap on top, but not always. Parts may be held in place with small setscrews.

Cleaning and removing debris can sometimes solve the problem of low water flow, and occasionally can solve a leak as well.

Apply plumber's grease (also known as faucet grease or valve grease), to new parts before installing them. Be especially sure to coat rubber parts like O-rings and washers.

COMPRESSION FAUCETS

Cap

Top screw

Handle

Valve

O-ring

Stem screw

A compression faucet has a stem assembly that includes a retaining nut, threaded spindle, O-ring, stem washer, and stem screw. Dripping at the spout occurs when the washer becomes worn. Leaks around the handle are caused by a worn O-ring.

Pry off the cap on top of the handle and remove the screw that holds the cap onto the stem. Pull the handle up and out. Use an adjustable wrench or pliers to unscrew the stem and pull it out.

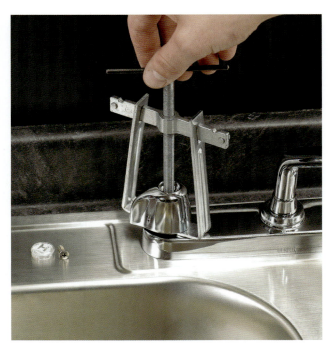

If the handle is stuck, try applying mineral cleaner from above. If that doesn't work, you may need to buy a handle puller. With the cap and the hold-down screw removed, position the wings of the puller under the handle and tighten the puller to slowly pull the handle up.

Remove the screw that holds the rubber washer in place, and pry out the washer. Replace a worn washer with an exact replacement—one that is the same diameter, thickness, and shape.

Replace any O-rings. A worn O-ring can cause water to leak out the handle. Gently pry out the old O-ring and reinstall an exact replacement. Apply plumber's grease to the rubber parts before reinstalling the stem.

If washers wear out quickly, the seat is likely worn. Use a seat wrench to unscrew the seat from inside the faucet. Replace it with an exact duplicate. If replacing the washer and O-ring doesn't solve the problem, you may need to replace the entire stem.

WASHERLESS TWO-HANDLE FAUCET

Handle

Set screw

Stem screw

Retaining nut

Cartridge

Housing

Retaining nut

Remove the faucet handle and withdraw the old cartridge. Make a note of how the cartridge is oriented before you remove it. Purchase a replacement cartridge.

Almost all two-handle faucets made today are "washerless." Instead of an older-type compression stem, there is a cartridge, usually with a plastic casing. Many of these cartridges contain ceramic discs, while others have metal or plastic pathways. No matter the type of cartridge, the repair is the same; instead of replacing small parts, you simply replace the entire cartridge.

Install the replacement cartridge. Clean the valve seat first and coat the valve seat and O-rings with faucet grease. Be sure the new cartridge is in the correct position, with its tabs seated in the slotted body of the faucet. Re-assemble the valve and handles.

ONE-HANDLE CARTRIDGE FAUCETS

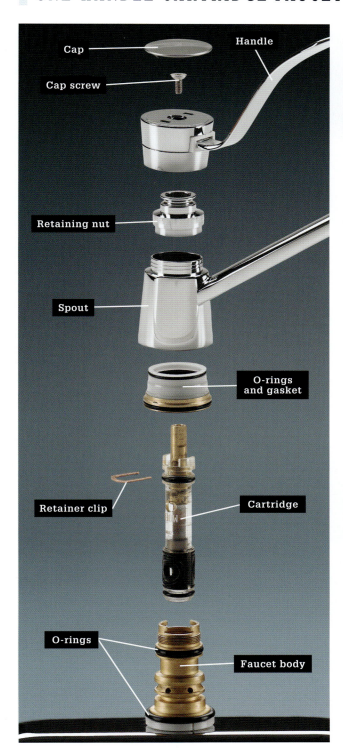

Cap
Handle
Cap screw

Retaining nut

Spout

O-rings
and gasket

Retainer clip

Cartridge

O-rings

Faucet body

To remove the spout, pry off the handle's cap and remove the screw below it. Pull the handle up and off. Use a crescent wrench to remove the pivot nut.

Single-handle cartridge faucets like this work by moving the cartridge up and down and side to side, which opens up pathways to direct varying amounts of hot and cold water to the spout. Moen, Price-Pfister, Delta, Peerless, Kohler, and others make many types of cartridges, some of which look very different from this one.

Lift out the spout. If the faucet has a diverter valve, remove it as well. Use a screwdriver to pry out the retainer clip, which holds the cartridge in place.

Remove the cartridge. If you simply pull up with pliers, you may leave part of the stem in the faucet body. If that happens, replace the cartridge and buy a stem puller made for your model.

Gently pry out and replace all O-rings on the faucet body. Smear plumber's grease onto the new replacement cartridge and the new O-rings, and reassemble the faucet.

Here is one of many other types of single-handle cartridges. In this model, all the parts are plastic except for the stem, and it's important to note the direction in which the cartridge is aligned. If you test the faucet and the hot and cold are reversed, disassemble and realign the cartridge.

BALL FAUCETS

Handle

Stem screw

Ball cap

Spout

Cam

Ball

Valve seats and springs

Faucet body and O-rings

Outlet

Ball

Cam

Remove the old ball and cam after removing the faucet handle and ball cap. Some faucets may require a ball faucet tool to remove the handle. Otherwise, simply use a pair of channel-type pliers to twist off the ball cap.

Pry out the neoprene valve seals and springs. Place thick towels around the faucet. Slowly turn on the water to flush out any debris in the faucet body. Replace the seals and springs with new parts. Also replace the O-rings on the valve body. You may want to replace the ball and cam, too, especially if you're purchasing a repair kit. Coat all rubber parts in faucet grease, and reassemble the faucet.

The ball-type faucet is used by Delta, Peerless, and a few others. The ball fits into the faucet body and is constructed with three holes (not visible here)—a hot inlet, a cold inlet, and the outlet, which fills the valve body with water that then flows to the spout or sprayer. Depending on the position of the ball, each inlet hole is open, closed, or somewhere in-between. The inlet holes are sealed to the ball with valve seats, which are pressed tight against the ball with springs. If water drips from the spout, replace the seats and springs. Or go ahead and purchase an entire replacement kit and replace all or most of the working parts.

DISC FAUCETS

Cap

Handle

Cap screw

Threaded nut

Cylinder

Cartridge

100908

Spout

Disc-type faucets are the most common single-handle faucets currently being made. A pair of ceramic discs encased in a cylinder often referred to as a "cartridge" rub together as they rotate to open ports for hot and cold water. The ceramic discs do wear out in time, causing leaks, and there is only one solution—replace the disc unit (or "cartridge"). This makes for an easy—through comparatively expensive—repair.

Other Cartridges ▸

Many modern cartridges do not have seals or O-rings that can be replaced, and some have a ball rather than a ceramic disk inside. For the repair, the cartridge's innards do not matter; just replace the whole cartridge.

Replace the cylinder with a new one, coating the rubber parts with faucet grease before installing the new cylinder. Make sure the rubber seals fit correctly in the cylinder openings before you install the cylinder. Assemble the faucet handle.

PLUMBING

FAUCETS: TUB & SHOWER: REPAIRING

Tub and shower faucets have the same basic designs as sink faucets, and the techniques for repairing leaks are the same as described in the faucet repair section of this book (pages 159 to 168). To identify your faucet design, you may have to take off the handle and disassemble the faucet.

When a tub and shower are combined, the showerhead and the tub spout share the same hot and cold water supply lines and handles. Combination faucets are available as three-handle, two-handle, or single-handle types (next page). The number of handles gives clues as to the design of the faucets and the kinds of repairs that may be necessary.

With combination faucets, a diverter valve or gate diverter is used to direct water flow to the tub spout or the showerhead. On three-handle faucet types, the middle handle controls a diverter valve. If water does not shift easily from tub to showerhead, or if water continues to run out the spout when the shower is on,

the diverter valve probably needs to be cleaned and repaired (page 171).

Two-handle and single-handle types use a gate diverter that is operated by a pull lever or knob on the tub spout. Although gate diverters rarely need repair, the lever occasionally may break, come loose, or refuse to stay in the up position. To repair a gate diverter set in a tub spout, replace the entire spout.

Tub and shower faucets and diverter valves may be set inside wall cavities. Removing them may require a deep-set ratchet wrench.

If spray from the showerhead is uneven, clean the spray holes. If the showerhead does not stay in an upright position, remove the head and replace the O-ring.

To add a shower to an existing tub, install a flexible shower adapter. Several manufacturers make complete conversion kits that allow a shower to be installed in less than one hour.

Tub/shower plumbing is notorious for developing drips from the tub spout and the showerhead. In most cases, the leak can be traced to the valves controlled by the faucet handles.

FIXING THREE-HANDLE TUB & SHOWER FAUCETS

A three-handle faucet type has two handles to control hot and cold water, and a third handle to control the diverter valve and direct water to either a tub spout or a shower head. The separate hot and cold handles indicate cartridge or compression faucet designs. To repair them, refer to the opposite page (compression) or page 115 (cartridge).

If a diverter valve sticks, if water flow is weak, or if water runs out of the tub spout when the flow is directed to the showerhead, the diverter needs to be repaired or replaced. Most diverter valves are similar to either compression or cartridge faucet valves. Compression-type diverters can be repaired, but cartridge types should be replaced.

Remember to turn off the water before beginning work.

Tools & Materials ▸

Screwdriver
Adjustable wrench
    or channel-type
    pliers
Deep-set
    ratchet wrench
Small wire brush
Replacement
    diverter cartridge
    or universal
    washer kit

Faucet grease
Vinegar
Protective
    equipment

Water line to shower head

Diverter valve

Hot water supply line

Cold water supply line

Diverter valve handle

A three-handle tub/shower faucet has individual controls for hot and cold water plus a third handle that operates the diverter valve.

HOW TO REPAIR A COMPRESSION DIVERTER VALVE

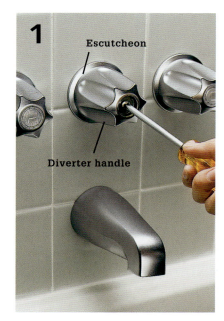

1

Escutcheon

Diverter handle

Remove the diverter valve handle with a screwdriver. Unscrew or pry off the escutcheon.

2

Bonnet nut

Remove bonnet nut with an adjustable wrench or channel-type pliers.

3

Unscrew the stem assembly, using a deep-set ratchet wrench. If necessary, chip away any mortar surrounding the bonnet nut.

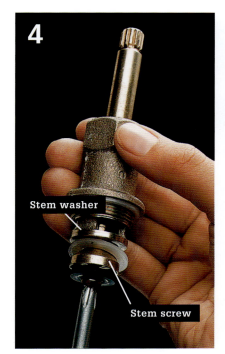

4

Stem washer

Stem screw

Remove brass stem screw. Replace stem washer with an exact duplicate. If stem screw is worn, replace it.

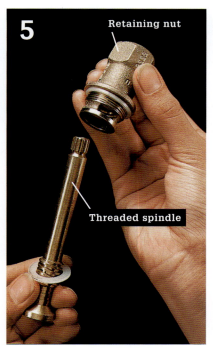

5

Retaining nut

Threaded spindle

Unscrew the threaded spindle from the retaining nut.

6

Clean sediment and lime buildup from nut, using a small wire brush dipped in vinegar. Coat all parts with faucet grease and reassemble diverter valve.

FIXING TWO-HANDLE TUB & SHOWER FAUCETS

Two-handle tub and shower faucets are either cartridge or compression design. They may be repaired following the directions on pages 171 and 175. Because the valves of two-handle tub and shower faucets may be set inside the wall cavity, a deep-set socket wrench may be required to remove the valve stem.

Two-handle tub and shower designs have a gate diverter. A gate diverter is a simple mechanism located in the tub spout. A gate diverter closes the supply of water to the tub spout and redirects the flow to the shower head. Gate diverters seldom need repair. Occasionally, the lever may break, come loose, or refuse to stay in the up position.

If the diverter fails to work properly, replace the tub spout. Tub spouts are inexpensive and easy to replace.

Remember to turn off the water before beginning any work.

Tools & Materials ▸

Screwdriver	Deep-set
Allen wrench	ratchet wrench
Pipe wrench	Pipe joint compound
Channel-type pliers	Replacement faucet
Small cold chisel	parts, as needed
Ball-peen hammer	Protective
Masking tape or cloth	equipment

Water line to shower head

Bonnet nut

Valve stem

Diverter lever

Cold water supply line

Hot water supply line

Gate diverter

A two-handle tub/shower faucet can operate with compression valves, but more often these days they contain cartridges that can be replaced. Unlike a three-handled model, the diverter is a simple gate valve that is operated by a lever.

Tips on Replacing a Tub Spout ▶

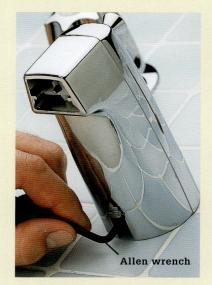

Check underneath tub spout for a small access slot. The slot indicates the spout is held in place with an Allen screw. Remove the screw, using an Allen wrench. Spout will slide off.

Unscrew faucet spout. Use a pipe wrench, or insert a large screwdriver or hammer handle into the spout opening and turn spout counterclockwise.

Spread pipe joint compound on threads of spout nipple before replacing spout. If you have a copper pipe or a short pipe, buy a spout retrofit kit, which can attach a spout to most any pipe.

HOW TO REMOVE A DEEP-SET FAUCET VALVE

Remove handle and unscrew the escutcheon with channel-type pliers. Pad the jaws of the pliers with masking tape to prevent scratching the escutcheon.

Chip away any mortar surrounding the bonnet nut using a ball-peen hammer and a small cold chisel.

Unscrew the bonnet nut with a deep-set ratchet wrench. Remove the bonnet nut and stem from the faucet body.

FIXING SINGLE-HANDLE TUB & SHOWER FAUCETS

A single-handle tub and shower faucet has one valve that controls both water flow and temperature. Single-handle faucets may be ball-type, cartridge, or disc designs.

If a single-handle control valve leaks or does not function properly, disassemble the faucet, clean the valve, and replace any worn parts. Use the repair techniques described on page 167 for ball-type, or page 168 for ceramic disc. Repairing a single-handle cartridge faucet is shown on the opposite page.

Direction of the water flow to either the tub spout or the showerhead is controlled by a gate diverter. Gate diverters seldom need repair. Occasionally, the lever may break, come loose, or refuse to stay in the up position. Remember to turn off the water before beginning any work; the shower faucet shown here has built-in shutoff valves, but many other valves do not. Open an access panel in an adjoining room or closet, behind the valve, and look for two shutoffs. If you can't find them there, you may have to shut off intermediate valves or the main shutoff valve.

Tools & Materials ▸

Screwdriver
Adjustable wrench
Channel-type pliers

Replacement faucet parts, as needed

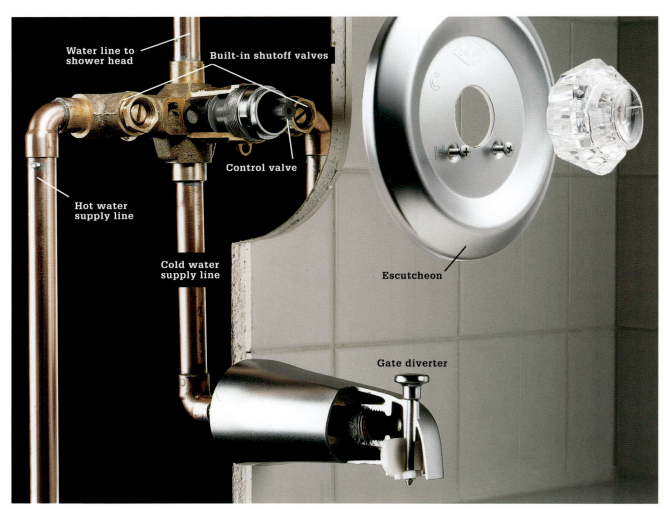

Water line to shower head

Built-in shutoff valves

Control valve

Hot water supply line

Cold water supply line

Escutcheon

Gate diverter

A single-handle tub/shower faucet is the simplest type to operate and to maintain. The handle controls the mixing ratio of both hot and cold water, and the diverter is a simple gate valve.

HOW TO REPAIR A SINGLE-HANDLE CARTRIDGE TUB & SHOWER FAUCET

1 Handle

Escutcheon

Use a screwdriver to remove the handle and escutcheon.

2 Built-in shutoff valves

Turn off water supply at the built-in shutoff valves or the main shutoff valve.

3 Bonnet nut

Unscrew and remove the retaining ring or bonnet nut using adjustable wrench.

4 Cartridge

O-ring

Remove the cartridge assembly by grasping the end of the valve with channel-type pliers and pulling gently.

5

Flush the valve body with clean water to remove sediment. Replace any worn O-rings. Reinstall the cartridge and test the valve. If the faucet fails to work properly, replace the cartridge.

SINGLE-HANDLE TUB & SHOWER FAUCET WITH SCALD CONTROL

In many plumbing systems, if someone flushes a nearby toilet or turns on the cold water of a nearby faucet while someone else is taking a shower, the shower water temperature can suddenly rise precipitously. This is not only uncomfortable; it can actually scald you. For that reason, many one-handle shower valves have a device, called a "balancing valve" or an "anti-scald valve," that keeps the water from getting too hot.

The temperature of your shower may drastically rise to dangerous scalding levels if a nearby toilet is flushed. A shower fixture equipped with an anti-scald valve prevents this sometimes dangerous situation.

HOW TO ADJUST THE SHOWER'S TEMPERATURE

1

To reduce or raise the maximum temperature, remove the handle and escutcheon. Some models have an adjustment screw, others have a handle that can be turned by hand.

2

To remove a balancing valve, you may need to buy a removal tool made for your faucet. Before replacing, slowly turn on water to flush out any debris; use a towel or bucket to keep water from entering inside the wall.

PLUMBING

FIXING & REPLACING SHOWERHEADS

If spray from the showerhead is uneven, clean the spray holes. The outlet or inlet holes of the showerhead may get clogged with mineral deposits. Showerheads pivot into different positions. If a showerhead does not stay in position, or if it leaks, replace the O-ring that seals against the swivel ball.

A tub can be equipped with a shower by installing a flexible shower adapter kit. Complete kits are available at hardware stores and home centers.

Tools & Materials ▸

Adjustable wrench or channel-type pliers
Pipe wrench
Drill
Glass and tile bit
Mallet
Screwdriver
Masking tape
Thin wire (paper clip)
Faucet grease
Rag
Replacement O-rings
Masonry anchors
Flexible shower adapter kit (optional)
Protective equipment

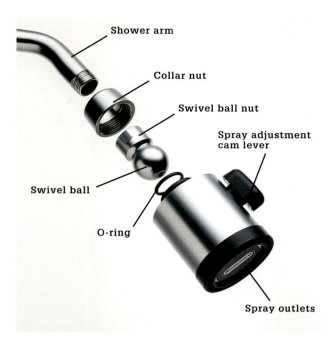

A typical showerhead can be disassembled easily for cleaning and repair. Some showerheads include a spray adjustment cam lever that is used to change the force of the spray.

HOW TO CLEAN & REPAIR A SHOWERHEAD

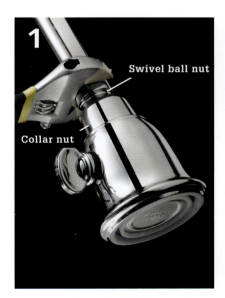

Unscrew the swivel ball nut, using an adjustable wrench or channel-type pliers. Wrap jaws of the tool with masking tape to prevent marring the finish. Unscrew collar nut from the showerhead.

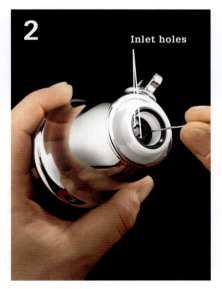

Clean outlet and inlet holes of showerhead with a thin wire. Flush the head with clean water.

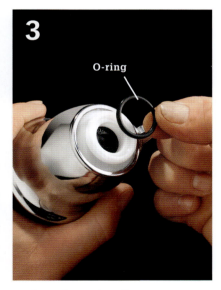

Replace the O-ring, if necessary. Lubricate the O-ring with faucet grease before installing.

FLOORS

FLOOR LEVELER

Self-leveling underlayment, otherwise referred to as self-leveling cement, is applied over uneven surfaces, such as cementitious backers and concrete slabs, to make them level prior to tile application. A similar product called concrete resurfacer accomplishes essentially the same thing. Levelers and resurfacer have fairly liquid viscosities. They are poured onto uneven surfaces, where gravity directs them to fill in the low areas of a subfloor. One 50-pound bag of floor leveler will typically cover a surface area of approximately 50 square feet, at ⅛-inch thick. Leveler can be applied in layers as thin as a feather edge and as thick as one inch, depending on the specific product you buy. Self-leveling underlayment cures very quickly,

usually within a few hours of application. In some cases, multiple applications are required to build up to the desired thickness.

A coat of paint-like primer should be applied prior to the leveler in almost all cases. This is usually rolled onto the substrate using a short-nap roller. The primer seals the substrate, which helps keep it from absorbing the moisture in the cement mixture too rapidly. It also improves the adhesive bond between the self-leveling cement and the surface it is applied to.

The leveler compound is best mixed using a ½-inch corded drill fitted with a mixing paddle. A garden rake and a trowel will also be necessary to spread the batch over the area in need of repair.

Cement-based tile products such as this floor leveler must be mixed well with water. A ½" power drill with a mixing paddle attachment is a great help in this regard.

Floor levelers and resurfacers are applied prior to installing tile backer to address dips, valleys, and other uneven areas in a concrete floor. An acrylic or latex fortifier helps the product flow more smoothly and gives it some extra flex, without sacrificing hardness.

HOW TO APPLY LEVELER

Patch any major cracks or large popouts with concrete patching compound before you apply the leveler. Once the patch dries, wash and rinse the floor according to the instructions on the leveler package. This may include the use of grease cutters and pressure washers.

Apply an even layer of concrete primer to the entire surface using a long-nap paint roller. Let the primer dry completely.

Following the manufacturer's instructions, mix the floor leveler with water. The batch should be large enough to cover the entire floor area to the desired thickness (up to 1"). Pour the leveler over the floor.

Distribute the leveler evenly, using a rake or spreader. Work quickly: the leveler begins to harden in 15 min. Use a trowel to feather the edges and create a smooth transition with an uncovered area. Let the leveler dry for 24 hrs.

FLOORS: LAMINATE

Plan your layout. In most cases, you'll need to trim one row of floorboards for width so the flooring fits into the room with the correct expansion gaps between it and the wall. Measure the width of the flooring installation area and subtract ½". Divide this distance by the actual width of a plank. If the leftover amount is more than one-half of a plank width, trim the planks for your first course to that width. If it is less than one-half, add the amount to the plank width, divide by two, and trim the planks in both the first and last rows to this width.

Clear out the installation room completely and vacuum the floor thoroughly to get rid of any debris that might interfere with the installation. A vacuum cleaner is the best tool for this.

Option: Install underlayment if the product you're installing doesn't have the pad preattached. Roll out underlayment pad from the starting corner to the opposite wall. Cut the pad to fit using a utility knife or scissors. Some manufacturers recommend overlapping the rows by 2 to 3". Otherwise, butt the seams together. Tape seams with 2 or 3" clear or duct tape. Smooth sheets out as you work.

Blade guard removed for clarity

Trim the tongues off the edges of the floorboards in the first course. If you need to trim the boards for width this can be done in the same cut. Check your manufacturer's instructions first: some recommend installing the boards with the groove side facing the wall.

Set spacers against the wall around the perimeter of the installation area. Spacers are ¼ to ½" thick. If you are installing the flooring over a wood subbase you can drive finish nails ¼" away from the walls to create stops. The point of the spacers is to create an expansion gap between the flooring and the wall. *Tip: Buy an installation kit (inset) to make laying your laminate flooring an easier job. A typical kit contains a pull bar, a tapping block, and a selection of spacers.*

Cross-cut a floorboard into a ⅔-length piece and a ⅓-length piece to start the second and third courses, respectively. Install the floorboards so the uncut edge with the tongue or groove intact will fit with the second board in the course. Alternating the length of the first board in each course will ensure that the butt joints where floorboard ends meet do not align from course to course.

⅓ length

Full length

⅔ length

Lay the first floorboard (use a full-length board) in the farthest corner of the installation. Make sure spacers are in place so there is a gap of approximately ¼" at each corner wall. Snap a ⅔-length floorboard next to it, and a ⅓-length next to that. This will establish a repeating pattern with a ⅓-length offset between all board ends.

Fill out the first three courses and then repeat the installation sequence to fill out the entire floor area. Mark the final board in each row for cutting by placing it upside down (tongue toward wall) on the previous plank. Push it flush to the spacer on the end wall. Line up a speed square with the bottom plank edge and trace the cut line.

(continued)

Work around door thresholds. At door openings, cut the bottoms of the door casing with a flush cutting saw to provide clearance for the flooring (left photo). When you reach the door as you lay floorboards, drive the flooring board that meets the door underneath the trimmed casing. Use a block and mallet to drive the board so the end is flush against the wall underneath the casing (right photo).

To fit the end plank for the row tightly into position, wedge one end of the pull bar between the spacer and the outside end of the plank. Tap the opposite end of the pull bar with a rubber mallet.

Finish installing floorboards. Rip-cut the floorboards for width if necessary (see next page). Test-fit the pieces in the last course and, if necessary, make adjustment cuts to fit using a utility knife. Finally, snap and lock the last course into place and remove all spacers. Work around obstacles as you go. Add transitions as needed.

CUTTING LAMINATE FLOORING

Rip-cut floorboards with a circular saw or table saw equipped with a fine-toothed, carbide-tipped wood blade. In either case, cut on the back side of the plank and make sure the board is clamped securely to a worksurface (when cutting with a circular saw). Cut along the waste side of the marked cut line. Use a straightedge as a guide, as shown.

Make internal cutouts with a jigsaw. If you're experienced with using power tools you can make a plunge cut with the saw blade, but to be on the safe side drill a starter hole near one corner and then make your cutout.

HOW TO MARK FOR CUTTING AROUND OBSTACLES

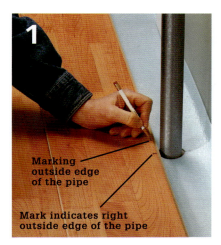

Marking outside edge of the pipe

Mark indicates right outside edge of the pipe

Position a plank end against the spacers on the wall next to the obstacle. Use a pencil to make two marks along the length of the plank, indicating the points where the obstacle begins and ends.

Once the plank is snapped into the previous row, position the plank end against the obstacle. Make two marks with a pencil, this time on the end of the plank to indicate where the obstacle falls along the width of the board.

Use a speed square to extend the four lines. The space at which they intersect is the part of the plank that needs to be removed to make room for the obstacle to go through it. Use a drill with a Forstner bit, or a hole saw the same diameter as the space within the intersecting lines, and drill through the plank at the X. You'll be left with a hole; extend the cut to the edges with a jigsaw.

FLOORS: UNDERLAYMENT

Underlayment is a thin layer of sheathing screwed or nailed to the subfloor to provide a smooth, stable surface for the floor covering. The type of underlayment you choose depends on the type of floor covering you plan to install. Ceramic and natural stone tile floors usually require an underlayment that stands up to moisture, such as cementboard. For vinyl flooring, use a quality-grade plywood; most warranties are void if the flooring is installed over substandard underlayments. If you want to use your old flooring as underlayment, apply an embossing leveler to prepare it for the new installation. Most wood flooring and carpeting do not require underlayment and are often placed on a plywood subfloor with only a cushion pad or rosin paper for underlayment.

When you install new underlayment, attach it securely to the subfloor in all areas, including under movable appliances. Notch the underlayment to fit the room's contours. Insert the underlayment beneath door casings and moldings. Once the underlayment is installed, use a latex patching compound to fill gaps, holes, and low spots. This compound is also used to cover screw heads, nail heads, and seams in underlayment. Some compounds include dry and wet ingredients that need to be mixed, while others are premixed. The compound is applied with a trowel or drywall knife.

¼" Plywood-AC

Fiber/cementboard

Cementboard

24 × 24" interlocking underlayment panels

Tools & Materials ▸

Drill	Latex additive
Circular saw	Thinset mortar
Drywall knife	Fiberglass-mesh
Power sander	wallboard tape
¼" notched trowel	Tape measure
Straightedge	Eye and ear
Utility knife	protection
Jigsaw with carbide-	Cementboard
tipped blade	screws, 1¼"
Flooring roller	Level
Underlayment	Mallet
1" deck screws	Dust mask
Floor-patching	Work gloves
compound	

HOW TO INSTALL PLYWOOD UNDERLAYMENT

Plywood is the most common underlayment for sheet vinyl flooring and resilient tile. For vinyl, use ¼" exterior-grade AC plywood. This type has one smooth, sanded side for a quality surface. Wood-based floor coverings, like parquet, can be installed over lower-quality plywood underlayment. When installing plywood, leave ¼" expansion gaps at the walls and between sheets. Make sure the seams in the underlayment are offset from the subfloor seams.

Install a piece of plywood along the longest wall, making sure the underlayment seams are not aligned with the subfloor seams. Fasten the plywood to the subfloor using 1" deck screws driven every 6" along the edges and at 8" intervals in the field of the sheet.

Continue fastening sheets of plywood to the subfloor, driving the screw heads slightly below the underlayment surface. Leave ¼" expansion gaps at the walls and between sheets. Offset seams in subsequent rows.

Using a circular saw or jigsaw, notch the plywood to meet the existing flooring in doorways. Fasten the notched sheets to the subfloor.

Mix floor-patching compound and latex or acrylic additive following the manufacturer's directions. Spread it over seams and screw heads using a wallboard knife.

Let the patching compound dry, then sand the patched areas using a power sander.

INSTALLING CEMENTBOARD

Ceramic and natural stone tile floors usually require an underlayment that stands up to moisture, such as cementboard. Fiber-cementboard is a thin, high-density underlayment used under ceramic tile and vinyl flooring in situations where floor height is a concern. Cementboard is used only for ceramic tile or stone tile installations. It remains stable even when wet, so it is the best underlayment to use in areas that are likely to get wet, such as bathrooms. Cementboard is more expensive than plywood, but a good investment for a large tile installation.

Tools & Materials ▸

Cementboard	Straightedge
Thinset mortar	Notched trowel
Fiberglass	Drill/driver
drywall tape	Drywall knife
1¼" cementboard	Tape measure
screws	Eye protection
Utility knife	and gloves

Common tile backers are cementboard, fiber-cementboard, and Dens-Shield. Cementboard is made from portland cement and sand reinforced by an outer layer of fiberglass mesh. Fiber-cementboard is made similarly, but with a fiber reinforcement integrated throughout the panel. Dens-Shield is a water-resistant gypsum board with a waterproof acrylic facing.

HOW TO INSTALL CEMENTBOARD

Cut cementboard by scoring through the mesh just below the surface using a utility knife or carbide-tipped cutter. Snap the panel back, then cut through the back-side mesh (inset). *Note: For tile applications, the rough face of the board is the front.*

Mix thin-set mortar according to the manufacturer's directions. Starting at the longest wall, spread the mortar on the subfloor in a figure eight pattern using a ¼" notched trowel. Spread only enough mortar for one sheet at a time. Set the cementboard on the mortar with the rough side up, making sure the edges are offset from the subfloor seams.

3

Fasten the cementboard to the subfloor using 1¼" cementboard screws driven every 6" along the edges and 8" throughout the sheet. Drive the screw heads flush with the surface. Continue spreading mortar and installing sheets along the wall. *Option: If installing fiber-cementboard underlayment, use a ³⁄₁₆" notched trowel to spread the mortar, and drill pilot holes for all screws.*

4

Cut cementboard pieces as necessary, leaving an ⅛" gap at all joints and a ¼" gap along the room perimeter.

5

To cut holes, notches, or irregular shapes, use a jigsaw with a carbide-tipped blade. Continue installing cementboard sheets to cover the entire floor.

6

Place fiberglass-mesh wallboard tape over the seams. Use a wallboard knife to apply thin-set mortar to the seams, filling the gaps between sheets and spreading a thin layer of mortar over the tape. Allow the mortar to set for two days before starting the tile installation.

FLOORS: UNDERLAYMENT: PANELS

When installing a new floor over a concrete base, raised underlayment panels that simply rest on the concrete can provide a great surface for other flooring materials. The tongue-and-groove plywood panels have dimpled plastic on the bottom.

This allows air to circulate underneath so that the concrete stays dry, and insulates the flooring above. The assembled panels can support laminates, resilient sheets, or tiles. And you can install them in a weekend.

HOW TO INSTALL UNDERLAYMENT PANELS

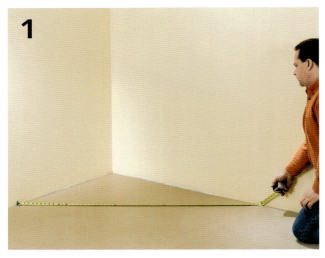

1

Start at one corner, and measure the length and width of the room from that starting point. Calculate the number of panels you will need to cover the space in both directions. If the starting corner is not square, trim the first row to create a straight starting line.

2

Create an expansion gap around the edges. Place ¼" spacers at all walls, doors, and other large obstacles. To make your own spacers, cut sheets of ¼" plywood to the thickness of the panels, and hold them in place temporarily with adhesive tape.

3

Dry-lay a row of panels across the room. If the last row will be less than 6" wide, balance it by trimming the first panel or the starting row, if necessary, to account for the row end pieces.

4

Starting in the corner, lay the first panel with the grooved side against the ¼" spacers. Slide the next panel into place and press-fit the groove of the second panel onto the tongue of the first. Check the edges against the wall.

5

Repeat these steps to complete the first row. If necessary, tap the panels into place with a scrap piece of lumber and a rubber mallet or hammer—just be careful not to damage the tongue or groove edges. Starting with the second row, stagger the seams so that the panels interlock.

6

Cut the last panel to fit snugly between the next-to-last panel and the ¼" spacer on the far wall. Install the last panel at an angle and tap it down. Continue working from the starting point, checking after each row to be sure the panels are square and level.

7

When you reach the last row and last panel to complete your installation, you may have to cut the panel to fit. Measure for fit, allowing for the ¼" expansion gap from the wall. Cut the panel and fit it into place.

8

When all the panels are in place, remove the spacers from around the perimeter of the room. *Note: You may choose to wait to remove the spacers until after your flooring project is finished, depending on the floor covering material.*

FLUORESCENT LIGHTS

Fluorescent lights are relatively trouble free and use less energy than incandescent lights. A typical fluorescent tube lasts about three years and produces two to four times as much light per watt as a standard incandescent light bulb.

The most frequent problem with a fluorescent light fixture is a worn-out tube. If a fluorescent light fixture begins to flicker or does not light fully, remove and examine the tube. If the tube has bent or broken pins or black discoloration near the ends, replace it. Light gray discoloration is normal in working fluorescent tubes. When replacing an old tube, read the wattage rating printed on the glass surface, and buy a new tube with a matching rating. Never dispose of old tubes by breaking them. Fluorescent tubes contain a small amount of hazardous mercury. Check with your local environmental control agency or health department for disposal guidelines.

Fluorescent light fixtures also can malfunction if the sockets are cracked or worn. Inexpensive replacement sockets are available at any hardware store and can be installed in a few minutes.

If a fixture does not work even after the tube and sockets have been serviced, the ballast probably is defective. Faulty ballasts may leak a black, oily substance and can cause a fluorescent light fixture to make a loud humming sound. Although ballasts can be replaced, always check prices before buying a new ballast. It may be cheaper to purchase and install a new fluorescent fixture rather than to replace the ballast in an old fluorescent light fixture.

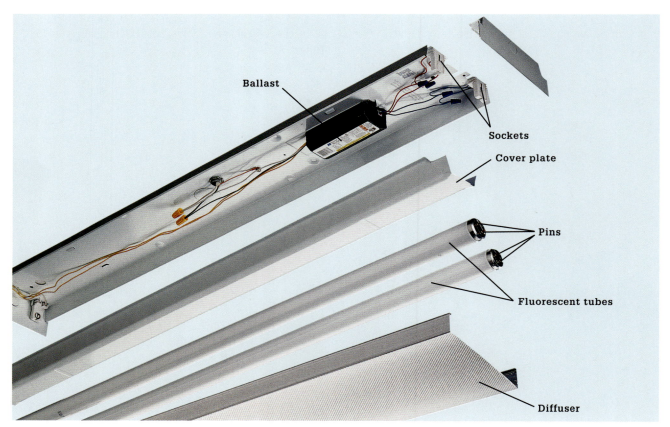

A fluorescent light works by directing electrical current through a special gas-filled tube that glows when energized. A white translucent diffuser protects the fluorescent tube and softens the light. A cover plate protects a special transformer, called a ballast. The ballast regulates the flow of 120-volt household current to the sockets. The sockets transfer power to metal pins that extend into the tube.

Problem	Repair
Tube flickers, or lights partially.	1. Rotate tube to make sure it is seated properly in the sockets. 2. Replace tube and the starter (where present) if tube is discolored or if pins are bent or broken. 3. Replace the ballast if replacement cost is reasonable. Otherwise, replace the entire fixture.
Tube does not light.	1. Check wall switch and repair or replace, if needed. 2. Rotate the tube to make sure it is seated properly in sockets. 3. Replace tube and the starter (where present) if tube is discolored or if pins are bent or broken. 4. Replace sockets if they are chipped or if tube does not seat properly. 5. Replace the ballast or the entire fixture.
Noticeable black substance around ballast.	Replace ballast if replacement cost is reasonable. Otherwise, replace the entire fixture.
Fixture hums.	Replace ballast if replacement cost is reasonable. Otherwise, replace the entire fixture.

Tools & Materials ▶

Screwdriver
Ratchet wrench
Combination tool
Circuit tester
Replacement tubes
Starters, or ballast
   (if needed)
Replacement fluorescent light fixture
   (if needed)
Protective equipment

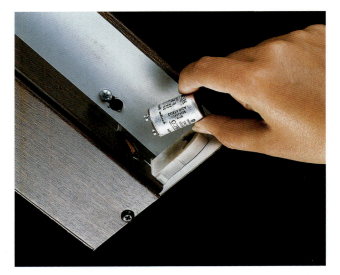

Older fluorescent lights may have a small cylindrical device, called a starter, located near one of the sockets. When a tube begins to flicker, replace both the tube and the starter. Turn off the power, then remove the starter by pushing it slightly and turning counterclockwise. Install a replacement that matches the old starter.

FOOD DISPOSERS

1

Mounting lug

Remove the old disposer if you have one. You'll need to disconnect the drain pipes and traps first. If your old disposer has a special wrench for the mounting lugs, use it to loosen the lugs. Otherwise, use a screwdriver. If you do not have a helper, place a solid object directly beneath the disposer to support it before you begin removal. *Important: Shut off electrical power at the main service panel before you begin removal. Disconnect the wire leads, cap them, and stuff them into the electrical box.*

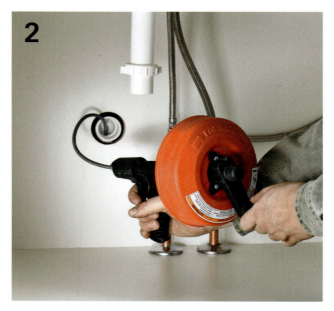

2

Clear the drain lines all the way to the branch drain before you begin the new installation. Remove the trap and trap arm first.

3

Upper mounting ring

Lower mounting ring

Snap ring

Disassemble the mounting assembly and then separate the upper and lower mounting rings and the backup ring. Also remove the snap ring from the sink sleeve.

4

Sink sleeve

Press the flange of the sink sleeve for your new disposer into a thin coil of plumber's putty that you have laid around the perimeter of the drain opening. The sleeve should be well-seated in the coil.

Slip the fiber gasket and then the backup ring onto the sink sleeve, working from inside the sink base cabinet. Make sure the backup ring is oriented the same way it was before you disassembled the mounting assembly.

Insert the upper mounting ring onto the sleeve with the slotted ends of the screws facing away from the backup ring so you can access them. Then, holding all three parts at the top of the sleeve, slide the snap ring onto the sleeve until it snaps into the groove.

Tighten the three mounting screws on the upper mounting ring until the tips press firmly against the backup ring. It is the tension created by these screws that keeps the disposer steady and minimizes vibrating.

Make electrical connections before you mount the disposer unit on the mounting assembly. Shut off the power at the service panel if you have turned it back on. Remove the access plate from the disposer. Attach the white and black feeder wires from the electrical box to the white and black wires (respectively) inside the disposer. Twist a small wire cap onto each connection and wrap it with electrical tape for good measure. Also attach the green ground wire from the box to the grounding terminal on your disposer.

(continued)

9

Knock out the plug in the disposer port if you will be connecting your dishwasher to the disposer. If you have no dishwasher, leave the plug in. Insert a large flathead screwdriver into the port opening and rap it with a mallet. Retrieve the knock-out plug from inside the disposer canister.

10

Hang the disposer from the mounting ring attached to the sink sleeve. To hang it, simply lift it up and position the unit so the three mounting ears are underneath the three mounting screws and then spin the unit so all three ears fit into the mounting assembly. Wait until after the plumbing hookups have been made to lock the unit in place.

11

Attach the discharge tube to the disposer according to the manufacturer's instructions. It is important to get a very good seal here, or the disposer will leak. Go ahead and spin the disposer if it helps you access the discharge port.

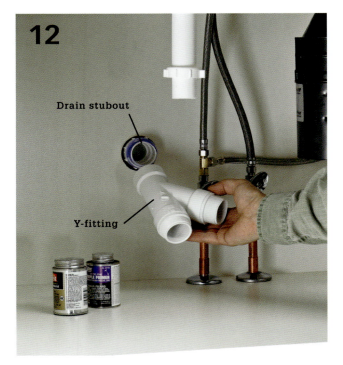

12

Drain stubout

Y-fitting

Attach a Y-fitting at the drain stubout. The Y-fitting should be sized to accept a drain line from the disposer and another from the sink. Adjust the sink drain plumbing as needed to get from the sink P-trap to one opening of the Y.

13

Outlet from sink

Y-fitting

Trap arm

P-trap

Install a trap arm for the disposer in the open port of the Y-fitting at the wall stubout. Then, attach a P-trap or a combination of a tube extension and a P-trap so the trap will align with the bottom of the disposer discharge tube.

14

P-trap

Spin the disposer so the end of the discharge tube is lined up over the open end of the P-trap and confirm that they will fit together correctly. If the discharge tube extends down too far, mark a line on it at the top of the P-trap and cut at the line with a hacksaw. If the tube is too short, attach an extension with a slip joint. You may need to further shorten the discharge tube first to create enough room for the slip joint on the extension. Slide a slip nut and beveled compression washer onto the discharge tube and attach the tube to the P-trap.

15

Dishwasher discharge tube

Connect the dishwasher discharge tube to the inlet port located at the top of the disposer unit. This may require a dishwasher hookup kit. Typically, a hose clamp is used to secure the connection.

16

Lock the disposer into position on the mounting ring assembly once you have tested to make sure it is functioning correctly and without leaks. Lock it by turning one of the mounting lugs until it makes contact with the locking notch.

FRAMING A WALL

Measurements are critical in framing a wall, but the actual components that go into the structure are fairly basic. Refer to your plans and be sure to account for all of the elements of your framed wall, including door and window openings. For any frame carpentry it usually works best to build the wall on the ground or floor, including the sill and cap plates. Then, raise the assembly, position it, and anchor it to the structural members beneath the subfloor.

Hand Nailing ▸

The best hand-nailing technique for joining framing members depends on whether you assemble the framed wall and then raise it, or you add boards one at a time in their final position. If you're assembling the wall on the floor or ground, end-nail the studs to the plates whenever you can (left sample). End-nailed joints, usually made with 10d common nails, are strong and fast to make. To double up wall studs or headers, facenail the parts (right sample) with 8d common nails. Facenailing is also used for attaching jack studs to king studs. To fasten a vertical stud to a top or sole plate that is already in place, toenailing (middle sample) is your best option.

Tools & Materials ▸

Hammer	2 × 6 lumber
Tape measure	16d nails
Level	8d common nails
Circular saw	10d common nails
Carpenter's pencil	Protective equipment

The wall raising is one of the more exciting moments in construction, as the shape of the structure begins to emerge. The basic idea is to build the addition as completely as you can before you cut into the house.

HOW TO FRAME A WALL

Sight down the studs and top and sole plates and replace any with warps or obvious imperfections. Cut the plates and studs to uniform lengths, using a stop block. If you have designed your addition with 8-ft.-tall walls, look for pre-cut 92⅝" studs. *Note: In most climates today, your wall framing members should be made of 2 × 6 lumber, not the 2 × 4 lumber seen here. Code requirements for minimum wall insulation generally require a deeper 2 × 6 stud bay.*

Gang-mark the wall stud locations on the sole and top plates. Cut the plates to length first and clamp the ends together, making sure they are flush. In most cases, the studs should be 16" on-center. Draw an X on the side of the marking lines where the stud will fit.

With sole plate lying on edge, face nail through the sole plate and into the bottoms of the studs. Use two or three 16d common nails per stud. Then, nail the top plate to the other end of the studs so that the wall is framed, lying down.

Build the wall corners. There are several ways you can create interlocking corners so the wall can be attached easily and accurately to the adjoining framed wall. Here, a pair of studs are installed perpendicular to the corner stud to create nailing surfaces for the adjoining wall and for the exterior wall sheathing at the corner.

(continued)

Measure the diagonals of the wall to check that it is square. If the diagonal measurements are not identical, use pressure (and clamps if necessary) to pull the wall frame into square. If the diagonals just won't match, measure the wall studs and make sure none of the studs is too long or too short.

Raise the first wall. Nail guide blocks to the outside edge of the rim joist to create stops for the soleplate. With a helper, raise the wall into position and check the studs for plumb and the wall for level. If the wall abuts the house make sure it fits cleanly against the wall (the siding should have been removed at the wall tie-in spot by this point).

Nail the soleplate to the structural members beneath the subfloor with pairs of 16d common nails spaced every 14" to 16". Attach a 2 × 4 brace to an intermediate stud and anchor the other end to a stake in the ground.

Plumb the wall, then nail the corner wall stud to the existing house structure. If you did not plan your addition so the wall meets the house at a house stud location, you'll need to remove the exterior wall sheathing in the installation area and install 2 × 4 or 2 × 6 nailing blocks between the wall studs on each side of the opening.

9

Begin building the second wall. If the wall includes an exterior door, nail king studs into place allowing for the rough-in width of the pre-hung door unit plus 3" (for the jack studs). Face nail jack studs in place.

Constructing a Header ▸

Door and window openings are wider than normal stud spacing, so they require a head beam, or header, to transfer the overhead weight to the studs at the sides of the opening. Professional builders commonly make their own headers by sandwiching ½" plywood between two 2× pieces. The width of the 2× depends on the width of the opening and how much overhead load the wall carries; check your local codes. The pieces are laminated with construction adhesive and then nailed from both sides to create a strong header that measures exactly as wide as the thickness of a 2 × 4 wall. For 2 × 6 walls, construct a box from parallel 2×s on all sides and fill it with insulation.

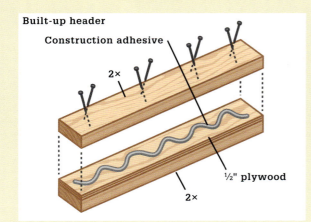

Built-up header

Construction adhesive

2×

½" plywood

2×

(continued)

Place the header on the tops of the jack studs with the ends flush against the king studs. Drive 10d common nails through the king studs and into the header. Then, cut cripple studs to fit between the header and the top plate, maintaining the 16" o.c. spacing. Toenail the cripple studs into position.

Add extra blocking next to the door opening for improved security.

Add framing for windows as needed. Nail king studs into place, allowing for the rough-in width of the window plus 3". Facenail jack studs into place above the sole plate to the bottom of the sill.

Nail a doubled 2 × 4 window sill into place on top of jack studs. Drive 10d common nails through the king studs and into the ends of the double sill.

Nail the window header into position above the top jack studs, facenailing it through the king studs.

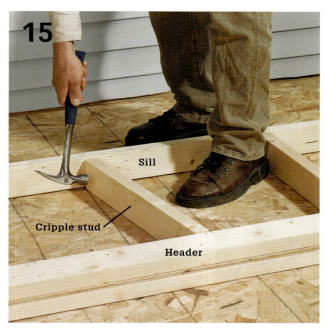

Nail cripple studs above the header and below the sill, adding more cripples as necessary to maintain at least 16" o.c. spacing for studs.

Tie adjoining wall frames together by nailing them at the corners, and add overlapping top plates to lock the walls together.

FRAMING A WALL: FURRED-OUT BASEMENT WALLS

Wall framing members can be attached directly to a concrete foundation wall to provide a support for wall coverings and to house wires and pipes. Because they have no significant structural purpose, they are usually made with smaller stock called furring strips, which can be 2 × 2 or 2 × 3 wood. Do not install furring strips in conjunction with a vapor barrier or insulation, and do not attach them to walls that are not dry walls (see definition, page 13) with insulation on the exterior side.

Furring strips serve primarily to create nailing surfaces for wallboard. Attach them to dry basement walls at web locations of block wall where possible.

▌ HOW TO ATTACH FURRING STRIPS TO DRY FOUNDATION WALLS

Cut a 2 × 2 top plate to span the length of the wall. Mark the furring-strip layout onto the bottom edge of the plate using 16"-on-center spacing. Attach the plate to the bottom of the joists with 2½" wallboard screws. The back edge of the plate should line up with the front of the blocks.

If the joists run parallel to the wall, you'll need to install backers between the outer joist and the sill plate to provide support for ceiling wallboard. Make T-shaped backers from short 2 × 4s and 2 × 2s. Install each so the bottom face of the 2 × 4 is flush with the bottom edge of the joists. Attach the top plate to the foundation wall with its top edge flush with the top of the blocks.

3

Install a bottom plate cut from pressure-treated 2 × 2 lumber so the plate spans the length of the wall. Apply construction adhesive to the back and bottom of the plate, then attach it to the floor with a nailer. Use a plumb bob to transfer the furring-strip layout marks from the top plate to the bottom plate.

4

Cut 2 × 2 furring strips to fit between the top and bottom plates. Apply construction adhesive to the back of each furring strip, and position it on the layout marks on the plates. Nail along the length of each strip at 16" intervals.

5

Option: Leave a channel for the installation of wires or supply pipes by installing pairs of vertically aligned furring strips with a 2" gap between each pair. *Note: Consult local codes to ensure proper installation of electrical or plumbing materials.*

Isolate the Wall ▶

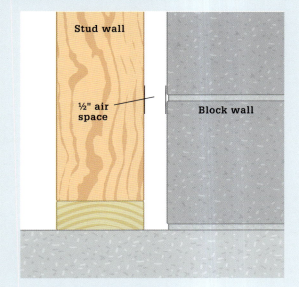

Stud wall

½" air space

Block wall

It consumes more floorspace, but a good alternative to a furred-out wall is to build a 2 x 4 stud wall parallel to the foundation wall, but ½" away from it. This eliminates any contact between the wall framing members and the foundation wall.

FRAMING A WALL: STUD SIZE & SPACING

WOOD GRADES
USED IN WALL CONSTRUCTION

1. Use Number 3, standard, or stud grade wood for most load-bearing walls not more than 10 feet tall. Do not use this wood for load-bearing walls more than 10 feet tall. Use Number 2 grade or better lumber for walls more than 10 feet tall.

2. You may use utility grade wood for nonload-bearing walls.

3. You may use utility grade wood for load-bearing exterior walls that support only a ceiling and a roof if the studs are spaced not more than 16 inches on center and the walls are not more than eight feet tall.

4. Refer to general codes for more information about other wall height and stud spacing combinations.

5. Refer to general codes for wall height and stud spacing requirements in high wind, heavy snow load, and seismic design areas.

STUD SIZE & SPACING
FOR LOAD-BEARING WALLS
NOT MORE THAN 10 FEET TALL

1. Use the table below to determine stud size and spacing when the unsupported vertical height of an exterior load-bearing wall is not more than 10 feet. Measure vertical height between points of horizontal (lateral) support between studs. Vertical wall height is usually measured between the bottom of the sole or sill plate and the bottom of the floor or ceiling. Consult a qualified engineer before measuring unsupported vertical wall height between points other than at floor levels.

Wall studs taller than 10 ft. require No. 2 or better grade construction lumber. Shorter walls may be built with cheaper No. 3 grade in most cases.

Stud Size & Spacing for Load-bearing Walls ▸

Stud size (inches)	Maximum stud spacing supporting only one floor, or supporting a ceiling and roof with or without a habitable attic	Maximum stud spacing supporting one floor and a ceiling and roof with or without a habitable attic	Maximum stud spacing supporting two floors and a ceiling and roof with or without a habitable attic
2 × 4	24"	16"	Not allowed
2 × 6	24"	24"	16"

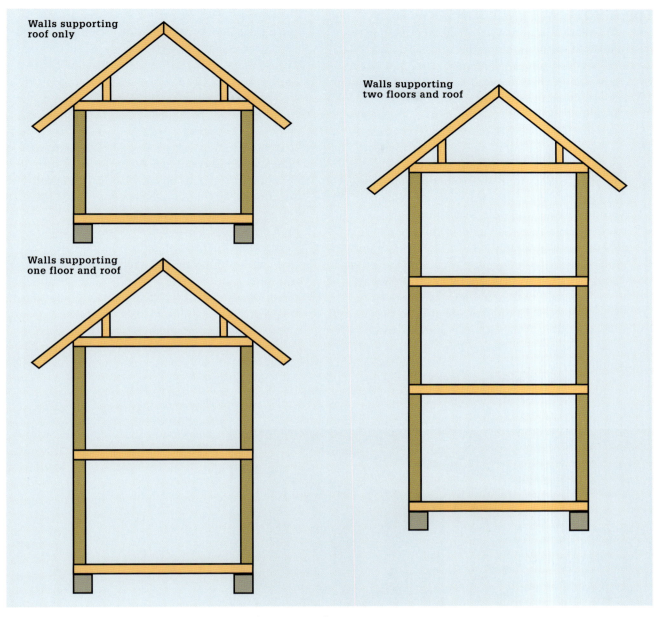

Walls supporting roof only

Walls supporting two floors and roof

Walls supporting one floor and roof

Stud size and spacing depends on what the studs are supporting.

STUD SIZE & SPACING FOR NONLOAD-BEARING WALLS

1. Use the adjacent table to determine stud size and spacing for nonload-bearing walls. Measure vertical height between points of horizontal (lateral) support between studs. Vertical wall height is usually measured between the bottom of the sole or sill plate and the bottom of the floor or ceiling. Consult a qualified engineer before measuring unsupported vertical wall height between points other than at floor levels.

Stud Size & Spacing for Nonload-bearing Walls ▶

Stud size	Maximum stud height	Maximum stud spacing
2 × 4	14 ft.	24"
2 × 6	20 ft.	24"

TOP & BOTTOM PLATE CONSTRUCTION

1. Use at least two 2-inch (nominal) depth top plates that are at least as wide as the studs at the top of load-bearing walls. Example: use two 2 × 4 top plates on top of a 2 × 4 wall and use 2 × 6 top plates on top of 2 × 6 walls.

2. Offset joints where two pieces of top plate meet by at least 24 inches. You do not need to place a stud under a joint in a top plate unless the stud would be placed there for other reasons.

3. Lap one top plate from one wall over the top plate of an intersecting wall at the wall corners and at the intersection with load-bearing walls.

4. You may use a single top plate at the top of nonload-bearing walls.

5. You may use a single top plate on load-bearing walls if wall joints and corners and top plate end joints are secured with at least a 3-inch by 6-inch by 0.036-inch thick galvanized steel plate secured by at least six 8d nails on each side of the connection; and if the supported framing above (such as joists or rafters) is not more than one inch from the stud below. This exception is not commonly used.

6. Install one galvanized metal strap at least 0.054-inch thick and 1½ inches wide on a top plate if it is cut more than 50 percent of its actual depth. These metal straps are sometimes called FHA straps. It is not necessary to install a strap on both top plates for purposes of this section. You may need to install shield plate to protect plumbing pipes and electrical wires.

7. Extend the strap at least six inches beyond each side of the cut opening. Secure the strap with at least eight 16d nails on each side of the strap.

8. Apply this strap requirement to top plates in exterior and interior load-bearing walls.

9. You do not need to install the strap if wood structural panel sheathing covers the entire side of the wall with the notched or cut top plates.

10. Use at least one 2-inch (nominal) depth bottom plate that is at least as wide as the studs. Note that some jurisdictions allow treated plywood to serve as the bottom plate for curved walls. Verify this local exception with the building official.

Offset joints where 2 top plates meet by at least 24".

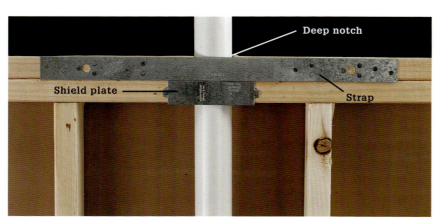

Install a strap across 1 top plate when it is notched more than half its width. Install another strap or a shield plate when required to protect pipes and electrical wires.

NOTCHES & HOLES IN WALL STUDS

BORING & NOTCHING DEFINITIONS

A bore is a hole drilled in a stud or joist. Use the actual dimensions to determine the depth of framing lumber and when calculating the maximum hole diameter.

A notch is a piece cut from the smaller dimension of framing lumber such as a stud or joist. Use the actual dimensions to determine the depth of framing lumber and when calculating the maximum notch depth. Actual dimensions are the dimensions of framing lumber after finishing at the mill. Example: the nominal dimensions of a 2 × 6 are 2 inches by 6 inches and the actual dimensions, after finishing, are about 1½ inches by 5½ inches.

WOOD STUD NOTCHING

1. Notch a load-bearing stud not more than 25 percent of its actual depth. Example: notch a 2 × 6 load-bearing stud not more than 1⅜ inches.
2. Notch a nonload-bearing stud not more than 40 percent of its actual depth. Example: notch a 2 × 6 nonload-bearing stud not more than 2¼ inches.

WOOD STUD BORING

1. Bore a hole in a single load-bearing stud not more than 40 percent of its actual depth. Example: bore a 2 × 6 load-bearing stud not more than 2¼ inches in diameter.
2. You may bore holes in load-bearing studs not more than 60 percent of their actual depth if you install a double stud and do not bore more than two successive studs.
3. Bore a hole in a nonload-bearing stud not more than 60 percent of its actual depth.Example: bore a 2 × 6 nonload-bearing stud not more than 3¼ inches in diameter.
4. Leave at least ⅝ inch of undisturbed wood between the hole and the stud edge.
5. Do not place a hole and a notch in the same horizontal section of the stud.

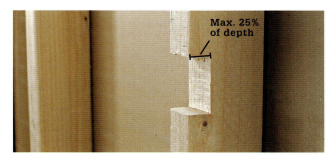

Notch a load-bearing stud not more than 25 percent of its actual depth.

Drill a hole in a load-bearing stud not more than 40 percent of its actual depth.

Double two load-bearing studs if the holes are not more than 60 percent of their actual depth.

VIOLATION! Do not locate a notch and a hole in the same part of the stud.

207

GARAGE DOOR TUNE UP

Begin the tune-up by lubricating the door tracks, pulleys, and rollers. Use a lightweight oil, not grease, for this job. The grease catches too much dust and dirt.

Remove clogged or damaged rollers from the door by loosening the nuts that hold the roller brackets. The roller will come with the bracket when the bracket is pulled free.

Mineral spirits and kerosene are good solvents for cleaning roller bearings. Let the bearing sit for a half-hour in the solvent. Then brush away the grime build-up with an old paintbrush or toothbrush.

4

If the rollers are making a lot of noise as they move over the tracks, the tracks are probably out of alignment. To fix this, check the tracks for plumb. If they are out of plumb, the track mounting brackets must be adjusted.

5

To adjust out-of-plumb tracks, loosen all the track mounting brackets (usually 3 or 4 per track) and push the brackets into alignment.

6

It's often easier to adjust the brackets by partially loosening the bolts and tapping the track with a soft-faced mallet. Once the track is plumb, tighten all the bolts.

(continued)

7

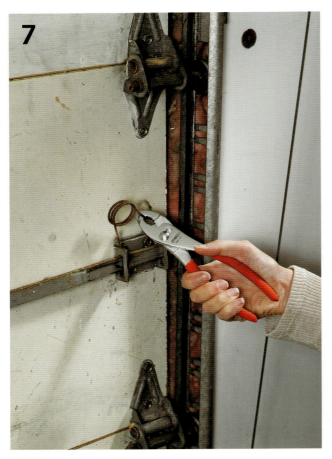

Sometimes the door lock bar opens sluggishly because the return spring has lost its tension. The only way to fix this is to replace the spring. One end is attached to the body of the lock; the other end hooks onto the lock bar.

8

If a latch needs lubrication, use graphite in powder or liquid form. Don't use oil because it attracts dust that will clog the lock even more.

Alternative: Sometimes the lock bar won't lock the door because it won't slide into its opening on the door track. To fix this, loosen the guide bracket that holds the lock bar and move it up or down until the bar hits the opening.

Worn or broken weather stripping on the bottom edge of the door can let in a lot of cold air and stiff breezes. Check to see if this strip is cracked, broken, or has holes along its edges. If so, remove the old strip and pull any nails left behind.

Measure the width of your garage door, then buy a piece of weather stripping to match. These strips are standard lumberyard and home center items. Sometimes they are sold in kit form, with fasteners included. If not, just nail the stripping in place with galvanized roofing nails.

If the chain on your garage door opener is sagging more than ½" below the bottom rail, it can make a lot of noise and cause drive sprocket wear. Tighten the chain according to the directions in the owner's manual.

(continued)

On openers with a chain, lubricate the entire length of the chain with lightweight oil. Do not use grease. Use the same lubricant if your opener has a drive screw instead.

Test the door's closing force sensitivity and make adjustments at the opener's motor case if needed. Because both the sensitivity and the adjustment mechanism vary greatly between opener models, you'll have to rely on your owner's manual for guidance. If you don't have the owner's manual, you can usually download one from the manufacturer's website.

Check for proper alignment on the safety sensors near the floor. They should be pointing directly at one another and their lenses should be clean of any dirt and grease.

Make sure that the sensors are "talking" to the opener properly. Start to close the door, then put your hand down between the two sensors. If the door stops immediately and reverses direction, it's working properly. If it's not, make the adjustment recommended in the owner's manual. If that doesn't do the trick, call a professional door installer and don't use the door until it passes this test.

GFCI RECEPTACLES

The ground-fault circuit-interrupter (GFCI) receptacle protects against electrical shock caused by a faulty appliance, or a worn cord or plug. It senses small changes in current flow and can shut off power in as little as $\frac{1}{40}$ of a second.

GFCIs are now required in bathrooms, kitchens, garages, crawl spaces, unfinished basements, and outdoor receptacle locations. Consult your local codes for any requirements regarding the installation of GFCI receptacles. Most GFCIs use standard screw terminal connections, but some have wire leads and are attached with wire connectors. Because the body of a GFCI receptacle is larger than a standard receptacle, small crowded electrical boxes may need to be replaced with more spacious boxes.

The GFCI receptacle may be wired to protect only itself (single location), or it can be wired to protect all receptacles, switches, and light fixtures from the GFCI "forward" to the end of the circuit (multiple locations).

Because the GFCI is so sensitive, it is most effective when wired to protect a single location. The more receptacles any one GFCI protects, the more susceptible it is to "phantom tripping," shutting off power because of tiny, normal fluctuations in current flow. GFCI receptacles installed in outdoor locations must be rated for outdoor use and weather resistance (WR) along with ground fault protection.

Tools & Materials ▶

Circuit tester
Screwdriver
Wire connectors
Masking tape
Protective equipment

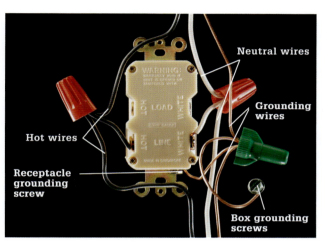

A GFCI wired for single-location protection (shown from the back) has hot and neutral wires connected only to the screw terminals marked LINE. A GFCI connected for single-location protection may be wired as either an end-of-run or middle-of-run configuration.

Modern GFCI receptacle have tamper-resistant slots. Look for a model that's rated "WR" (for weather resistance) if you'll be installing it outdoors or in a wet location.

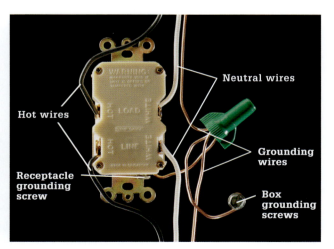

A GFCI wired for multiple-location protection (shown from the back) has one set of hot and neutral wires connected to the LINE pair of screw terminals, and the other set connected to the LOAD pair of screw terminals. A GFCI receptacle connected for multiple-location protection may be wired only as a middle-of-run configuration.

213

HOW TO INSTALL A GFCI FOR SINGLE-LOCATION PROTECTION

1

Shut off power to the receptacle at the main service panel. Test for power with a neon circuit tester. Be sure to check both halves of the receptacle.

2

Remove cover plate. Loosen mounting screws, and gently pull receptacle from the box. Do not touch wires. Confirm power is off with a circuit tester.

3

Disconnect all white neutral wires from the silver screw terminals of the old receptacle.

4

Pigtail all the white neutral wires together, and connect the pigtail to the terminal marked WHITE LINE on the GFCI (see photo on page 216).

5

Disconnect all black hot wires from the brass screw terminals of the old receptacle. Pigtail these wires together, and connect them to the terminal marked HOT LINE on the GFCI.

6

If a grounding wire is available, connect it to the green grounding screw terminal of the GFCI. Mount the GFCI in the receptacle box, and reattach the cover plate. Restore power, and test the GFCI according to the manufacturer's instructions.

HOW TO INSTALL A GFCI FOR MULTIPLE-LOCATION PROTECTION

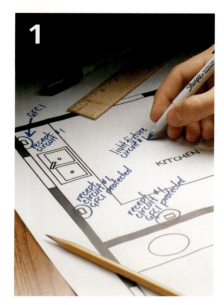

Use a map of your house circuits to determine a location for your GFCI. Indicate all receptacles that will be protected by the GFCI installation.

Turn off power to the correct circuit at the main service panel. Test all the receptacles in the circuit with a neon circuit tester to make sure the power is off. Always check both halves of each duplex receptacle.

Remove the cover plate from the receptacle that will be replaced with the GFCI. Loosen the mounting screws and gently pull the receptacle from its box. Take care not to touch any bare wires. Confirm the power is off with a neon circuit tester.

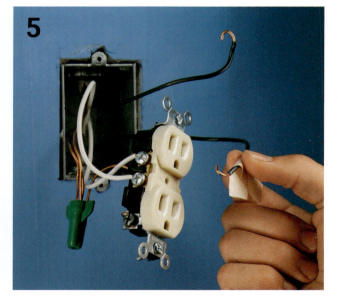

Disconnect all black hot wires. Carefully separate the hot wires and position them so that the bare ends do not touch anything. Restore power to the circuit at the main service panel. Determine which black wire is the feed wire by testing for hot wires. The feed wire brings power to the receptacle from the service panel. Use caution: This is a live wire test, during which the power is turned on temporarily.

When you have found the hot feed wire, turn off power at the main service panel. Identify the feed wire by marking it with masking tape.

(continued)

6

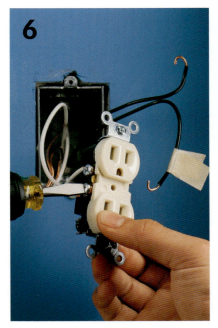

Disconnect the white neutral wires from the old receptacle. Identify the white feed wire and label it with masking tape. The white feed wire will be the one that shares the same cable as the black feed wire.

7

Disconnect the grounding wire from the grounding screw terminal of the old receptacle. Remove the old receptacle. Connect the grounding wire to the grounding screw terminal of the GFCI.

8

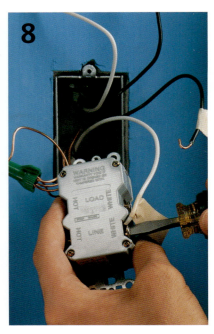

Connect the white feed wire to the terminal marked WHITE LINE on the GFCI. Connect the black feed wire to the terminal marked HOT LINE on the GFCI.

9

Connect the other white neutral wire to the terminal marked WHITE LOAD on the GFCI.

10

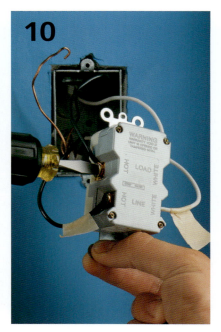

Connect the other black hot wire to the terminal marked HOT LOAD on the GFCI.

11

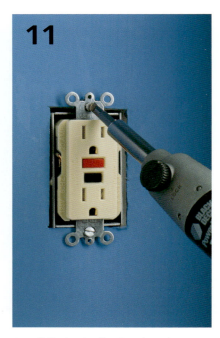

Carefully tuck all wires into the receptacle box. Mount the GFCI in the box and attach the cover plate. Turn on power to the circuit at the main service panel. Test the GFCI according to the manufacturer's instructions.

GRAB BARS

Bathrooms are beautiful with their shiny ceramic tubs, showers, and floors, but add water and moisture to the mix and you've created the perfect conditions for a fall. The good news is many falls in the bathroom can be avoided by installing grab bars at key locations.

Grab bars help family members steady themselves on slippery shower, tub, and other floor surfaces. Plus, they provide support for people transferring from a wheelchair or walker to the shower, tub, or toilet.

Grab bars come in a variety of colors, shapes, sizes, and textures. Choose a style with a 1¼-inch to 1½-inch diameter that fits comfortably between your thumb and fingers. Then properly install it 1½-inch from the wall with anchors that can support at least 250 pounds.

The easiest way to install grab bars is to screw them into wall studs or into blocking or backing attached to studs. Blocking is a good option if you are framing a new bathroom or have the wall surface removed during a major remodel (see Illustration A). Use 2 × 6 or 2 × 8 lumber to provide room for adjustments, and fasten the blocks to the framing with 16d nails. Note the locations of your blocking for future reference.

As an alternative, cover the entire wall with ¾" plywood backing secured with screws to the wall framing, so you can install grab bars virtually anywhere on the wall (see Illustration B).

Grab bars can be installed in areas without studs. For these installations, use specialized heavy-duty hollow-wall anchors designed to support at least 250 pounds.

Grab bars promote independence in the bathroom, where privacy is especially important. Grab bars not only help prevent slips and falls, they also help people steady themselves in showers and lower themselves into tubs.

Tools & Materials ▶

Measuring tape	Hollow-wall
Pencil	anchors
Stud finder	#12 stainless steel
Level	screws
Drill	Silicone caulk
Masonry bit	Protective
Grab bar	equipment

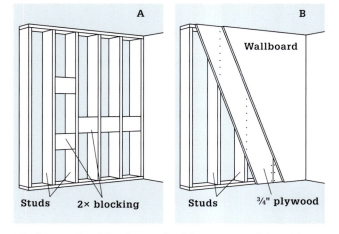

Blocking or backing is required for secure grab bars. If you know where the grab bars will be located, add 2× blocking between studs (Illustration A). You also can cover the entire wall with ¾" plywood backing, which allows you to install grab bars virtually anywhere on the wall.

HOW TO INSTALL GRAB BARS

Locate the wall studs in the installation area using a stud finder. If the area is tiled, the stud finder may not detect studs, so try to locate the studs above the tile, if possible, then use a level to transfer the marks lower on the wall. Otherwise, you can drill small, exploratory holes through grout joints in the tile, then fill the holes with silicone caulk to seal them. Be careful not to drill into pipes.

Mark the grab bar height at one stud location, then use a level to transfer the height mark to the stud that will receive the other end of the bar. Position the grab bar on the height marks so at least two of the three mounting holes are aligned with the stud centers. Mark the mounting hole locations onto the wall.

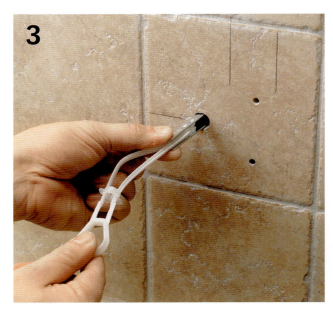

Drill pilot holes for the mounting screws. If you are drilling through tile, start with a small bit (about ⅛"), then redrill the hole with the larger bit. For screws that won't hit studs, drill holes for wall anchors, following the manufacturer's directions for sizing. Install anchors, if necessary.

Apply a continuous bead of silicone caulk to the back side of each bar end (inset). Secure the bar to the studs using #12 stainless steel screws (the screws should penetrate the stud by at least 1"). Install a stainless steel screw or bolt into the wall anchors. Test the bar to make sure it's secure.

GUTTERS (VINYL): INSTALLING

Installing a snap-together vinyl gutter system is a manageable task for most do-it-yourselfers. Snap-together gutter systems are designed for ease of installation, requiring no fasteners other than the screws used to attach the gutter hangers to the fascia.

Before you purchase new gutters, create a detailed plan and cost estimate. Include all of the necessary parts, not just the gutter and drain pipe sections—they make up only part of the total system. Test-fit the pieces on the ground before you begin the actual installation.

Tools & Materials ▸

Chalk line	Drain pipes
Tape measure	Connectors
Drill	Fittings
Hacksaw	Hangers
1¼" deck screws	Protective
Gutters	equipment

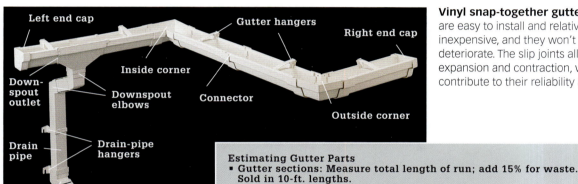

Vinyl snap-together gutter systems are easy to install and relatively inexpensive, and they won't rot or deteriorate. The slip joints allow for expansion and contraction, which contribute to their reliability and longevity.

Left end cap • Gutter hangers • Right end cap • Inside corner • Downspout outlet • Downspout elbows • Connector • Outside corner • Drain pipe • Drain-pipe hangers • Swing-up elbow • Splash block • Splash block outlet

Estimating Gutter Parts
- **Gutter sections:** Measure total length of run; add 15% for waste. Sold in 10-ft. lengths.
- **Gutter hangers:** One for every 2 ft. of gutter.
- **Inside/outside corners:** One per corner with no outlet.
- **Connectors:** Two per corner; one per 10 ft. of gutter.
- **End caps (right or left):** One per end.
- **Downspout outlets:** One for every 35 ft. of gutter.
- **Downspout elbows:** Three per downspout.
- **Drainpipe:** One pipe per downspout outlet. Measure gutter height and add 5 ft. for each pipe (for splash block outlet and waste). Sold in 10-ft. lengths.
- **Drainpipe hangers:** Two per drainpipe.

HOW TO INSTALL VINYL GUTTERS

Mark a point at the high end of each gutter run, 1" from the top of the fascia. Snap chalk lines that slope ¼" per 10 ft. toward downspouts. For runs longer than 35 ft., mark a slope from a high point in the center toward downspouts at each end.

Install downspout outlets near the ends of gutter runs (at least one outlet for every 35 ft. of run). The tops of the outlets should be flush with the slope line, and they should align with end caps on the corners of the house.

(continued)

Following the slope line, attach hangers or support clips for hangers for a complete run. Attach them to the fascia at 24" intervals using deck screws.

Following the slope line, attach outside and inside corners at all corner locations that don't have end caps.

Use a hacksaw to cut gutter sections to fit between outlets and corners. Attach the end caps and connect the gutter sections to the outlets. Cut and test-fit gutter sections to fit between outlets, allowing for expansion gaps.

Working on the ground, join the gutter sections together using connectors. Attach gutter hangers to the gutter (for models with support clips mounted on the fascia). Hang the gutters, connecting them to the outlets.

Cut a section of drainpipe to fit between two downspout elbows. One elbow should fit over the tail of the downspout outlet and the other should fit against the wall. Assemble the parts, slip the top elbow onto the outlet, and secure the other to the siding with a drainpipe hanger.

Cut a piece of drainpipe to fit between the elbow at the top of the wall and the end of the drainpipe run, staying at least 12" above the ground. Attach an elbow, and secure the pipe to the wall with a drainpipe hanger. Add accessories, such as splash blocks, to help channel water away from the house (inset).

GUTTERS (SEAMLESS): INSTALLING

Seamless gutters are continuous lengths of gutters, rather than two or more sections fastened together. By eliminating the seams, you eliminate the potential for leaks. However, "seamless" is a bit of a misnomer. There are still seams at the corners and ends, which need to be sealed.

The gutters should extend slightly past the edge of the fascia, aligning with the edges of the roofing. The back edge of the gutter slides behind the drip edge. When preparing the gutters, zip screws are preferred over rivets. They don't require predrilling, and they can be unscrewed later.

Seamless gutters are fabricated on-site, or they can be delivered to your home at the specified length.

Tools & Materials ▸

Tape measure	Gutter sealant or
Drill with ¼"	silicone caulk
hex-drive bit	Hangers
Caulk gun	Gutter outlets
Chalk line	Downspouts
Hammer	End caps
Aviation snips	Elbows
Rotary saw	Hangers
Hacksaw	Downspout brackets
Gutters	End box
Zip screws	Protective equipment

HOW TO INSTALL SEAMLESS GUTTERS

At the fascia's midpoint, measure down from the drip edge and make a mark for the bottom of the gutter. Mark both ends of the fascia, adding a ¼" slope for every 10 ft. of gutter. Snap chalk lines between the marks.

Mark the downspout locations on the gutter. Set a gutter outlet at each mark, centered from front to back, and trace around it. Cut out the holes using aviation snips or a rotary saw.

Apply a bead of sealant under the lip of the outlet. Place the outlet in the hole in the gutter. Press firmly in place, then attach from the bottom side of the gutter using zip screws.

(continued)

Place an end cap over the end of the gutter. Drive zip screws through the flange into the gutter. Apply ample sealant along the inside edges of the cap.

Apply a small bead of sealant on the bottom and sides inside a corner box. Slide the end of the gutter inside the box. Fasten the gutter and box together using zip screws. Apply ample sealant along the inside seam.

Clip gutter hangers to the gutter every 24". Lift the gutter into place, sliding the back side under the drip edge and aligning the bottom with the chalk line. Drive the nail or screw in each hanger through the fascia to install.

Fasten an elbow to the gutter outlet, driving a zip screw through each side. Hold another elbow in place against the house. Measure the distance between the elbows, adding 2" at each end for overlap. Cut a downspout to this length using a hacksaw. Crimp the corners of the downspout for easy insertion and fasten together. *Tip: Assemble the elbows and downspout so the top pieces always fit inside bottom pieces.*

Fasten downspout brackets to the wall for the top and bottom of the downspout and every 8 ft. in between. Cut a downspout that spans the length of the wall, and attach it to the elbow at the top. Install another elbow at the end of the downspout. Fasten the brackets to the downspout.

GUTTERS: REPAIRING

Gutters perform the important task of channeling water away from your house. A good gutter system prevents damage to your siding, foundation, and landscaping, and it helps prevent water from leaking into your basement. When gutters fail, evaluate the type and extent of damage to select the best repair method. Clean your gutters and downspouts as often as necessary to keep the system working efficiently.

Tools & Materials ▸

Flat pry bar	Wood scraps
2 hacksaw	Replacement
Caulk gun	gutter materials
Pop rivet gun	Siliconized
Drill	acrylic caulk
Hammer	Roofing cement
Stiff-bristle brush	Metal flashing
Putty knife	Sheet-metal screws
Steel wool	or pop rivets
Aviation snips	Gutter hangers
Level	Primer and paint
Paintbrush	Gutter patching kit
Trowel	Gutter guards
Garden hose	Gutter caulk
Chalk line	Protective equipment

Use a trowel to clean leaves, twigs, and other debris out of the gutters before starting the repairs.

Keep gutters and downspouts clean so rain falling on the roof is directed well away from the foundation. Nearly all wet basement problems are caused by water collecting near the foundation, a situation that can frequently be traced to clogged and overflowing gutters and downspouts.

HOW TO UNCLOG GUTTERS

Flush clogged downspouts with water. Wrap a large rag around a garden hose and insert it in the downspout opening. Arrange the rag so it fills the opening, then turn on the water full force.

Check the slope of the gutters using a level. Gutters should slope slightly toward the downspouts. Adjust the hangers, if necessary.

Place gutter guards over the gutters to prevent future clogs.

HOW TO REHANG SAGGING GUTTERS & PATCH LEAKS

For sagging gutters, snap a chalk line on the fascia that follows the correct slope. Remove hangers in and near the sag. Lift the gutter until it's flush with the chalk line. *Tip: A good slope for gutters is a ¼" drop every 10 ft. toward the downspouts.*

Reattach hangers every 24" and within 12" of seams. Use new hangers, if necessary. Avoid using the original nail holes. Fill small holes and seal minor leaks using gutter caulk.

Use a gutter patching kit to make temporary repairs to a gutter with minor damage. Follow manufacturer's directions. For permanent repairs, see pages 219 to 222.

HOW TO REPAIR LEAKY JOINTS

Drill out the rivets or unfasten the metal screws to disassemble the leaky joint. Scrub both parts of the joint with a stiff-bristle brush. Clean the damaged area with water, and allow to dry completely.

Apply caulk to the joining parts, then reassemble the joint. Secure the connection with pop rivets or sheet-metal screws.

HOW TO PATCH METAL GUTTERS

Clean the area around the damage with a stiff-bristle brush. Scrub it with steel wool or an abrasive pad to loosen residue, then rinse it with water.

Apply a ⅛"-thick layer of roofing cement evenly over the damage. Spread the roofing cement a few inches past the damaged area on all sides.

Cut and bend a piece of flashing to fit inside the gutter. Bed the patch in the roofing cement. Feather out the cement to reduce ridges so it won't cause significant damming. *Tip: To prevent corrosion, make sure the patch is the same type of metal as the gutter.*

HOW TO REPLACE A SECTION OF METAL GUTTER

Remove gutter hangers in and near the damaged area. Insert wood spacers in the gutter near each hanger before prying. *Tip: If the damaged area is more than 2 ft. long, replace the entire section with new material.*

Slip spacers between the gutter and fascia near each end of the damaged area, so you won't damage the roof when cutting the gutter. Cut out the damaged section using a hacksaw.

Cut a new gutter section at least 4" longer than the damaged section.

Clean the cut ends of the old gutter using a wire brush. Caulk the ends, then center the gutter patch over the cutout area and press into the caulk.

Secure the gutter patch with pop rivets or sheet-metal screws. Use at least three fasteners at each joint. On the inside surfaces of the gutter, caulk over the heads of the fasteners.

Reinstall gutter hangers. If necessary, use new hangers but don't use old holes. Prime and paint the patch to match the existing gutter.

HARDWOOD FLOOR INSTALLING

1

Acclimate the flooring by stacking planks in the installation room. Separate the rows of flooring with wood scraps. Allow the material to rest in the space for several days, or as directed by the manufacturer's instructions. *Tip: Inspect your wood flooring as soon as it arrives. Look for any major defects such as knots, cracks, and damaged, warped, or bowed boards. It's easier to replace inadequate boards during the acclimation period than in mid-installation.*

2

Install a layer of rosin paper over the entire subfloor, stapling it down and overlapping the edges by 4". The purpose of this layer is mostly to eliminate noise caused by the floorboards scraping or pressing on the wood underlayment, which should be installed and leveled before the flooring installation begins (see pages 184 to 189).

3

Check that the room is square using the 3-4-5 rule (measure out 3 ft. from a corner in one direction and 4 ft. in the other direction—the distance between the marks should be exactly 5 ft.). If the room is out of square, you'll have to decide which wall (usually the longest) to follow as a baseline for laying the flooring.

4

Determine the location of the floor joists and drive a nail in at each end, centered on the joists. Snap chalk lines along the centerlines of each joist, connecting the nails. Use these as a reference for installing floorboards.

(continued)

5

Snap a starter line. Measure ¾" out from the longest wall, perpendicular to the floor joists, to allow for an expansion gap. Drive a nail at each end, and snap a chalk line parallel to the wall.

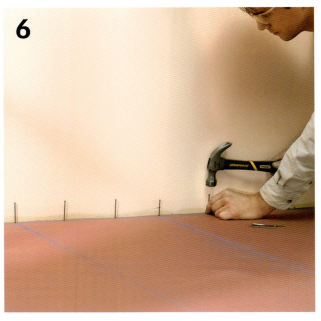

6

Drive spacer nails, such as 8d finish nails, every 4 to 5" along the chalk line, as a guide for placement of the first row of planks. Drive the nails in far enough to be stable, but with enough of the nail protruding to serve as a bumper for the flooring (and to make the nail easier to remove later).

7

Lay down a dry run for the first two or three rows to determine plank positions for best appearance. Mark the backs of planks with a pencil to keep them in your preferred order and remove them from the work area.

Variation: Some manufacturers recommend that you apply a bead of flooring adhesive to the backs of wider planks prior to nailing them. Use the recommended adhesive and lay beads across the width of the plank; keep adhesive at least ½" from the edges and 1½" from the ends.

8

Install the first row. Choose the longest planks available for this row. Lay the planks in place and drill holes every 8" for face nailing along the wall edge. Locate the holes ¼ to ½" in from the edge, where they'll be covered up by the base molding and shoe.

9

Attach the first floorboards by facenailing 8d finish nails into the pilot holes along the wall edge. Sink the nail heads with a nail set.

10

Predrill pilot holes through the tongues of the first row planks and blind-nail 8d finish or flooring nails. Make sure the heads of the nails do not stick up through the tops of the tongues, where they would interfere with the tongue-and-groove joint.

Plugging Counterbores ▸

Wider plank floors frequently require that you fasten the ends of floorboards by screwing down through the board and into the subfloor. This is most commonly needed when you are installing wood flooring that does not have tongue-and-groove ends. In such cases, drill counterbored pilot holes for the screws, making sure the counterbores are deep enough to accept a wood plug. After the floorboards are installed, check to make sure the screws are tight (but be careful not to overdrive them) and then glue a wood plug into each counterbore. Wood plugs should be the same species as the flooring (or, if that's not available, make them a contrasting species). Sand the plugs so the tops are even with surrounding floor and finish them at the same time. *Note: If you are using matching plugs, orient them in the counterbores with the wood grain running parallel to the floorboards; if you are using contrasting plugs, make the grains perpendicular.*

Wood plugs and counterbore bit

(continued)

Cut the end planks for each row to length, so that the butt end faces the wall. In other words, try and preserve the tongue-and-groove profiles if your flooring has them on the ends. Saw the planks with a fine-tooth blade, making sure to orient the workpiece so you'll be cutting into the face, minimizing tearout on the surface.

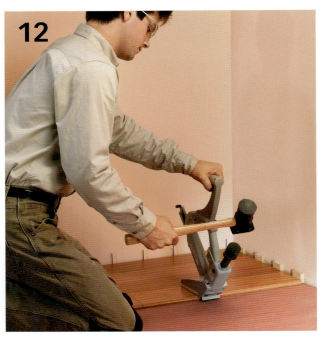

After the second row, use a flooring nailer to blind-nail the tongues of each plank. Flooring nailers are struck with a mallet to drive and set the flooring nails through the floorboard tongues. They can be rented at most home centers or rental centers. *Note: You can continue to hand-nail if you choose, but be sure to continue pre-drilling pilot holes as well to avoid damaging the tongues.*

Keep joints tight. As you install each successive plank in a row, use a flooring pull bar at the open end of the plank. Drive the end of the board toward the joint by rapping on the pull bar with a mallet.

At the end of rows and along walls, use a pull bar to seat the boards. For the last row, rip the planks as necessary, use the pull bar to seat them, and facenail along the edge as you did with the first row.

15

16

17

If a plank is slightly bowed, cut fitting wedges to force the wayward board into position before nailing it. Make wedges by cutting two triangles from a 1 ft. or longer scrap of flooring (inset). Attach one half of the wedge pair with the outside edge parallel to the bowed plank. Slide the groove of the other wedge piece onto the tongue of the bowed plank, and hammer until the plank sits flush against its neighbor. Nail the plank into place. Remove the wedge parts.

Install a reducer strip or other transition as needed between the plank floor and adjoining rooms. Cut the strip to size and fit the strip's groove over the plank's tongue. Drill pilot holes and facenail the strip with 8d finishing nails. Sink the nails with a nail set, putty, and sand smooth.

Install a quarter-round shoe molding to cover all the expansion gaps between the floor and walls at the edge of the floor. Paint, stain, or finish the molding before installing.

18

To reverse the direction of the tongue and groove at doorways or other openings, glue a spline into the groove of the plank. Fit the groove of the following board onto the spline and nail into place as before.

Finishing Unfinished Planks ▶

Standard strip floors are normally finished with clear or amber polyurethane finish, but the unusual look of a plank floor makes it worth considering other finishing options.

Wax is an age-old wood floor finish, one that protects the surface but needs to be renewed regularly. Wax is labor intensive, but not tricky to apply. The finish emphasizes variations in grain—a plus for many of the woods used in plank floors. It also gives the wood a deep rich glow that emphasizes the character of the species used.

Tung oil and linseed oil don't protect as well as wax, although they can be supplemented with hardeners, sealers, and other agents for a tougher finish in a range of sheens. They don't have the plastic look of polyurethane that some wood enthusiasts object to.

HARDWOOD FLOOR: REFINISHING

1

Wedge a pry bar between the shoe molding and baseboards. Move along the wall as nails loosen. Once removed, place a scrap 2 × 4 board against the wall and pry out baseboard at nails. Maintain the gap with wood shims. Number the sections for easy replacement. Place wide masking tape along the baseboards. Drive protruding nails in the floor ⅛" below the surface with a nail set.

2

Practice with the drum sander turned off. Move forward and backward. Tilt or raise it off the floor a couple of times. A drum sander is heavy, bulky, and awkward. Once it touches the floor, it walks forward; if you stop it, it gouges the floor.

3

For the initial pass with the drum sander, sand with the grain using 40- or 60-grit paper; if there are large scratches, use 20 or 30. Start two-thirds down the room length on the right side; work your way to the left. Raise drum. Start motor. Slowly lower drum to floor. Lift the sander off the floor when you reach the wall. Move to the left 2 to 4" and then walk it backwards the same distance you just walked forward. Repeat.

Sandpapers for Drum Sanders & Edgers ▸

Grits	Grade	Use
20, 30, 40, 60	Coarse	To level uneven boards
100, 120	Medium	To minimize scratches from coarse grits
150, 180	Fine	To eliminate scratches from medium grits

Sandpaper becomes less effective over time; it may even rip. Buy 3–5 sheets of every grade for each room you want to refinish. You won't use them all, but most rentals allow you to return what you don't use. It's far better to have too many than to find yourself unable to continue until the next day because you ran out and the hardware store is closed.

Reminder: Before you leave the rental shop, have an employee show you how to load the paper. Every machine is a little different.

When you get to the far left side of the room, turn the machine around and repeat the process. Overlap the sanded section two-thirds to feather out the ridgeline. Repeat the sanding process 3 or 4 more times using 120-grit sandpaper. Sand the entire floor. For the final passes, use finer sandpaper (150- to 180-grit) to remove scratches left by coarser papers.

Power edge sander

To sand hard-to-reach spots, first use a power edge sander along the walls, using the same grit that you last used with the drum sander. Make a succession of overlapping half-circles starting in the corner on one wall. Pull out in an arc and then swirl back to the wall. Continue around the room. Blend together any lines left by the drum and edge sanders by running a rotary buffer over the floor twice: first with an 80-grit screen and then with a 100-grit screen. Finally, use a 5" random orbital sander to smooth out the floor. The random motion naturally feathers out bumps.

Use a paint scraper to get to corners and hard-to-reach nooks and crannies. Pull the scraper toward you with a steady downward pressure. Pull with the grain. Next, sand with a sanding block.

Prepare the room for finish by sweeping and vacuuming. Remove plastic on the doors, windows, and fixtures. Sweep and vacuum again. Wipe up fine particles with a tack cloth.

(continued)

8

Apply polyurethane finish. Mix equal parts water-based polyurethane and water. Use a natural bristle brush to apply the mixture along walls and around obstacles. To apply the mixture in the middle of the room, use a painting pad on a pole. Apply 2 coats diagonally across the grain and a final coat in the direction of the grain.

9

Allow the finish to dry after each coat. Lightly buff the floor with a fine to medium abrasive pad. Clean the floor with a damp cloth and wipe the area dry with a towel.

10

Apply at least two coats of undiluted polyurethane finish to get a hard, durable finish. Allow the finish to dry; repeat step 9 and then add a final coat. Do not overbrush.

11

After the final coat is dry, buff the surface with water and a fine abrasive pad. This removes surface imperfections and diminishes gloss. After finishing, wait at least 72 hours before replacing the shoe molding.

HARDWOOD FLOOR: REPAIRING

Use a straightedge to draw cut lines above and below the damaged portion of the board. To avoid nails, be sure to mark cut lines at least ¾" inside the outermost edge of any joints. The goal is not to cut out the entire section of floorboard, but to remove a strip down the middle so you can create room to pry it out.

Determine the depth of the boards to be cut. With a drill and ¾"-wide spade bit, slowly drill through a damaged board. Drill until you see the top of the subfloor. Measure the depth. A common depth is ⅝" or ¾". Set your circular saw to this depth.

To prevent boards from chipping, place painter's tape along the outside of the pencil lines. To create a wood cutting guide, tack a straight wood strip inside the damaged area (for easy removal, allow nails to slightly stick up). Set the guide back the distance between the saw blade and the guide edge of the circular saw.

Align the circular saw with the wood cutting guide. Turn on the saw. Lower the blade into the cutline. Do not cut the last ¼" of the corners. Remove cutting guide. Repeat with other sides.

(continued)

Complete the cuts. Use a hammer and sharp chisel to completely loosen the boards from the subfloor. Make sure the chisel's beveled side is facing the damaged area for a clean edge.

Remove split boards. Use a scrap 2 × 4 block for leverage and to protect the floor. With a hammer, tap a pry bar into and under the split board. Most boards pop out easily, but some may require a little pressure. Remove exposed nails with the hammer claw.

Use a chisel to remove the 2 remaining strips. Again, make sure the bevel side of the chisel is facing the interior of the damaged area. Set any exposed nails with your nail set.

Trimming Tongues & Grooves ▶

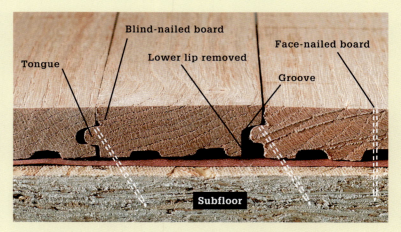

Blind-nailed board

Tongue

Lower lip removed

Face-nailed board

Groove

Subfloor

When tongue-and-groove hardwood floors are installed, each new course is blind-nailed through the tongue before the next course is placed. The process is called "blind-nailing" because you can't see the nail after the floor is finished because it is angled into the tongue-and-groove joint. This brings up two points: 1. You should be aware of the nails angled into the groove side of every board, so you have a better chance of avoiding them when you are cutting or drilling into floorboards. 2. The last board you install has to be "facenailed" (nailed through the top of the board) because you no longer have access to the tongue. The lower lip of this board is first removed, to fit into place.

Cut strips of new flooring to the length and width and slip the patch strip into the repair opening, forming the tongue-and-groove joint with the board at the edge of the opening. If you are installing a single board, trim off the bottom shoulder of the groove edge first.

To install the last board, hook the tongue into the groove of the old floor and then use a soft mallet to tap the groove side down into the previous board installed.

Drill pilot holes angled outward: two side-by-side holes about ½" from the edges of each board, and one hole every 12" along the groove side of each board. Drive 1½"-long, 8d finish nails through the holes. Set nails with a nail set. Fill holes with wood putty.

Once putty is dry, sand the patch smooth with fine-grit sandpaper. Feather sand neighboring boards. Vacuum and wipe the area with a clean cloth. Apply matching wood stain or restorer; then apply 2 coats of matching finish.

HEATERS: BASEBOARD

Baseboard heaters are a popular way to provide additional heating for an existing room or primary heat to a converted basement.

Heaters are generally wired on a dedicated 240-volt circuit controlled by a thermostat. Several heaters can be wired in parallel and controlled by a single thermostat.

Baseboard heaters are generally surface mounted without boxes, so in a remodeling situation, you only need to run cables. Be sure to mark cable locations on the floor before installing drywall. Retrofit installations are also not difficult. You can remove existing baseboard and run new cable in the space behind.

Tools & Materials ▸

Drill/driver	Basic wiring supplies
Wire stripper	Flathead screws
Cable ripper	Combination tool
Wallboard saw	Protective
Baseboard heater	equipment
or heaters	
Thermostat	
(in-heater	
or in-wall)	
12/2 NM cable	
Electrical tape	

How Much Heater Do You Need? ▸

If you don't mind doing a little math, determining how many lineal feet of baseboard heater a room requires is not hard.

1. Measure the area of the room in sq ft. (length × width): _____
2. Divide the area by 10 to get the baseline minimum wattage: _____
3. Add 5% for each newer window or 10% for each older window: _____
4. Add 10% for each exterior wall in the room: _____
5. Add 10% for each exterior door: _____
6. Add 10% if the space below is not insulated: _____

7. Add 20% if the space above is not well insulated: _____
8. Add 10% if ceiling is more than 8 ft. high: _____
9. Total of the baseline wattage plus all additions: _____
10. Divide this number by 250 (the wattage produced per ft. of standard baseboard heater): _____
11. Round up to a whole number. This is the minimum number of feet of heater you need. _____

Note: It is much better to have more feet of heater than is required than fewer. Having more footage of heater does not consume more energy; it does allow the heaters to work more efficiently.

Planning Tips for Baseboard Heaters ▸

- 240-volt heaters are much more energy efficient than 120-volt heaters.
- Baseboard heaters require a dedicated circuit. A 20-amp, 240-volt circuit of 12-gauge copper wire will power up to 16 ft. of heater.
- Do not install a heater beneath a wall receptacle. Cords hanging down from the receptacle are a fire hazard.

- Do not mount heaters directly on the floor. You should maintain at least 1" of clear space between the baseboard heater and the floor covering.
- Installing heaters directly beneath windows is a good practice.
- Locate wall thermostats on interior walls only, and do not install directly above a heat source.

HOW TO INSTALL A 240-VOLT BASEBOARD HEATER

1

Cut a small hole in the drywall 3 to 4" above the floor at heater locations. Pull 12/2 NM cables through the first hole: one from the thermostat, the other to the next heater. Pull all the cables for subsequent heaters. Middle-of-run heaters will have two cables, while end-of-run heaters have only one cable.

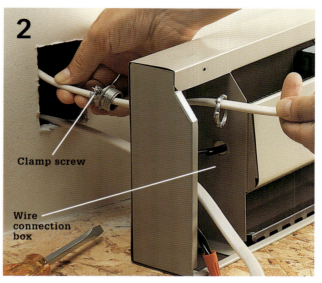

2

Clamp screw

Wire connection box

Remove the cover on the wire connection box. Open a knockout for each cable that will enter the box, then feed the cables through the cable clamps and into the wire connection box. Attach the clamps to the wire connection box and tighten the clamp screws until the cables are gripped firmly.

3

Anchor heater against wall about 1" off the floor by driving flathead screws through back of housing and into studs. Strip away cable sheathing so at least ½" of sheathing extends into the heater. Strip ¾" of insulation from each wire using a combination tool.

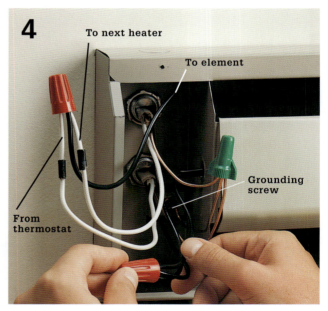

4

To next heater

To element

From thermostat

Grounding screw

Make connections to the heating element if the power wires are coming from a thermostat or another heater controlled by a thermostat. Connect the white circuit wires to one of the wire leads on the heater. Tag white wires with black tape to indicate they are hot. Connect the black circuit wires to the other wire lead. Connect a grounding pigtail to the green grounding screw in the box, then join all grounding wires with a wire connector. Reattach cover.

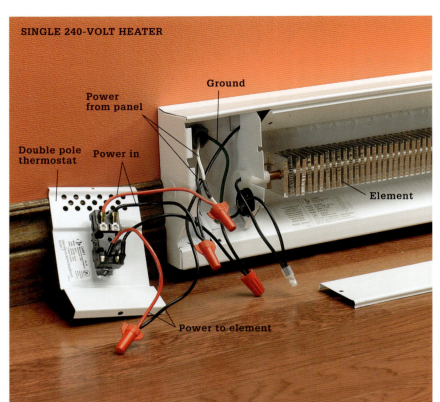

SINGLE 240-VOLT HEATER

Power from panel

Ground

Power in

Double pole thermostat

Power to element

Element

One heater with end-cap thermostat.
Run both power leads (black plus tagged neutral) into the connection box at either end of the heater. If installing a single-pole thermostat, connect one power lead to one thermostat wire and connect the other thermostat wire to one of the heater leads. Connect the other hot LINE wire to the other heater lead. If you are installing a double-pole thermostat, make connections with both legs of the power supply.

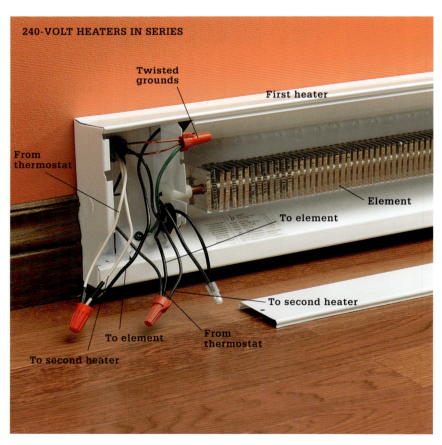

240-VOLT HEATERS IN SERIES

Twisted grounds

First heater

From thermostat

Element

To element

From thermostat

To second heater

To element

To second heater

Multiple heaters. At the first heater, join both hot wires from the thermostat to the wires leading to the second heater in line. Be sure to tag all white neutrals hot. Twist copper ground wires together and pigtail them to the grounding screw in the baseboard heater junction box. This parallel wiring configuration ensures that power flow will not be interrupted to the downstream heaters if an upstream heater fails.

WIRING

HOUSEWRAP: INSTALLING

Housewrap is a specially engineered fabric that blocks air and water infiltration from the outside but allows moisture vapor to pass through from the inside. It's best to apply the housewrap before installing windows and doors, but since that's not always possible with a remodeling or siding replacement job, you can cut the housewrap to fit around them. Most siding materials need to be nailed to studs, and the marks on the housewrap identify their locations. Staples are permissible for fastening housewrap, but cap nails are recommended and have better holding power.

Felt paper is not the same as housewrap. It's not necessarily designed to work as an air barrier, and it may absorb water. Do not substitute felt paper when housewrap is supposed to be used.

Tools & Materials ▶

Hammer
Utility knife
Tape dispenser
Housewrap

Cap nails
Housewrap tape
Protective
    equipment

Make sure the stud marks on the housewrap are aligned with the wall studs.

HOW TO INSTALL HOUSEWRAP

Starting 6 to 12" around a corner and 3" over the foundation to cover the sill plate, unroll the housewrap along the side of the house with the printed side facing out. Align the printed stud marks on the housewrap with the stud marks on the sheathing. Keep the roll straight as you unwrap it.

Nail the housewrap every 12 to 18" on the vertical stud lines using cap nails. Keep the housewrap pulled snug as it's unrolled. Cut holes in the housewrap for extrusions such as hose spigots and the electric meter.

(continued)

EXTERIOR

Tip ▶

Housewrap helps protect the house from its worst enemies—water, moisture, and cold air drafts. Covering exterior walls with housewrap before installing siding can also reduce your energy bills.

3

When starting a new roll, overlap vertical seams by 6 to 12", aligning the stud marks. Begin the second course by overlapping the bottom course by 6". Once again, make sure stud marks are lined up.

4

At window and door locations, cut the housewrap at the middle of the nailing flanges. At the bottom, cut the housewrap at the sill. Pull the sill and jamb flashing over the housewrap. Be careful not to slice the nailing flanges and windowsills when cutting the housewrap.

5

Tape all horizontal and vertical seams, accidental tears, and seams around doors, windows, and plumbing and electrical protrusions using housewrap tape. Tape the bottom of the protrusion first, then the sides, then place a piece of tape over the top.

ICEMAKER: INSTALLING

Most expensive refrigerators come with icemakers as standard equipment, and practically every model features them as an option (a refrigerator with an icemaker usually costs about $100 more). It is also possible to purchase an icemaker as a retrofit feature for your old fridge.

Hooking up an existing icemaker to a cold-water supply involves drilling holes and connecting to a cold-water pipe. Most often, a pipe can be found in the basement below the kitchen, perhaps under the kitchen sink. To make the connection, some local codes allow the installation of a saddle Tee valve, but many do not, and a compression Tee valve is not difficult to install, as we show. In many kitchens the flexible line running from the valve to the fridge is copper, but plastic icemaker tubing is easier to install and less likely to kink or crack. To be sure everything fits, you can buy a connection kit from the refrigerator manufacturer.

Most icemakers either come preinstalled or are purchased as an accessory when you buy your new refrigerator. But if you have an older refrigerator with no icemaker and you'd like it to have one, all is not lost. Inspect the back of the unit, behind the freezer compartment. If your refrigerator has the required plumbing to support an icemaker, you will see a port or a port that is covered with backing. In that case, all you need to do is take the make and model information to an appliance parts dealer and they can sell you an aftermarket icemaker. Plan to spend $100 to $200.

A built-in icemaker is easy to install as a retrofit appliance in most modern refrigerators. If you want to have an endless supply of ice for home use, you'll wonder how you ever got along without one.

Tools & Materials ▶

Screwdrivers	Electric drill and	Open-end or	Putty knife
Nut drivers	assorted bits	adjustable wrench	Long ½" drill bit
Needle-nose pliers	Icemaker kit (or icemaker	T-valve	Electrician's tape
Duct or masking tape	tubing with ferrules	(for supply tube)	Protective equipment
Channel-type pliers	and nuts)		

How Icemakers Work ▸

An icemaker receives its supply of water for making cubes through a ¼" copper supply line that runs from the icemaker to a water pipe. The supply line runs through a valve in the refrigerator and is controlled by a solenoid that monitors the water supply and sends the water into the icemaker itself, where it is turned into ice cubes. The cubes drop down into a bin, and as the ice level rises, they also raise a bail wire that's connected to a shutoff. When the bin is full, the bail wire will be high enough to trigger a mechanism that shuts off the water supply.

Aftermarket automatic icemakers are simple to install as long as your refrigerator is icemaker ready. Make sure to buy the correct model for your appliance and do careful installation work—icemaker water supply lines are very common sources for leaks.

HOW TO CONNECT AN ICEMAKER

1

Locate a nearby cold-water pipe, usually in the basement or crawl space below the kitchen. Behind the refrigerator and near the wall, use a long ½" bit to drill a hole through the floor. Do not pull the bit out.

2

Pull upward

From below, fasten plastic icemaker tubing to the end of the drill bit by wrapping firmly with electrician's tape. From above, carefully pull the bit up, to thread the tubing up into the kitchen.

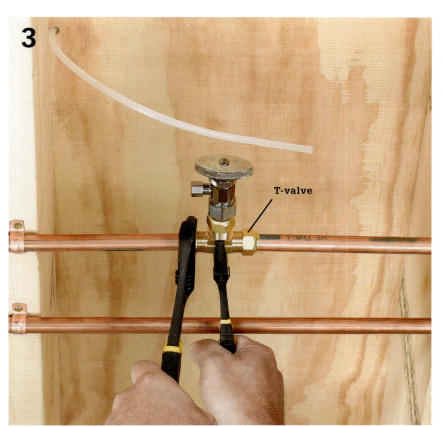

3

Shut off the water and open nearby faucets to drain the line. Cut into a cold-water pipe and install a compression T-valve. Tighten all the nuts, close the valve and nearby faucets, and restore water to test for leaks.

T-valve

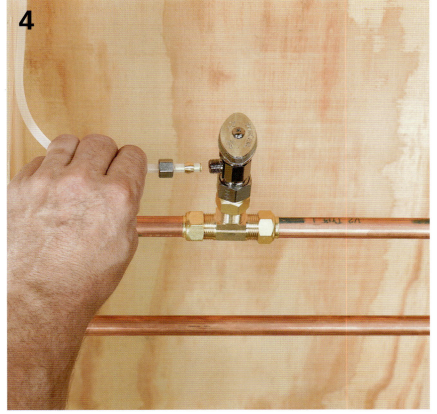

4

Connect the tubing. Arrange the tubing behind the fridge so you have about 6 ft. of slack, making it easy to pull the fridge out for cleaning. Cut the tubing with a knife. Slide on a nut and a ferrule. Insert the tubing into the valve, slide the ferrule tight against the valve, and tighten the nut. To finish the installation, connect the tubing to the refrigerator, using a nut and ferrule. Keep the tubing neatly coiled and kink-free for future maintenance.

HOW TO INSTALL A NEW ICEMAKER

Remove all the contents from the refrigerator and freezer. Unplug the unit and pull it out from the wall. Open the freezer door and remove the icemaker cover plate (inset). On the back of the refrigerator, remove the backing or unscrew the icemaker access panel.

Install the tube assembly. Remove two insulation plugs to expose two openings, one for the water line and the other for a wiring harness. Install the water tube assembly (part of the icemaker kit) in its access hole; it has a plastic elbow attached to the plastic tube that reaches into the freezer compartment.

Hook up the harness. Icemaker kits usually come with a wiring harness that joins the icemaker motor inside the freezer box to the power supply wires. Push this harness through its access hole and into the freezer compartment. Then seal the hole with the plastic grommet that comes with the harness.

Join the end of the icemaker wiring harness to the power connector that was preinstalled on the back of the refrigerator. This connection should lay flat against the back. If it doesn't, just tape it down with some duct tape or masking tape.

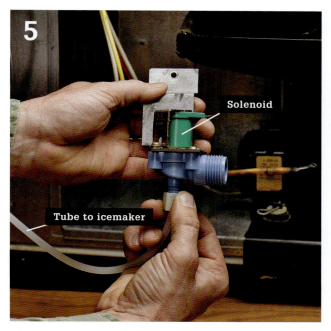

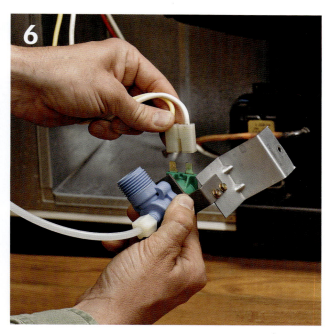

The water tube at the top of the refrigerator is attached to the solenoid that is mounted at the bottom with a plastic water line. To install the line, first attach it to the water tube, then run it down the back of the refrigerator and attach it to the solenoid valve with a compression fitting. This job is easier to do before you attach the solenoid assembly to the refrigerator cabinet.

The icemaker wiring harness comes with two snap connectors. One goes to the preinstalled wires on the refrigerator and the other is attached to the solenoid. Just push this second connector onto the brass tabs, usually at the top of the solenoid.

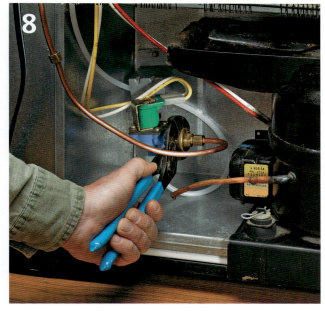

Attach the solenoid to a mounting bracket that should be installed on the cabinet wall at the bottom of the refrigerator. Mounting holes may be predrilled in the cabinet for this purpose. But if not, drill holes to match the bracket and the size of the screws. Then attach the bracket and make sure to attach the solenoid ground wire to one of these screws.

Install the water-inlet copper tube once the solenoid is mounted. Attach it by tightening the nut on one end with channel-type pliers. The other end of the tube is held to the refrigerator cabinet with a simple clamp. Make sure the end of this tubing is pointing straight up.

(continued)

The end of the water-inlet tube is joined to the water supply tubing (from the house plumbing system) with a brass compression coupling. Tighten the compression nuts with an open-end or adjustable wrench.

From inside the freezer compartment, make sure the water tube and the wiring harness (from the back of the refrigerator) are free. If they are caught on the cabinet, loosen them until they are easily accessible.

Connect the wire harness to the plug on the icemaker unit. Also connect the water supply tube to the back of the icemaker with a spring clip or hose clamp.

Install the icemaker. Remove any small rubber caps that may be installed in the mounting screw holes with a narrow putty knife. Lift the unit and screw it to the freezer wall. The mounting bracket holes are usually slotted to permit leveling the unit. Plug in the refrigerator and test the icemaker.

INSULATION

Common Insulation Types ▸

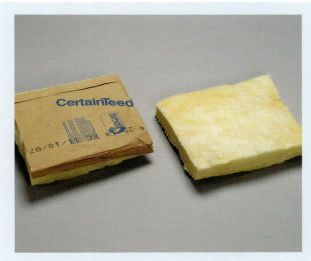

Blankets and batts: Batts are precut panels in standard widths and lengths to fit inside studs spaced 16" or 24" on center, and walls 8 ft. or 9 ft. high. Some manufacturers offer batts with vertical seams that make tearing the batts to fit much easier. Blankets are rolls of insulation that are more efficient when you need to fill long spaces. Both styles are available in fiberglass, spun mineral wool, recycled plastic, and natural fibers. Fiberglass batts are the most common and least expensive type, and are lightweight and easy to work with. Blankets and batts come faced or unfaced, in a wide range of R-values.

Loose fill: As the name implies, this is particulate insulation that is blown into walls and other spaces. Fiberglass and mineral wool are usually blown in dry, while cellulose insulation—shredded bits of paper and cardboard added to water, flame-retardants, and other chemicals and fillers—may be blown in wet or dry. Loose fill is ideal for tight and unusual spaces that are difficult to insulate with batts. R-values vary depending on how the material is prepared and how it is blown in, and the spraying of loose fill is generally best left to professionals.

Spray foam: A combination of polymer and foaming agent, this insulation is mixed on site by special installers and sprayed into walls, floors, and ceilings. The foam expands and solidifies, forming a plastic barrier with millions of air pockets. Foam is more expensive than other types of insulation. But R-values are generally higher and there's no air movement, so overall performance is better. The process is quick, and foam does not need a vapor barrier.

HOW TO INSTALL FIBERGLASS BATT INSULATION

1

Stuff the batt into the wall or ceiling cavity. Whenever handling fiberglass wear proper safety gear, including respirator, enclosed safety glasses, gloves, and a long-sleeved shirt.

2

Cut batts to fit, rather than compressing them, which can reduce R-value. Use a sharp utility knife to trim the batt ¼" wider and longer than the space. Use a stud as a straightedge and cutting surface, or measure and cut on the subfloor. Cut the unfaced side on faced batts.

3

Install polyethelene vapor barrier over unfaced batts by draping it across the entire wall, a few inches over on all sides, and stapling it to framing. Cut around obstructions and seal with vapor barrier tape.

4

Facing flange

Install faced batts by tucking along the edges so that the flange is flush with the edge of the studs. Staple flanges to the face of framing members, spacing staples every 8". Patch gaps or tears with vapor barrier tape.

INTERIOR DOOR: INSTALLING

Install prehung interior doors after the framing work is complete and the wallboard has been installed. If the rough opening for the door has been framed accurately, installing the door takes about an hour.

Standard prehung doors have 4½-inch-wide jambs and are sized to fit walls with 2 × 4 construction and ½" wallboard. If you have 2 × 6 construction or thicker wall surface material, you can special-order a door to match, or you can add jamb extensions to a standard-sized door (see Tip, next page).

Tools & Materials ▶

Level	Wood shims
Hammer	8d casing nails
Handsaw	Protective equipment
Prehung interior door	

Prehung doors save you time and effort during installation because the jamb is already installed on the door.

HOW TO INSTALL A PREHUNG INTERIOR DOOR

1

Slide the door unit into the framed opening so the edges of the jambs are flush with the wall surface and the hinge-side jamb is plumb.

2

Insert pairs of wood shims driven from opposite directions into the gap between the framing members and the hinge-side jamb, spaced every 12". Check the hinge-side jamb to make sure it is still plumb and does not bow.

(continued)

3

Anchor the hinge-side jamb with 8d casing nails driven through the jamb and shims and into the jack stud. You may want to predrill the nail holes to prevent splitting the shims.

4

Insert pairs of shims in the gap between the framing members and the latch-side jamb and top jamb, spaced every 12". With the door closed, adjust the shims so the gap between the door edge and jamb is ⅛" wide. Drive 8d casing nails through the jambs and shims into the framing members.

5

Cut the shims flush with the wall surface using a handsaw. Hold the saw vertically to prevent damage to the door jamb or wall. Finish the door and install the lockset as directed by the manufacturer. Install trim.

KITCHEN CABINETS

Position a corner upper cabinet on a ledger and hold it in place, making sure it is resting cleanly on the ledger. Drill ³⁄₁₆" pilot holes into the wall studs through the hanging strips at the top rear of the cabinet. Attach the cabinet to the wall with 2½" screws. Do not tighten fully until all cabinets are hung.

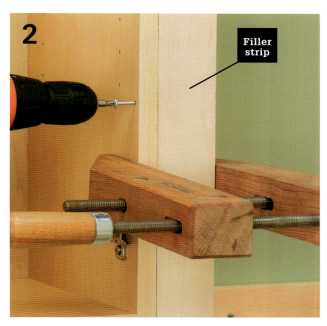

Filler strip

Attach a filler strip to the front edge of the cabinet, if needed. Clamp the filler in place and drill counterbored pilot holes through the cabinet face frame near hinge locations. Attach filler to cabinet with 2½" cabinet screws or flathead wood screws.

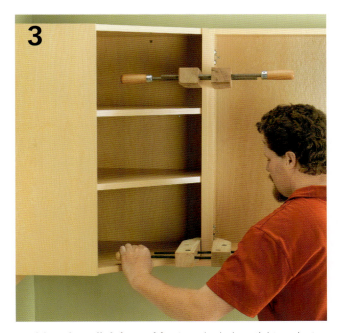

Position the adjoining cabinet on the ledger, tight against the corner cabinet or filler strip. Clamp the corner cabinet and the adjoining cabinet together at the top and bottom. Handscrew clamps will not damage wood face frames.

Check the front cabinet edges or face frames for plumb. Drill ³⁄₁₆" pilot holes into the wall studs through the hanging strips in the rear of the cabinet. Attach the cabinet with 2½" screws. Do not tighten the wall screws fully until all the cabinets are hung.

(continued)

Attach the corner cabinet to the adjoining cabinet. From the inside corner cabinet, drill pilot holes through the face frame. Join the cabinets with sheet-metal screws.

Position and attach each additional cabinet. Clamp frames together, and drill counterbored pilot holes through the side of the face frame. Join the cabinets with wood screws. Drill ³⁄₁₆" pilot holes in the hanging strips, and attach the cabinet to the studs with wood screws.

Join the frameless cabinets with #8 × 1¼" panhead wood screws or wood screws with decorative washers. Each pair of cabinets should be joined by at least four screws.

Fill the gaps between the cabinet and wall or neighboring appliance with a filler strip. Cut the filler strip to fit the space, then wedge wood shims between the filler and the wall to create a friction fit that holds it in place temporarily. Drill counterbored pilot holes through the side of the cabinet (or the edge of the face frame) and attach filler with screws.

Remove the temporary ledger. Check the cabinet run for plumb, and adjust if necessary by placing wood shims behind the cabinet, near the stud locations. Tighten the wall screws completely. Cut off the shims with a utility knife.

Use trim moldings to cover any gaps between the cabinets and the walls. Stain the moldings to match the cabinet finish.

Attach decorative valance above the sink. Clamp the valance to the edge of cabinet frames and drill counterbored pilot holes through the cabinet frames and into the end of the valance. Attach with sheet-metal screws.

Install the cabinet doors. If necessary, adjust the hinges so that the doors are straight and plumb.

HOW TO INSTALL BASE CABINETS

1

Begin the installation with a corner cabinet. Draw plumb lines that intersect the 34½" reference line (measured from the high point of the floor) at the locations for the cabinet sides.

2

Place the cabinet in the corner. Make sure the cabinet is plumb and level. If necessary, adjust by driving wood shims under the cabinet base. Be careful not to damage the flooring. Drill ³⁄₁₆" pilot holes through the hanging strip and into the wall studs. Tack the cabinet to the wall with wood screws or wallboard screws.

3

Clamp the adjoining cabinet to the corner cabinet. Make sure the new cabinet is plumb, then drill counterbored pilot holes through the cabinet sides or the face frame and filler strip. Screw the cabinets together. Drill ³⁄₁₆" pilot holes through the hanging strips and into the wall studs. Tack the cabinets loosely to the wall studs with wood screws or wallboard screws.

4

Use a jigsaw to cut any cabinet openings needed in the cabinet backs (for example, in the sink base seen here) for plumbing, wiring, or heating ducts.

5

Position and attach additional cabinets, making sure the frames are aligned and the cabinet tops are level. Clamp cabinets together, then attach the face frames or cabinet sides with screws driven into pilot holes. Tack the cabinets to the wall studs, but don't drive screws too tight—you may need to make adjustments once the entire bank is installed.

6

Make sure all the cabinets are level. If necessary, adjust by driving shims underneath the cabinets. Place the shims behind the cabinets near the stud locations to fill any gaps. Tighten the wall screws. Cut off the shims with a utility knife.

7

Toe-kick molding

Use trim moldings to cover gaps between the cabinets and the wall or floor. The toe-kick area is often covered with a strip of wood finished to match the cabinets or painted black.

8

Hang the cabinet doors and mount the drawer fronts, then test to make sure they close smoothly and the doors fit evenly and flush. Self-closing cabinet hinges (by far the most common type installed today) have adjustment screws that allow you to make minor changes to the hardware to correct any problems.

VARIATION: INSTALLING FACE-FRAME CABINETS

The more traditional-looking face-frame cabinets differ only slightly from frameless cabinets in terms of installation. The opening of the cabinet is surrounded by vertical and horizontal frames called "stiles" and "rails." The face frame typically overhangs the cabinet case on the outside by $\frac{1}{16}$" to $\frac{1}{8}$". Because of this overhang, the frames must be the connection point rather than the cabinet case. Use $2\frac{1}{2}$" No.10 wood screws to connect the frames (or use special $2\frac{1}{2}$"- or 3"-long cabinet screws). Do not screw the cabinet sides together at any other point than the face frame, as this will skew the cabinets and create structural stress.

Most face-frame cabinets use overlay doors. The hinges for these doors simply attach to the back of the door and to the side or face of the cabinet face-frame with screws. They are called "overlay wrap" or "partial wrap" hinges if they attach to the side of the face frame, and they are called "semi-concealed" if they attach to the front of the face-frame. Cup or Euro-style hinges are available for face-frame cabinets, but are somewhat more difficult to install if the doors have not been predrilled for this hinge style. The best way to attach the door hardware uniformly is to use a drilling template. You can usually purchase one where you purchase the cabinets or hardware.

Tools & Materials ▸

Drill	Filler strip (if needed)
No. 10 counterbore bit	¾" finish-grade plywood
⁵⁄₆₄" self-centering vix bit	Finish materials
Cabinet screws (or 2½"	Drilling template
No. 10 screws)	

To join face-frame cabinets, set the cabinets in position, aligned with the frame faces flush and the frame tops flush. Clamp the frames together at the top and bottom. Using a drill with a No.10 counterbore bit, drill two pilot holes through the sides of the frame into the adjoining frame. Attach the frames with cabinet screws or 2½" No. 10 screws.

Start at the corner when installing a bank of cabinets that includes a blind corner cabinet. Attach the cabinet adjoining the corner by driving screws through the face frame (see photo at the top of this page). If a filler strip is necessary to fill a gap between the two cabinets, attach the filler strip to the base cabinet first and then run screws through the corner cabinet face frame and into the filler strip only after the adjoining cabinet is positioned and shimmed.

To install partial wrap overlay hinges, use a template to mark the hinge locations on the back of the door. Drill ⁵⁄₆₄"-dia. pilot holes no more than ⅜" deep using a self-centering vix bit. Screw the hinge to the door back. Place the hinge against the face frame and mark the screw holes. Drill ⁵⁄₆₄" pilot holes. Drive all the screws for both hinges partially, then tighten all.

Adjusting European Hinges ▸

European hinges (also called cup hinges) are the standard hinges used on frameless cabinets and some face-frame cabinets. One advantage of these hinges is their adjustability. This adjustability means that you will need some patience to tackle this project.

At first glance, European hinges appear to need a Phillips screwdriver to be adjusted, but you will have more success if you use a Pozidrive #2 screwdriver. This looks like a Phillips driver, but it is engineered with extra blade tips for reduced slippage. Never use a power screwdriver for hinge adjustments.

European hinges have three adjustment screws that secure the hinge to the door and cabinet while moving the door in and out, up and down, or right to left. If you own face-frame cabinets, the hinges may be more compact than frameless cabinet hinges. Some of the most compact hinges have unique adjustment systems, so you may have more trial and error in installing them.

Before making any adjustments, try tightening the anchoring screw or the vertical adjustment screws. Often these screws have worked loose over time and are affecting the door alignment and function.

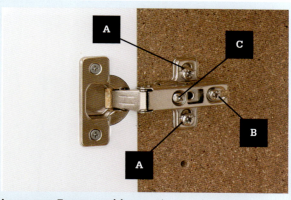

Long-arm European hinges. The standard long-arm European hinge has four adjustment screws. The first pair (A) attach the mounting plate to the side of the cabinet. Loosen these screws slightly on both hinges to move the cabinet up and down vertically. Retighten the screws when you have the hinge aligned as desired. The third adjustment screw (B) attaches the hinge to the mounting plate. If this screw is loose, the door will move in and out and seem floppy. This screw should be in the same relative position in its slot as the B screw on the other hinge, and they should both always be tight. The fourth screw (C) adjusts the door left and right horizontally. Adjust one hinge at a time in small increments by turning the screw. Check the adjustment results frequently by closing the door.

European hinges. Cabinet doors with European hinges can be adjusted in three dimensions: vertical (up and down) (A); depth (in and out) (B); and horizontal (right and left) (C). If your cabinets are slightly out of alignment, begin door installation with the center cabinet and work your way out to one side and then the other.

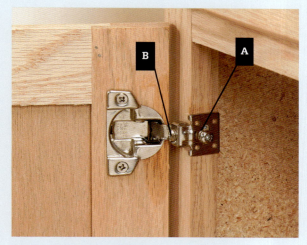

Compact European hinges. The compact European hinge for overlay doors on face-frame cabinets has three adjustment screws. The first screw (A) attaches the mounting clip to the side or front of the face frame. Screw B attaches the hinge to the mounting plate and serves as the left and right adjustment. Loosen all the A screws slightly to adjust the door up or down, then tighten. Loosen or tighten one B screw in small increments to move the door left or right. Check the adjustment results frequently by closing the door.

KITCHEN CABINETS: ISLAND

Set two base cabinets back-to-back in position on the floor and outline the cabinet corners onto the flooring. Remove the cabinets and draw a new outline inside of the one you just created to allow for the thickness of the cabinet sides (usually ¾").

Cut 2 × 4 cleats to fit inside the inner outline to provide nailing surfaces for the cabinets. Attach the cleats to the floor with screws or nails. Tip: Create an L-shaped cleat for each inside corner.

Join the two base cabinets together by driving 1¼" wallboard screws through the nailing strips on the backs of the cabinets from each direction. Make sure the cabinet sides are flush and aligned. Lower the base cabinets over the cleats. Check the cabinets for level, and shim underneath the edges of the base if necessary.

Attach the cabinets to the floor cleats using 6d finish nails. Drill pilot holes for nails, and recess the nail heads with a nail set. Install your preferred countertop on the cabinets.

KITCHEN SINK

1

Invert the sink and trace around the edges as a reference for making the sink cutout cutting lines, which should be parallel to the outlines, but about 1" inside of them to create a 1" ledge. If your sink comes with a template for the cutout, use it.

2

Drill a starter hole and cut out the sink opening with a jigsaw. Cut right up to the line. Because the sink flange fits over the edges of the cutout, the opening doesn't need to be perfect, but as always you should try to do a nice, neat job.

3

Attach as much of the plumbing as makes sense to install prior to setting the sink into the opening. Having access to the underside of the flange is a great help when it comes to attaching the faucet body, sprayer, and strainer, in particular.

4

Apply a bead of silicone caulk around the edges of the sink opening. The sink flange most likely is not flat, so try and apply the caulk in the area that will make contact with the flange.

5

Place the sink in the opening. Try to get the sink centered right away so you don't need to move it around and disturb the caulk, which can break the seal. If you are installing a heavy cast-iron sink, it's best to leave the strainers off so you can grab onto the sink at the drain openings.

6

For sinks with mounting clips, tighten the clips from below using a screwdriver or wrench (depending on the type of clip your sink has). There should be at least three clips on every side. Don't overtighten the clips—this can cause the sink flange to flatten or become warped.

KITCHEN SPRAYER: REPLACING

To replace a sprayer hose, start by shutting off the water at the shutoff valves. Clear out the cabinet under your sink and put on eye protection. Unthread the coupling nut that attaches the old hose to a nipple or tube below the faucet spout. Use a basin wrench if you can't get your channel-type pliers on the nut.

Unscrew the mounting nut of the old sprayer from below and remove the old sprayer body. Clean the sink deck and then apply plumber's putty to the base of the new sprayer. Insert the new sprayer tailpiece into the opening in the sink deck.

From below, slip the friction washer up over the sprayer tailpiece. Screw the mounting nut onto the tailpiece and tighten with a basin wrench or channel-type pliers. Do not overtighten. Wipe away any excess plumber's putty.

Screw the coupling for the sprayer hose onto the hose nipple underneath the faucet body. For a good seal, apply pipe joint compound to the nipple threads first. Tighten the coupling with a basin wrench, turn on the water supply at the shutoff valves, and test the new sprayer.

LAMP SOCKET: REPLACING

Next to the cord plug, the most common source of trouble in a lamp is a worn light bulb socket. When a lamp socket assembly fails, the problem is usually with the socket-switch unit, although replacement sockets may include other parts you do not need.

Lamp failure is not always caused by a bad socket. You can avoid unnecessary repairs by checking the lamp cord, plug, and light bulb before replacing the socket.

Tools & Materials ▶

Replacement socket
Continuity tester
Screwdriver

Socket-mounted switch types are usually interchangeable: choose a replacement you prefer. Clockwise from top left: twist knob, remote switch, pull chain, push lever.

Tip ▶

When replacing a lamp socket, you can improve a standard ON-OFF lamp by installing a three-way socket.

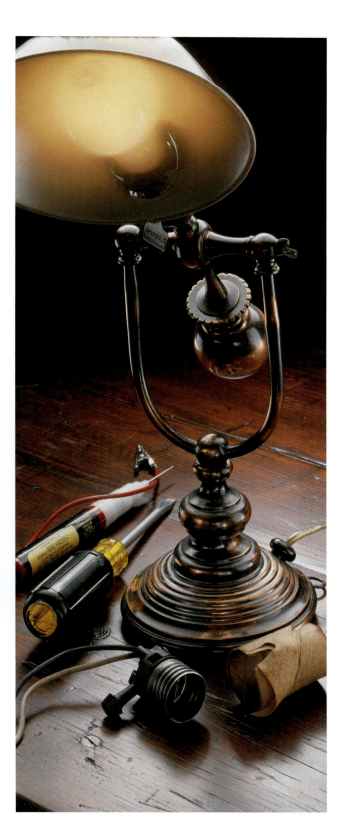

HOW TO REPAIR OR REPLACE A LAMP SOCKET

1 Contact tab

Unplug lamp. Remove shade, light bulb, and harp (shade bracket). Scrape contact tab clean with a small screwdriver. Pry contact tab up slightly if flattened inside socket. Replace bulb, plug in lamp, and test. If lamp does not work, unplug, remove bulb, and continue with next step.

2 Outer shell

Insulating sleeve

Squeeze outer shell of socket near Press marking, and lift it off. On older lamps, socket may be held by screws found at the base of the screw socket. Slip off cardboard insulating sleeve. If sleeve is damaged, replace entire socket.

3

Check for loose wire connections on screw terminals. Refasten any loose connections, then reassemble lamp, and test. If connections are not loose, remove the wires, lift out the socket, and continue with the next step.

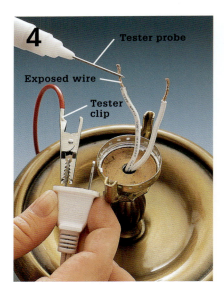

4 Tester probe

Exposed wire

Tester clip

Test for lamp cord problems with continuity tester. Place clip of tester on one prong of plug. Touch probe to one exposed wire, then to the other wire. Repeat test with other prong of plug. If tester fails to light for either prong, then replace the cord and plug. Retest the lamp.

5 Silver screw

Ridged insulation   Smooth insulation

If cord and plug are functional, then choose a replacement socket marked with the same amp and volt ratings as the old socket. One half of flat-cord lamp wire is covered by insulation that is ridged or marked: attach this wire to the silver screw terminal. Connect other wire to brass screw.

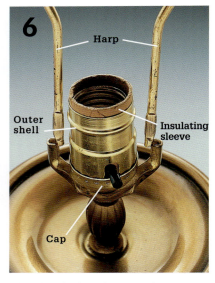

6 Harp

Outer shell   Insulating sleeve

Cap

Slide insulating sleeve and outer shell over socket so that socket and screw terminals are fully covered and switch fits into sleeve slot. Press socket assembly down into cap until socket locks into place. Replace harp, light bulb, and shade.

LAP SIDING: INSTALLING

1

Cover the exterior walls with housewrap so the stud marks fall on the studs (see pages 241 to 242). Starting at the lowest corner of the house, snap a level line at the bottom of the wall where the siding will begin. The siding should cover the sill plate but stay above grade and concrete surfaces.

2

Install a corner trim board flush with the outside wall and flush with the chalk line at the bottom. Keep nails 1" from each end and ¾" from the edges. Drive two nails every 16". Overlap a second trim board on the adjacent side, aligning the edge with the face of the first board, and nail in place.

3

When two or more corner trim pieces are needed to complete a wall, cut a 45° bevel on the end of each board. Apply primer to the cut ends. Install the first board so the bevel faces away from the house. Place the top piece over the first board, aligning the bevels. Stagger seams between adjacent sides.

4

Place a corner trim board in an inside corner. Drive nails every 16".

(continued)

5

Measure and cut trim to fit around a window. Install trim along the bottom of the window first, then measure and cut trim to fit along the sides, flush with the bottom edge of the first trim piece and ⅛" above the top of the drip cap. Measure and cut trim to fit over the window, flush with the outside edges of the side trim. Drive two nails in the trim pieces every 16". Repeat for each window and door.

Option: Rather than install the trim first, wait until after the siding is in place. Then, nail the trim directly over the siding. Make sure the nails are long enough to penetrate through the siding and sheathing and into the studs by at least 1".

6

On horizontal eaves, install frieze boards directly under the soffits. Butt the frieze boards against the corner trim, and drive two nails every 16" into studs.

7

Use a T-bevel to determine the angle on the gable end of the house. Cut this angle on the end of a frieze board, and install under the soffits.

8

Install wood lath along the base of the walls. Align the bottom edge of the lath with the chalk line and nail in place using 6d nails. Keep the lath ⅛" from the corner trim. *Tip: Rather than buying lath, rip panels of wood or fiber-cement siding to 1½"-wide strips, and use them as lath.*

9

Cut the first siding panel so it ends halfway over a stud when the other end is placed ⅛" from a corner trim board. Apply primer to the cut end. Align the siding with the bottom edge of the lath. Keep a ⅛" gap between the siding and corner trim. Nail the panel at each stud location 1" from the top edge using siding nails.

10

Stud
location

Measure and cut the next panel so it reaches the opposite corner or falls at the midpoint of a stud. Set the panel over the lath, keeping a ⅛" gap between the first panel and the second panel. Nail the panel ⅜" from the seam edge and at every stud.

11

Set the measuring gauge (inset photo) to give the panels a minimum of 1¼" overlap. Place the second row of panels over the first, using the measuring gauge to set the amount of overlap. Offset seams by at least one stud. Repeat this procedure for subsequent rows. Check every five or six rows for level. Make adjustments in small increments. Cut or notch panels as necessary to fit around protrusions in the walls.

(continued)

For windows, slide the siding panel against the bottom window trim. Mark the panel ⅛" from the outside edges of the side trim. Place a scrap piece of siding next to the window trim at the proper overlap. Mark the depth of the cut ⅛" below the bottom trim. Transfer the measurement to the siding panel and cut it to fit. Install the cutout panel around the window. Do the same at the top of the window.

Option: Siding 12" or wider, or siding nailed 24" on center, needs to be facenailed. The siding is overlapped a minimum of 1¼" and nailed ¾ to 1" from the bottom. Drive the nail through both planks of siding into the stud using corrosion-resistant siding nails.

When installing the siding over a roof line, keep the panels 1 to 2" above the roofing. Use a T-bevel to determine the angle of the roof line, and transfer the angle to the siding. Cut the panels to fit. Place the bottom edge of the siding over the roof flashing, and nail the panel in place.

14

Frieze

Rip the last row of panels to fit ⅛" below the frieze boards under the horizontal eaves. Nail the panels in place.

15

Use a T-bevel to determine the angle of the roof line on the gable ends of the house. Transfer the angle to the panels, and cut them to fit.

16

Keep the panels ⅛" from the rake boards, and nail them in place along the gable end.

17

Fill all gaps between panels and trim with flexible, paintable caulk. Paint the siding as desired (see Painting & Staining Siding, beginning on page 298).

LIGHTS: CEILING

Ceiling fixtures don't have any moving parts and their wiring is very simple, so, other than changing bulbs, you're likely to get decades of trouble-free service from a fixture. This sounds like a good thing, but it also means that the fixture probably won't fail and give you an excuse to update a room's look with a new one. Fortunately, you don't need an excuse. Upgrading a fixture is easy and can make a dramatic impact on a room. You can substantially increase the light in a room by replacing a globe-style fixture by one with separate spot lights, or you can simply install a new fixture that matches the room's décor.

Tools & Materials ▸

Replacement light fixture	Hacksaw
Wire stripper	Pliers
Voltage sensor	Hammer
Insulated screwdrivers	
Wire connectors	
Eye protection	

Installing a new ceiling fixture can provide more light to a space, not to mention an aesthetic lift. It's one of the easiest upgrades you can do.

HOW TO REPLACE A CEILING LIGHT

1

Shut off power to the ceiling light and remove the shade or diffuser. Loosen the mounting screws and carefully lower the fixture, supporting it as you work (do not let light fixtures hang by their electrical wires alone). Test with a voltage sensor to make sure no power is reaching the connections.

2

Remove the twist connectors from the fixture wires or unscrew the screw terminals and remove the white neutral wire and the black lead wire (inset).

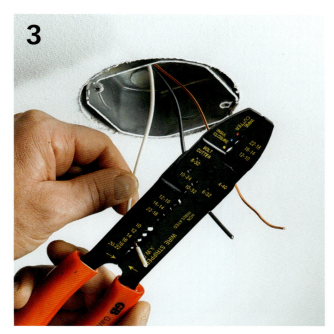

3

Before you install the new fixture, check the ends of the wires coming from the ceiling electrical box. They should be clean and free of nicks or scorch marks. If they're dirty or worn, clip off the stripped portion with your combination tool. Then strip away about ¾" of insulation from the end of each wire.

4

Attach a mounting strap to the ceiling fixture box if there is not one already present. Your new light may come equipped with a strap, otherwise you can find one for purchase at any hardware store.

(continued)

5

Lift the new fixture up to the ceiling (you may want a helper for this) and attach the bare copper ground wire from the power supply cable to the grounding screw or clip on the mounting strap. Also attach the ground wire from the fixture to the screw or clip.

6

With the fixture supported by a ladder or a helper, join the white wire lead and the white fixture wire with a wire connector (often supplied with the fixture).

7

Connect the black power supply wire to the black fixture wire with a wire connector.

8

Position the new fixture mounting plate over the box so the mounting screw holes align. Drive the screws until the fixture is secure against the ceiling. *Note: Some fixtures are supported by a threaded rod or nipple in the center that screws into a female threaded opening in the mounting strap (inset).*

LIGHTS: CEILING: RECESSED

Mark the location for the light canister. If you are installing multiple lights, measure out from the wall at the start and end of the run, and connect them with a chalkline snapped parallel to the wall. If the ceiling is finished with a surface (wallboard), see next page.

Install the housing for the recessed fixture. Housings for new construction (or remodeling installations where the installation area is fully accessible from either above or below) have integral hanger bars that you attach to the each joist in the joist bay.

Run electric cable from the switch to each canister location. Multiple lights are generally installed in series so there is no need to make pigtail connections in the individual boxes. Make sure to leave enough extra cable at each location to feed the wire into the housing and make the connection.

Run the feeder cables into the electrical boxes attached to the canister housings. You'll need to remove knockouts first and make sure to secure the cable with a wire staple within 8" of the entry point to the box.

(continued)

Connect the feeder wires to the fixture wires inside the junction box. Twist the hot lead together with the black fixture wire, as well as the black lead to other fixtures further downline. Also connect the neutral white wires. Join the ground wires and pigtail them to the grounding screw or clip in the box. Finish the ceiling, as desired.

Attach your trim kit of choice. Normally, these are hung with torsion spring clips from notches or hooks inside the canister. This should be done after the ceiling is installed and finished for new construction projects. With certain types of trim kits, such as eyeball trim, you'll need to install the light bulb before the trim kit.

HOW TO CONNECT A RECESSED FIXTURE CAN IN A FINISHED CEILING

Make the hole for the can. Most fixtures will include a template for sizing the hole. Fish 14/2 cable from the switch location to the hole. Pull about 16" of cable out of the hole for making the connection.

Remove a knockout from the electrical box attached to the can. Thread the cable into the box; secure it with a cable clamp. Remove sheathing insulation. Connect the black fixture wire to the black circuit wire, the white fixture wire to the white circuit wire, and then connect the ground wire to the grounding screw or grounding wire attached to the box.

Retrofit cans secure themselves in the hole with spring-loaded clips. Install the can in the ceiling by depressing the mounting clips so the can will fit into the hole. Insert the can so that its edge is tight to the ceiling. Push the mounting clips back out so they grip the drywall and hold the fixture in place. Install the trim piece.

LIGHTS: CEILING: TRACK

Disconnect the old ceiling light fixture (for remodeling projects) after shutting off power to the circuit at the main service panel. The globe or diffuser and the lamps should be removed before the fixture mounting mechanism is detached.

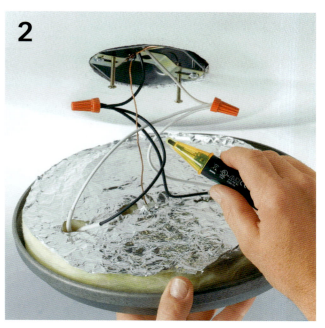

Test the fixture wires with a voltage sensor to make sure the circuit is dead. Support the fixture from below while you work—never allow a light fixture to hang by its electrical wires alone. Remove the wire connectors and pull the wires apart. Remove the old light fixture.

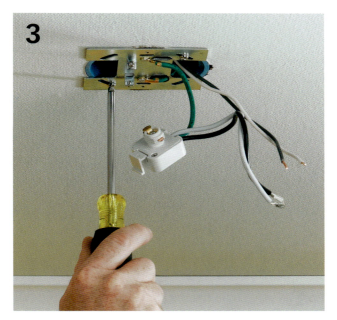

Attach the mounting strap for the new track light to the old ceiling box. If the mounting strap has a hole in the center, thread the circuit wires through the hole before screwing the strap to the box. The green or bare copper ground from the circuit should be attached to the grounding screw or clip on the strap or box.

Cut the track section to length, if necessary, using a hack saw. Deburr the cut end with a metal file. If you are installing multiple sections of track, assemble the sections with the correct connector fittings (sold separately from your kit). You can also purchase T-fittings or L-fittings (inset photo) if you wish to install tracks in either of these configurations.

(continued)

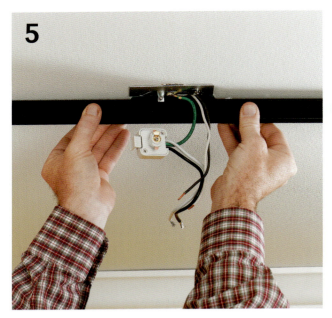

Position the track section in the mounting saddle on the mounting strap and hold it temporarily in place in the location where it will be installed. The track section will have predrilled mounting holes in the back. Draw a marking point on the ceiling at each of these locations. If your track does not have predrilled mounting holes, remove it and drill a ³⁄₁₆" hole in the back every 16".

Insert the bolt from a toggle bolt or molly bolt into each predrilled screw location and twist the toggle or molly back onto the free end. These types of hardware have greater holding power than anchor sleeves. Drill a ⅝" dia. access hole in the ceiling at each of the mounting hole locations you marked on the ceiling in step 5.

Insert the toggle or molly into the access hole far enough so it clears the top of the hole and the wings snap outward. Then tighten each bolt so the track is snug against the ceiling. If the mounting hole happens to fall over a ceiling joint, simply drive a wallboard screw at that hole location.

Hook up wires from the track's power supply fitting to the circuit wires. Connect black to black and white to white. The grounding wire from the power supply fitting can either be pigtailed to the circuit ground wire and connected to the grounding screw or clip, or it can be twisted together with the circuit grounding wire at the grounding terminal. Snap the fitting into the track if you have not already done so.

9

Attach the protective cover that came with your kit to conceal the ceiling box and the electrical connections. Some covers simply snap in place, others require a mounting screw.

10

Dead end

Cap the open ends of the track with a dead end cap fitting. These also may require a mounting screw. Leaving track ends open is a safety violation.

11

Insert the light heads into the track by slipping the stem into the track slot and then twisting it so the electrical contact points on the head press against the electrified inner rails of the track slot. Tug lightly on the head to make sure it is secure before releasing it.

12

Arrange the track light heads so their light falls in the manner you choose, and then depress the locking tab on each fixture to secure it in position. Restore power and test the lights.

LIGHTS: UNDERCABINET

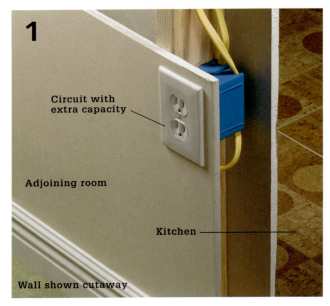

Look in the adjoining room for a usable power source in the form of a receptacle that has a box located in the wall behind your base cabinets. Unlike the small-appliance circuit with outlets in your backsplash area, these typically are not dedicated circuits (which can't be expanded). Make sure that the receptacle's circuit has enough capacity to support another load. Shut the power to the receptacle off at the main service panel and test for power.

Cut a hole in the base cabinet back panel to get access to the wall behind it in roughly the area where you know the next-door receptacle to be. Use a keyhole saw or drywall saw and make very shallow cuts until you have positively identified the locations of the electrical box and cables. Then finish the cuts with a jigsaw.

Drill an access hole into the kitchen wall for the cable that will feed the undercabinet light. A ½" dia. hole should be about the right size if you are using 12-ga. or 14-ga. sheathed NM cable.

Cut a small access hole (4 × 4" or so) in the back panel of the base cabinet directly below the undercabinet light location.

Feed the cable into the access hole at the light location until the end reaches the access hole below. Don't cut the cable yet. Reach into the access hole and feel around for the free cable end and then pull it out through the access hole once you've found it. Cut the cable, making sure to leave plenty of extra on both ends.

String the cable into a piece of flexible conduit that's long enough to reach between the two access holes in the base cabinets. Attach a connector to each end of the conduit to protect the cable sheathing from the sharp edges of the cut metal. Tip: *To make patching the cabinet back easier, drill a new access hole for the cable near the square access hole.*

Hang the conduit with hanger straps attached to the base cabinet frame or back panel, drilling holes in the side walls of the cabinet where necessary to thread the conduit through. On back panels, use small screws to hang the straps instead of brads or nails. Support the conduit near both the entrance and the exit holes (the conduit should extend past the back panels by a couple of inches).

Variation: If you are installing more than one undercabinet light, run the cable down from each installation point as you did for the first light. Mount an electrical junction box to the cabinet back near the receptacle providing the power. Run the power cables from each light through flexible conduit and make connections inside the junction box. Be sure to attach the junction box cover once the connections are made.

(continued)

Remove the receptacle from the box you are tying into and insert the new circuit cable into one of the knockouts using a cable clamp. Check a wire capacity chart to make sure the box is big enough for the new conductors. Replace it with a larger box if necessary. Reinstall the receptacle once the connections are made.

Install the undercabinet light. Some models have a removable diffuser that allows access to the fixture wires, and these should be screwed to the upper cabinet prior to making your wiring hookups. Other models need to be connected to the circuit wires before installation. Check your manufacturer's installations.

Connect wires inside the light fixture according to the light manufacturer's directions. Make sure the incoming cable is stapled just before it enters the light box and that a cable clamp is used at the knockout in the box to protect the cable. Restore the power and test the light.

Cut patches of hardboard and fit them over the access holes, overlapping the edges of the cutouts. Adhere them to the cabinet backs with panel adhesive.

LINOLEUM TILE: INSTALLING

Like sheet linoleum, linoleum tile is a natural floor covering produced from sustainable resources that include linseed oil, pine resin, and other organic additives. These ingredients make for an exceptionally green floor covering with little or no negative impact in air quality in your home. Linoleum is also antistatic and has antimicrobial properties that inhibit the growth of germs and harmful microorganisms.

Although linoleum is still offered as sheet flooring, the far easier option to install is linoleum tile in the form of "click" panels, such as the Marmoleum product seen here. These tiles are comprised of a linoleum surface bonded over moisture-resistant, high-density fiberboard. A cork layer also adds a comfortable feel underfoot and dampens sound transmission. The flooring is available in 12-inch square tiles and panels sized at 12 inches by 36 inches.

These formats—and a noteworthy palette of available colors—give you a great deal of flexibility in designing a floor to fit your décor. Although the moisture-resistant nature of linoleum tile makes it a great choice for kitchens and baths, the dusky colors, appealing finish, and comfortable, warm feel make it appropriate for just about any room or décor. The tiles and panels can be mixed and matched to create a complex pattern of shapes and shades, or you can use one or the other to create a floor design that's more restful visually.

No matter what colors or design you choose, installing a linoleum click floor is an easy process. The panels can be installed over any clean, dry, structurally sound surface with no more than $\frac{3}{32}$-inch of height variation per six feet of surface. The panels are simply snapped together row by row. And because the process uses no glue or adhesive, the floor can be walked on as soon as you're done installing it.

Tools & Materials ▸

Circular saw, jigsaw, or handsaw	Eye and ear protection	Speed square	Glue
Clamps	$\frac{3}{8}$" spacers	Wedge	Tape measure
	Linoleum click tiles	2 × 4 scrap lumber	

Click-together planks with linoleum for the top layer make striped floor patterns very easy to create. You can choose two colors to alternate, or several colors, preferably within a single family of tones.

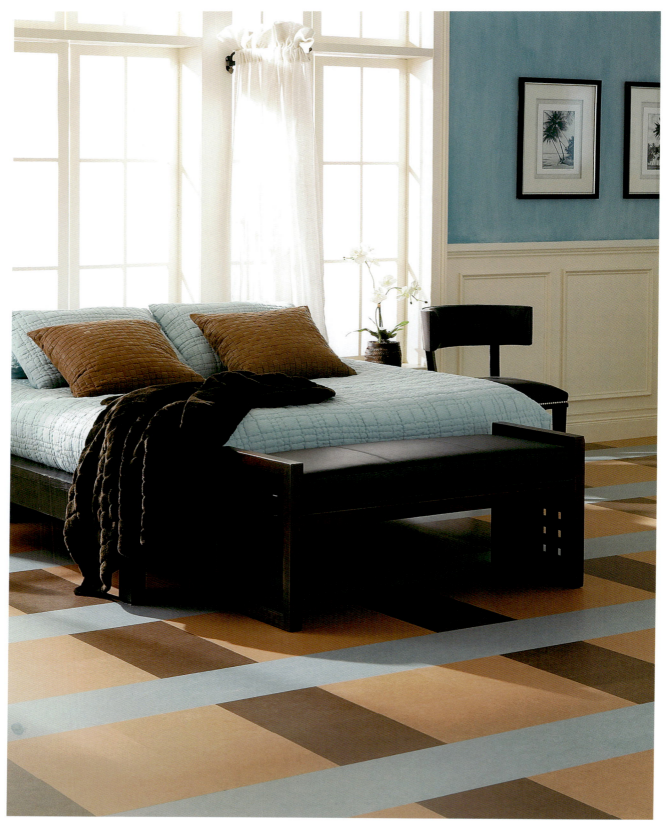

Visually, this floor features the soft, natural beauty of linoleum. But where sheets of linoleum typically require a professional installer, the click-together tiles used here are as easy to install as any laminate flooring made for DIYers.

INSTALLING LINOLEUM TILES OR STRIPS

1

Prepare the subfloor and the flooring. Ensure that the subfloor surface is clean and free of protrusions. Remove tiles or panels from the box and inspect each one for damage. Choose the first panel or tile in the starter row and saw off the tongue from the sides that will butt against walls. Make sure the workpiece is clamped securely and use a circular saw, jigsaw, or handsaw to trim off the tongues.

2

Position the first panel or tile in the corner of the longest wall (preferably opposite to the largest window in the room), positioning the sides from which the tongue has been removed against the walls. Use ⅜" spacers to maintain an expansion gap between the panels and the walls.

3

Position the tongue end of the second panel or tile inside the groove in the first, with the far end raised about 30°. Lower the raised end to lock the second panel into the first. Continue installing the row in this fashion, positioning two spacers evenly along the length of each panel.

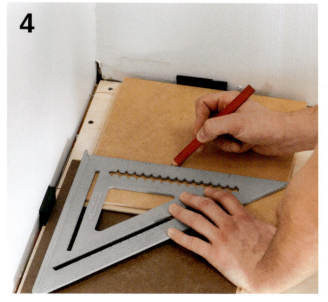

4

Measure the last panel or tile in the row for cutting by placing it on top of the preceding panel and butting it to the corner walls. The end panel should be marked on the top side (linoleum surface), with the groove side facing the wall. This is to ensure that the tongue of the end panel piece matches the preceding panel's groove. Click the end panel into place.

(continued)

Begin the second row. Set the edge tongue on the preceding row's lip. Slide the wedge under the tile. Connect the next tile in the row to the first tile, set on the preceding row's lip, and slide the wedge under the strip.

Continue connecting second-row panels or tiles to each other until you have completed the row. Slide wedges out from underneath the row. Use a 2 × 4 scrap piece to brace against the second row edges and push the entire row forward to engage with the lips on the first row's panels. Lower the second row to lock the rows together.

Install the remaining rows in the same manner, changing the measurement of the first panel in each row by 12" from the preceding row if you are installing strip panels. Measure, mark, and rip the pieces in the final row, using a circular saw and cutting on the faces of the pieces to prevent tearout. The final row is installed in the same way as previous rows.

Door Casings ▸

Glue

Where final panels must slide under door casings or other obstructions, remove the locking ridge from the groove side of the previous row. Lay a bead of glue along the modified groove. Slide the final row panel into place under the obstruction and pull it back snug against the glue-coated groove.

MEDICINE CABINETS

Common bathroom cabinets include vanities, medicine cabinets, linen cabinets, and "tank topper" cabinets that mount over the toilet area. See pages 253 to 259 for more information on cabinets.

When installing cabinets in a damp location, like a bathroom, choose the best cabinets you can afford. Look for quality indicators, like doweled construction, hardwood doors and drawers, and high-gloss, moisture-resistant finishes. Avoid cabinets with sides or doors that are painted on one side and finished with laminate or veneer on the other because these cabinets are more likely to warp.

Tools & Materials ▶

Electronic stud finder	Framing square
Level	Duplex nails
Pry bar	10d common nails
Hammer	Finish nails
Screwdriver	1 × 4 lumber
Drill	2½" wood screws
Circular saw	Wood shims
Reciprocating saw	Cabinet
Pencil	Measuring tape
Bar clamp	Protective equipment

A medicine cabinet is wall-mounted or recessed above a lavatory sink. They are better suited for storing toiletries than medicine.

HOW TO INSTALL A SURFACE-MOUNTED MEDICINE CABINET

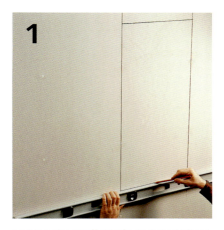

1

Locate the wall studs and mark them clearly on the wall surface. Draw a level line at the desired top height of the cabinet body, then measure and mark a second line to indicate the bottom of the cabinet.

2

Attach a temporary ledger board (usually 1 × 4) just below the lower level line using duplex nails. Rest the base of the cabinet on the ledger and hold it in place or brace it with 2 × 4s.

3

Attach the cabinet to the wall at the stud locations by drilling pilot holes and driving wood screws. Remove the ledger when finished, and patch the nail holes with drywall compound.

HOW TO INSTALL A RECESSED MEDICINE CABINET

Locate the first stud beyond either side of the planned cabinet location, then remove the wall surface between the studs. (Removing the wall surface all the way to the ceiling simplifies patch work.) Cut along the center of the studs, using a circular saw with the blade depth set to the thickness of the wall surface.

Mark a rough opening ½" taller than the cabinet frame onto the exposed wall studs. Add 1½" for each header and sill plate, then cut out the studs in the rough opening area.

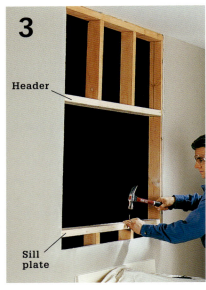

Frame out the top and bottom of the rough opening by installing a header and a sill plate between the cut wall studs. Make sure the header and sill plate are level, then nail them in place with 10d common nails.

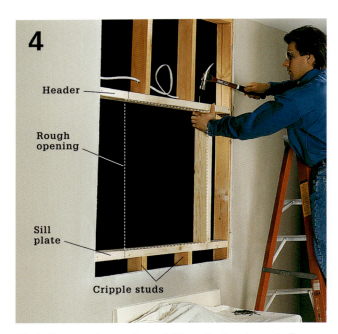

Mark the rough opening width on the header and sill plates, centering the opening over the sink. Cut and nail jack studs between the header and the sill plate, just outside the rough opening marks. Install any wiring for new light fixtures and receptacles, then patch the wall where necessary.

Position the cabinet in the opening. Check it for level with a carpenter's level, then attach the cabinet by drilling pilot holes and driving wood screws through the top and bottom of the cabinet sides and into the wall studs, header, and sill plate. Attach the doors, shelves, and hardware.

MITERED CASING FOR WINDOWS & DOORS

On each jamb, mark a reveal line ³⁄₁₆" to ¼" from the inside edge. The casings will be installed flush with these lines.

Place a length of casing along one side jamb, flush with the reveal line. At the top and bottom of the molding, mark the points where horizontal and vertical reveal lines meet. (When working with doors, mark the molding at the top only.)

Make 45° miter cuts on the ends of the moldings. Measure and cut the other vertical molding piece, using the same method.

Drill pilot holes spaced every 12" to prevent splitting, and attach the vertical casings with 4d finish nails driven through the casings and into the jambs. Drive 6d finish nails into the framing members near the outside edge of the casings.

Measure the distance between the side casings and cut top and bottom casings to fit, with ends mitered at 45°. If the window or door unit is not perfectly square, make test cuts on scrap pieces to find the correct angle of the joints. Drill pilot holes and attach with 4d and 6d finish nails.

Locknail the corner joints by drilling pilot holes and driving 4d finish nails through each corner, as shown. Drive all nail heads below the wood surface, using a nail set, then fill the nail holes with wood putty.

MITERED RETURNS

Mitered returns are a decorative treatment used to hide the end grain of wood and provide a finished appearance when molding stops prior to the end of a wall. Mitered returns range from tiny pieces of base shoe up to very large crown moldings. They are also commonly used when installing a stool and apron treatment or on decorative friezes above doors.

Bevel returns are another simple return option for chair rails, baseboards, and base shoe. A bevel return is simply a cut at the end of the molding that "returns" the workpiece back to the wall at an angle. The biggest advantage to using mitered returns rather than bevel returns is that mitered returns already have a finish applied. Bevel returns require more touchups.

Cutting mitered returns for small moldings, such as quarter round, or for thin stock, such as baseboard, can be tricky when using a power miter saw. The final cut of the process leaves the return loose where it can sometimes be thrown from the saw by the air current of the blade. Plan on using a piece of trim that is long enough to cut comfortably, or you will find yourself fighting the saw.

Tools & Materials ›

Combination square	Pneumatic finish
Utility knife	nail gun
Power miter saw	Air compressor
Miter box and	Air hose
back saw	T-bevel
Pencil	Molding
Tape measure	Wood glue
	Eye protection

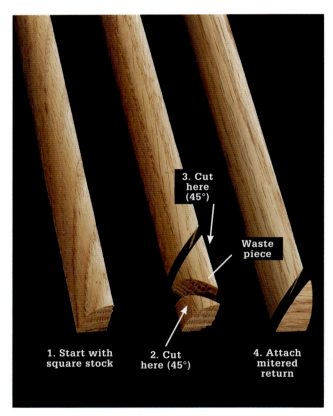

1. Start with square stock
2. Cut here (45°)
3. Cut here (45°)
Waste piece
4. Attach mitered return

Returns are made from two 45° angle cuts. The scrap piece is removed and the return piece is glued into place.

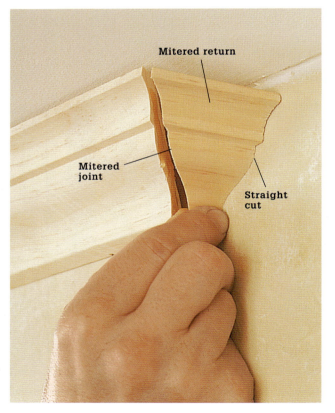

Mitered return
Mitered joint
Straight cut

Mitered returns finish molding ends that would otherwise be exposed. Miter the main piece as you would at an outside corner. Cut a miter on the return piece, then cut it to length with a straight cut so it butts to the wall. Attach the return piece with wood glue.

MITERING INSIDE CORNERS

Although most professionals prefer to cope-cut inside corners, it is common to see moldings that are mitered to inside corners. These joints are more likely to separate over time and to allow gaps to show. For that reason it is not advised to use inside corner miters when installing a stain-grade trim product. The gaps will be visible and are very difficult to fill with putty. For paint-grade projects, mitering inside corners makes more sense because joints can be filled and sanded before the top coats of paint are applied.

Tools & Materials ▸

Miter saw	Air compressor
Pencil	Air hose
Tape measure	Molding
Utility knife	T-bevel
Pneumatic finish	Eye protection
nail gun	Work gloves

HOW TO MITER SQUARE INSIDE CORNERS

Set the miter saw to 45° and place the first piece of trim on edge, flat on the miter box table and flush against the fence. Hold the piece firmly in place with your left hand and cut the trim with a slow, steady motion. Release the power button and remove the molding after the blade stops.

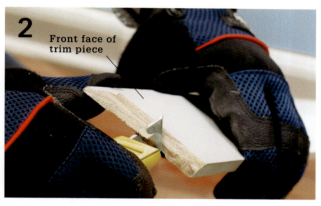

Back-cut the inside edge of the trim piece with a utility knife so that the top corner will sit flush against the wall corner.

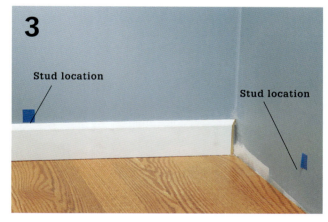

Butt the molding tightly against the wall and tack it into place. Adjust the blade of the miter saw to the opposite 45° angle and cut the mating piece.

Test the fit of the joint, adjusting the miter angle if necessary. Once the fit is tight, nail both pieces at stud locations.

OUT-OF-PLUMB CORNER CUTS

Out-of-plumb walls are concave, convex, or simply not perpendicular to the floor and ceiling at one or more points. It is a common condition. In some cases, the condition is caused by the fact that drywall sheets have tapered edges to make taping joints easier and the tapers fall at the edge of a work area where trim is installed. In other cases, the condition may be caused by wall framing issues. In either case, you'll find that it's easier to adapt your trim pieces to the wall than to try and straighten the finished wall surface. To do this, the trim pieces need to be cut to match the out-of-plumb area, to compensate for the taper in the panel. Another option is to install a running spacer along the bottom edge and then to cut your molding square, as shown on the previous page.

Bevel gauge

TIP: Occasionally, a compound cut is necessary for cutting miters on out-of-plumb corners. When this situation arises, set the bevel of the miter saw to match the out-of-plumb wall and miter the angle at the appropriate degree. Compound cuts can be difficult to get right the first time, so test the fit with a piece of scrap material first.

HOW TO MAKE OUT-OF-PLUMB CORNER CUTS

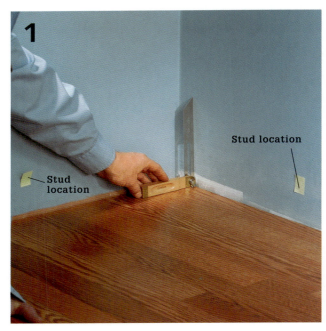

Stud location

Stud location

Place a T-bevel into the corner and press the blade flush to the wall surface. Tighten the adjustment knob so the blade conforms to the angle of the profile of the wall.

Transfer the angle of the T-bevel to the miter saw blade by locking the saw in the down position and adjusting the angle to match the angle of the T-bevel. Cut the molding to match the angle.

MITERING OUTSIDE CORNERS

Cutting outside miters is one of the main functions of a power miter saw. Most saws have positive stops (called detents) at 45° in each direction, so standard outside corners are practically cut for you by the saw. Keep in mind that your saw must be accurately set up to cut joints squarely. Read the owner's manual for setting up your saw as well as for safety precautions. Before you begin, check the walls for square with a combination square or a framing square. If the corner is very close to square, proceed with the square corner installation. If the corner is badly out of square, follow the "Out of Square" procedure on the following page.

Tools & Materials ▸

Combination square or framing square	Air compressor
	Air hose
Miter saw	T-bevel
Pencil	Molding
Tape measure	Masking tape
Pneumatic finish nail gun	1 × 4
	Eye protection

HOW TO MITER OUTSIDE CORNERS

Set the miter saw to 45°. Position the first piece on edge, flat on the miter box table, flush against the fence. Hold the piece firmly in place with your left hand and cut the trim with a slow, steady motion. Release the power button of the saw and remove the molding after the blade stops.

Set the miter saw blade to the opposing 45° positive stop. Place the second piece of molding on edge, flat on the saw table, flush against the fence. Fasten the piece tightly in place with a hold-down or clamp. Cut the molding with a slow, steady motion.

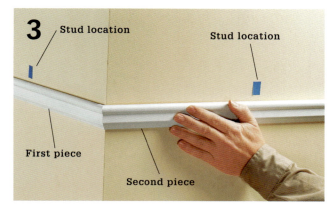

With the first piece of molding tacked in place, hold the second piece in position and check the fit of the joint. If the joint is tight, nail both pieces at stud locations with a pneumatic finish nail gun.

If the corner joint does not fit tightly, shim the workpiece away from the fence to make minor adjustments until the joint fits tightly. Shims should be a uniform thickness. Playing cards work well as shims.

HOW TO MITER OUT-OF-SQUARE OUTSIDE CORNERS: METHOD 1

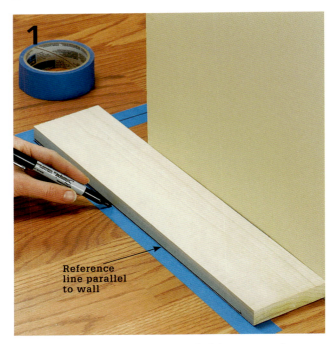

Draw a reference line off each wall of the corner using a straight 1 × 4. Put masking tape down on the finished floor to avoid scuffing it and to see your lines clearly. Trace along each wall, connecting the traced lines at a point out from the tip of the corner.

To find the angle you need to miter your moldings, place a T-bevel with the handle flush against one wall, and adjust the blade so that it intersects the point where your reference lines meet. Lock the blade in place at this angle.

HOW TO MITER OUT-OF-SQUARE OUTSIDE CORNERS: METHOD 2

Use a digital angle finder to record the exact outside corner angle. These tools are sold in a wide price range, with some costing as little as $30.

Do some math. If the outside corner angle is not a whole number (most angle finders give readings in 0.1° increments), then round up. For example, if the angle finder measures the outside angle at 91.4°, round up to 92° and cut the miter at 44° (180° - 92° = 88° and the miter is half of this, which is 44°). A big mistake is to divide the angle in half without subtracting it from 180. In this case, a 92° angle readout divided in half would yield 46°, which at 2° off the mark would easily cause a visible mistake in the miter.

WALLS & CEILINGS

NOTCHING JOISTS & RAFTERS

BORING & NOTCHING DEFINITIONS

A bore is a hole drilled in a stud or joist. Use the actual dimensions to determine the depth of framing lumber and when calculating the maximum hole diameter.

A notch is a piece cut from the smaller dimension of framing lumber such as a stud or joist. Use the actual dimensions to determine the depth of framing lumber and when calculating the maximum notch depth. Actual dimensions are the dimensions of framing lumber after finishing at the mill. Example: the nominal dimensions of a 2 × 6 are two inches by six inches and the actual dimensions, after finishing, are about 1½ inches by 5½ inches.

WOOD JOIST NOTCHING & BORING

1. You may notch solid lumber rafters, floor and ceiling joists, and beams not deeper than one-sixth the depth of the member. You may notch the ends of the member not deeper than one fourth the depth of the member. Example: notch a 2 × 10 joist not deeper than 1½ inches, except at the ends where you may notch not deeper than 2⁵⁄₁₆ inches.

2. You may notch solid lumber rafters, floor and ceiling joists, and beams not longer than one-third the depth of the member. Example: notch the top or bottom of a 2 × 10 joist not longer than 3¹⁄₁₆ inches.

3. You may notch solid lumber rafters, floor and ceiling joists, and beams only within the outer one-third of the span. Example: notch a 10-foot long joist only within 40 inches from each end.

4. You may notch the tension side (bottom) of solid lumber rafters, floor and ceiling joists, and beams more than four inches thick only at the ends.

5. You may drill holes in solid lumber rafters, floor and ceiling joists, and beams with a diameter not more than one-third of the depth of the member. Example: drill a hole with a diameter not more than 3⅛ inches in a 2 × 10 joist.

6. Locate holes at least two inches from the edge of the member and at least two inches from any other hole or notch.

7. Use actual joist depths, not nominal joist depths. Example: use 9¼ inches for a 2 × 10 joist, not the nominal depth of 10 inches.

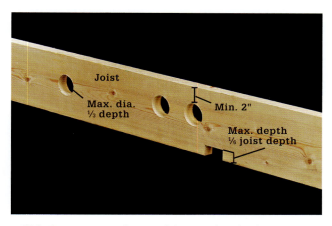

Drill holes not more than ⅓ of the member depth and cut member notches not deeper than ⅙ of the member depth.

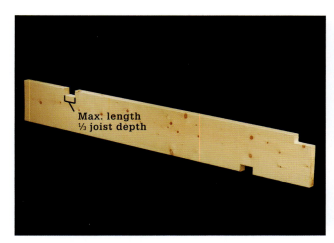

Notch wood joists and rafters not longer than ⅓ of the depth and only in the outer ⅓ of the member.

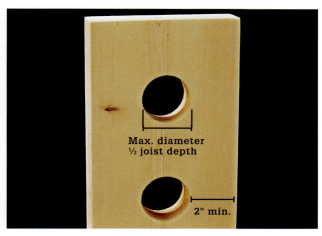

Drill holes in wood joists and rafters not larger than ⅓ the depth and at least 2" from the edge of the member.

PAINTING EXTERIORS: PREPARING

The key to an even paint job is to work on a smooth, clean, dry surface—so preparing the surface is essential. Generally, the more preparation work you do, the smoother the final finish will be and the longer it will last.

For the smoothest finish, sand all the way down to the bare wood with a power sander. For a less time-consuming (but rougher) finish, scrape off any loose paint, then spot-sand rough areas. You can use pressure washing to remove some of the flaking paint, but by itself, pressure washing won't create a smooth surface for painting.

Tools & Materials ▸

Pressure washer	Heat gun
Scrapers	Coarse abrasive pad
Siding sander	Wire-wheel attachment
Finishing sander	Proper respiratory protection
Sanding block	Sandpaper (80-, 120-, 150-grit)
Putty knife	Putty
Stiff-bristle brush	Paintable siliconized caulk
Wire brush	Muriatic acid
Steel wool	Sealant
Drill	Colored push pins or tape
Caulk gun	Protective equipment

The amount of surface preparation you do will largely determine the final appearance of your paint job. Decide how much sanding and scraping you're willing to do to obtain a finish you'll be happy with.

HOW TO REMOVE PAINT

Use a heat gun to loosen thick layers of old paint. Aim the gun at the surface, warm the paint until it starts to bubble, then scrape the paint as soon as it releases.

To remove large areas of paint on wood lap siding, use a siding sander with a disk that's as wide as the reveal on your siding.

HOW TO PREPARE SURFACES FOR PAINT

Clean the surface and remove loose paint by pressure washing the house. As you work, direct the water stream downward, and don't get too close to the surface with the sprayer head. Allow all surfaces to dry thoroughly before continuing.

Scrape off loose paint using a paint scraper. Be careful not to damage the surface by scraping too hard.

Smooth out rough paint with a finishing sander and 80-grit sandpaper. Use sanding blocks and 80- to 120-grit sandpaper to sand hard-to-reach areas of trim. *Tip: You can make sanding blocks from dowels, wood scraps, or garden hoses.*

Use detail scrapers to remove loose paint in hard-to-reach areas. Some of these scrapers have interchangeable heads that match common trim profiles.

Inspect all surfaces for cracks, rot, and other damage. Mark affected areas with colored pushpins or tape. Fill the holes and cracks with epoxy wood filler.

Use a finishing sander with 120-grit sandpaper to sand down repaired areas, ridges, and hard edges left from the scraping process, creating a smooth surface.

HOW TO PREPARE WINDOW & DOOR TRIM FOR PAINT

Scuff-sand glossy surfaces on doors, window casings, and all surfaces painted with enamel paint. Use a coarse abrasive pad or 150-grit sandpaper.

Fill cracks in siding and gaps around window and door trim with paintable siliconized acrylic caulk.

HOW TO REMOVE CLEAR FINISHES

Pressure wash stained or unpainted surfaces that have been treated with a wood preservative or protectant before recoating them with fresh sealant.

Use a stiff-bristle brush to dislodge any flakes of loosened surface coating that weren't removed by pressure washing. Don't use a wire brush on wood surfaces.

HOW TO PREPARE METAL & MASONRY FOR PAINT

Remove rust and loose paint from metal hardware, such as railings and ornate trim, using a wire brush. Cover the surface with metal primer immediately after brushing to prevent the formation of new rust.

Scuff-sand metal siding and trim with medium-coarse steel wool or a coarse abrasive pad. Wash the surface and let dry before priming and painting.

Remove loose mortar, mineral deposits, or paint from mortar lines in masonry surfaces with a drill and wire-wheel attachment. Clean broad, flat masonry surfaces with a wire brush. Correct any minor damage before repainting.

Dissolve rust on metal hardware with diluted muriatic acid solution. When working with muriatic acid, it's important to wear safety equipment, work in a well-ventilated area, and follow all manufacturer's directions and precautions.

PAINTING: EXTERIORS

Schedule priming and painting tasks so that you can paint within two weeks of priming surfaces. If more than two weeks pass, wash the surface with soap and water before applying the next coat.

Check the weather forecast and keep an eye on the sky while you work. Damp weather or rain within two hours of application will ruin a paint job. Don't paint when the temperature is below 50° or above 90°F. Avoid painting on windy days—it's dangerous to be on a ladder in high winds, and wind blows dirt onto the fresh paint.

Plan each day's work so you can follow the shade. Prepare, prime, and paint one face of the house at a time, and follow a logical painting order. Work from the top of the house down to the foundation, covering an entire section before you move the ladder or scaffolding.

Tools & Materials ▸

Paintbrush (4", 2½", 3")	Primer
Sash brush	House paint
Scaffolding	Trim paint
Ladders	Cleanup materials
Paint roller	Protective equipment

Paint in a logical order, starting from the top and working your way down. Cover as much surface as you can reach comfortably without moving your ladder or scaffolding. After the paint or primer dries, touch up any unpainted areas that were covered by the ladder or ladder stabilizer.

TIPS FOR APPLYING PRIMER & PAINT

Use the right primer and paint for each job. Always read the manufacturer's recommendations.

Plan your painting sequence so you paint the walls, doors, and trim before painting stairs and porch floors. This prevents the need to touch up spills.

Apply primer and paint in the shade or indirect sunlight. Direct sun can dry primers and paints too quickly and trap moisture below the surface, which leads to blistering and peeling.

TIPS FOR SELECTING BRUSHES & ROLLERS

Wall brushes, which are thick, square brushes 3 to 5" wide, are designed to carry a lot of paint and distribute it widely. *Tip: It's good to keep a variety of clean brushes on hand, including 2½", 3", and 4" flat brushes, 2" and 3" trim brushes, and tapered sash brushes.*

Trim and tapered sash brushes, which are 2 to 3" wide, are good for painting doors and trim, and for cutting in small areas.

Paint rollers work best for quickly painting smooth surfaces. Use an 8 or 9" roller sleeve for broad surfaces.

Use a 3" roller to paint flat-surfaced trim, such as end caps and corner trim.

TIPS FOR LOADING & DISTRIBUTING PAINT

Load your brush with the right amount of paint for the area you're covering. Use a full load of paint for broad areas, a moderate load for smaller areas and feathering strokes, and a light load when painting or working around trim.

Hold the brush at a 45° angle and apply just enough downward pressure to flex the bristles and squeeze the paint from the brush.

HOW TO USE A PAINTBRUSH

Load the brush with a full load of paint. Starting at one end of the surface, make a long, smooth stroke until the paint begins to feather out. *Tip: Paint color can vary from one can to the next. To avoid problems, pour all of your paint into one large container and mix it thoroughly. Pour the mixed paint back into the individual cans and seal them carefully. Stir each can before use.*

At the end of the stroke, lift the brush without leaving a definite ending point. If the paint appears uneven or contains heavy brush marks, smooth it out without overbrushing.

Reload the brush and make a stroke from the opposite direction, painting over the feathered end of the first stroke to create a smooth, even surface. If the junction of the two strokes is visible, rebrush with a light coat of paint. Feather out the starting point of the second stroke.

TIPS FOR USING PAINT ROLLERS

Wet the roller nap, then squeeze out the excess water. Position a roller screen inside a 5-gal. bucket. Dip the roller into the paint, then roll it back and forth across the roller screen. The roller sleeve should be full but not dripping when lifted from the bucket.

Cone-shaped rollers work well for painting the joints between intersecting surfaces.

Doughnut-shaped rollers work well for painting the edges of lap siding and moldings.

HOW TO PAINT FASCIA, SOFFITS & TRIM

Prime all surfaces to be painted, and allow ample drying time. Paint the face of the fascia first, then cut in paint at the bottom edges of the soffit panels. *Tip: Fascia and soffits are usually painted the same color as the trim.*

Paint the soffit panels and trim with a 4" brush. Start by cutting in around the edges of the panels using the narrow edge of the brush, then feather in the broad surfaces of the soffit panels with full loads of paint. Be sure to get good coverage in the grooves.

Paint any decorative trim near the top of the house at the same time you paint the soffits and fascia. Use a 2½" or 3" paintbrush for broader surfaces, and a sash brush for more intricate trim areas.

HOW TO PAINT SIDING

Paint the bottom edges of lap siding by holding the paintbrush flat against the wall. Paint the bottom edges of several siding pieces before returning to paint the faces of the same boards.

Paint the broad faces of the siding boards with a 4" brush using the painting technique shown on page 300. Working down from the top of the house, paint as much surface as you can reach without leaning beyond the sides of the ladder.

Paint the siding all the way down to the foundation, working from top to bottom. Shift the ladder or scaffolding, then paint the next section. *Tip: Paint up to the edges of end caps and window or door trim that will be painted later.*

On board and batten or vertical panel siding, paint the edges of the battens, or top boards, first. Paint the faces of the battens before the sides dry, then use a roller with a ⅝"-nap sleeve to paint the large, broad surfaces between the battens.

PAINTING: INTERIORS

1

Scrape away loose paint with a putty knife or paint scraper.

2

Apply spackle to the edges of the chipped paint with a putty knife or a flexible wallboard knife.

3

Sand the patch area with 150-grit production sandpaper. The patch area should feel smooth to the touch.

HOW TO MASK TRIM

Masking and draping materials include (clockwise from top left): plastic and canvas drop cloths, self-adhesive plastic, masking tape, and pregummed masking papers.

1

Use pregummed paper or wide masking tape to protect wood moldings from paint splatters. Leave the outside edge of the masking tape loose.

2

After applying the tape, run the tip of a putty knife along the inside edge of the tape to seal it against seeping paint. After painting, remove the tape as soon as the paint is too dry to run.

WALLS & CEILINGS

HOW TO USE A PAINTBRUSH

Dip the brush, loading one-third of its bristle length. Tap the bristles against the side of the can. Dipping deeper overloads the brush. Dragging the brush against the lip of the can causes the bristles to wear.

Cut in the edges using the narrow edge of the brush, pressing just enough to flex the bristles. Keep an eye on the paint edge, and paint with long, slow strokes. Always paint from a dry area back into wet paint to avoid lap marks.

Brush wall corners using the wide edge of the brush. Paint open areas with a brush or roller before the brushed paint dries.

HOW TO PAINT WITH A PAINT ROLLER

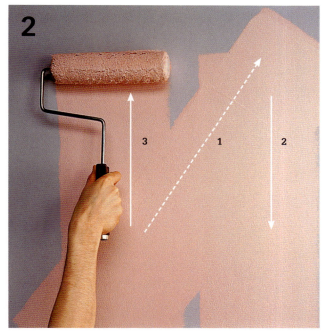

With the loaded roller, make a diagonal sweep (1) about 4 ft. long on the surface. On walls, roll upward on the first stroke to avoid spilling paint. Use slow roller strokes to avoid splattering.

Draw the roller straight down (2) from the top of the diagonal sweep. Shift the roller to the beginning of the diagonal and roll up (3) to complete the unloading of the roller. Distribute paint over the rest of the section with horizontal back-and-forth strokes.

HOW TO PAINT CEILINGS

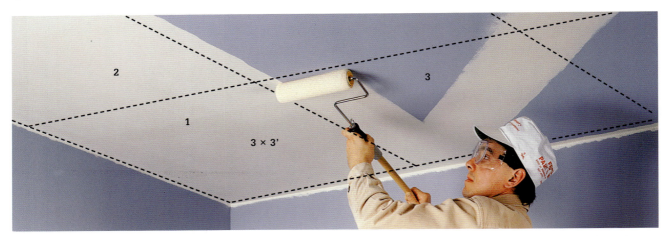

Paint ceilings with a roller handle extension. Use eye protection while painting overhead. Start at the corner farthest from the entry door. Cut in the edges with a brush, then paint the ceiling along the narrow end in 3-ft. × 3-ft. sections. Apply the paint with a diagonal stroke. Distribute the paint evenly with back-and-forth strokes. For the final smoothing strokes, roll each section toward the wall containing the entry door, lifting the roller at the end of each sweep.

HOW TO PAINT WALLS

Paint walls in 2-ft. × 4-ft. sections. Start in an upper corner, cutting in the ceiling and wall corners with a brush, then rolling the section. Make the initial diagonal roller stroke from the bottom of the section upward, to avoid dripping paint. Distribute the paint evenly with horizontal strokes, then finish with downward sweeps of the roller. Next, cut in and roll the section directly underneath. Continue with adjacent areas, cutting in and rolling the top sections before the bottom sections. Roll all finish strokes toward the floor.

PATIO DOOR: INSTALLING

A walkout basement without a patio door seems incomplete. Yet many homes with direct access into the basement do not take full advantage of the feature. A sliding or swingout patio door allows several times the amount of natural light into a room that a single door lets in, even if the single door has a large bright panel. If there is a patio or deck on the exterior side of your basement door, enlarging the door will make moving guests and supplies through the doorway much easier and more comfortable.

When choosing a new patio door, you'll need to decide between models with hinged doors that swing out and close together or ones with sliding door panels. Swinging doors tend to require less maintenance than sliding doors, and they offer better security. Sliding doors are a good choice if ventilation is one of your requirements, because the amount of air they let in is easy to regulate. You can also leave a sliding door open without the wind catching it and causing it to slam or break.

Enlarging a door opening requires that you make structural changes to your house, so it almost always requires a building permit. During construction you will need to provide temporary support to replace the bearing being done by the wall studs you'll need to cut. And when you install the new door, the framed opening must have a substantial header. Check with your local building department for the header requirements. Because basement ceilings may be shorter than eight feet, you may need to use a header that's fabricated from engineered beams to meet the load bearing requirements within the available space.

Tools & Materials ▶

Circular saw	Self-adhesive
Reciprocating saw	rubber flashing
with bi-metal blade	Drip edge molding
Handsaw	Panel adhesive
10d, 16d nails	Fiberglass insulation
2½" deck screws	Case molding
½" plywood	Temporary ceiling support
Building paper	Protective equipment

BEFORE

AFTER

Replacing a single door with a sliding patio door is a great way to add light to a walkout basement and create an inviting entryway into your home.

HOW TO INSTALL A PATIO DOOR

Build a temporary support wall. Use doubled 2 x 4s (or 4 x 4s) for the top plate and support posts. The wall should extend at least 2 ft. past the planned door opening in each direction and cannot be more than 24" away from the bearing wall. Secure the support wall to the floor and to the ceiling.

Remove the old door and the wallcoverings in the project area. If there are light switches or receptacles in the demolition area, shut off their power supply at the main service panel and then remove cover plates. To remove the old door, take off the case molding and then cut through the nails by sawing between the jambs and the frame with a reciprocating saw and bi-metal blade (inset).

Relocate wiring elements such as switches and receptacles so they are safely outside the new door area. You will need an electrical permit for this and possibly an on-site inspection. If you are not experienced with home wiring, hire an electrician for this part of the job.

Remove wall studs in the project area. If they are difficult to remove, cut them through the center with a reciprocating saw first. Watch out for nails driven in through the exterior side.

Frame the rough opening so it is sized according to the door manufacturer's recommendation. Install the new king studs if needed and then install the jack studs.

King stud

Jack studs

Install the new header by driving 16d nails through the king stud and into the ends of the header. You can make your own structural header by sandwiching a strip of ½" plywood between two pieces of dimensional lumber (inset). Assemble the header with construction adhesive and 10d nails or 2½" deck screws. You can also purchase an engineered header.

Cut through the exterior wall materials. You can either mark the corners of the framed opening by driving a nail out from the side, or simply use the framed opening as guidance for your reciprocating saw. Also cut through the sole plate at the edges of the opening so the cut end is flush with the jack stud face.

Lift the door unit or frame into the opening, with a helper. Test the fit. Trace the edges of the preattached brickmold onto the outside wall, or place a piece of brickmold next to the door and trace around the perimeter to establish cutting lines (inset). Remove the door.

(continued)

9

Cut along the brickmold cutting lines with a saw set to a cutting depth equal to the thickness of the siding and the wall sheathing. Finish the cuts at the corners with a handsaw. Thoroughly vacuum the floor in the door opening.

10

Seal the framed opening by installing strips of building paper or self-adhesive rubber flashing product. Make sure that the top strip overlaps any seams you create. If the patio door is exposed, attach drip edge molding to the top of the framed opening.

11

Apply a bead of exterior-rated panel adhesive to the door threshold. Also apply adhesive to the back surface of the preattached brickmold or the nailing flange (whichever your door has).

12

Set the door in position so the brickmold or nailing flange is flush against the outside of the framed opening. Center it in the opening, side to side. Tack the door near the top of each side and then check with a level. Install shims where necessary so the door is plumb. Re-hang the door in the frame, if it has been removed.

13

Fill the gaps around the door with minimal expanding foam or with loosely backed fiberglass insulation (foam makes a better seal). Patch the wall and attach case molding (see brickmold pages 86 to 87). If your door does not have preattached brickmold, cut and attach molding on the outside.

PEDASTAL SINK: INSTALLING

Install 2 × 6 blocking between the wall studs, behind the planned sink location where you will drive screws to mount the sink. Cover the wall with water-resistant drywall. Waste and supply lines may need to be moved, depending on the sink.

Set the basin and pedestal in position and brace it with 2 × 4s. Outline the top of the basin on the wall, and mark the base of the pedestal on the floor. Mark reference points on the wall and floor through the mounting holes found on the back of the sink and the bottom of the pedestal.

Set aside the basin and pedestal. Drill pilot holes in the wall and floor at the reference points, then reposition the pedestal. Anchor the pedestal to the floor with lag screws.

Attach the faucet, then set the sink on the pedestal. Align the holes in the back of the sink with the pilot holes drilled in the wall, then drive lag screws and washers into the wall brace using a ratchet wrench. Do not overtighten the screws.

Hook up the drain and supply fittings. Caulk between the back of the sink and the wall when installation is finished. You may choose to apply caulk between the sink and the wall, or between the bottom of the pedestal and the floor.

PEX WATER SUPPLY

Cross-linked polyethylene (PEX) is growing quickly in acceptance as a supply pipe for residential plumbing. It's not hard to understand why. Developed in the 1960s but relatively new to the United States, this supply pipe combines the ease of use of flexible tubing with the durability of rigid pipe. It can withstand a wide temperature range (from subfreezing to 180°F); it is inexpensive; and it's quieter than rigid supply pipe.

PEX is flexible plastic (polyethylene, or PE) tubing that's reinforced by a chemical reaction that creates long fibers to increase the strength of the material. It has been allowed by code in Europe and the southern United States for many years, but has won approval for residential supply use in most major plumbing codes only recently. It's frequently used in manufactured housing and recreational vehicles and in radiant heating systems. Because it is so flexible, PEX can easily be bent to follow corners and make other changes in direction. From the water main and heater, it is connected into manifold fittings that redistribute the water in much the same manner as a lawn irrigation system.

For standard residential installations, PEX can be joined with very simple fittings and tools. Unions are generally made with a crimping tool and a crimping ring. You simply insert the ends of the pipe you're joining into the ring, then clamp down on the ring with the crimping tool. PEX pipe, tools, and fittings can be purchased from most wholesale plumbing suppliers and at many home centers. Coils of PEX are sold in several diameters from ¼" to 1". PEX tubing and fittings from different manufacturers are not interchangeable. Any warranty coverage will be voided if products are mixed.

Tools & Materials ▸

Tape measure	Protector plates
Felt-tipped pen	PEX fittings
Full-circle crimping tool	Utility knife
Go/no-go gauge	Plastic hangers
Tubing cutter	Crimp ring
PEX pipe	Protective
Manifolds	equipment

PEX pipe is a relatively new water supply material that's growing in popularity in part because it can be installed with simple mechanical connections.

PEX TOOLS & MATERIALS

Specialty tools for installing PEX are available wherever PEX is sold. The basic set includes a full-circle crimping tool (A), a tubing cutter (B), and a go/no-go gauge (C) to test connections after they've been crimped. Competing manufacturers make several types of fittings, with proprietary tools that only work with their fittings. The tools and fittings you use may differ from those shown on these pages.

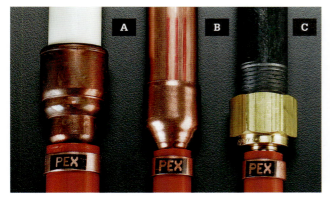

PEX is connected to other water supply materials with transition fittings, including CPVC-to-PEX (A), copper-to-PEX (B), and iron-to-PEX (C).

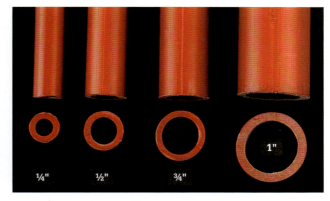

Generally, you should use the same diameter PEX as is specified for rigid supply tubing, but in some "home run" installations (see next page) you can use ⅜" PEX where ½" rigid copper would normally be used.

PEX INSTALLATION

Check with your local plumbing inspector to verify that PEX is allowed in your municipality. PEX has been endorsed by all major plumbing codes in North America, but your municipality may still be using an older set of codes. Follow the guidelines below when installing PEX:

- Do not install PEX in above-ground exterior applications because it degrades quickly from UV exposure.
- Do not use PEX for gas lines.
- Do not use plastic solvents or petroleum-based products with PEX (they can dissolve the plastic).
- Keep PEX at least 12" away from recessed light fixtures and other potential sources of high heat.

- Do not attach PEX directly to a water heater. Make connections at the heater with metallic tubing (either flexible water-heater connector tubing or rigid copper) at least 18" long; then join it to PEX with a transition fitting.
- Do not install PEX in areas where there is a possibility of mechanical damage or puncture. Always fasten protective plates to wall studs that house PEX.
- Always leave some slack in installed PEX lines to allow for contraction and in case you need to cut off a bad crimp.
- Use the same minimum branch and distribution supply-pipe dimensions for PEX that you'd use for copper or CPVC, according to your local plumbing codes.
- You can use push fittings to join PEX to itself or to CPVC or copper.

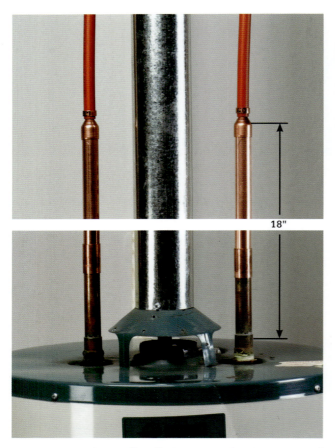

Do not connect PEX directly to a water heater. Use metal connector tubes. Solder the connector tubes to the water heater before attaching PEX. Never solder metal tubing that is already connected to PEX lines.

Bundle PEX together with plastic ties when running pipe through wall cavities. PEX can contract slightly, so leave some slack in the lines.

BUYING PEX

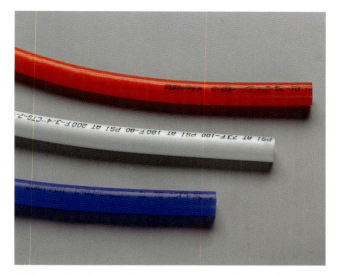

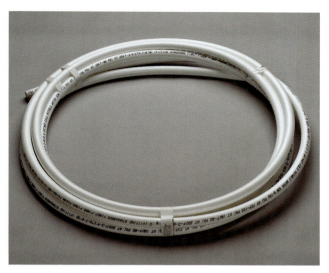

Color coding is a practice many PEX manufacturers have embraced to make identification easier. Because the material is identical except for the color, you can buy only one color (red is more common) and use it for both hot and cold supply lines.

PEX combines the flexibility of plastic tubing with the durability of rigid supply pipe. It is sold in coils of common supply-pipe diameters.

The PEX Advantage ▸

PEX supply tubing offers a number of advantages over traditional rigid supply tubing:

- Easy to install. PEX does not require coupling joints for long runs or elbows and sweeps for turns. The mechanical connections do not require solvents or soldering.
- Easy to transport. Large coils are lightweight and much easier to move around than 10 ft. lengths of pipe.
- Good insulation. The PEX material has better thermal properties than copper for lessened heat loss.

- Quiet. PEX will not rattle or clang from trapped air or kinetic energy.
- Good for retrofit jobs. PEX is easier to snake through walls than rigid supply tubing and is compatible with copper, PVC, or iron supply systems if the correct transition fittings are used. If your metal supply tubes are used to ground your electrical system, you'll need to provide a jumper if PEX is installed in midrun. Check with a plumber or electrician.
- Freeze resistance. PEX retains some flexibility in subfreezing conditions and is less likely to be damaged than rigid pipe, but it is not frostproof.

General Codes for PEX ▸

PEX has been endorsed for residential use by all major building codes, although some municipal codes may be more restrictive. The specific design standards may also vary, but here are some general rules:

- For PEX, maximum horizontal support spacing is 32" and maximum vertical support spacing is 10 ft.

- Maximum length of individual distribution lines is 60 ft.
- PEX is designed to withstand 210°F water for up to 48 hours. For ongoing use, most PEX is rated for 180 degree water up to 100 pounds per square inch of pressure.
- Directional changes of more than 90 degrees require a guide fitting.

HOW TO MAKE PEX CONNECTIONS

Cut the pipe to length, making sure to leave enough extra material so the line will have a small amount of slack once the connections are made. A straight, clean cut is very important. For best results, use a tubing cutter.

Inspect the cut end to make sure it is clean and smooth. If necessary, deburr the end of the pipe with a sharp utility knife. Slip a crimp ring over the end.

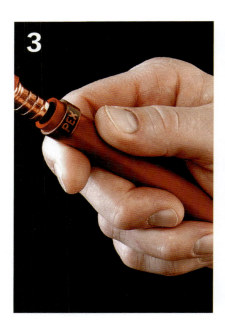

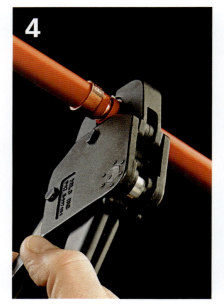

Insert the barbed end of the fitting into the pipe until it is snug against the cut edges. Position the crimp ring so it is ⅛" to ¼" from the end of the pipe, covering the barbed end of the fitting. Pinch the fitting to hold it in place.

Align the jaws of a full-circle crimping tool over the crimp ring and squeeze the handles together to apply strong, even pressure to the ring.

Test the connection to make sure it is mechanically acceptable, using a go/no-go gauge. If the ring does not fit into the gauge properly, cut the pipe near the connection and try again.

PICTURE RAIL MOLDING

Measure down the desired distance from the ceiling and draw a level reference line around the room using a pencil and a 4-ft. level or use a laser level. Use a stud finder to locate the framing members, and mark the locations on the walls with blue painter's tape.

Use a T-bevel to measure the angle of the corner, tightening the lock nut with the blade and the handle on the reference line. Place the T-bevel on the table of your power miter saw and adjust the miter blade so that it matches the angle.

Calculate the cutting angle. First, adjust the saw blade so it is parallel to the arm of the T-bevel when the handle is flush against the saw fence. Note the number of degrees, if any, away from zero that the blade location reads. Subtract this number from 180 and divide by 2; this is your cutting angle.

Cut both mating parts at the same bevel angle, arrived at in step 3. When cutting picture rail, the molding should be positioned with the bottom edge resting on the table and the back face flat against the saw fence.

Nail the molding at the stud locations covering the level line around the room (if you're using a laser level, you simply keep it in position and turned on to cast a reference line you can follow). After each molding is completely nailed in place, go back to each stud location and drive 1⅝" drywall screws into the molding through counter-bored pilot holes.

Fill nail holes with wood filler. Let the filler dry and sand it smooth. Then apply a final coat of paint over the molding face.

PIPE: COPPER: CUTTING & SOLDERING

1

Place the tubing cutter over the pipe and tighten the handle so that the pipe rests on both rollers and the cutting wheel is on the marked line.

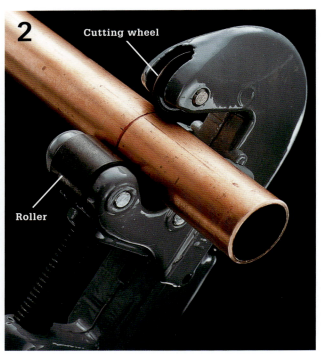

2

Cutting wheel

Roller

Turn the tubing cutter one rotation so that the cutting wheel scores a continuous straight line around the pipe.

3

Rotate the cutter in the opposite direction, tightening the handle slightly after every two rotations, until the cut is complete.

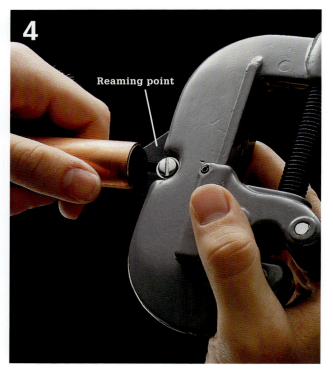

4

Reaming point

Remove sharp metal burrs from the inside edge of the cut pipe, using the reaming point on the tubing cutter, or a round file.

HOW TO SOLDER COPPER PIPES & FITTINGS

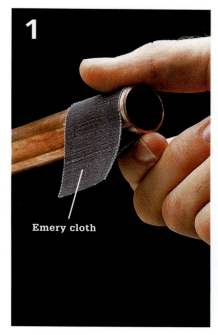

Clean the end of each pipe by sanding with emery cloth. Ends must be free of dirt and grease to ensure that the solder forms a good seal.

Clean the inside of each fitting by scouring with a wire brush or emery cloth.

Apply a thin layer of soldering paste (flux) to end of each pipe, using a flux brush. Soldering paste should cover about 1" of pipe end.

Apply a thin layer of flux to the inside of the fitting.

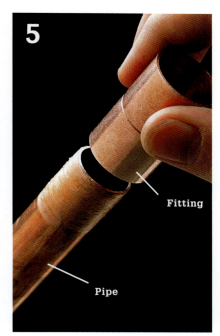

Assemble each joint by inserting the pipe into the fitting so it is tight against the bottom of the fitting sockets. Twist each fitting slightly to spread soldering paste.

Use a clean dry cloth to remove excess flux before soldering the assembled fitting.

(continued)

7

Prepare the wire solder by unwinding 8" to 10" of wire from spool. Bend the first 2" of the wire to a 90º angle.

8

Open the gas valve and trigger the spark lighter to ignite the torch. Adjust the torch valve until the inner portion of the flame is 1" to 2" long.

9

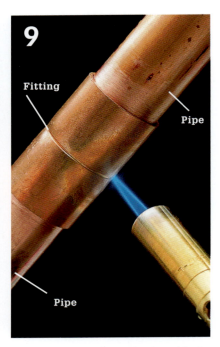

Fitting

Pipe

Pipe

Move the torch flame back and forth and around the pipe and the fitting to heat the area evenly.

10

Heat the other side of the copper fitting to ensure that heat is distributed evenly. Touch solder to pipe. Solder will melt when the pipe is at the right temperature.

11

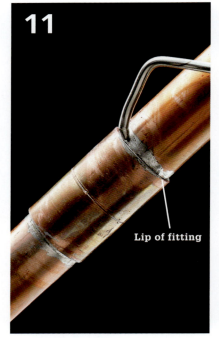

Lip of fitting

When solder melts, remove the torch and quickly push ½" to ¾" of solder into each joint. Capillary action fills the joint with liquid solder. A correctly soldered joint should show a thin bead of solder around the lips of the fitting.

12

Allow the joint to cool briefly, then wipe away excess solder with a dry rag. *Caution: Pipes will be hot. If joints leak after water is turned on, disassemble and resolder.*

HOW TO SOLDER BRASS VALVES

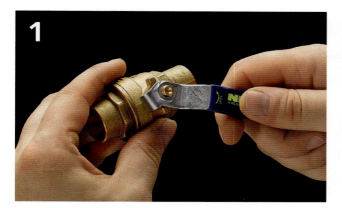

Valves should be fully open during all stages of the soldering process. If a valve has any plastic or rubber parts, remove them prior to soldering.

To prevent valve damage, quickly heat the pipe and the flanges of the valve, not the valve body. After soldering, cool the valve by spraying with water.

HOW TO TAKE APART SOLDERED JOINTS

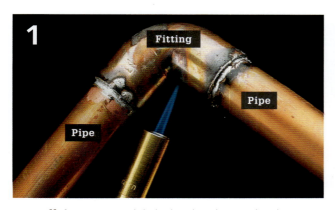

Fitting

Pipe

Pipe

Turn off the water and drain the pipes by opening the highest and lowest faucets in the house. Light your torch. Hold the flame tip to the fitting until the solder becomes shiny and begins to melt.

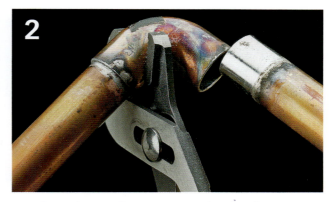

Use channel-type pliers to separate the pipes from the fitting.

Remove old solder by heating the ends of the pipe with your torch. Use a dry rag to wipe away melted solder quickly. *Caution: Pipes will be hot.*

Use emery cloth to polish the ends of the pipe down to bare metal. Never reuse fittings.

PIPE: JOINING: COMPRESSION FITTINGS

Compression fittings are used to make connections that may need to be taken apart. Compression fittings are easy to disconnect and often are used to install supply tubes and fixture shutoff valves. Use compression fittings in places where it is unsafe or difficult to solder, such as in crawl spaces.

Compression fittings are used most often with flexible copper pipe. Flexible copper is soft enough to allow the compression ring to seat snugly, creating a watertight seal. Compression fittings also may be used to make connections with Type M rigid copper pipe.

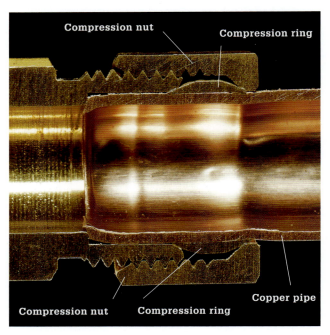

Compression fitting (shown in cutaway) shows how threaded compression nut forms a seal by forcing the compression ring against the copper pipe. Compression ring is covered with pipe joint compound before assembling to ensure a perfect seal.

Tools & Materials ▶

Felt-tipped pen	Pipe joint
Tubing cutter	compound or
or hacksaw	Teflon tape
Adjustable wrenches	Protective
Brass compression fittings	equipment

HOW TO ATTACH SUPPLY TUBES TO FIXTURE SHUTOFF VALVES WITH COMPRESSION FITTINGS

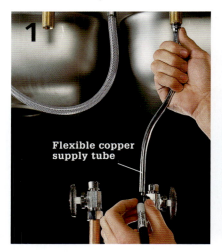

Bend flexible copper supply tube and mark to length. Include ½" for portion that will fit inside valve. Cut tube.

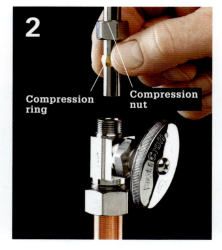

Slide the compression nut and then the compression ring over end of the pipe. The threads of the nut should face the valve.

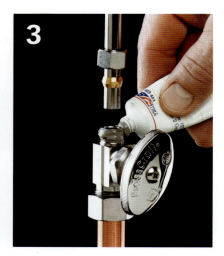

Apply a layer of pipe joint compound or Teflon tape over the threads on the valve. This helps ensure a watertight seal.

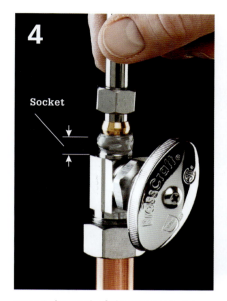

Insert the end of the pipe into the fitting so it fits flush against the bottom of the fitting socket.

Slide the compression ring and nut against the threads of the valve. Hand-tighten the nut onto the valve.

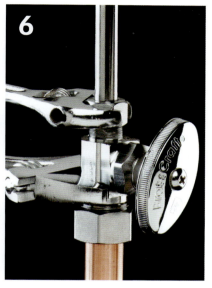

Tighten the compression nut with adjustable wrenches. Do not overtighten. Turn on the water and watch for leaks. If the fitting leaks, tighten the nut gently.

HOW TO JOIN TWO COPPER PIPES WITH A COMPRESSION UNION FITTING

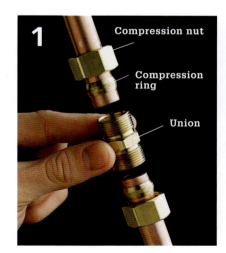

Slide compression nuts and rings over the ends of pipes. Place a threaded union between the pipes.

Apply a layer of pipe joint compound or Teflon tape to the union's threads, then screw compression nuts onto the union.

Hold the center of the union fitting with an adjustable wrench and use another wrench to tighten each compression nut one complete turn. Turn on the water. If the fitting leaks, tighten the nuts gently.

PIPE: JOINING: FLARE FITTINGS

Flare fittings are used more often for flexible copper gas lines. Flare fittings may be used with flexible copper water supply pipes, but they cannot be used where the connections will be concealed inside walls. Always check your local code regarding the use of flare fittings.

Flare fittings are easy to disconnect. Use flare fittings in places where it is unsafe or difficult to solder, such as in crawl spaces.

Tools & Materials ▸

Two-piece flaring tool
Adjustable wrenches

Brass flare fittings
Protective equipment

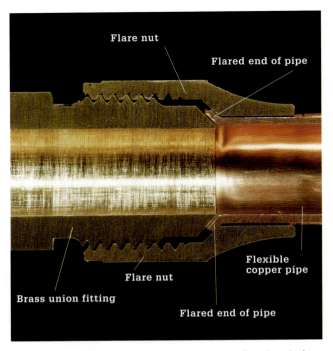

Flare fitting (shown in cutaway) shows how flared end of flexible copper pipe forms seal against the head of a brass union fitting.

HOW TO JOIN TWO COPPER PIPES WITH A FLARE UNION FITTING

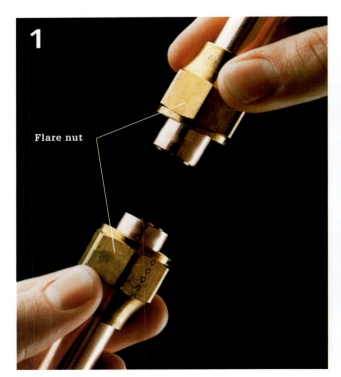

Slide flare nuts onto ends of pipes. Nuts must be placed on pipes before ends can be flared. Ream inside of pipe to create smooth edge.

Select hole in flaring tool base that matches outside diameter of pipe. Open base, and place end of pipe inside hole.

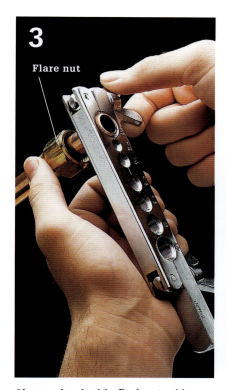

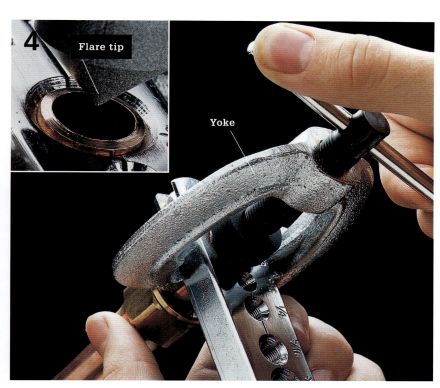

Clamp pipe inside flaring tool base.
End of pipe must be flush with flat
surface of base.

Slip yoke of flaring tool around base. Center flaring tip of yoke over end of pipe
(inset photo above). Tighten handle of yoke to shape the end of the pipe. Flare is
completed when handle cannot be turned farther.

Remove yoke and remove pipe from
base. Repeat flaring for other pipe.

Place flare union between flared ends
of pipe and screw flare nuts onto union.

Hold center of flare union with
adjustable wrench and use another
wrench to tighten flare nuts one
complete turn. Turn on water. If fitting
leaks, tighten nuts.

PLUGS & CORDS: REPLACING

Replace an electrical plug whenever you notice bent or loose prongs, a cracked or damaged casing, or a missing insulating faceplate. A damaged plug poses a shock and fire hazard.

Replacement plugs are available in different styles to match common appliance cords. Always choose a replacement that is similar to the original plug. Flat-cord and quick-connect plugs are used with light-duty appliances, like lamps and radios. Round-cord plugs are used with larger appliances, including those that have three-prong grounding plugs.

Some tools and appliances use polarized plugs. A polarized plug has one wide prong and one narrow prong, corresponding to the hot and neutral slots found in a standard receptacle.

If there is room in the plug body, tie the individual wires in an underwriter's knot to secure the plug to the cord.

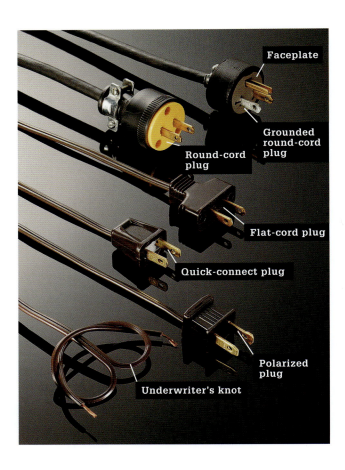

Faceplate
Grounded round-cord plug
Round-cord plug
Flat-cord plug
Quick-connect plug
Underwriter's knot
Polarized plug

Tools & Materials ▸

Combination tool
Needlenose pliers
Screwdriver
Replacement plug

HOW TO INSTALL A QUICK-CONNECT PLUG

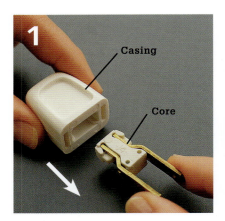

Casing
Core

Squeeze the prongs of the new quick-connect plug together slightly and pull the plug core from the casing. Cut the old plug from the flat-cord wire with a combination tool, leaving a clean cut end.

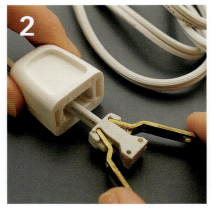

Feed unstripped wire through rear of plug casing. Spread prongs, then insert wire into opening in rear of core. Squeeze prongs together; spikes inside core penetrate cord. Slide casing over core until it snaps into place.

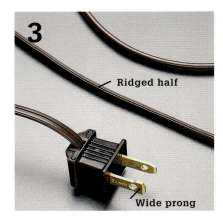

Ridged half
Wide prong

When replacing a polarized plug, make sure that the ridged half of the cord lines up with the wider (neutral) prong of the plug.

HOW TO REPLACE A ROUND-CORD PLUG

Cut off round cord near the old plug using a combination tool. Remove the insulating faceplate on the new plug and feed cord through rear of plug. Strip about 3" of outer insulation from the round cord. Strip ¾" insulation from the individual wires.

Tie an underwriter's knot with the black and the white wires. Make sure the knot is located close to the edge of the stripped outer insulation. Pull the cord so that the knot slides into the plug body.

Hook end of black wire clockwise around brass screw and white wire around silver screw. On a three-prong plug, attach third wire to grounding screw. If necessary, excess grounding wire can be cut away.

Tighten the screws securely, making sure the copper wires do not touch each other. Replace the insulating faceplate.

HOW TO REPLACE A FLAT-CORD PLUG

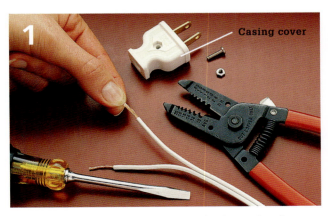

Cut old plug from cord using a combination tool. Pull apart the two halves of the flat cord so that about 2" of wire are separated. Strip ¾" insulation from each half. Remove casing cover on new plug.

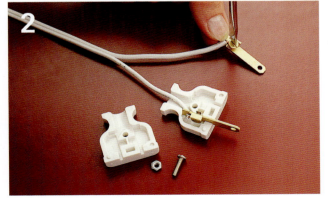

Hook ends of wires clockwise around the screw terminals, and tighten the screw terminals securely. Reassemble the plug casing. Some plugs may have an insulating faceplate that must be installed.

PLUGS & CORDS: REPLACING: LAMP

With the lamp unplugged, the shade off, and the bulb out, you can remove the socket. Squeeze the outer shell of the socket just above the base and pull the shell out of the base. The shell is often marked Press at some point along its perimeter. Press there and then pull.

Under the outer shell there is a cardboard insulating sleeve. Pull this off and you'll reveal the socket attached to the end of the cord.

With the shell and insulation set aside, pull the socket away from the lamp (it will still be connected to the cord). Unscrew the two screws to completely disconnect the socket from the cord. Set the socket aside with its shell (you'll need them to reassemble the lamp)

Remove the old cord from the lamp by grasping the cord near the base and pulling the cord through the lamp.

5

Bring your damaged cord to a hardware store or home center and purchase a similar cord set. (A cord set is simply a replacement cord with a plug already attached.) Snake the end of the cord up from the base of the lamp through the top so that about 3" of cord is visible above the top.

6

Carefully separate the two halves of the cord. If the halves won't pull apart, you can carefully make a cut in the middle with a knife. Strip away about ¾" of insulation from the end of each wire.

7

Connect the ends of the new cord to the two screws on the side of the socket (one of which will be silver in color, the other brass-colored). One half of the cord will have ribbing or markings along its length; wrap that wire clockwise around the silver screw and tighten the screw. The other half of the cord will be smooth; wrap it around the copper screw and tighten the screw.

8

Outer sleeve

Insulating sleeve

Set the socket on the base. Make sure the switch isn't blocked by the harp—the part that holds the shade on some lamps. Slide the cardboard insulating sleeve over the socket so the sleeve's notch aligns with the switch. Now slide the outer sleeve over the socket, aligning the notch with the switch. It should snap into the base securely. Screw in a light bulb, plug the lamp in, and test it.

WIRING

PLUMBING: BASICS

Because most of a plumbing system is hidden inside walls and floors, it may seem to be a complex maze of pipes and fittings. But spend a few minutes with us and you'll gain a basic understanding of your system. Understanding how home plumbing

works is an important first step toward doing routine maintenance and money-saving repairs.

A typical home plumbing system includes three basic parts: a water supply system, a fixture and appliance set, and a drain system. These three parts can be seen clearly in the photograph of the cut-away house on the opposite page.

Fresh water enters a home through a main supply line (1). This fresh water source is provided by either a municipal water company or a private underground well. If the source is a municipal supplier, the water passes through a meter (2) that registers the amount of water used. A family of four uses about 400 gallons of water each day.

Immediately after the main supply enters the house, a branch line splits off (3) and is joined to a water heater (4). From the water heater, a hot water line runs parallel to the cold water line to bring the water supply to fixtures and appliances throughout the house. Fixtures include sinks, bathtubs, showers, and laundry tubs. Appliances include water heaters, dishwashers, clothes washers, and water softeners. Toilets and exterior sillcocks are examples of fixtures that require only a cold water line.

The water supply to fixtures and appliances is controlled with faucets and valves. Faucets and valves have moving parts and seals that eventually may wear out or break, but they are easily repaired or replaced.

Waste water then enters the drain system. It first must flow past a drain trap (5), a U-shaped piece of pipe that holds standing water and prevents sewer gases from entering the home. Every fixture must have a drain trap.

The drain system works entirely by gravity, allowing waste water to flow downhill through a series of large-diameter pipes. These drain pipes are attached to a system of vent pipes. Vent pipes (6) bring fresh air to the drain system, preventing suction that would slow or stop drain water from flowing freely. Vent pipes usually exit the house at a roof vent (7).

All waste water eventually reaches a main waste and vent stack (8). The main stack curves to become a sewer line (9) that exits the house near the foundation. In a municipal system, this sewer line joins a main sewer line located near the street. Where sewer service is not available, waste water empties into a septic system.

Water meters and main shutoff valves are located where the main water supply pipe enters the house. The water meter is the property of your local municipal water company. If the water meter leaks, or if you suspect it is not functioning properly, call your water company for repairs.

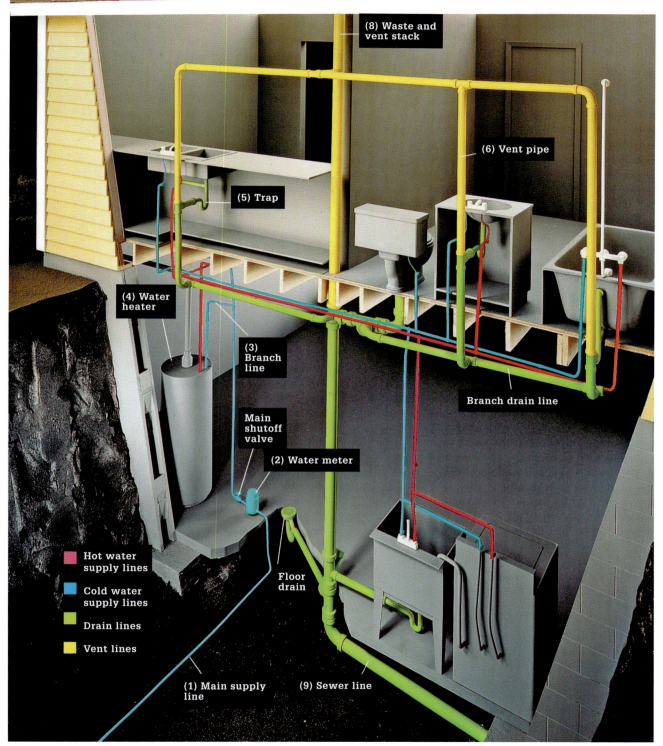

(7) Roof vent

(8) Waste and vent stack

(6) Vent pipe

(5) Trap

(4) Water heater

(3) Branch line

Main shutoff valve

(2) Water meter

Branch drain line

Floor drain

(1) Main supply line

(9) Sewer line

Hot water supply lines

Cold water supply lines

Drain lines

Vent lines

POWDER-ACTUATED TOOLS

Powder-Actuated Tools ▸

Basement floors and walls are almost always made of concrete or concrete products, which can present some difficulty when it comes time to attach walls. You can use hardened masonry screws for fastening, but that involves lots of tedious drilling and usually a few broken or stripped screw heads. An easier alternative is to use small charges of gunpowder to drive hardened nails into metal or concrete with a powder-actuated nail gun.

Powder-actuated nailers look and work a bit like a pile driver or handgun. A steel barrel holds specially designed hardened nails called drive pins. The nails are equipped with a plastic sleeve to keep them centered in the barrel. Driving force is delivered by a small gunpowder charge, called a powder load, which looks like a rifle shell with a crimped tip. The powder loads fit into a magazine behind the barrel on the tool. Squeezing the tool's trigger, or hitting the end with a hammer (depending on the tool style), activates a firing pin that ignites the gunpowder. The expanding gases drive a piston against the nail at great force. Powder-actuated nailers can drive only one fastener at a time, but some styles will hold a clip of multiple power loads for faster operation.

Powder loads are made in a range of color-coded calibers to suit different nailing applications and drive pin sizes. Follow the manufacturer's recommendations carefully to choose the correct load and fastener for your task. Generally, the safest method is to start with the lowest energy load that will work for your nailing situation and see if it's sufficient to fully drive the nail. Use the next stronger load, if necessary.

Powder-actuated nailers are easy to use for do-it-yourselfers and safe for indoor projects, provided you wear hearing and eye protection and follow all manufacturer's instructions. Most home centers sell the nail guns and supplies, or you can rent these tools.

Powder-actuated nailers offer the quickest and easiest method for fastening framing to block, poured concrete, and steel.

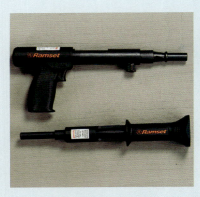

Powder-actuated nail guns (PATs) are designed in two styles. Plunger types are activated by hitting the end of the shaft with a hammer, while trigger styles function like a handgun. With either type, the barrel must be depressed against the work surface to release a safety before a drive pin can be fired.

Powder loads contain various amounts of gunpowder inside a crimped shell. Color coding ensures that you're using the right amount of charge for your drive pin size and the materials you're fastening together. Follow the color charts carefully, starting with a low-powder charge.

PATs use hardened nails, called drive pins, in a range of sizes. A plastic finned sleeve centers the drive pin in the tool barrel.

HOW TO USE A PAT

To prepare a PAT for use, slide a drive pin into the barrel first. Push it in until the nail tip is flush with the end of the barrel. Be sure there's no powder load in the magazine.

Slide the magazine open and insert a powder load into the barrel. A rim on the load shell ensures that it can only be loaded one way. Close the magazine.

Press the end of the barrel firmly against the work surface to release the safety. Squeeze the trigger or strike the end of the tool sharply with a hammer to fire the drive pin. Once the pin is fired, slide open the magazine to eject the spent load shell.

Driving Nails ▸

Occasionally, your first powder load selection won't completely set the nail. In this situation, use a hand maul to drive it in the rest of the way. Choose a stronger powder load for driving subsequent fasteners.

RACEWAYS: SURFACE-MOUNTED WIRING

Surface-mounted wiring is a network of electrical circuits that run through small, decorative tubes that function much like conduit. The systems include matching elbows, T-connectors, and various other fittings and boxes that are also surface-mounted. The main advantage to a surface-mounted wiring system is that you can add a new fixture onto a circuit without cutting into your walls.

Although they are extremely convenient and can even contribute to a room's decor when used thoughtfully, surface-mounted wiring systems do have some limitations. They are not allowed for some specific applications (such as damp areas like bathrooms) in many areas, so check with the local building authorities before beginning a

project. And, the boxes that house the switches and receptacles tend to be very shallow and more difficult to work with than ordinary boxes.

In some cases, you may choose to run an entirely new circuit with surface-mounted wiring components (at least starting at the point where the feeder wire reaches the room from the service panel). But more often, a surface-mounted wiring circuit ties into an existing receptacle or switch. If you are tying into a standard switch box for power, make sure the load wire for the new surface-mounted wiring circuit is connected to the hot wire in the switch box before it is connected to the switch (otherwise, the surface-mounted wiring circuit will be off whenever the switch is off).

After   **Before**

Surface-mounted wiring circuits are networks of cable channels and electrical boxes that allow you to run new wiring without cutting into walls. If you have a room with too much demand on a single receptacle (inset), installing a surface-mounted circuit with one or more new outlets is a good solution.

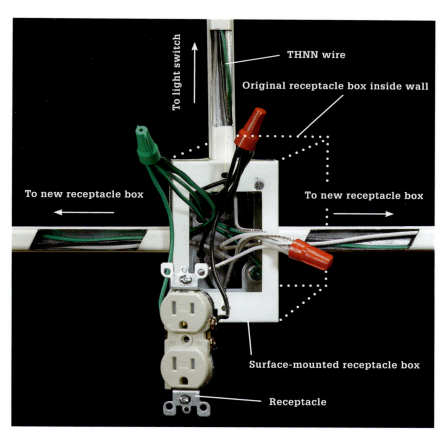

A surface-mounted receptacle box is mounted directly to the original electrical box (usually for a receptacle) and raceway tracks are attached to it. The tracks house THNN wires that run from the new box to new receptacles and light switches.

Labels in image: THNN wire · To light switch · Original receptacle box inside wall · To new receptacle box · To new receptacle box · Surface-mounted receptacle box · Receptacle

PARTS OF A SURFACE-MOUNTED SYSTEM

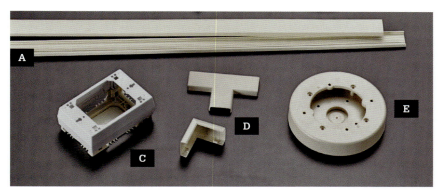

Surface-mounted wiring systems employ two-part tracks that are mounted directly to the wall surface to house cable. Lighter-duty plastic raceways (A), used frequently in office buildings, are made of snap-together plastic components. For home wiring, look for a heavier metal-component system (B). Both systems include box extenders for tying in to a receptacle (C), elbows, T-connectors, and couplings (D), and boxes for fixtures (E).

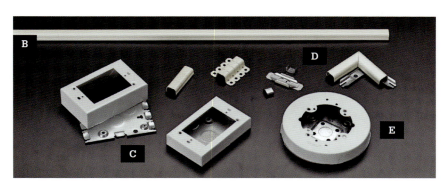

RADIANT HEAT SYSTEMS

Floor-warming systems require very little energy to run and are designed to heat ceramic tile floors only; they generally are not used as sole heat sources for rooms.

A typical floor-warming system consists of one or more thin mats containing electric resistance wires that heat up when energized like an electric blanket. The mats are installed beneath the tile and are hardwired to a 120-volt GFCI circuit. A thermostat controls the temperature, and a timer turns the system off automatically.

The system shown in this project includes two plastic mesh mats, each with its own power lead that is wired directly to the thermostat. Radiant mats may be installed over a plywood subfloor, but if you plan to install floor tile you should put down a base of cementboard first, and then install the mats on top of the cementboard.

A crucial part of installing this system is to use a multimeter to perform several resistance checks to make sure the heating wires have not been damaged during shipping or installation.

Electrical service required for a floor-warming system is based on size. A smaller system may connect to an existing GFCI circuit, but a larger one will need a dedicated circuit; follow the manufacturer's requirements.

To order a floor-warming system, contact the manufacturer or dealer. In most cases, you can send them plans and they'll custom-fit a system for your project area.

Tools & Materials ▸

Vacuum cleaner	Conduit
Multimeter	Thinset mortar
Tape measure	Thermostat with sensor
Scissors	Junction box(es)
Router/rotary tool	Tile or stone
Marker	floorcovering
Electric wire fault	Drill
indicator (optional)	Double-sided
Hot glue gun	carpet tape
Radiant floor mats	Cable clamps
12/2 NM cable	Protective equipment
Trowel or rubber float	

A radiant floor-warming system employs electric heating mats that are covered with floor tile to create a floor that's cozy underfoot.

Installation Tips ▶

- Thermostat
- Timer
- Dedicated circuit cable
- Thermostat sensor wire
- Electrical conduit
- Power lead
- Heating mats
- Floor tile
- Thinset mortar
- Heating mat
- Concrete or cementboard underlayment

A floor-warming system requires a dedicated circuit to power and control its heating mats, thermostat, and timer.

- Each radiant mat must have a direct connection to the power lead from the thermostat, with the connection made in a junction box in the wall cavity. Do not install mats in series.
- Do not install radiant floor mats under shower areas.
- Do not overlap mats or let them touch.
- Do not cut heating wire or damage heating wire insulation.
- The distance between wires in adjoining mats should equal the distance between wire loops measured center to center.

RADIATORS: DRAINING

Hot water and steam systems, also known as hydronic systems, feature a boiler that heats water and circulates it through a closed network of pipes to a set of radiators or convectors. Because water expands and contracts as it heats and cools, these systems include expansion tanks to ensure a constant volume of water circulating through the pipes.

Hot water and steam systems warm the surrounding air through a process called convection. Hot water radiators (photo 1) are linked to the system by pipes connected near the bottom of the radiator. As water cools inside the radiator, it is drawn back to the boiler for reheating. The radiators in steam systems (photo 2) have pipes connected near the top of the radiator. These radiators can be very hot to the touch. Convectors (photo 3) are smaller and lighter and may be used to replace hot water radiators, or to extend an existing hot water system.

Although the delivery of hot water or steam to the rooms in your house is considered a closed system, some air will make its way into the system. Steam radiators have an automatic release valve that periodically releases hot, moist air. Hot water radiators contain a bleed valve that must periodically be opened to release trapped air. It is usually necessary to bleed convector systems using a valve near the boiler.

Today's hot water and steam systems are often fueled by natural gas. Older systems may use fuel oil. Fuel oil systems require more frequent maintenance of the filter and blower.

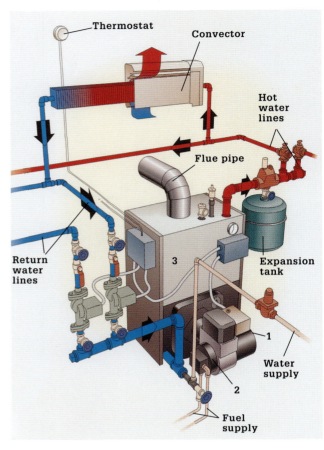

A blower draws in air through the air intake (1) while a fuel pump (2) maintains a constant supply of fuel oil. The mixture is ignited by a high-voltage spark as it enters the combustion chamber (3) and heats water.

Hot-water radiators circulate heated water through pipes. As it cools, water is drawn back to the boiler for reheating.

Steam radiators operate at a higher temperature. Steam cools in the radiators, returns to a liquid state, and then flows back to the boiler.

Space-saving hot water convectors work on the same principle as radiators, but use thin sheet-metal fins to transfer heat to the air.

DRAINING & FILLING A SYSTEM

Sediment gradually accumulates in any water-based system, reducing the system's efficiency and damaging internal parts. Draining the boiler every season reduces the accumulation of sediment. Be aware that draining the system can take a long time, and the water often has an unpleasant odor. This doesn't indicate a problem. Drain the system during warm weather, and open the windows and run a fan to reduce any odor.

Start by shutting off the boiler and allowing the hot system to cool. Attach a garden hose to the drain at the bottom of the boiler (photo 1), and place the other end in a floor drain or utility sink. Open a bleed valve on the highest radiator in the house (page 338).

When water stops draining, open a bleed valve on a radiator closer to the boiler. When the flow stops, locate the valve or gauge on top of the boiler, and remove it with a wrench (photo 2).

Make sure the system is cool before you add water. Close the drain valve on the boiler. Insert a funnel into the gauge fitting and add rust inhibitor, available from heating supply dealers (photo 3). Check the container for special instructions. Reinstall the valve or gauge in the top of the boiler, close all radiator bleed valves, and slowly reopen the water supply to the boiler.

When the water pressure gauge reads 5 psi, bleed the air from the radiators on the first floor, then do the same on the upper floors. Let the boiler reach 20 psi before you turn the power on (photo 4). Allow 12 hours for water to circulate fully, then bleed the radiators again.

Tools & Materials ▸

Open-end wrench set	Plastic bucket
Pipe wrenches	Drop cloth
Garden hose	Boiler rust inhibitor
Funnel	Protective equipment

Use a garden hose to drain water from the boiler. Keep the drain end of the hose lower than the drain cock on the boiler.

If the valve or gauge on top of the boiler is attached to a separate fitting, hold the fitting still with one wrench while removing the valve or gauge with another.

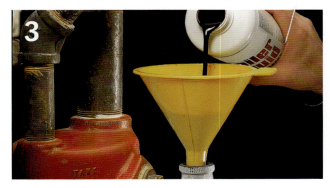

Using a funnel, add a recommended rust inhibitor to the boiler through the valve or gauge fitting.

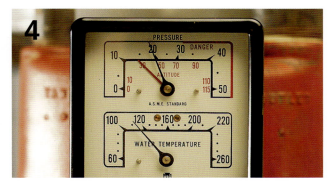

The boiler should reach a pressure of 20 psi before you turn the power back on.

RADIATORS: HOT WATER HEATING SYSTEMS

Hot water systems operate more quietly and efficiently if you bleed them of trapped air once a year. To bleed a hot water system, the boiler must be on. Start with the radiator that's highest in the house and farthest from the boiler. Place a cloth under the bleed valve, and open the valve slowly (photo 1). Close it as soon as water squirts out. Some bleed valves have knobs, which open with a half turn; others must be opened with a screwdriver or valve key, available at hardware stores.

Steam radiators have automatic bleed valves. To clear a clogged valve, close the shutoff at the radiator and let unit cool. Unscrew the bleed valve and clear the orifice with a fine wire or needle (photo 2).

Older hot water convector systems may have bleed valves on or near the convectors. Bleed these convectors as you would radiators.

Most convector systems today don't have bleed valves. For these, locate the hose bib where the return water line reaches the boiler. Close the gate valve between the bib and the boiler. Attach a short section of hose to the bib and immerse the other end in a bucket of water. Open the bib while adding water to the boiler by opening the supply valve. The supply valve is located on the supply pipe, usually the smallest pipe in the system. Flush the system until no air bubbles come out of the hose in the bucket (photo 3). Open the gate valve to bleed any remaining air. Close the hose bib before restarting the boiler.

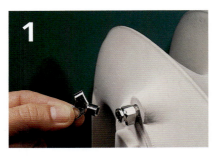

1

If you can't find a key for your radiators, a local hardware store or home center may have a replacement.

2

If the radiator isn't heating, clear the orifice with a fine wire or needle.

3

A convector-based heating system is usually bled at the boiler by holding a hose underwater and flushing the system until there are no more air bubbles coming from the hose.

Replace Radiator Control Valves ▸

A radiator control valve that won't operate should be replaced. To replace the valve, you'll first need to drain the system (page 337). Then use a pipe wrench to disconnect the nut on the outlet side of the valve, then disconnect the valve body from the supply pipe (photo 1, right). Thread the tailpiece of the new valve into the radiator. Thread the valve body onto the supply pipe. Make sure the arrow on the valve body points in the direction of the water flow. Thread the connecting nut on the tailpiece onto the outlet side of the valve (photo 2). When you recharge the system, open the bleed valve on the radiator until a trickle of water runs out.

1

Use a pipe wrench to remove the control valve (left). Thread the tailpiece of the new valve into the radiator (right).

2

Fasten the valve to the supply tube, then secure the connecting nut on the tailpiece to the valve.

RANGE HOOD

Install the vent duct in the wall first, then cut a hole in the back of the range hood cabinet and mount the cabinet over the duct. Cut a vent hole in the bottom of the cabinet to match the opening on the top of the hood.

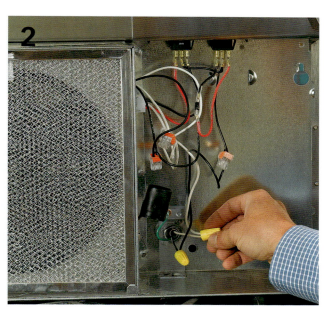

Make sure the circuit power is turned off at the service panel, then join the power cable wires to the lead wires inside the range hood. Use wire connectors for this job.

Get someone to help lift the range hood into place and hold it there while you attach it. Drive two screws through both sides and into the adjacent cabinets. If the hood is slightly small for the opening, slip a shim between the hood and the walls, trying to keep the gaps even.

Run ductwork from the cabinet to the exhaust exit point. Use two 45° adjustable elbows to join the duct in the wall to the top of the range hood. Use sheet metal screws and duct tape to hold all parts together and keep them from moving.

(continued)

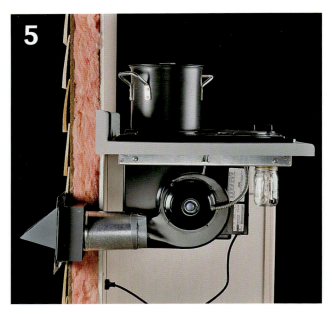

Downdraft cooktop: With a built-in blower unit that vents through the back or bottom of a base cabinet. A downdraft cooktop is a good choice for a kitchen island or peninsula.

Wall vent: If the duct comes out through the sidewall of the house, install a vertical duct cap. Make sure to seal around the perimeter of the cap with exterior caulk.

Ceiling vent: If the duct goes through an overhang soffit, you'll need a transition fitting to connect the round duct to a short piece of rectangular duct. Once these parts are installed, add a protective grille to keep animals and insects from getting into the duct.

Roof vent: For ducts that pass through the roof, cut an access hole through the roofing and sheathing, then install a weatherproof cap on top of the duct and under the roofing shingles. Make a waterproof seal by caulking the cap with plastic roof cement.

RECEPTACLES

Several different types of receptacles are found in the typical home. Each has a unique arrangement of slots that accepts only a certain kind of plug, and each is designed for a specific job.

Household receptacles provide two types of voltage: normal and high voltage. Although voltage ratings have changed slightly over the years, normal receptacles should be rated for 110, 115, 120, or 125 volts. For purposes of replacement, these ratings are considered identical. High-voltage receptacles are rated at 220, 240, or 250 volts. These ratings are considered identical.

When replacing a receptacle, check the amperage rating of the circuit at the main service panel, and buy a receptacle with the correct amperage rating.

15 amps, 120 volts. Polarized two-slot receptacle is common in homes built before 1960. Slots are different sizes to accept polarized plugs.

15 amps, 120 volts. Three-slot grounded receptacle has two different sized slots and a U-shaped hole for grounding. It is required in all new wiring installations.

20 amps, 120 volts. This three-slot grounded receptacle features a special T-shaped slot. It is installed for use with large appliances or portable tools that require 20 amps of current.

15 amps, 250 volts. This receptacle is used primarily for window air conditioners. It is available as a single unit or as half of a duplex receptacle with the other half wired for 120 volts.

30 amps, 125/250 volts. This receptacle is used for clothes dryers. It provides high-voltage current for heating coils and 125-volt current to run lights and timers.

50 amps, 125/250 volts. This receptacle is used for ranges. The high-voltage current powers heating coils, and the 125-volt current runs clocks and lights.

RECEPTACLES: HIGH-VOLTAGE

High-voltage receptacles provide current to large appliances like clothes dryers, ranges, water heaters, and air conditioners. The slot configuration of a high-voltage receptacle (page 341) will not accept a plug rated for 120 volts.

A high-voltage receptacle can be wired in one of two ways. In a standard high-voltage receptacle, voltage is brought to the receptacle with two hot wires, each carrying a maximum of 120 volts. No white neutral wire is necessary, but a grounding wire should be attached to the receptacle and to the metal receptacle box. Conduit can also act as a ground from the metal receptacle box back to the service panel.

A clothes dryer or range also may require normal current (a maximum of 120 volts) to run lights, timers, and clocks. If so, a white neutral wire will be attached to the receptacle. The appliance itself will split the incoming current into a 120-volt circuit and a 240-volt circuit.

It is important to identify and tag all wires on the existing receptacle so that the new receptacle will be properly wired.

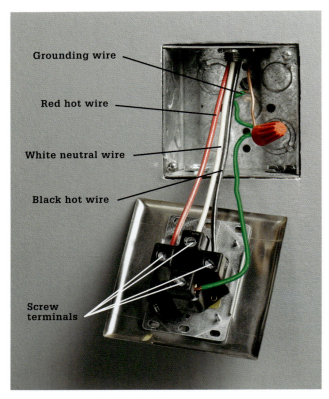

A receptacle rated for 120/240 volts has two incoming hot wires, each carrying 120 volts, a white neutral wire, and a copper grounding wire. Connections are made with setscrew terminals at the back of the receptacle.

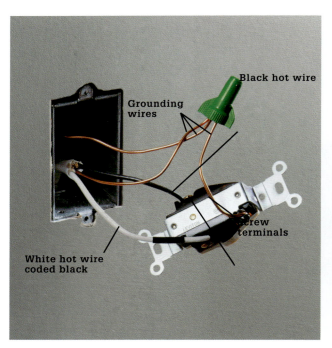

Standard receptacle rated for 240 volts has two incoming hot wires and no neutral wire. A grounding wire is pigtailed to the receptacle and to the metal receptacle box.

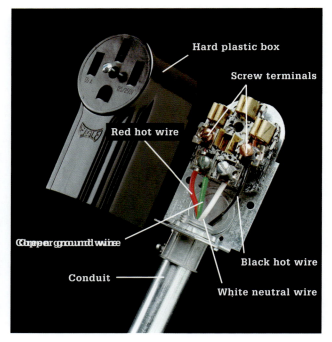

Surface-mounted receptacle rated for 240 volts has a hard plastic box that can be installed on concrete or block walls. Surface-mounted receptacles are often found in basements and utility rooms.

RECEPTACLES: REPLACING

A 120-volt duplex receptacle can be wired to the electrical system in a number of ways. The most common are shown on these pages.

Wiring configurations may vary slightly from these photographs, depending on the kind of receptacles used, the type of cable, or the technique of the electrician who installed the wiring. To make dependable repairs or replacements, use masking tape and label each wire according to its location on the terminals of the existing receptacle.

Receptacles are wired as either end-of-run or middle-of-run. These two basic configurations are easily identified by counting the number of cables entering the receptacle box. End-of-run wiring has only one cable, indicating that the circuit ends. Middle-of-run wiring has two cables, indicating that the circuit continues on to other receptacles, switches, or fixtures.

A split-circuit receptacle is shown on the next page. Each half of a split-circuit receptacle is wired to a separate circuit. This allows two appliances of high wattage to be plugged into the same receptacle without blowing a fuse or tripping a breaker. This wiring configuration is similar to a receptacle that is controlled by a wall switch. Code requires a switch-controlled receptacle in any room that does not have a built-in light fixture operated by a wall switch.

Split-circuit and switch-controlled receptacles are connected to two hot wires, so use caution during repairs or replacements. Make sure the connecting tab between the hot screw terminals is removed.

Two-slot receptacles are common in older homes. There is no grounding wire attached to the receptacle, but the box may be grounded with armored cable or conduit. Tamper-resistant receptacles are now required in all new residential installations.

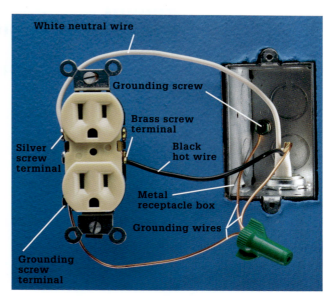

Single cable entering the box indicates end-of-run wiring. The black hot wire is attached to a brass screw terminal, and the white neutral wire is connected to a silver screw terminal. If the box is metal, the grounding wire is pigtailed to the grounding screws of the receptacle and the box. In a plastic box, the grounding wire is attached directly to the grounding screw terminal of the receptacle.

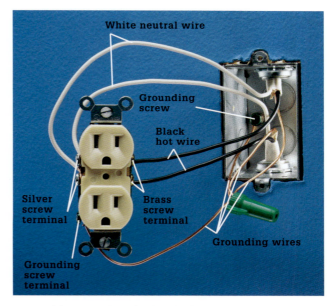

Two cables entering the box indicate middle-of-run wiring. Black hot wires are connected to brass screw terminals, and white neutral wires to silver screw terminals. The grounding wire is pigtailed to the grounding screws of the receptacle and the box.

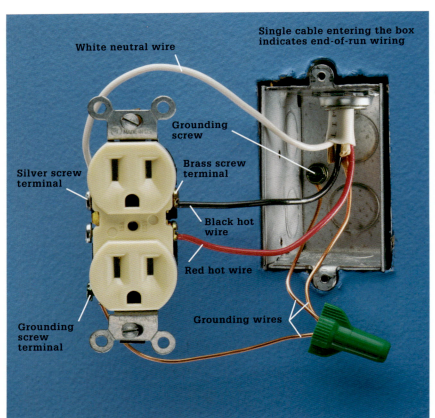

White neutral wire

Single cable entering the box indicates end-of-run wiring

Grounding screw

Silver screw terminal

Brass screw terminal

Black hot wire

Red hot wire

Grounding screw terminal

Grounding wires

A split-circuit receptacle is attached to a black hot wire, a red hot wire, a white neutral wire, and a bare grounding wire. The wiring is similar to a switch-controlled receptacle. The hot wires are attached to the brass screw terminals, and the connecting tab or fin between the brass terminals is removed. The white wire is attached to a silver screw terminal, and the connecting tab on the neutral side remains intact. The grounding wire is pigtailed to the grounding screw terminal of the receptacle and to the grounding screw attached to the box.

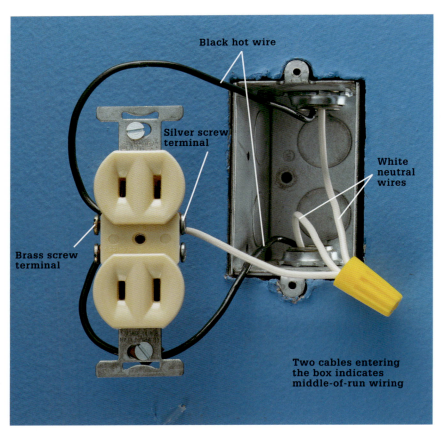

Black hot wire

Silver screw terminal

White neutral wires

Brass screw terminal

Two cables entering the box indicates middle-of-run wiring

A two-slot receptacle is often found in older homes. The black hot wires are connected to the brass screw terminals, and the white neutral wires are pigtailed to a silver screw terminal. Two-slot receptacles may be replaced with three-slot types, but only if a means of grounding exists at the receptacle box. In some municipalities, you may replace a two-slot receptacle with a GFCI receptacle as long as the receptacle has a sticker that reads "No equipment ground."

ROOFING: PREPARING

ORDERING ROOFING MATERIALS

Roofing materials are ordered in squares, with one square equaling 100 square feet. To determine how many squares are needed, first figure out the square footage of your roof. The easiest way to make this calculation is to multiply the length by the width of each section of roof, and then add the numbers together.

For steep roofs and those with complex designs, do your measuring from the ground and multiply by a number based on the slope of your roof. Measure the length and width of your house, include the overhangs, then multiply the numbers together to determine the overall square footage. Using the chart at the lower right, multiply the square footage by a number based on the roof's slope. Add 10 percent for waste, then divide the total square footage by 100 to determine the number of squares you need. Don't spend time calculating and subtracting the areas that won't be covered, such as skylights and chimneys. They're usually small enough that they don't impact the number of squares you need. Besides, it's good to have extra materials for waste, mistakes, and later repairs.

To determine how much flashing you'll need, measure the length of the valley to figure valley flashing, the lengths of the eaves and rakes to figure drip edge, and the number and size of vent pipes to figure vent flashing.

Asphalt shingles come in packaged bundles weighing around 65 pounds each. For typical three-tab shingles, three bundles will cover one square (100 sq. ft.) of roof.

Calculate the roof's surface by multiplying the height of the roof by the width. Do this for each section, then add the totals together. Divide that number by 100, add 10 percent for waste, and that's the number of squares of roofing materials you need.

Conversion Chart

Slope	Multiply by	Slope	Multiply by
2 in 12	1.02	8 in 12	1.20
3 in 12	1.03	9 in 12	1.25
4 in 12	1.06	10 in 12	1.30
5 in 12	1.08	11 in 12	1.36
6 in 12	1.12	12 in 12	1.41
7 in 12	1.16		

HOW TO TEAR OFF OLD SHINGLES

1

Remove the ridge cap using a flat pry bar. Pry up the cap shingles at the nail locations.

2

Working downward from the peak, tear off the felt paper and old shingles with a roofing shovel or pitchfork.

3

Unless flashing is in exceptional condition, remove it by slicing through the roofing cement that attaches it to the shingles. You may be able to salvage flashing pieces, such as chimney saddles and crickets, and reuse them.

4

After removing the shingles, felt paper, and flashing from the entire tear-off section, pry out any remaining nails and sweep the roof with a broom.

5

If an unexpected delay keeps you from finishing a section before nightfall, cover any unshingled sections using tarps weighted down with shingle bundles.

EXTERIOR

R

HOW TO INSTALL UNDERLAYMENT

Snap a chalk line 35⅝" up from the eaves, so the first course of the 36"-wide membrane will overhang the eaves by ⅜". Install a course of ice and water shield, using the chalk line as a reference, and peeling back the protective backing as you unroll it.

Measuring up from the eaves, make a mark 32" above the top of the last row of underlayment, and snap another chalk line. Roll out the next course of felt paper (or ice guard, if required) along the chalk line, overlapping the first course by 4". *Tip: Drive staples every 6 to 12" along the edges of felt paper, and one staple per sq. ft. in the field area.*

At valleys, roll felt paper across from both sides, overlapping the ends by 36". Install felt paper up to the ridge—ruled side up—snapping horizontal lines every two or three rows to check alignment. Overlap horizontal seams by 4", vertical seams by 12", and hips and ridges by 6". Trim the courses flush with the rake edges.

Apply felt paper up to an obstruction, then resume laying the course on the opposite side (make sure to maintain the line). Cut a patch that overlaps the felt paper by 12" on all sides. Make a crosshatch cutout for the obstruction. Position the patch over the obstruction, staple it in place, then caulk the seams with roofing cement.

At the bottom of dormers and sidewalls, tuck the felt paper under the siding where it intersects with the roof. Carefully pry up the siding and tuck at least 2" of paper under it. Also tuck the paper under counter flashing or siding on chimneys and skylights. Leave the siding or counter flashing or siding unfastened until after you install the step flashing.

HOW TO INSTALL DRIP EDGE

Cut a 45° miter at one end of the drip edge using aviation snips. Place the drip edge along the eaves end of the roof, aligning the mitered end with the rake edge. Nail the drip edge in place every 12".

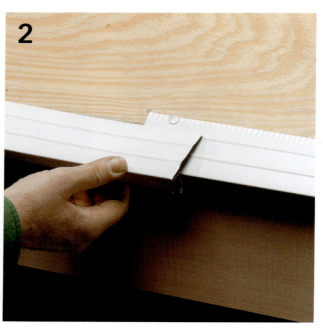

Overlap pieces of drip edge by 2". Install drip edge across the entire eaves, ending with a mitered cut on the opposite corner.

Apply felt paper, and ice guard if needed, to the roof, overhanging the eaves by ⅜" (see page 347).

Cut a 45° miter in a piece of drip edge and install it along the rake edge, forming a miter joint with the drip edge along the eaves. Overlap pieces by 2", making sure the higher piece is on top at the overlap. Apply drip edge all the way to the peak. Install drip edge along the other rake edges the same way.

ROOFING: PREPARING: FLASHING

Flashing is a metal or rubber barrier used to protect the seams around roof elements or between adjoining roof surfaces. Metal flashings are made of either galvanized steel, copper, or aluminum. Whatever metal you choose, use nails made of the same material. Mixing metals can cause corrosion and discoloration.

Flashing's primary job is to channel water off the roof and away from seams. It's installed in areas where shingles can't be applied and would otherwise be prone to leaks. Some flashing, such as the valley flashing shown on the next page, is installed over the underlayment, prior to the installation of the shingles. Other flashing, such as flashing for vent pipes, is installed in conjunction with the shingles, and is shown as part of the roofing sequences throughout this chapter.

While most flashing is preformed, you'll sometimes need to bend your own. This is especially true for flashing around roof elements, such as chimneys and dormers, that often need to be custom fit. Building a bending jig, as shown on the next page, allows you to easily bend flashing to fit your needs.

When installing flashing around roof elements, the flashing should be secured to one surface only—usually the roof deck. Use only roofing cement to bond the flashing to the roof elements. The flashing must be able to flex as the roof element and the roof deck expand and contract. If the flashing is fastened to both the roof deck and roof element, it will tear or loosen.

Tools & Materials ▸

Aviation snips	Galvanized metal
Caulk gun	valley flashing
Flat pry bar	Roofing cement
Roofing hammer	Roofing nails or
Tape measure	rubber gasket nails
Trowel	Screws
Clamp	Protective equipment
Scrap wood	

Flashing is a critical component of roofs that helps keep the structure watertight. Most roofs have flashing in the valleys and around dormers. This roof uses several valley flashings as well as flashing around the window and around the bump-out in the roof.

HOW TO BEND FLASHING

To bend flashing, make a bending jig by driving screws into a piece of wood, creating a space one-half the width of the flashing when measured from the edge of the board. Clamp the bending jig to a work surface. Lay a piece of flashing flat on the board and bend it over the edge.

Use the old flashing as a template for making replacement pieces. This is especially useful for reproducing complicated flashing, such as saddle flashing for chimneys and dormers.

HOW TO INSTALL VALLEY FLASHING

Spine

Starting at the eaves, set a piece of valley flashing into the valley so the bottom of the V rests in the crease of the valley. Nail the flashing at 12" intervals along each side. Trim the end of the flashing at the eaves so it's flush with the drip edge at each side. Working toward the top of the valley, add flashing pieces so they overlap by at least 8" until you reach the ridge.

Let the top edge of the flashing extend a few inches beyond the ridge. Bend the flashing over the ridge so it lies flat on the opposite side of the roof. If you're installing preformed flashing, make a small cut in the spine for easier bending. Cover nail heads with roofing cement (unless you're using rubber gasket nails). Apply roofing cement along the side edges of the flashing.

ROOFING: REPAIRING

A roof system is composed of several elements that work together to provide three basic, essential functions for your home: shelter, drainage, and ventilation. The roof covering and flashing are designed to shed water, directing it to gutters and downspouts. Air intake and outtake vents keep fresh air circulating below the roof sheathing, preventing moisture and heat buildup.

When your roof system develops problems that compromise its ability to protect your home—cracked shingles, incomplete ventilation, or damaged flashing—the damage quickly spreads to other parts of your house. Routine inspections are the best way to make sure the roof continues to do its job effectively.

Tools & Materials ▸

Tape measure	Replacement flashing
Wire brush	Replacement shingles
Aviation snips	Plywood
Trowel	Double-headed nails
Flat pry bar	Rubber gasket nails
Hammer	Lath strips
Utility knife	Wood chisel
Caulk gun	Zinc strip (if needed)
Tarp	Hacksaw blade (for repairing
Roofing cement	wood shakes or shingles)
Roofing nails	Protective equipment

▌ TIPS FOR IDENTIFYING ROOFING PROBLEMS

Ice dams occur when melting snow refreezes near the eaves, causing ice to back up under the shingles, where it melts onto the sheathing and seeps into the house.

Inspect both the interior and the exterior of the roof to spot problems. From inside the attic, check the rafters and sheathing for signs of water damage. Symptoms will appear in the form of streaking or discoloration. A moist or wet area also signals water damage.

COMMON ROOFING PROBLEMS

Wind, weather, and flying debris can damage shingles. The areas along valleys and ridges tend to take the most weather-related abuse. Torn, loose, or cracked shingles are common in these areas.

Buckled and cupped shingles are usually caused by moisture beneath the shingles. Loosened areas create an entry point for moisture and leave shingles vulnerable to wind damage.

A sagging ridge might be caused by the weight of too many roofing layers. It might also be the result of a more significant problem, such as a rotting ridge board or insufficient support for the ridge board.

Dirt and debris attract moisture and decay, which shorten a roof's life. To protect shingles, carefully wash the roof once a year using a pressure washer. Pay particular attention to areas where moss and mildew may accumulate.

In damp climates, it's a good idea to nail a zinc strip along the center ridge of a roof, under the ridge caps. Minute quantities of zinc wash down the roof each time it rains, killing moss and mildew.

Overhanging tree limbs drop debris and provide shade that encourages moss and mildew. To reduce chances of decay, trim any limbs that overhang the roof.

HOW TO LOCATE & EVALUATE LEAKS

If you have an unfinished attic, examine the underside of your roof with a flashlight on a rainy day. If you find wetness, discoloration, or other signs of moisture, trace the trail up to where the water is making its entrance.

Water that flows toward a wall can be temporarily diverted to minimize damage. Nail a small block of wood in the path of the water, and place a bucket underneath to catch the drip. On a dry day, drive a nail through the underside of the roof decking to mark the hole.

If the leak is finding its way to a finished ceiling, take steps to minimize damage until the leak can be repaired. As soon as possible, reduce the accumulation of water behind a ceiling by poking a small hole in the wallboard or plaster and draining the water.

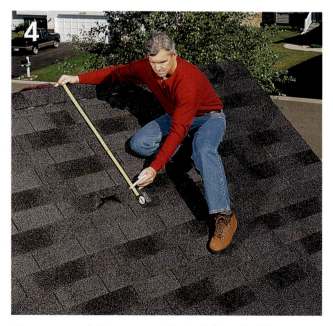

Once you mark the source of a leak from inside, measure from that spot to a point that will be visible and identifiable from outside the house, such as a chimney, vent pipe, or the peak of the roof. Get up on the roof and use that measurement to locate the leak.

HOW TO MAKE EMERGENCY REPAIRS

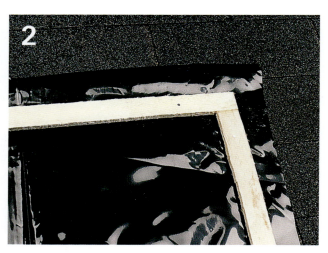

If your roof is severely damaged, the primary goal is to prevent additional damage until permanent repairs are made. Nail a sheet of plywood to the roof to serve as emergency cover to keep out the wind and water. *Tip: For temporary repairs, use double-headed nails, which can be easily removed. Fill nail holes with roofing cement when the repair is complete.*

Cover the damaged area by nailing strips of lath around the edges of a plastic sheet or tarp.

HOW TO MAKE SPOT REPAIRS WITH ROOFING CEMENT

To reattach a loose shingle, wipe down the felt paper and the underside of the shingle. Let each dry, then apply a liberal coat of roofing cement. Press the shingle down to seat it in the bed of cement. *Tip: Heat softens the roof's surface, and cold makes it brittle. If needed, warm shingles slightly with a hair dryer to make them easier to work with and less likely to crack.*

Tack down buckled shingles by cleaning below the buckled area, filling the area with roofing cement, then pressing the shingle into the cement. Patch cracks and splits in shingles with roofing cement.

Check the joints around flashing, which are common places for roof leaks to occur. Seal any gaps by cleaning out and replacing any failed roofing cement.

HOW TO REPLACE ASPHALT SHINGLES

Pull out damaged shingles, starting with the uppermost shingle in the damaged area. Be careful not to damage surrounding shingles that are still in good condition.

Remove old nails in and above the repair area using a flat pry bar. Patch damaged felt paper with roofing cement.

Install the replacement shingles, beginning with the lowest shingle in the repair area. Nail above the tab slots using ⅞ or 1" roofing nails.

Install all but the top shingle with nails, then apply roofing cement to the underside of the top shingle, above the seal line.

Slip the last shingle into place, under the overlapping shingle. Lift the shingles immediately above the repair area, and nail the top replacement shingle.

HOW TO REPLACE WOOD SHAKES & SHINGLES

Split the damaged wood shingles or shakes with a wood chisel and mallet so they can be removed.

Remove the pieces. Slide a hacksaw blade under the overlapping shingles and cut the nail heads. Pry out the remaining pieces of the shakes or shingles.

Gently pry up, but don't remove, the shakes or shingles above the repair area. Cut new pieces for the lowest course, leaving a ⅜" gap between pieces. Nail replacements in place with ring-shank siding nails. Fill in all but the top course in the repair area.

Cut the shakes or shingles for the top course. Because the top course can't be nailed, use roofing cement to fasten the pieces in place. Apply a coat of roofing cement where the shakes or shingles will sit, then slip them beneath the overlapping pieces. Press down to seat them in the roofing cement.

ROOFING: RIDGE VENTS

If you need attic ventilation, installing a continuous ridge vent will get the job done. Since they're installed along the entire ridge of the roof, they provide an even flow of air along the entire underside of the roof decking. Combined with continuous soffit vents, this is the most effective type of ventilation system.

Since the vents are installed along the ridge, they're practically invisible, eliminating any disruptions to the roof. Other vent types, such as roof louvers and turbines, often distract from the roof's aesthetics.

Installing one continuous ridge vent is quicker and easier than installing other types of vents that need to be placed in several locations across the roof. It also saves you from having to make numerous cuts in your finished roof, which can disturb surrounding shingles.

Tools & Materials ▶

Hammer	Flat pry bar
Circular saw	Ridge vents
Tape measure	1½" roofing nails
Chalk line	Protective equipment

Continuous ridge vents work in conjunction with the soffits to allow airflow under the roof decking. Installed at the roof peak and covered with cap shingles, ridge vents are less conspicuous than other roof vents.

HOW TO INSTALL A RIDGE VENT

Remove the ridge caps using a flat pry bar. Measure down from the peak the width of the manufacturer's recommended opening, and mark each end of the roof. Snap a chalk line between the marks. Repeat for the other side of the peak. Remove any nails in your path.

Set the blade depth of a circular saw to cut the sheathing but not the rafters. Cut along each chalk line, staying 12" from the edges of the roof. Remove the cut sheathing using a pry bar.

(continued)

Measure down from the peak half the width of the ridge vent, and make a mark on both ends of the roof. Snap a line between the marks. Do this on both sides of the peak.

Center the ridge vent over the peak, aligning the edges with the chalk lines. Install using roofing nails that are long enough to penetrate the roof sheathing. *Tip: If a chimney extends through the peak, leave 12" of sheathing around the chimney.*

Butt sections of ridge vents together and nail the ends. Install vents across the entire peak, including the 12" sections at each end of the roof that were not cut away.

Place ridge cap shingles over the ridge vents. Nail them with two 1½" roofing nails per cap. Overlap the caps as you would on a normal ridge. If the caps you removed in step 1 are still in good shape, you can reuse them. Otherwise, use new ones.

ROOFING: ROOF VENTS

Ridge pole

Mark the location for the roof vent by driving a nail through the roof sheathing. Center the nail between rafters 16" to 24" from the ridge pole.

Center a vent cover over the nail on the outside of the roof. Outline the base flange of the vent cover on the shingles, then remove shingles in an area 2" inside the outline. Mark the roof vent hole using the marker nail as a centerpoint. Cut the hole using a reciprocating saw or jigsaw.

Apply roof cement to the underside of the base flange. Set the vent cover in position, slipping the flange under the shingles, centered over the vent-hole cutout.

Secure the roof vent to the sheathing with rubber gasket nails on all sides of the flange. Tack down any loose shingles. Do not nail through the flange when attaching shingles.

ROOFING: SAFETY EQUIPMENT

Working on the exterior of a house presents challenges not faced in the interior, such as dealing with the weather, working at heights, and staying clear of power lines. By taking a few commonsense safety precautions, you can perform exterior work safely.

Dress appropriately for the job and weather. Avoid working in extreme temperatures, hot or cold, and never work outdoors during a storm or high winds.

Work with a helper whenever possible—especially when working at heights. If you must work alone, tell a family member or friend so the person can check in with you periodically. Keep your cell phone handy at all times.

Don't use tools or work at heights after consuming alcohol. If you're taking medications, read the label and follow the recommendations regarding the use of tools and equipment.

When using ladders, extend the top of the ladder 3 feet above the roof edge for greater stability. Climb on and off the ladder at a point as close to the ground as possible. Use caution and keep your center of gravity low when moving from a ladder onto a roof. Keep your hips between the side rails when reaching over the side of a ladder, and be careful not to extend yourself too far or it could throw off your balance. Move the ladder as often as necessary to avoid overreaching. Finally, don't exceed the workload rating for your ladder. Read and follow the load limits and safety instructions listed on the label.

Wear appropriate clothing and safety equipment whenever working high above ground. Eye protection and hearing protection are very important when using power tools or pneumatic tools. And if you'll be climbing on a roof, wear tennis shoes or any sturdy shoe with a soft sole designed for gripping. When roofing, always avoid hard-soled shoes or boots, which can damage shingles and are prone to slipping.

Safety Tips ▶

Use a GFCI extension cord when working outdoors. GFCIs (ground-fault circuit-interrupters) shut off power if a short circuit occurs.

Use cordless tools to eliminate the hazards of extension cords, especially when working from ladders.

Use fiberglass or wood ladders when working near power cables. Exercise extreme caution around these cables, and only work near them when absolutely necessary.

Never climb a ladder with a loaded air nailer attached to a pressurized air hose. Even with trigger safeties, air guns pose a serious danger to the operator as well as anyone who may be standing near the ladder.

FALL-ARRESTING GEAR

Even if you consider yourself dexterous and are comfortable working in high places, all it takes is one misstep on a roof to lead to a tragic fall. Despite the fact that many professional roofers never don safety harnesses, you should seriously consider investing in personal fall-arresting gear if you plan to reroof your home. Fall-arresting gear consists of several components. You wear a webbed body harness that spreads the impact of a fall over your shoulders, thighs, and back to reduce injury. Harnesses are made to fit average adult builds. The harness connects to a shock absorber and a lanyard around 6 feet in length. A self-locking, rope-grab mechanism attaches the lanyard to a lifeline that must be fastened securely to a ridge anchor screwed to roof framing. In the event that you slip or fall, the rope grab will limit your fall to the length of the lanyard because it will not move down the lifeline unless you override the locking mechanism by hand.

Most rental centers will not carry fall-arresting gear, and a complete system will cost several hundred dollars. When compared with the loss of life or limb, however, your real investment is small. Better yet, you'll have it available any time you need to get on the roof for cleaning tasks or to make repairs.

Tools & Materials ▸

Drill/driver
Harness
Lanyard
Rope grab

Synthetic fiber lifeline
Ridge anchor

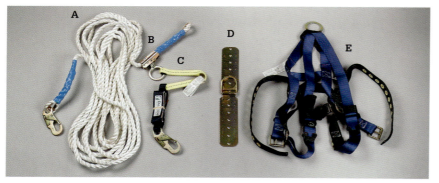

Personal fall-arresting gear consists of a lifeline (A) with mechanical rope grab (B) and lanyard (C); a metal ridge anchor (D); and a body harness (E).

A metal ridge anchor must be secured with screws to the roof framing. Follow the manufacturer's recommendations for proper screw sizing, and make sure your attachment points go beyond the roof sheathing into the roof trusses or rafters.

The rope-grab mechanism allows you to move up a roof along the lifeline without interference. To move down the roof, you'll need to override the grab by hand. As soon as you release it, the lock engages again.

ROOFING: SAFETY EQUIPMENT: ROOF JACKS

Sure footing isn't an issue when you're working on a low-pitched roof, but it becomes a real safety concern for roofs with 7-in-12 or steeper pitches. In these situations, you need to install roof jacks to create a stable work area and navigate the roof safely. Roof jacks are steel braces that nail temporarily to roof decking to support a 2 × 8 or 2 × 10 perch. In addition to improving your footing, roof jacks also provide a flatter surface to stand on, which can help reduce ankle strain. Roof jacks should be installed every 4 feet of plank length with 16d nails. They're inexpensive and available wherever roofing products are sold.

Roof jacks are steel braces that you nail to the roof deck. Installed in pairs, they support a dimensional board (usually a 2 × 8) to create a sturdy work platform on a sloped roof.

Tools & Materials ▸

Pry bar
Hammer
16d nails
Roof jacks
2 × 8 or 2 × 10 lumber

HOW TO INSTALL ROOF JACKS

Nail roof jacks to the roof at the fourth or fifth course. Drive 16d nails into the overlap, or dead area, where they won't be exposed. Install one jack every 4 ft., with a 6" to 12" overhang at the ends of the boards.

Shingle over the tops of the roof jacks. Rest a 2 × 8 or 2 × 10 board on the jacks. Fasten the board with a nail driven through the hole in the lip of each roof jack.

When the project is complete, remove the boards and jacks. Position the end of a flat pry bar over each nail and drive in the nail by rapping the shank with a hammer.

ROOFING: THREE-TAB SHINGLES

If you want to install asphalt shingles on your roof, then you're in good company. Asphalt shingles, also known as composition shingles, are the roofing of choice for nearly four out of five homeowners in America. They perform well in all types of climate, are available in a multitude of colors, shapes, and textures to complement every housing design, and are less expensive than most other roofing products.

Asphalt shingles are available as either fiberglass shingles or organic shingles. Both types are made with asphalt, the difference being that one uses a fiberglass reinforcing mat, while the other uses a cellulose-fiber mat. Fiberglass shingles are lighter, thinner, and have a better fire rating. Organic shingles have a higher tear strength, are more flexible in cold climates, and are used more often in northern regions.

Although the roofing market has exploded with innovative new asphalt shingle designs, such as the architectural or laminated shingle that offers a three-dimensional look, the standard three-tab asphalt shingle is still the most common, which is the project we're featuring here. The tabs provide an easy reference for aligning shingles for installation.

To help the job get done faster, rent an air compressor and pneumatic roofing gun. This will greatly reduce the time you spend nailing.

Tools & Materials ▶

Aviation snips	Chalk gun
Carpenter's square	Flashing
Chalk line	Shingles
Flat bar	Nailing cartridges
Roofer's hatchet or	Roofing cement
pneumatic nailer	Roofing nails
Utility knife	(⅞", 1¼")
Straightedge	Rubber gasket nails
Tape measure	Protective equipment

Stagger shingles for effective protection against leaks. If the tab slots are aligned in successive rows, water forms channels, increasing erosion of the mineral surface of the shingles. Creating a 6" offset between rows of shingles—with the three-tab shingles shown above—ensures that the tab slots do not align.

HOW TO INSTALL THREE-TAB SHINGLES

Cover the roof with felt paper (pages 70 to 71) and install drip edge (pages 72 to 73). Snap a chalk line onto the felt paper or ice guard 11½" up from the eaves edge, to mark the alignment of the starter course. This will result in a ½" shingle overhang for standard 12" shingles. *Tip: Use blue chalk rather than red. Red chalk will stain roofing materials.*

Trim off one-half (6") of an end tab on a shingle. Position the shingle upside down, so the tabs are aligned with the chalk line and the half-tab is flush against the rake edge. Drive ⅞" roofing nails near each end, 1" down from each slot between tabs. Butt a full upside-down shingle next to the trimmed shingle, and nail it. Fill out the row, trimming the last shingle flush with the opposite rake edge.

Apply the first full course of shingles over the starter course with the tabs pointing down. Begin at the rake edge where you began the starter row. Place the first shingle so it overhangs the rake edge by ⅜" and the eaves edge by ½". Make sure the top of each shingle is flush with the top of the starter course, following the chalk line.

Snap a chalk line from the eaves edge to the ridge to create a vertical line to align the shingles. Choose an area with no obstructions, as close as possible to the center of the roof. The chalk line should pass through a slot or a shingle edge on the first full shingle course. Use a carpenter's square to establish a line perpendicular to the eaves edge.

(continued)

Use the vertical reference line to establish a shingle pattern with slots that are offset by 6" in succeeding courses. Tack down a shingle 6" to one side of the vertical line, 5" above the bottom edge of the first-course shingles to start the second row. Tack down shingles for the third and fourth courses, 12" and 18" from the vertical line. Butt the fifth course against the line.

Fill in shingles in the second through fifth courses, working upward from the second course and maintaining a consistent 5" reveal. Slide lower-course shingles under any upper-course shingles left partially nailed, and then nail them down. *Tip: Install roof jacks, if needed, after filling out the fifth course.*

Check the alignment of the shingles after each four-course cycle. In several spots on the last installed course, measure from the bottom edge of a shingle to the nearest felt paper line. If you discover any misalignment, make minor adjustments over the next few rows until it's corrected.

When you reach obstructions, such as dormers, install a full course of shingles above them so you can retain your shingle offset pattern. On the unshingled side of the obstruction, snap another vertical reference line using the shingles above the obstruction as a guide.

Shingle upward from the eaves on the unshingled side of the obstruction using the vertical line as a reference for reestablishing your shingle slot offset pattern. Fill out the shingle courses past the rake edges of the roof, then trim off the excess.

Trim off excess shingle material at the V in the valley flashing using a utility knife and straightedge. Do not cut into the flashing. The edges will be trimmed back farther at a slight taper after both roof decks are completely shingled.

Install shingles on adjoining roof decks, starting at the bottom edge using the same offset alignment pattern shown in steps 1 to 6. Install shingles until courses overlap the center of the valley flashing. Trim shingles at both sides of the valley when finished.

Install shingles up to the vent pipe so the flashing rests on at least one row of shingles. Apply a heavy double bead of roofing cement along the bottom edge of the flange.

(continued)

13

Sleeve

Place the flashing over the vent pipe. Position the flashing collar so the longer portion of the tapered neck slopes down the roof and the flange lies over the shingles. Nail the perimeter of the flange using rubber gasket nails.

14

Cut shingles to fit around the neck of the flashing so they lie flat against the flange. Do not drive roofing nails through the flashing. Instead, apply roofing cement to the back of shingles where they lie over the flashing.

15

Outline of shape for first piece of step flashing

Base flashing

Trim line

Waste section

Shingle up to an element that requires flashing so the top of the reveal areas are within 5" of the element. Install base flashing using the old base flashing as a template. Bend a piece of step flashing in half and set it next to the lowest corner of the element. Mark a trim line on the flashing, following the vertical edge of the element. Cut the flashing to fit.

16

Spacer

Pry out the lowest courses of siding and any trim at the base of the element. Insert spacers to prop the trim or siding away from the work area. Apply roofing cement to the base flashing in the area where the overlap with the step flashing will be formed. Tuck the trimmed piece of step flashing under the propped area, and secure the flashing. Fasten the flashing with one rubber gasket nail driven near the top and into the roof deck.

Apply roofing cement to the top side of the first piece of step flashing where it will be covered by the next shingle course. Install the shingle by pressing it firmly into the roofing cement. Do not nail through the flashing underneath.

Tuck another piece of flashing under the trim or siding, overlapping the first piece of flashing at least 2". Set the flashing into roofing cement applied on the top of the shingle. Nail the shingle in place without driving nails through the flashing. Install flashing up to the top of the element the same way. Trim the last piece of flashing to fit the top corner of the element. Reattach the siding and trim.

Counterflashing

Base flashing

Shingle up to the chimney base. Use the old base flashing as a template to cut new flashing. Bend up the counter flashing. Apply roofing cement to the base of the chimney and the shingles just below the base. Press the base flashing into the roofing cement and bend the flashing around the edges of the chimney. Drive rubber gasket nails through the flashing flange into the roof deck.

Step flashing

Install step flashing and shingles, working up to the high side of the chimney. Fasten flashing to the chimney with roofing cement. Fold down the counter flashing as you go.

(continued)

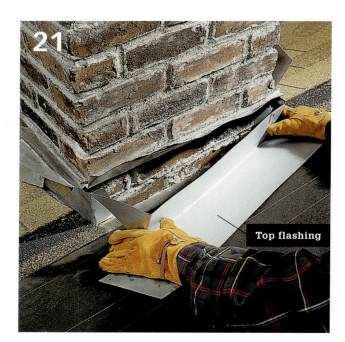

Cut and install top flashing (also called a saddle) around the high side of the chimney. Overlap the final piece of flashing along each side. Attach the flashing with roofing cement applied to the deck and chimney and with rubber gasket nails driven through the flashing base into the roof deck. Shingle past the chimney using roofing cement (not nails) to attach shingles over the flashing.

When you reach a hip or ridge, shingle up the first side until the top of the uppermost reveal area is within 5" of the hip or ridge. Trim the shingles along the peak. Install shingles on the opposite side of the hip or ridge. Overlap the peak no more than 5".

Cut three 12"-sq. cap shingles from each three-tab shingle. With the back surface facing up, cut the shingles at the tab lines. Trim the top corners of each square with an angled cut, starting just below the seal strip to avoid overlaps in the reveal area.

Snap a chalk line 6" down from the ridge, parallel to the peak. Attach cap shingles, starting at one end of the ridge, aligned with the chalk line. Drive two 1¼" roofing nails per cap about 1" from each edge, just below the seal strip.

Following the chalk line, install cap shingles halfway along the ridge, creating a 5" reveal for each cap. Then, starting at the opposite end, install caps over the other half of the ridge to meet the first run in the center. Cut a 5"-wide section from the reveal area of a shingle tab, and use it as a "closure cap" to cover the joint where the caps meet.

Shingle the hips in the same manner using a chalk reference line and cap shingles. Start at the bottom of each hip and work to the peak. Where hips join with roof ridges, install a custom shingle cut from the center of a cap shingle. Set the cap at the end of the ridge and bend the corners so they fit over the hips. Secure each corner with a roofing nail, and cover the nail heads with roofing cement.

After all shingles are installed, trim them at the valleys to create a gap that's 3" wide at the top and widens at a rate of 1⁄8" per foot as it moves downward. Use a utility knife and straightedge to cut the shingles, making sure not to cut through the valley flashing. At the valleys, seal the undersides and edges of shingles with roofing cement. Also cover exposed nail heads with roofing cement.

Mark and trim the shingles at the rake edges of the roof. Snap a chalk line 3⁄8" from the edge to make an overhang, then trim the shingles.

RUBBER ROOFS

Prepare the roof deck for membrane roofing by removing the old roofing material down to bare decking. Look closely for signs of deterioration. Replace deteriorated decking. For a smooth surface, cover the roof with a new layer of high-density fiberboard (sold at roofing materials suppliers). Secure with fasteners recommended by the manufacturer for this purpose—usually long screws with large insulation plates.

Sweep the roof deck thoroughly, and spread out the membrane so it has a chance to relax. Make any cutouts in the membrane that may be necessary to allow for vent pipes or other protrusions. Overlap the sheets by 3" and wipe them down with the recommended cleaner to prepare the surfaces for adhesive.

Apply the latex adhesive. Fold half of the first membrane sheet over on itself to expose the roof deck, and roll a heavy coat of adhesive onto both the deck and membrane surfaces with a medium-nap paint roller. However, do not apply adhesive to the overlapped section of membrane. Once the adhesive begins to set (about 20 minutes in normal conditions), carefully roll the folded rubber down into place. Avoid wrinkling the membrane.

Use a stiff-bristle push broom to brush out any air pockets that may be evident under the bonded half of the membrane. Brush from the middle of the roof outward to the edges. Then fold the other unbonded half over, apply adhesive to the rubber and roof deck again, and adhere this half of the membrane to the roof. Apply all sections of membrane to the roof deck in this fashion, but do not apply adhesive within 3" of the edges of any overlapping sections of rubber; these must be accessible for applying seaming tape along the seams.

Roll the top section of overlapping membrane back along the seam area, and chalk a reference line 3" from the edge of the bottom membrane. This marks the area for applying seaming tape.

Tape the seams. Use the recommended cleaning solvent to clean both halves of the overlapping membrane in the tape areas, then apply seaming tape sticky side down to the bottom membrane within the marked area. Press the tape down firmly to ensure good adhesion to the membrane.

Fold the top membrane overlap back in place on the tape. Slowly pull off the tape's paper backing with the membrane edges now overlapping. Press the overlapping edges down to create a tighter, smooth seam. Roll the seamed areas with a J-roller or seam rolling tool to bond the seam.

If the roof meets a vertical wall, you may need to remove siding so you can bond the membrane to wall sheathing. Use contact adhesive to apply the membrane 12" up the wall. Seal the edge with a metal termination bar fastened to the wall with exterior screws. Trim off overhanging membrane around the roof edges, and flash it according to the manufacturer's recommendations using rubber adhesive flashing and rubber boots.

SHEET VINYL: FLOORING: INSTALLING

Preparing a perfect underlayment is the most important phase of resilient sheet vinyl installation (see pages 184 to 189). Cutting the material to fit the contours of the room is a close second.

The best way to ensure accurate cuts is to make a cutting template. Some manufacturers offer template kits, or you can make one by following the instructions on page 377. Be sure to use the recommended adhesive for the sheet vinyl you are installing. Many manufacturers require that you use the glue they provide for installation.

Use extreme care when handling the sheet vinyl, especially felt-backed products, to avoid creasing and tearing.

Tools & Materials ▶

Linoleum knife	Heat gun
Framing square	Straightedge
Compass	Vinyl flooring
Scissors	Masking tape
Non-permanent	Heavy butcher paper
felt-tipped pen	Duct tape
Utility knife	Flooring adhesive
¼" V-notched trowel	⅜" staples
J-roller	Metal threshold bars
Stapler	Nails
Flooring roller	Wallboard knife
Sponge	Wallboard saw
Chalk line	Protective equipment
Hammer	

Sheet vinyl is a classic flooring material that is easy to install and simple to maintain.

TOOLS FOR INSTALLING RESILIENT FLOORS

Tools for resilient flooring installation include a heat gun (A), J-roller (B), floor roller (C), framing square (D), sponge (E), notched trowel (F), hammer (G), stapler (H), linoleum knife (I), utility knife (J), wallboard saw (K), chalk line (L), and straightedge (M).

RESILIENT FLOORING TYPES

Perimeter-bond flooring

Full-spread sheet vinyl

Dry-back tile

Self-adhesive tile

Resilient sheet vinyl comes in full-spread and perimeter-bond styles. Full-spread sheet vinyl has a felt-paper backing and is secured with adhesive that is spread over the floor before installation. Perimeter-bond flooring, identifiable by its smooth, white PVC backing, is laid directly on underlayment and is secured by a special adhesive spread along the edges and seams.

Resilient tile comes in self-adhesive and dry-back styles. Self-adhesive tile has a pre-applied adhesive protected by wax paper backing that is peeled off as the tiles are installed. Dry-back tile is secured with adhesive spread onto the underlayment before installation. Self-adhesive tile is easier to install than dry-back tile, but the bond is less reliable. Don't use additional adhesives with self-adhesive tile.

Installation Tips ▸

Sweep and vacuum the underlayment thoroughly before installing resilient flooring to ensure a smooth, flawless finish (left). Small pieces of debris can create noticeable bumps in the flooring (right).

Handle resilient sheet vinyl carefully to avoid creasing or tearing (right). Working with a helper can help prevent costly mistakes (left). Make sure the sheet vinyl is at room temperature before you handle it.

HOW TO MAKE A CUTTING TEMPLATE

Place sheets of heavy butcher paper or brown wrapping paper along the walls, leaving a ⅛" expansion gap. Cut triangular holes in the paper with a utility knife. Fasten the template to the floor by placing masking tape over the holes.

Follow the outline of the room, working with one sheet of paper at a time. Overlap the edges of adjoining sheets by about 2" and tape the sheets together.

To fit the template around pipes, tape sheets of paper on either side. Measure the distance from the wall to the center of the pipe, then subtract ⅛".

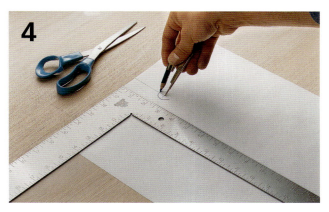

Transfer the measurement to a separate piece of paper. Use a compass to draw the pipe diameter on the paper, then cut out the hole with scissors or a utility knife. Cut a slit from the edge of the paper to the hole.

Fit the hole cutout around the pipe. Tape the hole template to the adjoining sheets.

When completed, roll or loosely fold the paper template for carrying.

HOW TO INSTALL PERIMETER-BOND SHEET VINYL

1

Unroll the flooring on any large, flat, clean surface. To prevent wrinkles, sheet vinyl comes from the manufacturer rolled with the pattern-side out. Unroll the sheet and turn it pattern-side up for marking.

2

For two-piece installations, overlap the edges of the sheets by at least 2". Plan to have the seams fall along the pattern lines or simulated grout joints. Align the sheets so the pattern matches, then tape the sheets together with duct tape.

3

Make a paper template (see page 377) and position it. Trace the outline of the template onto the flooring using a non-permanent felt-tipped pen.

4

Remove the template. Cut the sheet vinyl with a sharp linoleum knife or a utility knife with a new blade. Use a straightedge as a guide for making longer cuts.

5

Cut holes for pipes and other permanent obstructions. Cut a slit from each hole to the nearest edge of the flooring. Whenever possible, make slits along pattern lines.

6

Roll up the flooring loosely and transfer it to the installation area. Do not fold the flooring. Unroll and position the sheet vinyl carefully. Slide the edges beneath undercut door casings.

FLOORS

Cut the seams for two-piece installations using a straightedge as a guide. Hold the straightedge tightly against the flooring, and cut along the pattern lines through both pieces of vinyl flooring.

Remove both pieces of scrap flooring. The pattern should now run continuously across the adjoining sheets of flooring.

Fold back the edges of both sheets. Apply a 3" band of multipurpose flooring adhesive to the underlayment or old flooring, using a ¼" V-notched trowel or wallboard knife.

Lay the seam edges one at a time onto the adhesive. Make sure the seam is tight, pressing the gaps together with your fingers, if needed. Roll the seam edges with a J-roller or wallpaper seam roller.

Apply flooring adhesive underneath flooring cuts at pipes or posts and around the entire perimeter of the room. Roll the flooring with the roller to ensure good contact with the adhesive.

If you're applying flooring over a wood underlayment, fasten the outer edges of the sheet with ⅜" staples driven every 3". Make sure the staples will be covered by the base molding.

NO-GLUE SHEET VINYL

The latest in the sheet-vinyl world is a "loose-lay" (no-glue) product. It has a fiberglass backing, which makes it cushier than standard felt-backed vinyl. The fiberglass backing also makes this sheet product thicker and more dimensionally stable. Consequently, it only needs to be adhered at seams or under heavy appliances. Also, rather than using glue, you use acrylic double-sided adhesive tape.

No-glue sheet vinyl is installed in much the same way as other resilient sheet goods. Cutting the material to size is the most difficult part of the project. Fortunately, the major manufacturers have kits available to help you do it right.

This loose-lay sheet vinyl can be installed over many surfaces, including a single layer of sheet vinyl or vinyl tile, underlayment-grade plywood, concrete, or ceramic tile. Do not install over particleboard, cushioned vinyl flooring, carpet, strip wood, or plank flooring. Use embossing leveler to fill textured vinyl or ceramic grout lines, or use patching compound on plywood to create a flat, smooth surface. Do not

use carpet tape for this product, as it will cause discoloration. Use standard threshold transition moldings where the sheet vinyl meets other floor surfaces.

Supplies for installing no-glue sheet vinyl include a floor leveler and patching compound for preparing the floor, reinforced double-sided tape, and a seaming kit for larger installations.

Thicker than standard sheet vinyl flooring, no-glue sheet vinyl is designed to remain flat and stay put without the use of glues or other adhesives.

Installation Notes for No-glue Vinyl Flooring ▸

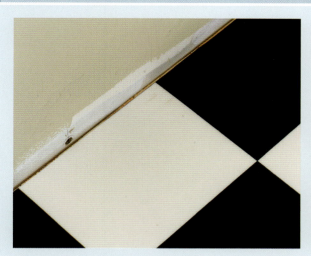

Leave gaps. To allow for the normal movement and expansion of the floor and wall surfaces, the flooring must be cut ³⁄₁₆ to ¼" away from all vertical surfaces such as walls, cabinets, or pipes. Use a jamb saw to undercut door trim—this will allow for expansion. Make sure vinyl is not contacting the wall surface behind the door trim. Check the fit of the no-glue flooring and then carefully remove the flooring.

Place acrylic double-face tape in areas that will be under heavy appliances such as stoves and refrigerators. Make an X with three pieces of tape—one long piece and two short pieces—so that the tape does not overlap. Place acrylic double-face tape at doorways and under seam lines. Leave the paper covering in place and press the tape down so it adheres well to the subfloor.

Center the tape under the two sides at seam lines. Press one side of the vinyl into place first. Place the second vinyl sheet and press it into place. Use a seam sealer kit to seal the seams.

Drive nails into the wall surface—not through the vinyl flooring—when installing the baseboard or base shoe. Anchoring the flooring with perimeter nails may result in buckling of the vinyl surface when the floor expands or contracts. Also, do not press the molding down into the vinyl. Leave a small gap between the molding and the floor surface so the vinyl is not constricted.

HOW TO INSTALL FULL-SPREAD SHEET VINYL

Cut the sheet vinyl using the techniques described on page 378 (steps 1 to 5), then lay the sheet vinyl into position, sliding the edges under door casings.

Pull back half of the flooring, then apply a layer of flooring adhesive over the underlayment or old flooring using a ¼" V-notched trowel. Lay the flooring back onto the adhesive.

Roll the bonded section with a weighted floor roller. The roller creates a stronger bond and eliminates air bubbles. Fold over the unbonded section of flooring, apply adhesive, then replace and roll the flooring. Wipe up any adhesive that oozes up around the edges of the vinyl using a damp rag.

Measure and cut metal threshold bars to fit across doorways. Position each bar over the edge of the vinyl flooring and nail it in place.

FLOORS

VINYL COVE MOLDING

Vinyl cove molding is popular in basements and other damp locations because it is moisture resistant. The plastic appearance and limited color selection make it less desirable from a design standpoint. Moldings are sold in strips and in rolls and are installed using trowel-on adhesive or adhesive caulk (inset).

To install, apply adhesive to the back side of the vinyl cove molding, not to the installation wall. If you bought your molding in a roll, roll the material out flat and let it rest for at least an hour or two before installing it. After you have applied the molding to the wall, roll the entire molding surface with a J-roller.

CUTTING VINYL COVE MOLDING

Use a backer board when cutting cove molding. Cut the molding where necessary to fit using a straightedge and sharp utility knife or flooring knife to create a butt joint.

At inside corners, lightly score the back of the molding from top to bottom at the joint of the corner. Notch the base of the molding at the bottom of the score, and press the molding firmly into the corner.

At outside corners, warm the molding with a hair dryer or paint stripping gun, and then fold it so that the back side is exposed, and shave a thin layer off the inside surface. Be careful not to cut all the way through the molding.

SHOWER DOOR: INSTALLING

1

Measure the width of the shower opening. If the walls of the shower slope inward slightly before meeting the base, take your measurement from a higher point at the full width of the opening so you don't cut the door base too short. Cut the base piece to fit using a hacksaw and a miter box. File the cut ends if necessary to deburr them.

2

Identify which side jamb will be the hinge jamb and which will be the strike jamb according to the direction you want your hinged door to swing—an outward swing is preferred. Prepare the jambs for installation as directed in your instructions.

3

Place the base jamb on the curb of the shower base. If the joint where the wall meets the curb is sloped, you'll need to trim the corners of the base piece to follow the profile. Place a jamb carefully onto the base and plumb it with a level. Then, mark a drilling point by tapping a centerpunch in the middle of each nail hole in each jamb. Remove the jambs, drill pilot holes, and then attach the jambs with the provided screws.

4

Remove the bottom track and prepare the shower base curb for installation of the base track, following the manufacturer's directions. Permanently install the bottom track. Bottom tracks (not all doors have them) are usually attached to the side jambs or held in place with adhesive. Never use fasteners to secure them to curb.

Working on the floor or another flat surface, attach the door hinge to the hinge jamb, if required. In most systems, the hinge is fitted over the hinge jamb after you attach it to the wall.

Attach the hinge to the door panel, according to the manufacturer's instructions. Attach any cap fitting that keeps water out of the jamb.

Fit the hinge jamb over the side jamb and adjust it as directed in your instruction manual. Once the clearances are correct, fasten the jambs to hang the door.

Sweep

Install the magnetic strike plate and any remaining caps or accessories such as towel rods. Also attach the sweep that seals the passage, if provided.

SHOWER ENCLOSURE: INSTALLING

Mark out the location of the shower, including any new walls, on the floor and walls. Most kits can be installed over wallboard, but you can usually achieve a more professional looking wall finish if you remove the wallcovering and floor covering in the installation area. Dispose of the materials immediately and thoroughly clean the area.

If you are adding a wall to create the alcove, lay out the locations for the studs and plumbing on the new wood sill plate. Also lay out the stud locations on the cap plate that will be attached to the ceiling. Refer to the enclosure kit instructions for exact locations and dimensions of studs. Attach the sill plate to the floor with deck screws and panel adhesive, making sure it is square to the back wall and the correct distance from the side wall.

Sill plate

New wall stud

Align a straight 2 × 4 right next to the sill plate and make a mark on the ceiling. Use a level to extend that line directly above the sill plate. Attach the cap plate at that point.

Install the 2 × 4 studs at the outlined locations. Check with a level to make sure each stud is plumb, and then attach them by driving deck screws toenail style into the sill plate and cap plate.

PLUMBING

S

Cut an access hole in the floor for the drain, according to the installation manual instructions. Drill openings in the sill plate of the wet wall (the new wall in this project) for the supply pipes, also according to the instructions.

Install a drain pipe and branch line and then trim the drain pipe flush with the floor. If you are not experienced with plumbing, hire a plumber to install the new drain line.

Faucet body

Cross brace

Ball valves

Supply riser

Install new supply risers as directed in the instruction manual (again, have a plumber do this if necessary). Also install cross braces between the studs in the wet wall for mounting the faucet body and shower arm.

If the supply plumbing is located in a wall (old or new) that is accessible from the non-shower side, install framing for a removable access panel.

(continued)

Attach the drain tailpiece that came with your receptor to the underside of the unit, following the manufacturer's instructions precisely. Here, an adjustable spud wrench is being used to tighten the tailpiece.

Option: To stabilize the receptor, especially if the floor is uneven, pour or trowel a layer of thinset mortar into the installation area, taking care to keep the mortar out of the drain access hole. Do not apply mortar in areas where the receptor has feet that are intended to make full contact with the floor.

Set the receptor in place, check to make sure it is level, and shim it if necessary. Secure the receptor with large-head roofing nails driven into the wall stud so the heads pin the flange against the stud. Do not overdrive the nails.

Lay out the locations for the valve hole or holes in the end wall panel that will be installed on the wet wall. Check your installation instructions. Some kits come with a template marked on the packaging carton. Cut the access hole with a hole saw and drill or with a jigsaw and fine-tooth blade. If using a jigsaw, orient the panel so the good surface is facing down.

Position the back wall so there is a slight gap (about 1⁄32") between the bottom of the panel and the rim of the receptor—set a few small spacers on the rim if need be. Tack a pair of roofing nails above the top of the back panel to hold it in place (or, use duct tape). Position both end walls and test the fits. Make clip connections between panels (inset) if your kit uses them.

Remove the end wall so you can prepare the installation area for them. If your kit recommends panel adhesive, apply it to the wall or studs. In the kit shown here, only a small bead of silicone sealant on the receptor flange is required.

Reinstall the end panels, permanently clipping them to the back panel according to the kit manufacturer's instructions. Make sure the front edges of the end panels are flush with the front of the receptor.

Once the panels are positioned correctly and snapped together, fasten them to the wall studs. If the panels have predrilled nail holes, drive roofing nails through them at each stud at the panel tops and every 4" to 6" along vertical surfaces.

(continued)

Install wallcovering material above the enclosure panels and anywhere else it is needed. Use moisture-resistant materials, and maintain a gap of ¼" between the shoulders of the top panel flanges and the wallcovering.

Finish the walls and then caulk between the enclosure panels and the wallcoverings with tub and tile caulk.

Install the faucet handles and escutcheon and caulk around the escutcheon plate. Install the shower arm escutcheon and showerhead.

Access panel

You can make an access panel out of plywood framed with mitered case molding, or buy a ready-made plumbing panel. Attach the panel to the opening created in step 8.

SIDING: REPAIRING

Damage to siding is fairly common, but fortunately, it's also easy to fix. Small to medium holes, cracks, and rotted areas can be repaired with filler or by replacing the damaged sections with matching siding.

If you cannot find matching siding for repairs at building centers, check with salvage yards or siding contractors. When repairing aluminum or vinyl siding, contact the manufacturer or the contractor who installed the siding to help you locate matching materials and parts. If you're unable to find an exact match, remove a section of original siding from a less visible area of the house, such as the back of the garage, and use it for the patch. Cover the gap in the less visible area with a close matching siding, where the mismatch will be less noticeable.

Tools & Materials ▸

Aviation snips	Paintbrush
Caulk gun	Epoxy wood filler
Drill	Epoxy glue
Flat pry bar	Galvanized ring-shank
Hammer	siding nails
Straightedge	Siliconized acrylic caulk
Tape measure	Roofing cement
Utility knife	30# felt paper
Zip-lock tool	Sheathing
Chisel	Trim
Trowel	Replacement siding
Screwdrivers	End caps
Hacksaw	Wood preservative
Circular saw	Primer
Jigsaw	Paint or stain
Key hole saw	Metal sandpaper
Nail set	Level
Stud finder	Protective equipment

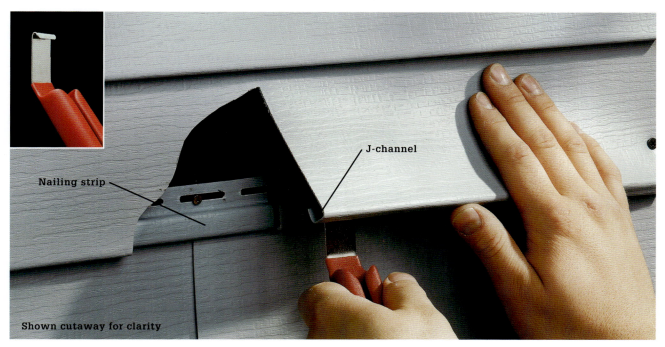

Vinyl and metal siding panels have a locking J-channel that fits over the bottom of the nailing strip on the underlying piece. Use a zip-lock tool (inset) to separate panels. Insert the tool at the seam nearest the repair area. Slide it over the J-channel, pulling outward slightly, to unlock the joint from the siding below.

HOW TO PATCH VINYL SIDING

Starting at the seam nearest the damaged area, unlock interlocking joints using a zip-lock tool. Insert spacers between the panels, then remove the fasteners in the damaged siding using a flat pry bar. Cut out the damaged area using aviation snips. Cut a replacement piece 4" longer than the open area, and trim 2" off the nailing strip from each end. Slide the piece into position.

Insert siding nails in the nailing strip, then position the end of a flat pry bar over each nail head. Drive the nails by tapping on the neck of the pry bar with a hammer. Place a scrap piece of wood between the pry bar and siding to avoid damaging the siding. Slip the locking channel on the overlapping piece over the nailing strip of the replacement piece. *Tip: If the damaged panel is near a corner, door, or window, replace the entire panel. This eliminates an extra seam.*

HOW TO PATCH ALUMINUM SIDING

Bonding surface left intact

Cut out the damaged area using aviation snips. Leave an exposed area on top of the uppermost piece to act as a bonding surface. Cut a patch 4" larger than the repair area. Remove the nailing strip. Smooth the edges with metal sandpaper.

Nail the lower patch in place by driving siding nails through the nailing flange. Apply roofing cement to the back of the top piece, then press it into place, slipping the locking channel over the nailing strip of the underlying piece. Caulk the seams.

HOW TO REPLACE ALUMINUM END CAPS

Remove the damaged end cap. If necessary, pry the bottom loose, then cut along the top with a hacksaw blade. Starting at the bottom, attach the replacement end caps by driving siding nails through the nailing tabs and into the framing members.

Trim the nailing tabs off the top replacement cap. Apply roofing cement to its back. Slide the cap over the locking channels of the siding panels. Press the top cap securely in place.

HOW TO REPLACE BOARD & BATTEN SIDING

Remove the battens over the damaged boards. Pry out the damaged boards in their entirety. Inspect the underlying housewrap, and patch if necessary.

Cut replacement boards from the same type of lumber, allowing a ⅛" gap at the side seams. Prime or seal the edges and the back side of the replacement boards. Let them dry.

Nail the new boards in place using ring-shank siding nails. Replace the battens and any other trim. Prime and paint or stain the new boards to blend with the surrounding siding.

HOW TO REPLACE WOOD SHAKES & SHINGLES

Split damaged shakes or shingles with a hammer and chisel, and remove them. Insert wood spacers under the shakes or shingles above the repair area, then slip a hacksaw blade under the top board to cut off any remaining nail heads.

Cut replacement shakes or shingles to fit, leaving a ⅛- to ¼"-wide gap at each side. Coat all sides and edges with wood preservative. Slip the patch pieces under the siding above the repair area. Drive siding nails near the top of the exposed area on the patches. Cover nail heads with caulk. Remove the spacers.

HOW TO REPLACE LAP SIDING

If the damage is caused by water, locate and repair the leak or other source of the water damage.

Mark the area of siding that needs to be replaced. Make the cutout lines over the center of the framing members on each side of the repair area, staggering the cuts to offset the joints. *Tip: Use an electronic stud finder to locate framing members, or look for the nail heads.*

Insert spacers beneath the board above the repair area. Make entry cuts at the top of the cutting lines with a key hole saw, then saw through the boards and remove them. Pry out any nails or cut off the nail heads using a hacksaw blade. Patch or replace the sheathing and building paper, if necessary.

Measure and cut replacement boards to fit, leaving an expansion gap of ⅛" at each end. Use the old boards as templates to trace cutouts for fixtures and openings. Use a jigsaw to make the cutouts. Apply wood sealer or primer to the ends and backs of the boards. Let them dry.

Nail the new boards in place with siding nails, starting with the lowest board in the repair area. At each framing member, drive nails through the bottom of the new board and the top of the board below. *Tip: If you removed the bottom row of siding, nail a 1 × 2 starter strip along the bottom of the patch area.*

Fill expansion joints with caulk (use paintable caulk for painted wood or tinted caulk for stained wood). Prime and paint or stain the replacement boards to match the surrounding siding.

SIDING: VINYL

Install housewrap following instructions on pages 241 to 242. Identify the lowest corner of the house that has sheathing, and partially drive a nail 1½" above the bottom edge of the sheathing. Run a level string to the opposite corner of the wall and partially drive a nail. Do this around the entire house. Snap chalk lines between the nails.

Place the top edge of the starter strip along the chalk line and nail every 10". Nail in the center of the slots and don't nail tight to the house. Keep a ¼" gap between strips, and leave space at the corners for a ½" gap between starter strips and corner posts.

Option: Install foam vinyl siding underlayment on the house using cap nails. Align the bottom of the underlayment with the starting strip. To cut panels to size, score them with a utility knife, then break them over your cutting table. Some panels need to be taped at the seams. Follow manufacturer's recommendations.

Install a corner post, keeping a ¼" gap between the top of the post and the soffit. Extend the bottom of the post ¼" below the bottom of the starter strip. Drive a nail at the top end of the uppermost slot on each side of the post (the post hangs from these nails). Make sure the post is plumb on both sides using a level. Secure the post by driving nails every 8 to 12" in the center of the slots. Do not nail the post tight. Install the other posts the same way.

(continued)

4

If more than one corner post is needed to span the length of a corner, the upper post overlaps the lower post. For an outside corner post, cut off 1" from the nailing flanges on the bottom edge of the top post. For an inside corner post, cut off 1" from the nailing flange on the upper edge of the bottom post. Overlap the posts by ¾", leaving ¼" for expansion.

5

Measure and cut two J-channels that are the length of a window plus the width of the J-channel. Place one of the J-channels against the side of the window, aligning the bottom edge with the bottom edge of the window. Nail the channel in place. Nail the second J-channel against the opposite side of the window the same way.

6

At the top of the window, measure between the outside edges of the side J-channels and cut a piece of J-channel to fit. Cut a ¾" tab at each end. Bend the tabs down to form a drip edge. Miter cut the face at each end at 45°. Center the J-channel over the window and nail it in place. The top J-channel overlaps the side pieces, and the drip edges fit inside the side pieces. Do this for each window and door.

7

Measure, cut, and install J-channel along the gable ends. Nail the channels every 8 to 12". To overlap J-channels, cut 1" from the nailing hem. Overlap the channels ¾", leaving ¼" for expansion. At the gable peak, cut one channel at an angle to butt against the peak. Miter the channel on the opposite side to overlap the first channel.

8

To install J-channel over a roof line, snap a chalk line along the roof flashing ½" above the roof. Align the bottom edge of the J-channel along the chalk line, and nail the channel in place. Make sure the channel does not make direct contact with the shingles.

9

Measure, cut, and install undersill beneath each window. The undersill should be flush with the outside lip of the side channels.

10

Measure, cut, and install undersill along the horizontal eaves on the house. If more than one undersill is needed, cut the nailing hem 1¼" from the end of one undersill. Overlap the undersills by 1".

11

Snap the locking leg on the bottom of the first panel onto the starter strip, making sure it's securely locked in place. Keep a ¼" gap between the end of the panel and the corner post. Nail the panel a minimum of every 16" on center. Don't drive the nails tight. *Note: This installation shows a vinyl siding underlayment in place.*

(continued)

12

13

Overlap panels by 1". Cut panels so the factory cut edge is the one that's visible. Keep nails at least 6" from the end of panels to allow for smooth overlap. Do not overlap panels directly under a window.

Place the second row over the first, snapping the locking leg into the lock of the underlying panels. Leave ¼" gap at corners and J-channels. Install subsequent rows, staggering seams at least 24" unless separated by more than three rows. Check every several rows for level. Make adjustments in slight increments, if necessary.

14

15

For hose spigots, pipes, and other protrusions, create a seam at the obstacle. Begin with a new panel to avoid extra seams. Cut an opening ¼" larger than the obstacle, planning for a 1" overlap of siding. Match the shape and contour as closely as possible. Fit the panels together around the obstruction and nail in place.

Place mounting blocks around outlets, lights, and doorbells. Assemble the base around the fixture, making sure it's level, and nail in place. Install siding panels, cutting them to fit around the mounting block with a ¼" gap on each side. Fasten the cover by snapping it over the block.

Where panels must be notched to fit below a window, position the panel below the window and mark the edges of the window, allowing for a ¼" gap. Place a scrap piece of siding alongside the window and mark the depth of the notch, keeping a ¼" gap. Transfer the measurement to the panel, mark the notch, and cut it out. Create tabs on the outside face every 6" using a snap lock punch. Install the panel, locking the tabs into the undersill.

Install cut panels between windows and between windows and corners as you would regular panels. Avoid overlapping panels and creating seams in small spaces. The panels need to align with panels on the opposite side of the window.

To fit siding over a window, hold the panel in place over the window and mark it. Use a scrap piece of siding to mark the depth of the cut. Transfer the measurement to the full panel and cut the opening. Fit the cut edge into the J-channel above the window, lock the panel in place, and nail it.

For dormers, measure up from the bottom of the J-channel the height of a panel and make a mark. Measure across to the opposite J-channel. Use this measurement to mark and cut the panel to size. Cut and install panels for the rest of the dormer the same way.

(continued)

20

Measure the distance between the lock on the last fully installed panel and the top of the undersill under the horizontal eaves. Subtract ¼", then mark and rip a panel to fit. Use a snap lock punch to punch tabs on the outside face every 6". Install the panel, locking the tabs into the undersill.

21

Place a scrap panel in the J-channel along the gable end of the house. Place another scrap over the last row of panels before the gable starts, slide it under the first scrap, and mark the angle where they intersect. Transfer this angle to full panels. Make a similar template for the other side. Cut the panels and set the cut edge into the J-channel, leaving a ¼" gap.

22

Cut the last piece of siding to fit the gable peak. Drive a single aluminum or stainless steel finish nail through the top of the panel to hold it in place. This is the only place where you will facenail the siding.

23

Apply caulk between all windows and J-channel, and between doors and J-channel.

SILLCOCK: INSTALLING

Anatomy of a Frost-proof Sillcock ▸

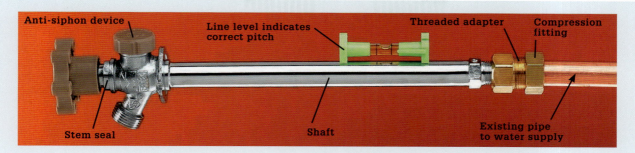

Anti-siphon device • Line level indicates correct pitch • Threaded adapter • Compression fitting • Stem seal • Shaft • Existing pipe to water supply

The frost-proof sillcock shown here can stay active all winter because the stem washer turns off the water in the warm interior of the house. The shaft needs to be pitched slightly down toward the outside to allow water to drain from the shaft. This supply pipe is connected to the threaded adapter with a compression fitting, which is secured to the pipe with two wrenches. Do not use the steps that follow if any of the following apply:

- Your pipes are made from steel instead of copper.
- The length of the pipe from the sillcock to where you can comfortably work on it is greater than 12".
- The pipe has a valve or change of direction fitting within 10" of the existing sillcock.
- The existing supply pipe is ⅝" outside diameter as measured with an adjustable wrench, and you are unable to make the hole in the wall bigger to accommodate the thicker shaft of the frost-proof sillcock. (For example, the hole is in a concrete foundation.)

1

Turn off the water to your outside faucet at a shutoff found inside the house or basement behind the faucet (see page 308 to locate shutoff). Open the faucet and a bleeder valve on the shutoff to drain any remaining water from the pipe.

2

When you are sure the water flow has been stopped, use a tubing cutter to sever the supply pipe between the shutoff valve and the faucet. Make this first cut close to the wall. Tighten the tubing cutter onto the pipe. Both wheels of the cutter should rest evenly on the pipe. Turn the cutter around the pipe. The line it cuts should make a perfect ring, not a spiral. If it doesn't track right, take it off and try in a slightly different spot. When the cutter is riding in a ring, tighten the cutter a little with each rotation until the pipe snaps.

(continued)

3

Spot where supply tubing was cut

3/4" I.D. / 7/8" O.D.

Remove the screws, holding the flange of the old sillcock to the house, and pull it and the pipe stub out of the hole. Measure the outside diameter of the pipe stub. It should be either ⅝", which means you have ½" nominal pipe, or ⅞", which means you have ¾" nominal pipe. Measure the diameter of the hole in the joist. (If it's less than an inch, you'll probably need to make it bigger.) Measure the length of the pipe stub from the cut end to where it enters the sillcock. This is the minimum length the new sillcock must be to reach the old pipe. Record all this information.

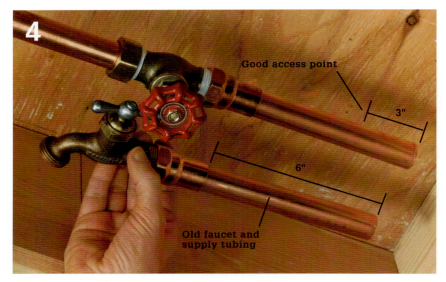

4

Good access point

3"

6"

Old faucet and supply tubing

Find a spot on the supply pipe where you have good access to work with a fitting and wrenches. The point of this is to help you select a new sillcock that is the best size for your project. In most cases, you'll have only two or three 6" to 12" shaft sizes to pick from. In the example above, we can see that the cut section of pipe is 6" long and the distance from the cut end to a spot with good access on the intact pipe is 3", so a new sillcock that's 9" long will fit perfectly.

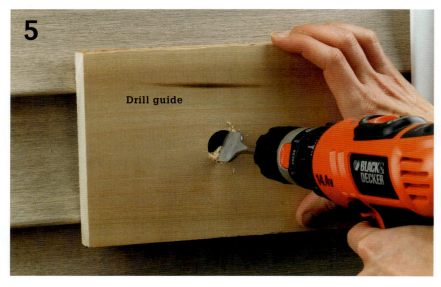

5

Drill guide

BLACK & DECKER

If you need to replace old pipe with a larger diameter size, simplify the job of enlarging the sillcock entry hole into your home with a simple drill guide. First, drill a perpendicular 1⅛" diameter hole in a short board. From outside, hold the board over the old hole so the tops are aligned (you can nail or screw it to the siding if you wish). Run the drill through your hole guide to make the new, wider and lower hole in the wall.

PLUMBING

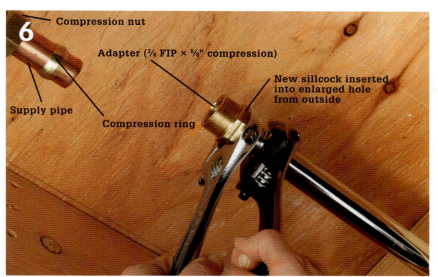

6

Compression nut

Adapter (¾ FIP × ⅝" compression)

New sillcock inserted into enlarged hole from outside

Supply pipe

Compression ring

Insert the sillcock into the hole from the outside. Cut the supply pipe where it will meet the end of the sillcock. From the inside, wrap Teflon tape clockwise onto the threads of the sillcock. Stabilize the sillcock with one wrench and fully tighten the adapter onto the threaded sillcock with the other wrench.

7

Apply pipe joint compound here

Insert the end of the supply pipe into the adapter and pull them together. Spin the sillcock shaft so the faucet outside is oriented correctly (there should be a reference line on the bottom or top of the shaft). Apply pipe joint compound to the male threads on the adapter body. Hand thread the nut onto the adapter body. Stabilize the adapter body with one wrench, then tighten the compression nut with the other about two full turns past hand tight.

8

Turn the water back on. With the sillcock off and then on, check for leaks. Tighten the compression nut a little more if this union drips with the sillcock off. From outside the house, push the sillcock down against the bottom of the entry hole in the wall. Drill small pilot holes into the siding through the slots on the sillcock flange. Now, pull out on the sillcock handle in order to squeeze a thick bead of silicone caulk between the sillcock flange and the house. Attach the sillcock flange to the house with No. 8 or No. 10 corrosion-resistant screws.

SINK DRAINS: BATHROOM: POP-UP

1 Lock nuts / Pop-up drain tailpiece / Trap arm / Trap J-bend

Put a basin under the trap to catch water. Loosen the nuts at the outlet and inlet to the trap J-bend by hand or with channel-type pliers and remove the bend. The trap will slide off the pop-up body tailpiece when the nuts are loose. Keep track of washers and nuts and their up/down orientation by leaving them on the tubes.

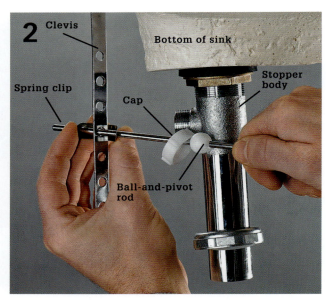

2 Clevis / Bottom of sink / Stopper body / Spring clip / Cap / Ball-and-pivot rod

Unscrew the cap holding the ball-and-pivot rod in the pop-up body and withdraw the ball. Compress the spring clip on the clevis and withdraw the pivot rod from the clevis.

3 Stopper / Flange

Remove the pop-up stopper. Then, from below, remove the lock nut on the stopper body. If needed, keep the flange from turning by inserting a large screwdriver in the drain from the top. Thrust the stopper body up through the hole to free the flange from the basin, and then remove the flange and the stopper body.

4 Wrap tape in clockwise direction / Stopper body

Clean the drain opening above and below, and then thread the locknut all the way down the new pop-up body, followed by the flat washer and the rubber gasket (beveled side up). Wrap three layers of Teflon tape clockwise onto the top of the threaded body. Make a ½"-dia. snake from plumber's putty, form it into a ring, and stick the ring underneath the drain flange.

5

Plumber's putty

From below, face the pivot rod opening directly back toward the middle of the faucet and pull the body straight down to seat the flange. Thread the locknut/washer assembly up under the sink, then fully tighten the locknut with channel-type pliers. Do not twist the flange in the process, as this can break the putty seal. Clean off the squeezeout of plumber's putty from around the flange.

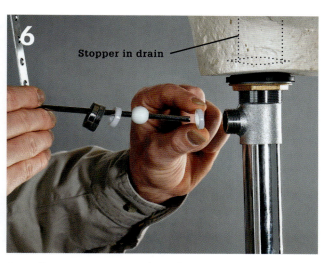

6

Stopper in drain

Drop the pop-up stopper into the drain hole so the hole at the bottom of its post is closest to the back of the sink. Put the beveled nylon washer into the opening in the back of the pop-up body with the bevel facing back.

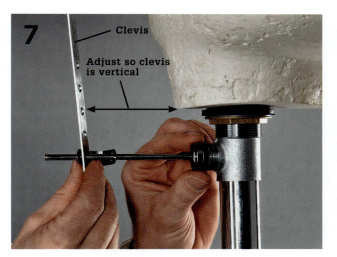

7

Clevis

Adjust so clevis is vertical

Put the cap behind the ball on the pivot rod as shown. Sandwich a hole in the clevis with the spring clip and thread the long end of the pivot rod through the clip and clevis. Put the ball end of the pivot rod into the pop-up body opening and into the hole in the the stopper stem. Screw the cap on to the pop-up body over the ball.

8

Clevis screw

Loosen the clevis screw holding the clevis to the lift rod. Push the pivot rod all the way down (which fully opens the pop-up stopper). With the lift rod also all the way down, tighten the clevis screw to the rod. If the clevis runs into the top of the trap, cut it short with your hacksaw or tin snips. Reassemble the J-bend trap.

Always Test Drain for Leaks ▸

To make sure the sink will not leak, do a thorough test. Close the stopper and turn on the faucet to fill the bowl. Once full, open the stopper and look carefully beneath the sink. Feel the trap parts; they should be dry. If there is any indication of moisture, tighten trap parts as needed.

PLUMBING

SINKS: CLEARING CLOGS

Every sink has a drain trap and a fixture drain line. Sink clogs usually are caused by a buildup of soap and hair in the trap or fixture drain line. Remove clogs by using a plunger, disconnecting and cleaning the trap (this page), or using a hand auger (page 407).

Many sinks hold water with a mechanical plug called a pop-up stopper. If the sink will not hold standing water, or if water in the sink drains too slowly, the pop-up stopper must be cleaned and adjusted (pages 404 to 405).

Tools & Materials ▶

Plunger	Rag
Channel-type pliers	Bucket
Small wire brush	Replacement gaskets
Screwdriver	Teflon tape
Flashlight	Hand auger
Bottle brush	Drain tube clamp
Wire	Protective equipment

Clogged lavatory sinks can be cleared with a plunger (not to be confused with a flanged force-cup). Remove the pop-up drain plug and strainer first, and plug the overflow hole by stuffing a wet rag into it, allowing you to create air pressure with the plunger.

HOW TO CLEAR A SINK TRAP

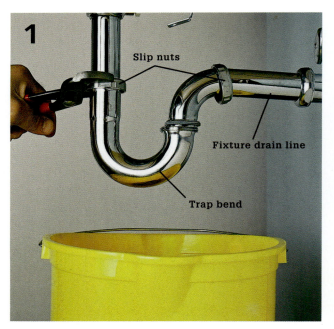

1

Slip nuts

Fixture drain line

Trap bend

Place bucket under trap to catch water and debris. Loosen slip nuts on trap bend with channel-type pliers. Unscrew nuts by hand and slide away from connections. Pull off trap bend.

2

Dump out debris. Clean trap bend with a small wire brush. Inspect slip nut washers for wear and replace if necessary. Reinstall trap bend and tighten slip nuts.

HOW TO CLEAR A KITCHEN SINK

Plunging a kitchen sink is not difficult, but you need to create an uninterrupted pressure lock between the plunger and the clog. If you have a dishwasher, the drain tube needs to be clamped shut and sealed off at the disposer or drainline. The pads on the clamp should be large enough to flatten the tube across its full diameter (or you can clamp the tube ends between small boards).

If there is a second basin, have a helper hold a basket strainer plug in its drain or put a large pot or bucket full of water on top of it. Unfold the skirt within the plunger and place this in the drain of the sink you are plunging. There should be enough water in the sink to cover the plunger head. Plunge rhythmically for six repetitions with increasing vigor, pulling up hard on the last repitition. Repeat this sequence until the clog is removed. Flush out a cleared clog with plenty of hot water.

HOW TO USE A HAND AUGER AT THE TRAP ARM

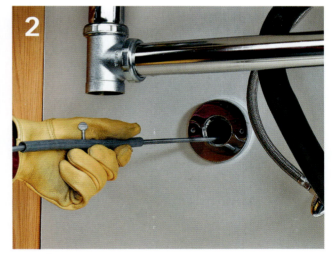

If plunging doesn't work, remove the trap and clean it out (see previous page). With the trap off, see if water flows freely from both sinks (if you have two). Sometimes clogs will lodge in the T-fitting or one of the waste pipes feeding it. These may be pulled out manually or cleared with a bottlebrush or wire. When reassembling the trap, apply Teflon tape clockwise to the male threads of metal waste pieces. Tighten with your channel-type pliers. Plastic pieces need no tape and should be hand tightened only.

If you suspect the clog is downstream of the trap, remove the trap arm from the fitting at the wall. Look in the fixture drain with a flashlight. If you see water, that means the fixture drain is plugged. Clear it with a hand-crank or drill-powered auger.

SINKS: KITCHEN DRAINS & TRAPS

Kitchen traps, also called sink drains or trap assemblies, are made of 1½-inch pipes (also called tubes), slip washers, and nuts, so they can be easily assembled and disassembled. Most plastic types can be tightened by hand, with no wrench required. Pipes made of chromed brass will corrode in time, and rubber washers will crumble, meaning they need to be replaced. Plastic pipes and plastic washers last virtually forever. All traps are liable to get bumped out of alignment; when this happens, they should be taken apart and reassembled.

A trap's configuration depends on how many bowls the sink has, whether or not you have a food disposer and/or a dishwasher drain line, and local codes. On this page we show three of the most common assembly types. T fittings on these traps often have a baffle, which reduces the water flow somewhat. Check local codes to make sure your trap is compliant.

Tools & Materials ▸

Flat screwdriver	Teflon tape
Spud wrench	Washers
Trap arm	Waste-T fitting
Mineral spirits	P-trap
Cloth	Saw
Strainer kit	Miter box
Plumber's putty	Protective
Utility knife	equipment

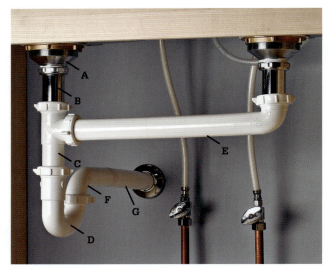

Kitchen sink drains include a strainer body (A), tailpiece (B), waste T (C), P-trap (D), outlet drain line (E), trap arm (F), and wall stubout with coupling (G).

In this arrangement, the dishwasher drain hose (A) attaches to the food disposer (B), and a trap arm (C) leads from the disposer to the P-trap (D).

A "center tee" arrangement has a single P-trap (A) that is connected to a waste T (B) and the trap arm (C).

Drain Kits ▸

Kits for installing a new sink drain include all the pipes, slip fittings, and washers you'll need to get from the sink tailpieces (most kits are equipped for a double bowl kitchen sink) to the trap arm that enters the wall or floor. For wall trap arms, you'll need a kit with a P-trap. Both drains normally are plumbed to share a trap. Chromed brass or PVC with slip fittings let you adjust the drain more easily and pull it apart and then reassemble if there is a clog. Some pipes have fittings on their ends that eliminate the need for a washer. Kitchen sink drains and traps should be 1½" o.d. pipe—the 1¼" pipe is for lavatories and doesn't have enough capacity for a kitchen sink.

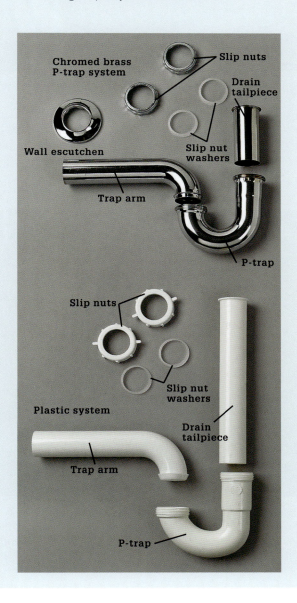

Chromed brass P-trap system — Slip nuts — Drain tailpiece — Wall escutchen — Slip nut washers — Trap arm — P-trap

Plastic system — Slip nuts — Slip nut washers — Drain tailpiece — Trap arm — P-trap

Tips for Choosing Drains ▸

Heavy plastic — Chromed brass — Light-duty plastic

Wall thickness varies in sink drain pipes.
The thinner plastic material is cheaper and more difficult to obtain a good seal with the thicker, more expensive tubing. The thin product is best reserved for lavatory drains, which are far less demanding.

Slip joints are formed by tightening a male-threaded slip nut over a female-threaded fitting, trapping and compressing a beveled nylon washer to seal the joint.

Use a spud wrench to tighten the strainer body against the underside of the sink bowl. Normally, the strainer flange has a layer of plumber's putty to seal beneath it above the sink drain, and a pair of washers (one rubber, one fibrous) to seal below.

HOW TO HOOK UP A KITCHEN SINK DRAIN

1

Slip nut washer

Threaded outlet

Tailpiece

If you are replacing the sink strainer body, remove the old one and clean the top and bottom of the sink deck around the drain opening with mineral spirits. Attach the drain tailpiece to the threaded outlet of the strainer body, inserting a nonbeveled washer between the parts if your strainer kits include one. Lubricate the threads or apply Teflon tape so you can get a good, snug fit.

2

Apply plumber's putty around the perimeter of the drain opening and seat the strainer assembly into it. Add washers below as directed and tighten the strainer locknut with a spud wrench (see photo, previous page) or by striking the mounting nubs at the top of the body with a flat screwdriver.

3

You may need to cut a trap arm or drain tailpiece to length. Cut metal tubing with a hacksaw. Cut plastic tubing with a handsaw, power miter saw, or a hand miter box and a backsaw or hacksaw. You can use a tubing cutter for any material. Deburr the cut end of plastic tubing with a utility knife.

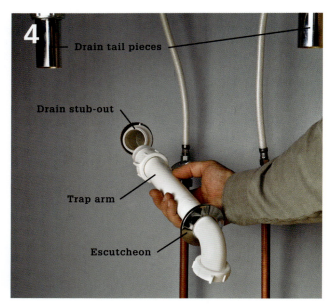

4

Drain tail pieces

Drain stub-out

Trap arm

Escutcheon

Attach the trap arm to the male-threaded drain stubout in the wall, using a slip nut and beveled compression washer. The outlet for the trap arm should point downward. *Note: The trap arm must be lower on the wall than any of the horizontal lines in the set-up, including lines to dishwasher, disposer, or the outlet line to the second sink bowl.*

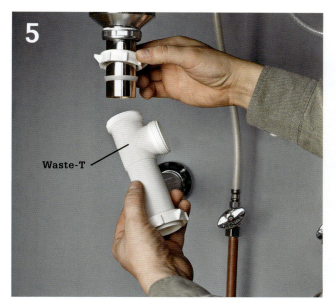

5

Attach a waste-T-fitting to the drain tailpiece, orienting the opening in the fitting side so it will accept the outlet drain line from the other sink bowl. If the waste-T is higher than the top of the trap arm, remove it and trim the drain tailpiece.

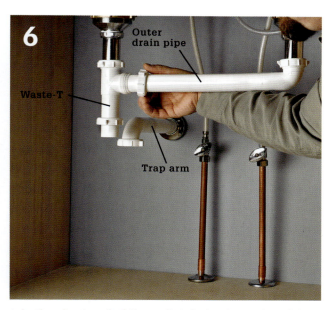

6

Join the short end of the outlet drain pipe to the tailpiece for the other sink bowl and then attach the end of the long run to the opening in the waste-T. The outlet tube should extend into the T ½"—make sure it does not extend in far enough to block water flow from above.

7

Attach the long leg of a P-trap to the waste-T and attach the shorter leg to the downward-facing opening of the trap arm. Adjust as necessary and test all joints to make sure they are still tight, and then test the system.

Variation: Drain in Floor ▶

If your drain stubout comes up out of the floor instead of the wall, you have an S-trap instead of a P-trap. This arrangement is illegal in many parts of the country, because a heavy surge of water can siphon the trap dry, rendering it unable to trap gases. However, if after draining the sink you run a slow to moderate stream of water for a few seconds, the trap will fill. An S-trap has two trap pipes that lead to a straight vertical pipe.

SKYLIGHT: INSTALLING

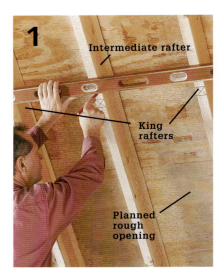

1 Intermediate rafter — King rafters — Planned rough opening

Use the first rafter on each side of the planned rough opening as a king rafter. Measure and mark where the double header and sill will fit against the king rafters. Then, use a level as a straightedge to extend the marks across the intermediate rafter.

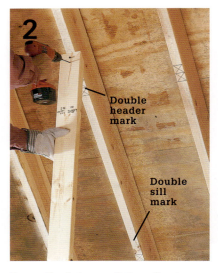

2 Double header mark — Double sill mark

Brace the intermediate rafter by installing two 2 × 4s between the rafter and the attic floor. Position the braces just above the header marks and just below the sill marks. Secure them temporarily to the rafter and subfloor (or joists) with screws.

3 Sister rafter

Reinforce each king rafter by attaching a full-length "sister" rafter against its outside face. Cut sister rafters from the same size of lumber as existing rafters, matching lengths and end cuts exactly. Work each one into position, flush against the outside face of the king rafters, then nail the sisters to the kings with pairs of 10d common nails spaced 12" apart.

4

Use a combination square to transfer the sill and header marks across the face of the intermediate rafter, then cut along the outermost lines with a reciprocating saw. Do not cut into the roof sheathing. Carefully remove the cutout section with a pry bar. The remaining rafter portions will serve as cripple rafters.

5

Build a double header and double sill to fit snugly between the king rafters, using 2× lumber that is the same size as the rafters. Nail the header pieces together using pairs of 10d nails spaced 6" apart.

6 Cripple rafter

Install the header and sill, anchoring them to the king rafters and cripple rafters with 16d common nails. Make sure the ends of the header and sill are aligned with the appropriate marks on the king rafters.

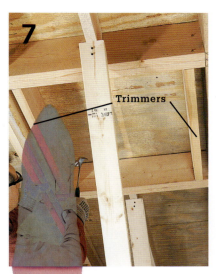

7

Trimmers

If your skylight unit is narrower than the opening between the king studs, measure and make marks for the trimmers: They should be centered in the opening and spaced according to the manufacturer's specifications. Cut the trimmers from the same 2× lumber used for the rest of the frame, and nail them in place with 10d common nails. Remove the 2 × 4 braces.

8

Mark the opening for the roof cutout by driving a screw through the sheathing at each corner of the frame. Then, tack a couple of scrap boards across the opening to prevent the roof cutout from falling and causing damage below.

9

Cut out the roof opening. Mount an old blade in a circular saw or cordless trim saw and plunge cut along the top and bottom cutting lines. Stop short of the corners so you don't overcut. Tack a piece of 1 × 4 across the opening to catch the waste piece and then make the side cuts. Finish the cuts at the corners with a jig saw or handsaw. Remove the waste.

10

Remove the shingles surrounding the opening, but try and maintain the integrity of the building paper beneath. Try to salvage the shingles if you can so they can be reinstalled (they'll match better than new shingles). Start with the row of shingles above the opening. Once these are removed you'll have access to the roofing nails on lower courses.

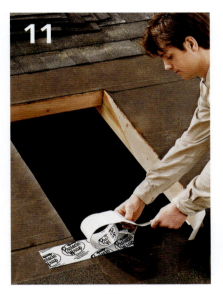

11

Seal the bottom of the rough frame opening. Apply a strip of self-adhesive flashing at the bottom of the roof opening to create a seal on the curb and to cover the seam between the underlayment and the roof deck. This is for extra protection.

12

Position the skylight in the opening. Different models use different fastening and centering devices. The one seen here is installed using pairs of adjustable brackets that are fastened to the roof deck and to the sides of the skylight frame.

(continued)

WINDOWS & DOORS

13

Fasten the skylight unit. Many models employ adjustable brackets like the ones seen here so the skylight can be raised or lowered and centered in the opening. The brackets seen here have a slot and several nail holes in the horizontal flange. Drive a ring shank nail in all four slots and then shift the unit side to side as necessary until it is centered in the opening.

14

Install self-adhesive flashing strips around the skylight curb. Start with the base strip, cutting slits in the corners so the flashing extends all the way up the curb (you'll need to remove metal cladding strips first). Install the head flashing last so all strips overlap from above.

15

Install the metal flashing beginning with the sill. Some skylights have a 4-piece flashing kit where the side flashing is simply shingled over. Others, like the one seen here, include solid base and head flashing components and step flashing that is woven in with the shingles as the roof coverings are installed.

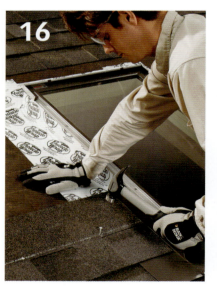

16

Replace shingles up to the skylight curb. Install shingles in complete rows, notching them to fit around the curb. Stop once the granular surfaces of the top row of shingles meet the curb.

17

Install side flashing. Here, metal step flashing is interwoven with the shingles during the shingling process. Whether it's the shingle layer or the step flashing layer, make sure that all components always overlap from above and the horizontal tabs on the step flashing are all covered with shingles. Do not nail through flashing.

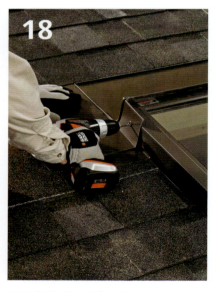

18

Install the head flashing piece so it overlaps the last course of shingle and step flashing. Finish shingling in the installation area, again taking care not to nail through any metal flashing. Replace the metal cladding and caulk if recommended by the manufacturer.

HOW TO BUILD A SKYLIGHT SHAFT

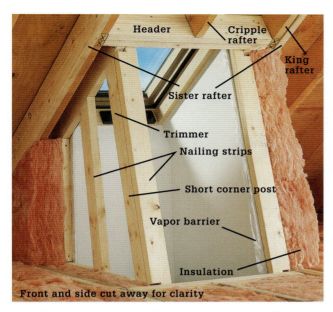

Header
Cripple rafter
King rafter
Sister rafter
Trimmer
Nailing strips
Short corner post
Vapor barrier
Insulation

Front and side cut away for clarity

A skylight shaft is made with 2 × 4 lumber and wallboard and includes a vapor barrier and fiberglass insulation. You can build a straight shaft with four vertical sides or an angled shaft that has a longer frame at ceiling level and one or more sides set at an angle. Since the ceiling opening is larger, an angled shaft lets in more direct light than a straight shaft.

Remove any insulation in the area where the skylight will be located; turn off and reroute electrical circuits as necessary. Use a plumb bob as a guide to mark reference points on the ceiling surface directly below the inside corners of the skylight frame.

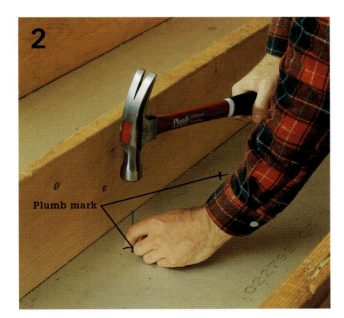

Plumb mark

If you are installing a straight shaft, use the plumb marks made in step 1 to define the corners of the ceiling opening; drive a finish nail through the ceiling surface at each mark. If you are installing an angled shaft, measure out from the plumb marks and make new marks that define the corners of the ceiling opening; drive finish nails at the new marks.

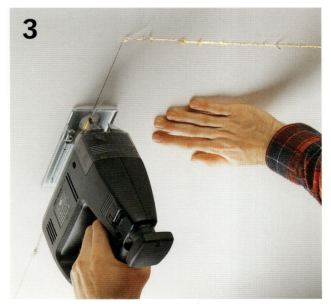

From the room below, mark cutting lines, then remove the ceiling surface.

(continued)

WINDOWS & DOORS

Use the nearest joists on either side of the ceiling opening to serve as king joists. Measure and mark where the double header and double sill will fit against the king joists and where the outside edge of the header and sill will cross any intermediate joists.

If you will be removing a section of an intermediate joist, reinforce the king joists by nailing full-length "sister" joists to the outside faces of the king joists using 10d nails.

Install temporary supports below the project area to support the intermediate rafter on both sides of the opening. Use a combination square to extend cutting lines down the sides of the intermediate joist, then cut out the joist section with a reciprocating saw. Pry loose the cutout portion of the joist, being careful not to damage the ceiling surface.

Build a double header and double sill to span the distance between the king joists using 2× dimensional lumber the same size as the joists.

8

Cripple joist

Install the double header and double sill, anchoring them to the king joists and cripple joists with 10d nails. The inside edges of the header and sill should be aligned with the edge of the ceiling cutout.

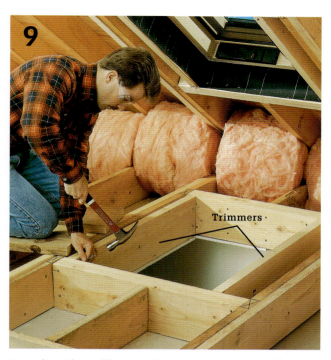

9

Trimmers

Complete the ceiling opening by cutting and attaching trimmers, if required, along the sides of the ceiling cutout between the header and sill. Toenail the trimmers to the header and sill with 10d nails.

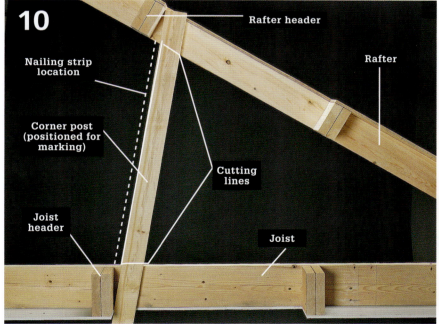

10

Rafter header

Nailing strip location

Rafter

Corner post (positioned for marking)

Cutting lines

Joist header

Joist

Install 2 × 4 corner posts for the skylight shaft. To measure for the posts, begin with a 2 × 4 that is long enough to reach from the top to the bottom of the shaft. Hold the 2 × 4 against the inside of the framed openings, so it is flush with the top of the rafter header and the bottom of the joist header (left photo). Mark cutting lines where the 2 × 4 meets the top of the joist or trimmer and the bottom of the rafter or trimmer (right photo). Cut along the lines, then toenail the posts to the top and bottom of the frame with 10d nails.

(continued)

Attach a 2 × 4 nailing strip to the outside edge of each corner post to provide a nailing surface for attaching the wallboard. Notch the ends of the nailing strips to fit around the trimmers; a perfect fit is not necessary.

Install additional 2 × 4 nailing strips between the corner posts if the distances between posts are more than 24". Miter the top ends of the nailing strips to fit against the rafter trimmers.

Insulation removed for clarity

Wallboard and insulation removed for clarity

Wrap the skylight shaft with fiberglass insulation. Secure the insulation by wrapping twine around the shaft and insulation.

From inside the shaft, staple a plastic vapor barrier of 6-mil polyethylene sheeting over the insulation.

Finish the inside of the shaft with wallboard. *Tip: To reflect light, paint the shaft interior with a light-colored, semigloss paint.*

SMOKE & CO DETECTORS

Smoke and carbon monoxide (CO) alarms are an essential safety component of any living facility. All national fire protection codes require that new homes have a hard-wired smoke alarm in every sleeping room and on every level of a residence, including basements, attics, and attached garages. A smoke alarm needs to be protected with an AFCI circuit if it is installed in a bedroom.

Most authorities also recommend CO detectors on every level of the house and in every sleeping area.

Heat alarms, which detect heat instead of smoke, are often specified for locations like utility rooms, basements, or unfinished attics, where conditions may cause nuisance tripping of smoke alarms.

Hard-wired alarms operate on your household electrical current but have battery backups in case of a power outage. On new homes, all smoke alarms must be wired in a series so that every alarm sounds regardless of the fire's location. When wiring a series of alarms, be sure to use alarms of the same brand to

ensure compatibility. Always check local codes before starting the job.

Ceiling-installed alarms should be 4" away from the nearest wall. Smoke alarms always need to be protected with an AFCI circuit.

Tools & Materials ▸

Screwdriver	Two- and three-wire
Combination tool	14-gauge
Fish tape	NM cable
Drywall saw	Alarms
Wall or ceiling	Wire connectors
outlet boxes	15-amp single-pole
Cable clamps	breaker
(if boxes are not	Eye protection
self-clamping)	

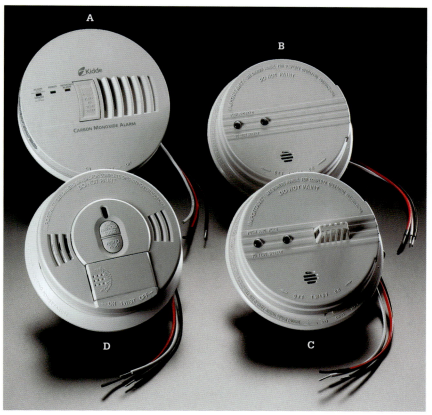

Smoke detectors and carbon monoxide (CO) detectors are required in new construction. Hard-wired carbon monoxide detectors (A) are triggered by the presence of carbon monoxide gas. Smoke detectors are available in photoelectric and ionizing models. In ionizing detectors (B), a small amount of current flows in an ionization chamber. When smoke enters the chamber, it interrupts the current, triggering the alarm. Photoelectric detectors (C) rely on a beam of light, which when interrupted by smoke triggers an alarm. Heat alarms (D) sound an alarm when they detect areas of high heat in the room.

HOW TO CONNECT A SERIES OF HARD-WIRED SMOKE ALARMS

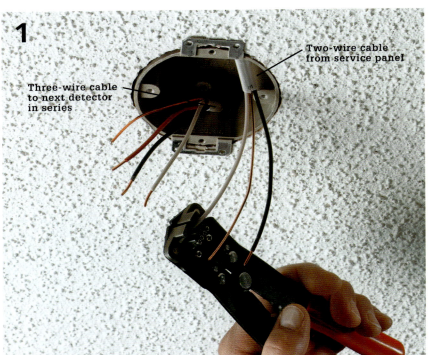

1

Three-wire cable to next detector in series

Two-wire cable from service panel

Pull 14/2 NM cable from the service panel into the first ceiling electrical box in the smoke alarm series. Pull 14/3 NM cable between the remaining alarm outlet boxes. Use cable clamps to secure the cable in each outlet box. Remove sheathing and strip insulation from wires.

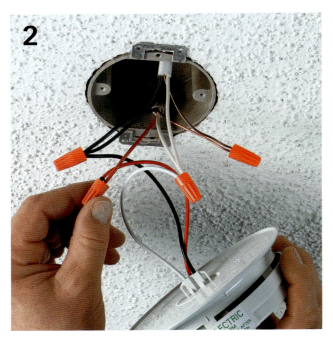

2

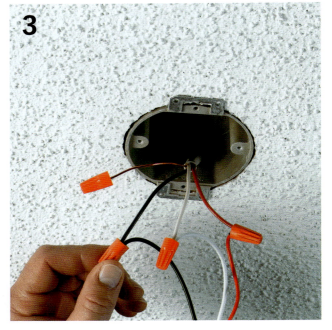

3

Ensure power is off and test for power. Wire the first alarm in the series. Use a wire connector to connect the ground wires. Splice the black circuit wire with the alarm's black lead and the black wire going to the next alarm in the series. Splice the white circuit wire with the alarm's white wire and the white (neutral) wire going to the next alarm in the series. Splice the red traveler wire with the odd-colored alarm wire (in this case, also a red wire).

Wire the remaining alarms in the series by connecting the like-colored wires in each outlet box. Always connect the red traveler wire to the odd-colored (in this case, red) alarm wire. This red traveler wire connects all the alarms together so that when one alarm sounds, all the alarms sound. If the alarm doesn't have a grounding wire, cap the ground with a wire connector. When all alarms are wired, install and connect the new 15-amp breaker.

SOFFITS: INTERIOR

A soffit is a structure that hangs down from a ceiling or overhang, usually filling the cornice area where the wall meets the ceiling. In your kitchen you may choose to install soffits above wall cabinets to create a solid wall surface. You may want to add a soffit to conceal the ductwork from an exhaust fan. Or, you might use a soffit to create a visual barrier (as well as a barrier to airborne food particles, odors, and grease) between kitchen and dining areas in an open floor plan. Soffits are also great for hiding recessed lighting fixtures if it is not possible to install recessed lighting in the existing ceiling.

If you are installing new cabinets, the soffits need to be built and installed first. That means you need to do the cabinet layout on the walls, then construct the soffits, taking care to make them level and plumb. Soffits above cabinets may be flush with the cabinets, extend a few inches for a slight visual reveal, or extend farther (at least 8") to accommodate canister light fixtures.

Tools & Materials ▸

Work gloves	6, 8, and 10"
Eye protection	mudding knives
Tape measure	Drywall compound
Chalk line	Carpenter's square
Level	Table saw
Stud finder	Lighting or ductwork
Lumber	Hammer
(2 × 2, 2 × 4)	Drywall tape
2½" screws	(if desired)
⅝" drywall	Sandpaper
Drywall screws	Primer and paint
Cordless drill	
Utility knife	

HOW TO INSTALL AN INTERIOR SOFFIT

1

Mark the desired outline of the soffits onto the ceiling. Use a carpenter's square to mark square corners. Use a chalk line to mark long straight sections. Use a stud finder to locate the ceiling joists and wall studs in the area of the soffits.

2

Build a ladder-like framework of 2 × 2s for the soffit sides. If you cannot find straight 2 × 2s, use a table saw to rip 2 × 4s in half. Attach the crossbars at regular intervals of 16 or 24" on center using 2½" screws. Create the ladder so the crossbars will not be aligned with the ceiling joists and wall studs when the framework is installed.

3

If the joists are perpendicular to the soffit, screw the soffit framework to the joists, aligned with the chalk lines. If not, go to the next step.

4

If the joists are parallel to the soffit location, cut 2 × 4s to a length 1½" shorter than the width of the soffit. Screw these boards into the ceiling joists and toe-screw the ends into the ceiling wall plate.

(continued)

Attach the soffit framework to the ends of the 2 × 4s with drywall screws.

Use a level or laser level to mark the wall even with the bottom of the installed soffit framework. Cut 2 × 2s to the length of the soffit and attach this cleat to the wall aligned with the mark.

Cut crossmembers to fit between the bottom of the framework and the wall cleat. Attach the crossmembers by toe-screwing into the cleat and end-screwing through the framework side. Place the crossmembers every 16" on center.

Install lighting or ductwork, if needed. Extend the mounting bars on recessed fixtures to reach framing members. Finish installing lights, and then check to make sure they work. Once you've determined that the lights work properly, have the work inspected by an electrician and/or a local building inspector. With approval, you can begin to close up the soffit.

Cut and install ⅝" drywall over the framework using drywall screws. Attach the bottom sections first, then cut and attach the sides. *Note: Required minimum drywall thickness is dictated by local building codes. Be sure to consult them before you begin installation.*

Apply joint compound and tape to the drywall. Use corner tape along all the edges. Sand smooth and finish with primer and paint.

SOFFITS: ROOF SYSTEM

Remove trim, soffits, and fascia along the eaves using a flat pry bar. If the eaves contain debris, such as bird nests or rotted wood, clean them out.

Check the rafters and rafter lookouts for decay or damage. Repair or replace them as needed.

Install new 1 × 8 or 2 × 8 subfascia over the rafters and rafter lookouts using 16d nails. Butt subfascia boards together at rafter or rafter lookout locations. Install drip edge at the top of the subfascia. Leave a ¹⁄₁₆" gap between the drip edge and the subfascia for the fascia to fit.

Install F-channels for the soffit panels along the bottom inside edge of the subfascia and along the outside wall of the house directly below the rafter lookouts. If more than one piece of channel is needed, butt pieces together.

(continued)

If the soffit panels will span more than 16", or if your house is subjected to high winds, add nailing strips to provide additional support.

Measure the distance between the mounting channels, subtract ⅛", and cut soffits to size. Slide the soffit panels in place, fitting the ends inside the mounting channels. Nail the panels to the nailing strips, if you've installed them.

Install soffit panels in the remaining spaces, cutting them to fit as needed. When finished, install the fascia (pages 147 to 148).

HOW TO INSTALL ALUMINUM SOFFITS (WITHOUT RAFTER LOOKOUTS)

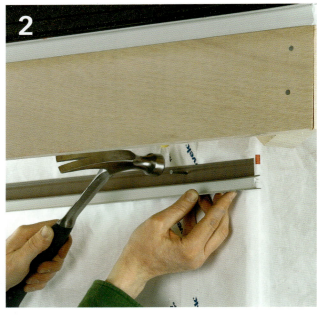

Remove the old soffits and fascia. Place a level at the bottom of the subfascia board level across to the house, and make a mark. Measure down from the mark a distance equal to the thickness of the soffits (usually about ¼"). Do this on each end of the wall. Snap a chalk line between the lower marks.

Start the F-channel at a corner and align the bottom edge with the chalk line. Nail the channel to the wall at stud locations using 8d box nails. If more than one F-channel is needed, butt the pieces together.

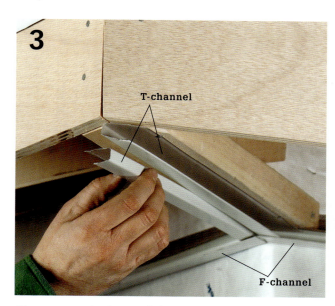

3

T-channel

F-channel

At corners, cut a 2 × 4 to fit between the house and the inside corner of the subfascia to provide support for the T-channel. Notch the 2 × 4 as needed, then nail in place so when the T-channel is installed, it will be aligned with the F-channel. Cut the T-channel to fit. Place it against the 2 × 4, setting the back edge inside the F-channel, and nail in place.

4

DuPo

Measure between the F-channel and the outside edge of the subfascia. Subtract ¼" and cut the soffits to size. For corners, miter the panels to fit the T-channel. Install the first panel inside the channel. Make sure the panel is square to the subfascia using a framing square. Nail the panel to the subfascia at the V-grooves. Slide the next panel against the first, locking them together. Nail the panel in place. Install remaining panels the same way.

VARIATIONS FOR INSTALLING ALUMINUM SOFFITS

Straight corners are made by installing the T-channel parallel with one of the F-channels. Align the outside edge of the T-channel with the outside edge of the installed F-channel. Keep the T-channel back ¼" from the outside of the subfascia, and nail it in place. Install the soffits in the channels.

Inclined overhangs allow soffits to run the same angle as the rafters. At the end of the rafter overhangs, measure from the bottom of the rafter to the bottom of the subfascia. Add the thickness of the soffits, then measure down from the rafters along the wall and make a mark at this distance. Do this on each end of the wall. Snap a chalk line between the marks. Align the bottom of the F-channel with the chalk line, nail the channel to the wall, then install the soffits.

SOUNDPROOFING

In making homes quieter, building professionals add soundproofing elements to combat everything from the hum of appliances to the roar of airliners. Many of the techniques they use are simple improvements involving common products and materials. What will work best in your home depends upon a few factors, including the types of noises involved, your home's construction and how much remodeling you have planned. For starters, it helps to know a little of the science behind sound control.

Sound is created by vibrations traveling through air. Consequently, the best ways to reduce sound transmission are by limiting airflow and blocking or absorbing vibrations. Effective soundproofing typically involves a combination of methods.

Stopping airflow—through walls, ceilings, floors, windows, and doors—is essential to any soundproofing effort. (Even a 2-foot-thick brick wall would not be very soundproof if it had cracks in the mortar.) It's also the simplest way to make minor improvements. Because you're dealing with air, this kind of soundproofing is a lot like weatherizing your home: add weatherstripping and door sweeps, seal air leaks with caulk, install storm doors and windows, etc. The same techniques that keep out the cold also block exterior noise and prevent sound from traveling between rooms.

After reducing airflow, the next level of soundproofing is to improve the sound-blocking qualities of your walls and ceilings. Engineers rate soundproofing performance of wall and ceiling

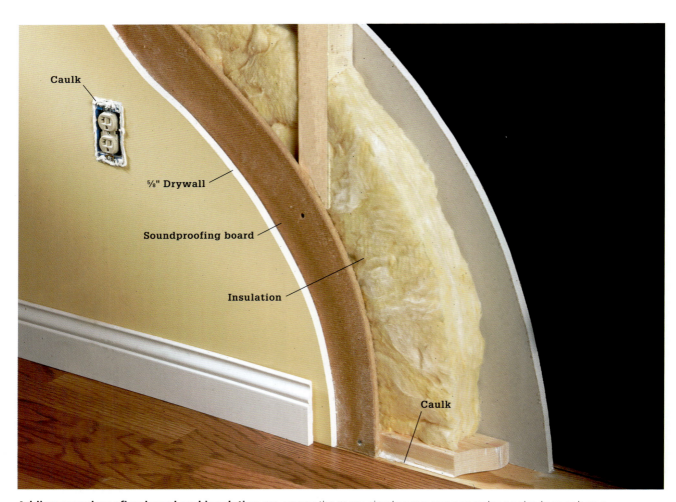

Caulk

⁵⁄₈" Drywall

Soundproofing board

Insulation

Caulk

Adding soundproofing board and insulation are among the many simple ways you can reduce noise in your home.

STC Ratings for Various Wall & Ceiling Constructions* ▶

Assembly	STC Rating
Wood-frame Walls	
2 × 4 wall; ½" drywall on both sides; no caulk	30
2 × 4 wall; ½" drywall on both sides; caulked	35
2 × 4 wall; ½" drywall on both sides; additional layer of ⅝" fire-resistant drywall on one side	38
2 × 4 wall; ½" drywall on both sides; additional layer of ⅝" fire-resistant drywall on both sides	40
2 × 4 wall; ½" drywall on both sides; insulated	39
Staggered-stud 2 × 4 wall; ⅝" fire-resistant drywall on each side; insulated	50
2 × 4 wall, soundproofing board (base layer) and ⅝" fire-resistant drywall on each side; insulated	50
2 × 4 wall with resilient steel channels on one side; ⅝" fire-resistant drywall on both sides; insulated	52
Steel-frame Walls	
3⅝" metal studs, spaced 24" on-center; ⅝" fire-resistant drywall on both sides	40
3⅝" metal studs, spaced 24" on-center, ½" fire-resistant drywall single layer on one side, doubled on other side; insulated	48
2½" metal studs, spaced 24" on-center; soundproofing board (base layer) and ½" fire-resistant drywall on both sides; insulated	50
Wood-frame Floor/Ceiling	
Drywall below; subfloor and resilient (vinyl) flooring above	32
⅝" fire-resistant drywall attached to resilient steel channels below; subfloor, pad, and carpet above	48
Double layer ⅝" fire-resistant drywall attached to resilient steel channels below; subfloor, pad, and carpet above	Up to 60

*All assemblies are sealed with caulk, except where noted. Ratings are approximate.

assemblies using a system called Sound Transmission Class, or STC. The higher the STC rating, the more sound is blocked by the assembly. For example, if a wall is rated at 30 to 35 STC, loud speech can be understood through the wall. At 42 STC, loud speech is reduced to a murmur. At 50 STC, loud speech cannot be heard through the wall.

Standard construction methods typically result in a 28 to 32 STC rating, while soundproofed walls and ceilings can carry ratings near 50. To give you an idea of how much soundproofing you need, a sleeping room at 40 to 50 STC is quiet enough for most people; a reading room is comfortable at 35 to 40 STC. For another gauge, consider the fact that increasing the STC rating of an assembly by 10 reduces the perceived sound levels by 50 percent. The chart above lists the STC ratings of several wall and ceiling assemblies.

Improvements to walls and ceilings usually involve increasing the mass, absorbancy, or resiliency of the assembly; often, a combination is best. Adding layers of drywall increases mass, helping a wall resist the vibrational force of sound (⅝-inch fire-resistant drywall works best because of its greater weight and density). Insulation and soundproofing board absorb sound. Soundproofing board is available through drywall suppliers and manufacturers. Some board products are gypsum-based; others are lightweight fiberboard. Installing resilient steel channels over the framing or old surface and adding a new layer of drywall increases mass, while the channels allow the surface to move slightly and absorb vibrations. New walls built with staggered studs and insulation are highly effective at reducing vibration.

In addition to these permanent improvements, you can reduce noise by decorating with soft materials that absorb sound. Rugs and carpet, drapery, fabric wall hangings, and soft furniture help reduce atmospheric noise within a room. Acoustical ceiling tiles effectively absorb and help contain sound within a room but do little to prevent sound from entering the room.

Stop airflow between rooms by sealing the joints where walls meet floors. With finished walls, remove the shoe molding and spray insulating foam, acoustic sealant, or nonhardening caulk under the baseboards. Also seal around door casings. With new walls, seal along the top and bottom plates.

Cover switch and receptacle boxes with foam gaskets to prevent air leaks. Otherwise, seal around the box perimeter with acoustic sealant or caulk and seal around the knockout where the cables enter the box.

Soundproof doors between rooms by adding a sweep at the bottom and weatherstripping along the stops. If doors are hollow-core, replacing them with solid-core units will increase soundproofing performance. Soundproof workshop and utility room doors with a layer of acoustical tiles.

Reduce sound transmission through ductwork by lining ducts with special insulation. If a duct supplying a quiet room has a takeoff point close to that of a noisy room, move one or both ducts so their takeoff points are as distant from each other as possible.

WALLS & CEILINGS

INSTALLING RESILIENT STEEL CHANNELS

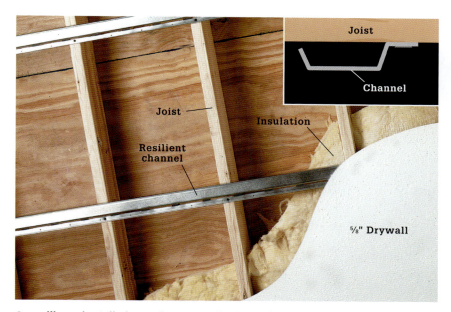

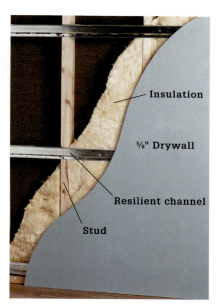

On ceilings, install channels perpendicular to the joists, spaced 24" on-center. Fasten at each joist with 1¼" Type W drywall screws, driven through the channel flange. Stop the channels 1" short of all walls. Join pieces on long runs by overlapping the ends and fastening through both pieces. Insulate the joist bays with unfaced fiberglass or other insulation and install ⅝" fire-resistant drywall, perpendicular to the channels. For double-layer application, install the second layer of drywall perpendicular to the first.

On walls, use the same installation techniques as with the ceiling application, installing the channels horizontally. Position the bottom channel 2" from the floor and the top channel within 6" of the ceiling. Insulate the stud cavities and install the drywall vertically.

HOW TO BUILD STAGGERED-STUD PARTITION WALLS

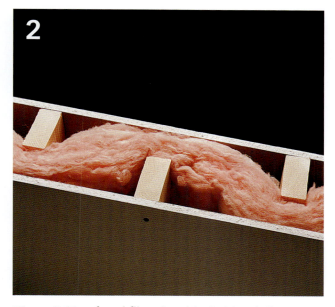

Frame new partition walls using 2 × 6 plates. Space the studs 12" apart, staggering them so alternate studs are aligned with opposite sides of the plates. Seal under and above the plates with acoustic sealant.

Weave R-11 unfaced fiberglass blanket insulation horizontally between the studs. Cover each side with one or more layers of ⅝" fire-resistant drywall.

STAIRWAYS: CODES FOR

Interior and exterior stairways are regulated closely by most codes because they are inherently very dangerous parts of a house. The regulations differ, even on very basic guidelines like the size ratio ranges of stair treads to risers. Many of the regulations deal with lighting issues, including the type and location of fixtures and switches. The size, grippability, and location of handrails and railing balusters also accounts for much of the regulatory wording on stairways.

INTERIOR STAIRWAY LIGHTING & SWITCHING

Codes are specific about the illumination of a stairway as well as the locations of switches that control stairway lights. You should locate a light fixture near each stairway landing, including the top, bottom, and any intermediate landings. You may locate a light fixture near each stairway flight instead of near each landing. This usually means installing a ceiling light near each stairway flight or installing a wall light above each stairway flight. The light must be capable of illuminating treads and landings to at least 1 foot-candle. *Note: A foot-candle is a unit of light measurement approximating the amount of light you* receive from a birthday cake candle when it is held 12 inches from your eyes. Photographer's light meters may be used to measure foot-candles.

You must locate a switch for interior stairway lights at the top and bottom of all interior stairs with at least six risers. Only one switch is required for interior stairs with fewer than six risers. Locate all stair switches so they can be used without climbing any steps. You are not required to install switches if lights are designed to be on continuously or are automatically controlled by motion sensors or other devices.

EXTERIOR STAIRWAY LIGHTING & SWITCHING

Codes for outdoor stairways differ somewhat from interior requirements and recommendations. In exterior areas, you must locate a light fixture near the top landing for stairs providing access to doors above grade level. You must also locate a light fixture near the bottom landing for stairs providing access to doors below grade level. Install stairway lights capable of illuminating treads and landings to at least one foot-candle. Locate the switch inside the dwelling for exterior stairs.

Definitions of Stairway Terms ▸

Landing: A landing is a flat surface at the top and bottom of a stairway, or it may also occur at points within a stairway. A landing must be at least as wide as the stairway and at least 36 inches deep.

Nosing: A tread nose (nosing) is the part of a horizontal stair surface that projects outward beyond a solid (closed) riser below.

Riser: A riser is the vertical part of a stair. A closed riser is created with solid material between adjacent treads. An open riser has no material (except for any required guards) between adjacent treads.

Stairway (flight of stairs): A series of risers and treads that is not interrupted by a landing. A flight of stairs includes the landings at the top and bottom of the flight. A stairway with only a top and bottom landing has one flight of stairs. A stairway with a landing in the middle has two flights of stairs.

Tread: A tread is the horizontal part of a stair. A tread is sometimes called the step.

Winder tread: A winder is a tread with one end wider than the other. Winders are often used at intermediate landings to change a stairway's direction.

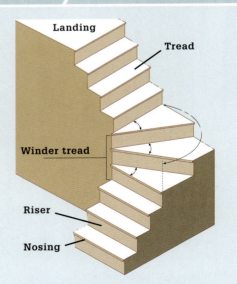

Stairway components include: tread, winder tread, nosing, riser, landing, flight of stairs.

Install a light switch at the top and bottom of stairways with at least six risers.

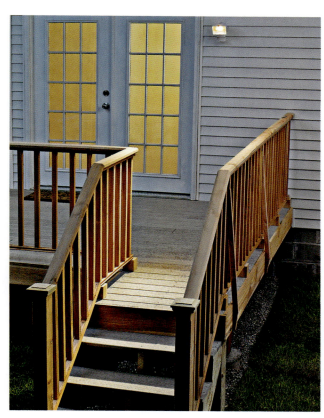

Install a light at the top landing of above-grade exterior stairs.

VIOLATION! Stairway lights. Locate a light near each flight of stairs or near the top, and any intermediate landing. The staircase seen here is in violation.

Provide a finished width of at least 36" above the handrail and at least 31½" at and below one handrail.

STAIRWAY WIDTH

1. Provide a finished stairway width of at least 36 inches above handrail to the minimum headroom height.
2. Provide a finished stairway width of at least 31½ inches at and below the handrail for stairs with one handrail, and at least 27 inches at and below both handrails for stairs with two handrails.

RISER HEIGHT

1. Provide a finished riser height of not more than 7¾ inches. Measure riser height vertically from leading edges of adjacent treads. The IRC does not mandate a minimum riser height.

2. Do not exceed ⅜-inch finished riser height difference between any two risers in a flight of stairs.

3. Do not allow open risers to fit a 4-inch-diameter sphere for passthrough. This includes interior stairs and exterior stairs, such as stairs for decks and balconies.

4. Do not include the height of carpets, carpet pads, rugs, and runners when measuring riser height.

Maximum riser height is 7¾".
Maximum difference between two risers in a flight of stairs is ⅜".

Open risers have the potential to trap the head of a small child. Do not allow an open riser to pass a 4" diameter sphere. Install filler strips to reduce riser opening size.

TREAD DEPTH

1. Provide a finished tread depth of at least 10 inches. Measure tread depth horizontally from the leading edges of adjacent treads and at a right angle to the tread's leading edge.

2. Do not exceed ⅜-inch finished tread depth difference between any two treads in a flight of stairs. This does not apply to consistently shaped winder treads contained within the same flight of stairs.

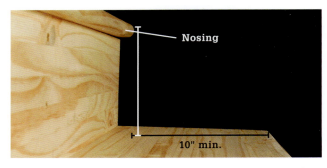

Provide a tread depth of at least 10" if treads have a nosing or at least 11" if treads have no nosing.

TREAD NOSING

1. Provide a finished tread nosing depth of at least ¾ inch and not more than 1¼ inches for stairs with solid risers. Add the nosing depth to the 10-inch minimum tread depth. You are not required to provide tread nosing if treads are at least 11 inches deep.
2. Do not exceed ⅜-inch finished tread nosing depth difference between any two treads for all treads between two stories, including at floors and landings. Note that this differs from the tread and riser maximum difference. The tread and riser differences are for a flight of stairs and the nosing depth difference is for all treads between two stories.
3. Do not exceed 9⁄16 inch for the curvature radius of a tread nosing and do not exceed ½ inch for the bevel of a tread nosing.

TREAD SLOPE

1. Slope treads and landings not more than 2 percent from horizontal in any direction.

WINDER STAIR TREADS

1. Provide a finished winder tread depth of at least 10 inches measured horizontally from the leading edges of adjacent treads at the walk line. The walk line is located 12 inches from the tread's narrow side.
2. Provide a finished winder tread depth of at least 6 inches at any point on a winder tread within the finished width of the stairway.
3. Do not exceed ⅜-inch finished tread depth difference between any two treads in a flight of stairs measured at the walk line.
4. Do not compare the depth of winder treads to the depth of rectangular treads in a flight of stairs if: (a) the winder treads all have a consistent shape, and if (b) the winder treads comply with the winder tread depth requirements. Winder treads will not have the same depth as the rectangular treads, so the winder tread depth will not be within ⅜ inch of the rectangular tread depth.

STAIRWAY HEADROOM HEIGHT

1. Provide a finished stairway headroom height of at least 80 inches measured vertically from a sloped plane connecting the tread nosing or from the finished floor of a landing. Projections from the ceiling are permitted above the minimum finished headroom height.

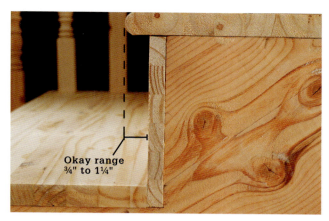

Provide a tread nosing depth of at least ¾" and not more than 1¼". Do not exceed 9⁄16" radius for a curved nosing or ½" depth for a beveled nosing.

The step up from landings should be not more than 7¾". Measure the step to the top of the threshold. Make landings at least as wide as the stairway and at least 36" deep.

STAIRWAY LANDINGS

1. Provide a landing or floor at the top and bottom of most stairs.
2. You are not required to provide a landing or floor at the top of interior stairs, including stairs in an attached garage, unless a door swings over stairs. This means you may terminate a flight of interior stairs directly into a door if the door swings away from the stairs.
3. Do not exceed 12 feet vertical rise of a flight of stairs without providing a landing or a floor. Example: do not install more than nineteen 7⅝-inch high risers without an intermediate landing.
4. Make rectangular and square landings width at least as wide as the stairway. Example: if the stairway is 36 inches wide, build the landing at least 36 inches wide.

5. Make rectangular and square landings depth at least 36 inches, measured in the direction of travel.
6. You may make landings with shapes other than rectangular and square if: (a) the depth of the landing at walk line is at least as wide as the stairway, and if (b) the total area of the landing is at least as large as a ¼ circle with a radius equal to the required width of the landing. The walk line is 12 inches from the narrow side of the landing. The area of a circle is 3.14 multiplied by the circle's radius squared. Example: the minimum area of a curved landing serving a 36-inch-wide stairway is calculated as follows: $(36 \text{ in.}^2 \times 3.14) \times .25 = 1{,}017.9$ square inches.

GUARDS: DEFINITION

A guard is a barrier that protects occupants from falling from a raised surface such as a stairway, deck, or balcony. Guards are often call guardrails when the guard also serves as a handrail; however, guards need not be an open rail. A guard may be a partial height solid wall, a partial height wall containing safety glazing, or any other structure that complies with IRC requirements.

HANDRAILS & GUARDS: LOCATION

1. Provide a handrail on at least one side of every continuous flight of stairs with four or more risers.
2. Provide a guard at raised floor surfaces more than 30 inches above an adjacent interior or exterior surface. Areas that require guards include porches, balconies, decks, hallways, screened enclosures, ramps, and the open sides of stairs with a total rise of more than 30 inches.
3. Provide a guard behind fixed benches and similar fixed seating areas when the surface behind the seating is more than 30 inches above an adjacent interior or exterior surface. Measure the guard height from the seating surface, not from the floor area adjacent to the seating.

HEIGHT

1. Install the handrail at least 34 inches and not more than 38 inches above the treads measured vertically from a sloped plane connecting the tread nosing or from the finished floor of a ramp.
2. You may exceed the 38-inch maximum height where a handrail connects with a guard to provide a continuous structure. Example: a handrail connects to a guard at an intermediate stairway landing. The handrail height at the beginning and ending of the intermediate landing guard may exceed 38 inches high.

3. Provide guards at least 36 inches tall at raised surfaces other than the open sides of stairs.
4. Provide guards at least 34 inches high on the open sides of stairs. Measure the guards vertically from the nosing of the treads.

Install a handrail on stairways with at least four risers. Provide a continuous handrail beginning above the first riser and ending at or above the last riser.

Install handrails at least 34" and not more than 38" above a sloped line connecting the stair treads.

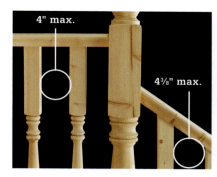

The maximum space between guard vertical members is a 4"-diameter sphere. The maximum space for stairway guards is a 4⅜" diameter sphere.

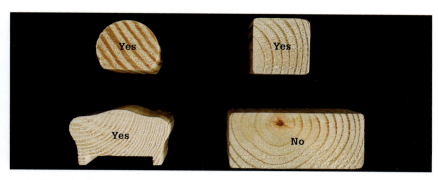

Install handrails that have the required gripping surface dimensions. Any of the above profiles will suffice. Handrails using 2 × 4 and larger lumber are too large to be grippable and thus do not meet the dimensions standard.

5. Limit the height of guards that are also handrails to not more than 38 inches. The IRC does not limit guard height other than for handrails.

CONTINUITY

1. Run the handrail continuously from at least a point directly above the top riser of the flight of stairs to at least a point directly above the lowest riser of the flight.
2. Provide all handrails with a return or terminate them in a newel post, volute, starting easing, or starting newel.
3. Project handrails at least 1½ inches and not more than 4½ inches from any adjacent wall.
4. You may interrupt a handrail by a newel post at a turn.
5. Provide continuous guards for open sides of the entire flight of stairs, even if some of the flight is less than 30 inches above an adjacent surface.
6. You need not provide a guard if the entire flight of stairs is less than 30 inches above an adjacent surface. This applies even if a lower flight of stairs connects with an upper flight of stairs at a landing. Example: a landing occurs before the last three risers of a stairway. The last three risers are a separate flight of stairs and do not require a guard or a handrail.

SHAPE

1. Use material with an outside diameter at least 1¼ inches and not more than two inches for Type 1 circular handrails.
2. Use material with a perimeter dimension of at least four inches and not more than 6¼ inches and a cross-section dimension of not more than 2¼ inches for Type 1 noncircular handrails.

3. Provide Type 2 handrails that have a perimeter dimension greater than 6¼ inches with a graspable finger recess on both sides of the profile.
4. Apply handrail shape requirements to interior and to exterior stairways, including stairways for decks and balconies.

OPENINGS

1. Do not allow openings in guards to pass a 4-inch diameter sphere.
2. Do not allow stair guard openings, such as balusters, to pass a 4⅜-inch diameter sphere.
3. Do not allow openings under stair guards formed by a riser, tread, and the guard's bottom rail to pass a 6-inch diameter sphere.

HANDRAILS & GUARDS LIVE LOADS

1. Install handrails and guards so they will resist a uniform distributed force of at least 200 pounds per square foot applied in any direction at any point along the top.

The maximum space in the triangle formed by a tread, riser, and stair guard bottom rail is a 6" diameter sphere.

STAIRWAYS: CONSTRUCTION

Transfer the location of the upper landing end to the floor below, using a plumb bob. Measure and mark the front of the run. If the stairs will be attached to the wall at one side, outline the layout of the undercarriage structure onto the wall.

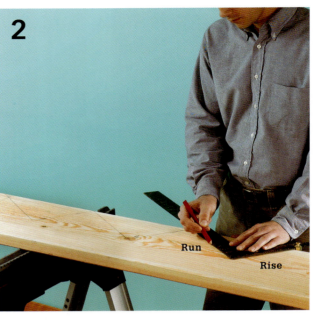

Begin marking cuts on a 2 × 10 stringer by positioning framing square with "unit-run" measurement intersecting the top edge near the bottom end of the stringer, and unit rise intersecting the top edge on the top end. The stringer should be construction grade lumber rated B or better.

Continue marking the first unit-run lines at the bottom edge of the stringer board. Mark the cut for the floor end of the stringer. Also mark cutouts for a 2 × 4 kickboard. Lay out the remaining unit-run and unit-rise lines on the stringer. Extend the last unit-rise line down to the lower edge of the board, to mark the spot where the stringer attaches to the header.

Make the cutouts in the stringer. Use a circular saw for the straight cuts, but stop cutting before the blade reaches the crotch of each cutout. Finish the cutouts with a jigsaw or hand saw.

Test-fit the first stringer in place, checking plumb of rise and level of run. Hold it against the wall if that is where it will be installed. When you've determined that it fits, use the first stringer as a template to mark the remaining two stringers. Align and clamp the boards before marking, and use a sharp pencil. Cut the other stringers.

Position the kickboard correctly and fasten it to the floor. Place the outside stringers in position and secure them to the header using metal hangers nailed on the inside of the stringers.

Position the center "carriage" stringer at the top of the stair opening and check across the tread runs to make sure they are level. Nail the carriage to hangers on the header. If the inside stringer runs along wall, secure it to the wall studs with lag screws.

Drill countersunk pilot holes, and then screw or finish nail the riser boards to the stringers. Do the same with the treads. Spread construction glue on the stringers to cut down on future squeaks.

HOW TO INSTALL STAIRCASE HANDRAILS

1

Measure and mark the peg holes for the balusters. Drill the holes and install the balusters, applying the glue directly to the dowel end or into the peg holes.

2

Position the newel post at the bottom of the staircase and drill holes for the four L brackets. Screw L brackets to the floor, and then to the base of the newel post, and cover with concealing trim nailed in place with finishing nails. *Note: The manufacturer may recommend a different method for attaching the newel post to the floor.*

3

Glue the underside of the handrail to the tops of balusters, and drill a small pilot hole for screws at an angle through the baluster into handrail. Drill holes for the newel mounting bracket and screw the handrail to the newel post. Plug the screwholes before finishing stairs.

4

If the stairs run against a wall, use a wall-mounted handrail on the wall side. Screw mounting brackets evenly spaced along the staircase, and screw the handrail to the mounting brackets.

STEEL STUDS: FRAMING WITH

Steel framing is quickly becoming a popular alternative to wood in residential construction due to the rising cost of wood and the advantages that steel offers. Steel framing is fireproof, insect proof, highly rot resistant, and lightweight. But the most significant advantage is that steel, unlike lumber, is always perfectly uniform and straight.

Steel studs and tracks (or plates) are commonly available at home centers and lumberyards in nominal widths comparable to their wooden counterparts: 1⅝" (2 × 2), 2½" (2 × 3), 3⅝" (2 × 4), and 5½" (2 × 6). Although 25-gauge (or 18-mil) and 20-gauge (or 33-mil) steel framing is suitable for most non-load-bearing partition walls and soffits that will be covered with wallboard, 20-gauge results in a somewhat sturdier wall. Use 20-gauge studs for walls that will receive cementboard.

With a few exceptions, the layout and framing methods used for a steel-frame partition wall are the same as those used for a wood-frame wall. For more information on framing partition walls, see pages 196 to 201; for help with framing soffits, see pages 421 to 422.

Here are a few tips for working with steel:

- Steel framing is fastened together with screws, not nails. Attach steel tracks to existing wood framing using long drywall screws.
- Even pressure and slow drill speed make it easy to start screws. Drive the screws down tight, but be careful not to strip the steel. Don't use drill-point screws with 25-gauge steel, which can strip easily.
- Most steel studs have punch-outs for running plumbing and electrical lines through the framing. Cut the studs to length from the same end to keep the punch-outs lined up.
- The hand-cut edges of steel framing are very sharp; wear heavy gloves when handling them.
- To provide support for electrical receptacle boxes, use boxes with special bracing for steel studs, or fasten boxes to wood framing installed between the studs.
- Use 16"-wide batts for insulating between steel studs. The added width allows for a friction fit, whereas standard batts would slide down.

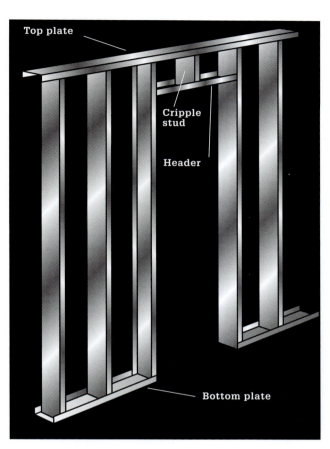

Steel framing, when coupled with wallboard, creates a rigid wall system as solid and strong as wood-framed walls. Steel track is used to create plates, headers, and sills. Steel studs are installed so the open side faces in the same direction, except at door, window, or other openings. The punch-outs in studs are for running utility lines through the framing.

Steel studs and tracks have the same basic structure—a web that spans two flange sides—however, studs also contain a ¼" lip to improve their rigidity.

Tools & Materials ▸

Steel framing requires a few specialty tools and materials. Aviation snips (A) are needed to cut tracks and studs, though a miter saw outfitted with a steel-cutting abrasive blade (B) can speed up the process. A drill or screwgun (C) is required for fastening framing. Handy for large projects, a stud crimper (D) creates mechanical joints between tracks and studs. Plastic grommets (E) are placed in punch-outs to help protected gas and power lines. Protective eyewear and heavy work gloves (F, G) are necessities when working with hand-cut steel framing. Use self-tapping screws (inset) to fasten steel components. To install wood trim, use Type S trim head screws (H); to fasten wallboard, Type S wallboard screws (I); and to fasten studs and tracks together, $7/16$" Type S panhead screws (J).

Tips for Framing with Steel ▸

When running metal plumbing pipe and electrical cable through steel studs, use plastic grommets at punch-outs to prevent galvanic action and electrification of the wall. Install wood blocking between studs for hanging decorative accessories or wainscoting.

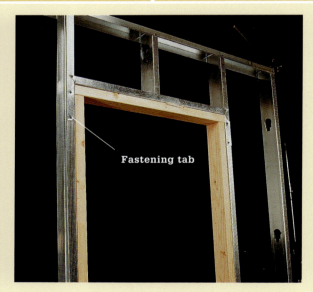

Fastening tab

Frame door openings 3" wider and 1½" taller than normal, then wrap the insides with 2 × 4s to provide a nailing surface for hanging the door and installing the casing.

HOW TO FRAME WALLS WITH STEEL STUDS

Mark the wall location on the floor or ceiling, following the same procedure used for a wood-frame wall. Cut the top and bottom tracks to length with aviation snips. Cut through the side flanges first, then bend the waste piece back and cut across the web. Use a marker to lay out the tracks with 16" on-center spacing.

Fasten the bottom track to the floor. For wood floors, use 2" coarse-thread drywall screws. For concrete floors, pin the track down with a powder-actuated nailer (see pages 330 to 331), or use 1¼" masonry screw. Drill pilot holes for screws using a masonry bit. Drive a fastener at each end of the track, then every 24" in between.

Plumb up from the bottom track with a plumb bob to position the top track. Fasten the top track to the ceiling joists with 1⅝" drywall screws. Drive two screws at each joist location.

At the first stud location, measure between the tracks and cut a stud to length. Insert the stud into the tracks at a slight angle and twist into place. *Note: Cut all subsequent studs from the same end so the punch-outs align.*

Clamp the stud flange to the track with C-clamp pliers and drive a ⁷⁄₁₆" Type S panhead screw through the tracks into the stud. Drive one screw on each side at both ends of the stud. Install remaining studs so the open sides face the same direction (except at door-frame studs).

(continued)

6

7

To install a door header, cut the track 8" longer than the opening. Measure in 4" at each end, cut the flanges at an angle toward the mark, then bend down the ends at 90°. Fasten the header in place with three screws at each stud—two through the fastening tab and one through the overlapping flange.

To provide running blocking for cabinets, wainscoting, or other fixtures, snap a chalk line across the face of the studs at the desired height, hold a track level at the line, then notch the flanges of the track to bypass the studs. Fasten the track in place with two screws at each stud location.

Steel Stud Corners & Joints ▸

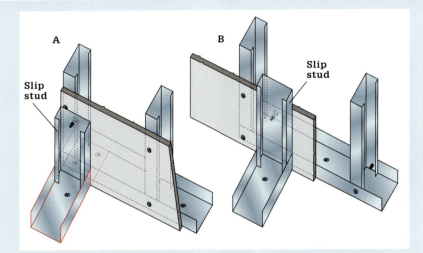

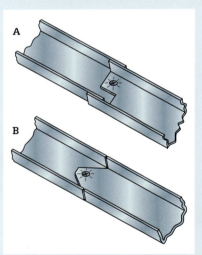

Build corners using a slip stud: A slip stud is not fastened until the adjacent drywall is in place. Form L-shaped corners (A) by overlapping the tracks. Cut off the flange on one side of one track, removing enough to allow room for the overlapping track and drywall. Form a T-shaped corner (B) by leaving a gap between the tracks for the drywall. Secure each slip stud by screwing through the stud into the tracks of the adjacent wall. Also screw through the back side of the drywall into the slip stud, if possible. Where there's no backing behind the slip stud, drive screws at a 45° angle through the back corners of the slip stud and into the drywall.

Join sections with a spliced joint (A) or notched joint (B). Make a spliced joint by cutting a 2" slit in the web of one track. Slip the other track into the slit and secure with a screw. For a notched joint cut back the flanges of one track and taper the web so it fits into the other track; secure with a screw.

WALLS & CEILINGS

STORM WINDOWS & DOORS: REPAIRING

Compared to removable wood storm windows and screens, repairing combination storm windows is a little more complex. But there are several repairs you can make without too much difficulty, as long as you find the right parts. Take the old corner keys, gaskets, or other original parts to a hardware store that repairs storm windows so the clerk can help you find the correct replacement parts. If you cannot find the right parts, have a new sash built.

Remove the metal storm window sash by pressing in the release hardware in the lower rail then lifting the sash out. Sash hangers on the corners of the top rail should be aligned with the notches in the side channels before removal.

Tools & Materials ▸

Tape measure	Hammer
Screwdriver	Spline cord
Scissors	Screening, glass
Drill	Rubber gasket
Utility knife	Replacement hardware
Spline roller	Protective equipment
Nail set	

HOW TO REPLACE SCREENING IN A METAL STORM WINDOW

1

Pry the vinyl spline from the groove around the edge of the frame with a screwdriver. Retain the old spline if it is still flexible, or replace it with a new spline.

2

Stretch the new screen tightly over the frame so that it overlaps the edges of the frame. Keeping the screen taut, use the convex side of a spline roller to press the screen into the retaining grooves.

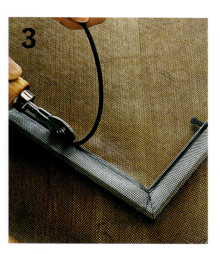

3

Use the concave side of the spline roller to press the spline into the groove (it helps to have a partner for this). Cut away excess screen using a utility knife.

HOW TO REPLACE GLASS IN A METAL STORM WINDOW

Remove the sash frame from the window, then completely remove the broken glass from the sash. Remove the rubber gasket that framed the old glass pane and remove any glass remnants. Find the dimensions for the replacement glass by measuring between the inside edges of the frame opening, then adding twice the thickness of the rubber gasket to each measurement.

Set the frame on a flat surface, and disconnect the top rail. Remove the retaining screws in the sides of the frame stiles where they join the top rail. After unscrewing the retaining screws, pull the top rail loose, pulling gently in a downward motion to avoid damaging the L-shaped corner keys that join the rail and the stiles. For glass replacement, you need only disconnect the top rail.

Fit the rubber gasket (buy a replacement if the original is in poor condition) around one edge of the replacement glass pane. At the corners, cut the spine of the gasket partway so it will bend around the corner. Continue fitting the gasket around the pane, cutting at the corners, until all four edges are covered. Trim off any excess gasket material.

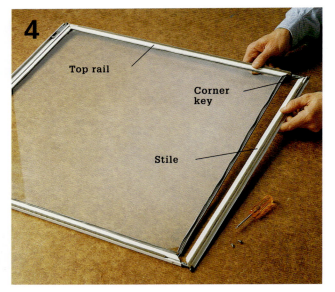

Slide the glass pane into the channels in the stiles and bottom rail of the sash frame. Insert corner keys into the top rail, then slip the other ends of the keys into the frame stiles. Press down on the top rail until the mitered corners are flush with the stiles. Drive the retaining screws back through the stiles and into the top rail to join the frame together. Reinsert the frame into the window.

HOW TO DISASSEMBLE & REPAIR A METAL SASH FRAME

1

Rail (bottom)

Broken corner key

Stile

Retaining screw

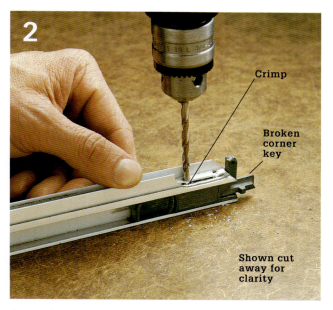

2

Crimp

Broken corner key

Shown cut away for clarity

Metal window sash are held together at the corner joints by L-shaped pieces of hardware that fit into grooves in the sash frame pieces. To disassemble a broken joint, start by disconnecting the stile and rail at the broken joint—there is usually a retaining screw driven through the stile that must be removed.

Corner keys are secured in the rail slots with crimps that are punched into the metal over the key. To remove keys, drill through the metal in the crimped area using a drill bit the same diameter as the crimp. Carefully knock the broken key pieces from the frame slots with a screwdriver and hammer.

3

Replacement corner key assembly

Original corner key assembly

4

5

Locate matching replacement parts for the broken corner key, which is usually an assembly of two or three pieces. There are dozens of different types, so it is important that you save the old parts for reference.

Insert the replacement corner key assembly into the slot in the rail. Use a nail set as a punch, and rap it into the metal over the corner key, creating a new crimp to hold the key in place.

Insert the glass and gasket into the frame slots, then reassemble the frame and drive in retainer screws (for screen windows, replace the screening).

STUCCO: REPAIRING

Although stucco siding is very durable, it can be damaged, and over time it can crumble or crack. The directions given below work well for patching small areas less than 2 square feet. For more extensive damage, the repair is done in layers, as shown on the opposite page.

Tools & Materials ▸

Caulk gun
Disposable paintbrush
Putty knife
Mason's trowel
Square-end trowel
Hammer
Whisk broom
Wire brush
Masonry chisel
Aviation snips
Pry bar
Drill with masonry bit
Scratching tool
Metal lath
Metal primer

Stucco patching
  compound
Bonding adhesive
Denatured alcohol
Metal primer
Stucco mix
Masonry paint
1½" roofing nails
15# building paper
Self-furring metal lath
Masonry caulk
Tint
Metal stop bead
Particle mask or respirator
Protective equipment

Fill thin cracks in stucco walls with masonry caulk. Overfill the crack with caulk and feather until it's flush with the stucco. Allow the caulk to set, then paint it to match the stucco. Masonry caulk stays semiflexible, preventing further cracking.

HOW TO PATCH SMALL AREAS

Remove loose material from the repair area using a wire brush. Use the brush to clean away rust from any exposed metal lath, then apply a coat of metal primer to the lath.

Apply premixed stucco repair compound to the repair area, slightly overfilling the hole using a putty knife or trowel. Read manufacturer's directions, as drying times vary.

Smooth the repair with a putty knife or trowel, feathering the edges to blend into the surrounding surface. Use a whisk broom or trowel to duplicate the original texture. Let the patch dry for several days, then touch it up with masonry paint.

HOW TO REPAIR LARGE AREAS

1

Make a starter hole with a drill and masonry bit, then use a masonry chisel and hammer to chip away stucco in the repair area. *Note: Wear safety glasses and a particle mask or respirator when cutting stucco.* Cut self-furring metal lath to size and attach it to the sheathing using roofing nails. Overlap pieces by 2". If the patch extends to the base of the wall, attach a metal stop bead at the bottom.

2

To mix your own stucco, combine three parts sand, two parts Portland cement, and one part masonry cement. Add just enough water so the mixture holds its shape when squeezed (inset). Mix only as much as you can use in 1 hour. *Tip: Premixed stucco works well for small jobs, but for large ones, it's more economical to mix your own.*

3

Apply a ⅜"-thick layer of stucco directly to the metal lath. Push the stucco into the mesh until it fills the gap between the mesh and the sheathing. Score horizontal grooves into the wet surface using a scratching tool. Let the stucco dry for two days, misting it with water every 2 to 4 hours.

4

Apply a second, smooth layer of stucco. Build up the stucco to within ¼" of the original surface. Let the patch dry for two days, misting every 2 to 4 hours.

5

Combine finish coat stucco mix with just enough water for the mixture to hold its shape. Dampen the patch area, then apply the finish coat to match the original surface. Dampen the patch periodically for a week. Let it dry for several more days before painting.

SUMP PUMP: INSTALLING

If water continues to accumulate in your basement despite all your efforts at regrading and sealing your basement walls, installing a sump pump may be your only option for resolving the problem. Permanently located in a pit that you dig beneath your basement floor, the sump pump automatically kicks in whenever enough water accumulates in the pit to trigger the pump float. The water is then pumped out of the basement through a pipe that runs through the rim joist of the house.

Because you'll be digging well beneath the basement floor, make certain there is no sewer pipe or water supply pipe in the digging area. Contact a plumber if you do not know for sure that the area is clear.

The purpose of a sump pump is to collect and eject water that accumulates beneath your basement floor (usually due to a high water table) before it can be drawn or forced up into the basement. The most effective sump installations have drain tile running around the entire perimeter of the house and channeling water to the pump pit. This system can be created as a retrofit job, but it is a major undertaking best left to a pro.

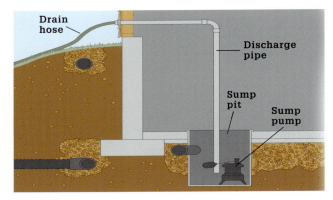

A submersible sump pump is installed in a pit beneath a basement floor to pump water out before it seeps up into the basement.

HOW TO INSTALL A SUMP PUMP

Dig the sump pit. Start by finding the lowest point of the floor (or the spot where water typically accumulates) that is at least 8" from a foundation wall. Outline an area that's about 6" wider than the pit liner all around. Remove the concrete in this area. Basement floors are typically 3 to 4" thick, so renting an electric jackhammer is a good idea.

Install the pit liner after digging a hole for it in the granular material under the floor. The hole should be a few inches wider than the liner. Remove the excavated material right away. Add gravel to the bottom of the hole as needed to bring the liner level with the top of its rim at floor level.

Pack the liner in place by pouring ½" gravel around it. Add a 1" base of gravel and then mix concrete to patch the floor. Trowel the concrete around the rim with a float so the patch is level and smooth.

Prepare the sump pump for installation. Thread a PVC adapter fitting onto the pump outlet, and then solvent glue a PVC standpipe to the adapter. The standpipe should be long enough to extend about 1 ft. past the liner rim when the pump is set on the bottom of the liner.

Attach a check valve to the top of the standpipe to prevent the backflow of water into the pump pit. Solvent weld another riser to fit into the top of the check valve and run upward to a point level with the rim joist, where the discharge tube will exit the basement.

Drill a hole in the rim joist for the discharge tube and finish routing the drainpipe out through the rim joist. Caulk around the tube on both the interior and exterior sides. On the exterior, attach an elbow fitting to the discharge tube and run drainpipe down from the elbow. Place a splash block beneath the drainpipe to direct water away from the house. Plug the pump in to a GFCI-protected receptacle.

SUSPENDED CEILING: INSTALLING

Suspended ceilings are traditionally popular ceiling finishes for basements because they hang below pipes and other mechanicals, providing easy access to them. Suspended ceiling tile manufacturers have a wide array of ceiling tiles to choose from. Popular styles mimic historical tin tiles and add depth to the ceiling while minimizing sound and vibration noise.

A suspended ceiling is a grid framework made of lightweight metal brackets hung on wires attached to ceiling or floor joists. The frame consists of T-shaped main beams (mains), cross tees (tees), and L-shaped wall angles. The grid supports ceiling panels, which rest on the flanges of the framing pieces. Panels are available in 2 × 2-ft. or 2 × 4-ft., in a variety of styles. Special options include insulated panels, acoustical panels that absorb sound, and light-diffuser screens for use with fluorescent lights. Generally, metal-frame ceiling systems are more durable than ones made of plastic.

To begin your ceiling project, devise the panel layout based on the size of the room, placing equally sized trimmed panels on opposite sides to create a balanced look. Your ceiling must also be level.

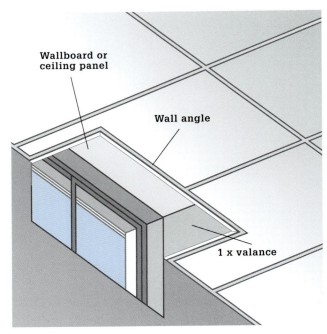

Build a valance around basement awning windows so they can be opened fully. Attach 1× lumber of an appropriate width to joists or blocking. Install drywall (or a suspended-ceiling panel trimmed to fit) to the joists inside the valance.

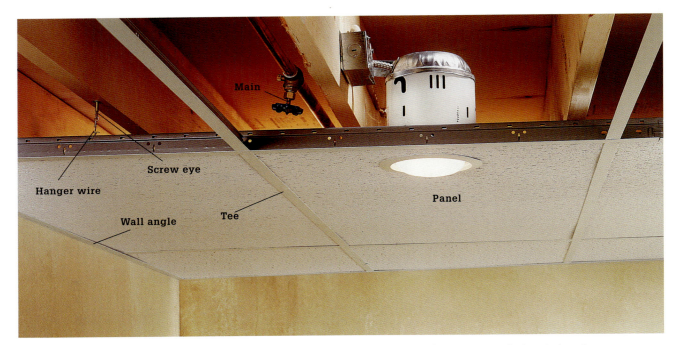

Suspended ceilings are very practical in basement rooms, and you can find them in many more design choices than you might expect.

HOW TO INSTALL A SUSPENDED CEILING

1

Make a mark on one wall that represents the ceiling height plus the height of the wall angle. Use a water level to transfer that height to both ends of each wall. Snap a chalk line to connect the marks. This line represents the top of the ceiling's wall angle.

2

Attach wall angle pieces to the studs on all walls, positioning the top of the wall angle flush with the chalk line. Use 1½" drywall screws (or short masonry nails driven into mortar joints on concrete block walls). Cut angle pieces using aviation snips.

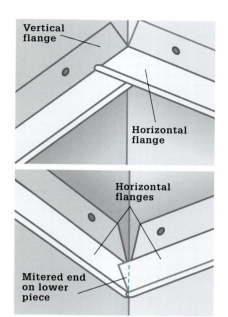

Tip: Trim wall angle pieces to fit around corners. At inside corners (top), back-cut the vertical flanges slightly, then overlap the horizontal flanges. At outside corners (bottom), miter-cut one horizontal flange, and overlap the flanges.

3

Mark the location of each main on the wall angles at the ends of the room. The mains must be parallel to each other and perpendicular to the ceiling joists. Set up a guide string for each main using a thin string and lock-type clamps (inset). Clamp the strings to the opposing wall angles, stretching them very taut so there's no sagging.

4

Install screw eyes for hanging the mains using a drill and screw eye driver. Drill pilot holes and drive the eyes into the joists every 4 ft., locating them directly above the guide strings. Attach hanger wire to the screw eyes by threading one end through the eye and twisting the wire on itself at least three times. Trim excess wire, leaving a few inches of wire hanging below the level of the guide string.

(continued)

Measure the distance from the bottom of a main's flange to the hanger hole in the web (inset). Use this measurement to prebend each hanger wire. Measure up from the guide string and make a 90° bend in the wire using pliers.

Following your ceiling plan, mark the placement of the first tee on opposite wall angles at one end of the room. Set up a guide string for the tee using a string and clamps, as before. This string must be perpendicular to the guide strings for the mains.

Trim one end of each main so that a tee slot in the main's web is aligned with the tee guide string, and the end of the main bears fully on a wall angle. Set the main in place to check the alignment of the tee slot with the string.

Cut the other end of each main to fit, so that it rests on the opposing wall angle. If a single main cannot span the room, splice two mains together end-to-end (the ends should be fashioned with male-female connectors). Make sure the tee slots remain aligned when splicing.

Install the mains by setting the ends on the wall angle and threading the hanger wires through the hanger holes in the webs. The wires should be as close to vertical as possible. Wrap each wire around itself three times, making sure the main's flange is level with the main guide string. Also install a hanger near each main splice.

Attach tees to the mains, slipping the tabbed ends into the tee slots on the mains. Align the first row of tees with the tee guide string; install the remaining rows at 4-ft. intervals. If you're using 2 × 2-ft. panels, install 2-ft. cross tees between the midpoints of the 4-ft. tees. Cut and install the border tees, setting the tee ends on the wall angles. Remove all guide strings and clamps.

Place full ceiling panels into the grid first, then install the border panels. Lift the panels in at an angle, and position them so they rest on the frame's flanges. Reach through adjacent openings to adjust the panels, if necessary.

To trim the border panels to size, cut them face-up using a straightedge and utility knife.

SWITCHES: ELECTRICAL

Wall switches are available in three general types. To repair or replace a switch, it is important to identify its type.

Single-pole switches are used to control a set of lights from one location. Three-way switches are used to control a set of lights from two different locations and are always installed in pairs. Four-way switches are used in combination with a pair of three-way switches to control a set of lights from three or more locations.

Identify switch types by counting the screw terminals. Single-pole switches have two screw terminals, three-way switches have three screw terminals, and four-way switches have four. Most switches include a grounding screw terminal, which is identified by its green color.

When replacing a switch, choose a new switch that has the same number of screw terminals as the old one. The location of the screws on the switch body varies depending on the manufacturer, but these differences will not affect the switch operation.

Whenever possible, connect switches using the screw terminals rather than push-in fittings. Some specialty switches have wire leads instead of screw terminals. They are connected to circuit wires with wire connectors.

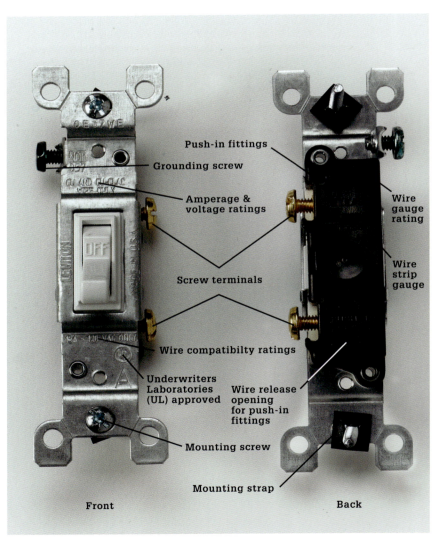

Push-in fittings

Grounding screw

Amperage & voltage ratings

Screw terminals

Wire compatibilty ratings

Underwriters Laboratories (UL) approved

Wire release opening for push-in fittings

Mounting screw

Mounting strap

Wire gauge rating

Wire strip gauge

Front

Back

A wall switch is connected to circuit wires with screw terminals or with push-in fittings on the back of the switch. A switch may have a stamped strip gauge that indicates how much insulation must be stripped from the circuit wires to make the connections.

The switch body is attached to a metal mounting strap that allows it to be mounted in an electrical box. Several rating stamps are found on the strap and on the back of the switch. The abbreviation UL or UND. LAB. INC. LIST means that the switch meets the safety standards of the Underwriters Laboratories. Switches also are stamped with maximum voltage and amperage ratings. Standard wall switches are rated 15A or 125V. Voltage ratings of 110, 120, and 125 are considered to be identical for purposes of identification.

For standard wall switch installations, choose a switch that has a wire gauge rating of #12 or #14. For wire systems with solid-core copper wiring, use only switches marked COPPER or CU. For aluminum wiring, use only switches marked CO/ALR. Switches marked AL/CU can no longer be used with aluminum wiring, according to the National Electrical Code.

SINGLE-POLE WALL SWITCHES

A single-pole switch is the most common type of wall switch. It has ON-OFF markings on the switch lever and is used to control a set of lights, an appliance, or a receptacle from a single location. A single-pole switch has two screw terminals and a grounding screw. When installing a single-pole switch, check to make sure the ON marking shows when the switch lever is in the up position.

In a correctly wired single-pole switch, a hot circuit wire is attached to each screw terminal. However, the color and number of wires inside the switch box will vary, depending on the location of the switch along the electrical circuit.

If two cables enter the box, then the switch lies in the middle of the circuit. In this installation, both of the hot wires attached to the switch are black.

If only one cable enters the box, then the switch lies at the end of the circuit. In this installation (sometimes called a switch loop), one of the hot wires is black, but the other hot wire usually is white. A white hot wire should be coded with black tape or paint.

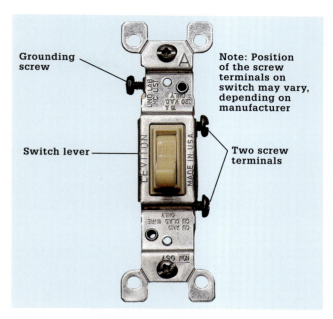

Grounding screw

Note: Position of the screw terminals on switch may vary, depending on manufacturer

Switch lever

Two screw terminals

A single-pole switch is essentially an interruption in the black power supply wire that is opened or closed with the toggle. Single-pole switches are the simplest of all home wiring switches.

TYPICAL SINGLE-POLE SWITCH INSTALLATIONS

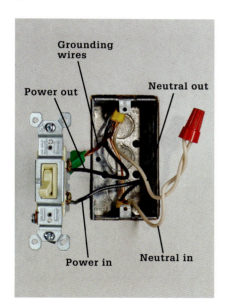

Grounding wires

Power out

Neutral out

Power in

Neutral in

Grounding wire

Grounding wire

Available neutral

Power out

Power in

Two cables enter the box when a switch is located in the middle of a circuit. Each cable has a white and a black insulated wire, plus a bare copper grounding wire. The black wires are hot and are connected to the screw terminals on the switch. The white wires are neutral and are joined together with a wire connector. Grounding wires are pigtailed to the switch.

One cable enters the box when a switch is located at the end of a circuit. The cable has a white and a black insulated wire, plus a bare copper grounding wire. In this installation, both of the insulated wires are hot. The white wire should be labeled with black tape or paint to identify it as a hot wire. The grounding wire is connected to the switch grounding screw.

Code change: In new switch wiring, the white wire should not supply current to the switched device and a separate neutral wire should be available in the switch box.

THREE-WAY WALL SWITCHES

Three-way switches have three screw terminals and do not have ON-OFF markings. Three-way switches are always installed in pairs and are used to control a set of lights from two locations.

One of the screw terminals on a three-way switch is darker than the others. This screw is the common screw terminal. The position of the common screw terminal on the switch body may vary, depending on the manufacturer. Before disconnecting a three-way switch, always label the wire that is connected to the common screw terminal. It must be reconnected to the common screw terminal on the new switch.

The two lighter-colored screw terminals on a three-way switch are called the traveler screw terminals. The traveler terminals are interchangeable, so there is no need to label the wires attached to them.

Because three-way switches are installed in pairs, it sometimes is difficult to determine which of the switches is causing a problem. The switch that receives greater use is more likely to fail, but you may need to inspect both switches to find the source of the problem.

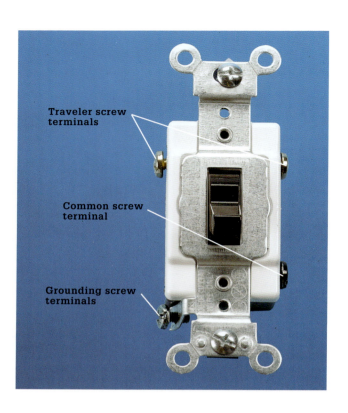

Traveler screw terminals

Common screw terminal

Grounding screw terminals

TYPICAL THREE-WAY SWITCH INSTALLATIONS

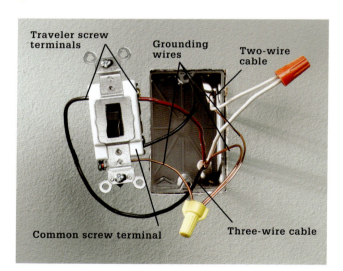

Traveler screw terminals

Grounding wires

Two-wire cable

Common screw terminal

Three-wire cable

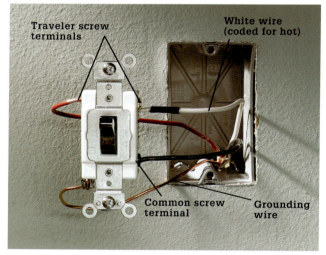

Traveler screw terminals

White wire (coded for hot)

Common screw terminal

Grounding wire

Two cables enter the box if the switch lies in the middle of a circuit. One cable has two wires, plus a bare copper grounding wire; the other cable has three wires, plus a ground. The black wire from the two-wire cable is connected to the dark common screw terminal. The red and black wires from the three-wire cable are connected to the traveler screw terminals. The white neutral wires are joined together with a wire connector, and the grounding wires are pigtailed to the grounded metal box.

One cable enters the box if the switch lies at the end of the circuit. The cable has a black wire, red wire, and white wire, plus a bare copper grounding wire. The black wire must be connected to the common screw terminal, which is darker than the other two screw terminals. The white and red wires are connected to the two traveler screw terminals. The white wire is taped to indicate that it is hot. The bare copper grounding wire is connected to the grounded metal box.

SWITCHES: ELECTRICAL: DIMMER

A dimmer switch makes it possible to vary the brightness of a light fixture. Dimmers are often installed in dining rooms, recreation areas, or bedrooms.

Any standard single-pole switch can be replaced with a dimmer, as long as the switch box is of adequate size. Dimmer switches have larger bodies than standard switches. They also generate a small amount of heat that must dissipate. For these reasons, dimmers should not be installed in undersized electrical boxes or in boxes that are crowded with circuit wires. Always follow the manufacturer's specifications for installation.

In lighting configurations that use three-way switches (opposite page), replace the standard switches with special three-way dimmers. If replacing both the switches with dimmers, buy a packaged pair of three-way dimmers designed to work together.

Dimmer switches are available in several styles (photo, right). All types have wire leads instead of screw terminals, and they are connected to circuit wires using wire connectors. Some types have a green grounding lead that should be connected to the grounded metal box or to the bare copper grounding wires.

Tools & Materials ▸

- Screwdriver
- Circuit tester
- Needlenose pliers
- Wire connectors
- Masking tape

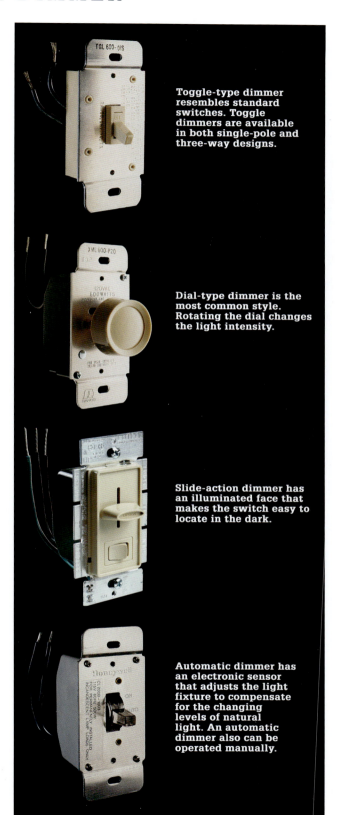

Toggle-type dimmer resembles standard switches. Toggle dimmers are available in both single-pole and three-way designs.

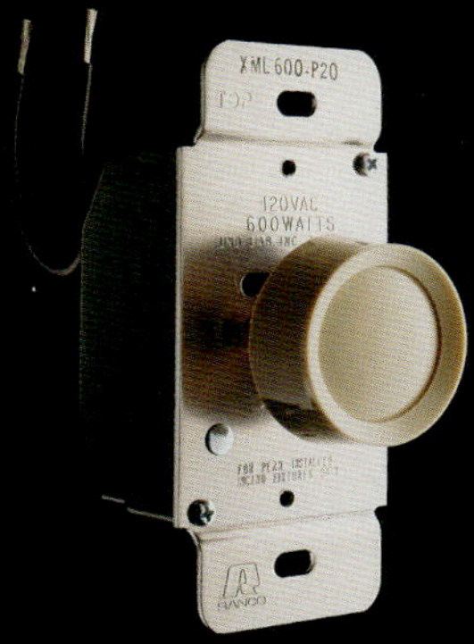

Dial-type dimmer is the most common style. Rotating the dial changes the light intensity.

Slide-action dimmer has an illuminated face that makes the switch easy to locate in the dark.

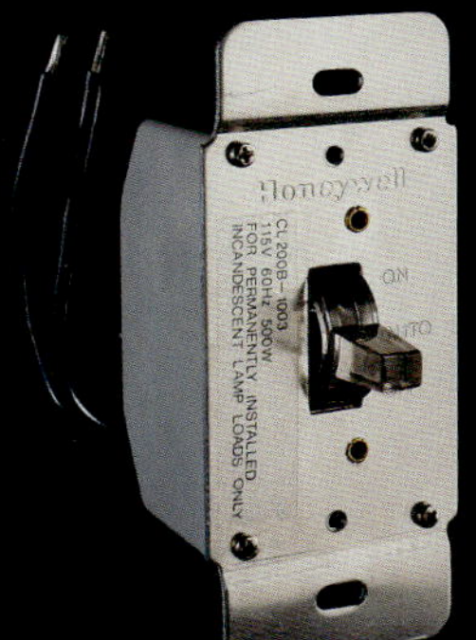

Automatic dimmer has an electronic sensor that adjusts the light fixture to compensate for the changing levels of natural light. An automatic dimmer also can be operated manually.

HOW TO INSTALL A DIMMER SWITCH

Turn off power to switch at the panel, then remove the cover plate and mounting screws. Holding the mounting straps carefully, pull switch from the box. Be careful not to touch bare wires or screw terminals until they have been tested for power. In new switch wiring, the white wire should not supply current to the switched device and a separate neutral wire should be available in the switch box.

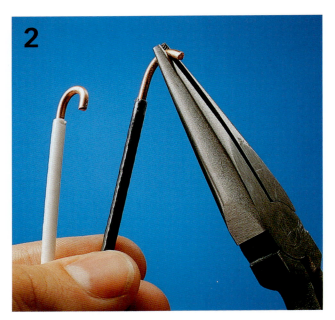

Disconnect the circuit wires and remove the switch. Straighten the circuit wires, and clip the ends, leaving about ½" of the bare wire end exposed.

Connect the wire leads on the dimmer switch to the circuit wires using wire connectors. The switch leads are interchangeable and can be attached to either of the two circuit wires.

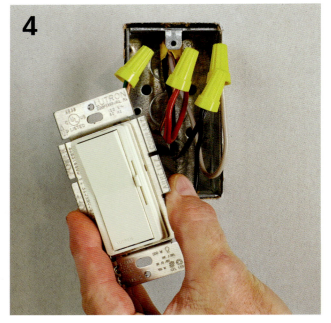

A three-way dimmer has an additional wire lead. This "common" lead is connected to the common circuit wire. When replacing a standard three-way switch with a dimmer, the common circuit wire is attached to the darkest screw terminal on the old switch. In new switch wiring, the white wire should not supply current to the switched device and a separate neutral wire should be available in the switch box.

THERMOSTATS

A thermostat is a temperature-sensitive switch that automatically controls home heating and air-conditioning systems. There are two types of thermostats used to control heating and air-conditioning systems. Low-voltage thermostats control whole-house heating and air conditioning from one central location. Line-voltage thermostats are used in zone heating systems, where each room has its own heating unit and thermostat.

A low-voltage thermostat is powered by a transformer (usually located inside the furnace) that reduces 120-volt current to about 24 volts. A low-voltage thermostat is very durable, but failures can occur if wire connections become loose or dirty, if thermostat parts become corroded, or if a transformer wears out. Some thermostat systems have two transformers. One transformer controls the heating unit, and the other controls the air-conditioning unit.

Line-voltage thermostats are powered by the same circuit as the heating unit, usually a 240-volt circuit. Always make sure to turn off the power before servicing a line-voltage thermostat (typically, these are found in electric heaters).

A thermostat can be replaced in about one hour. Many homeowners choose to replace standard low-voltage or line-voltage thermostats with programmable setback thermostats. These programmable thermostats can cut energy use by up to 35 percent.

When buying a new thermostat, make sure the new unit is compatible with your heating/air-conditioning system. For reference, take along the brand name and model number of the old thermostat and of your heating/air-conditioning units. When buying a new low-voltage transformer, choose a replacement with voltage and amperage ratings that match the old thermostat.

Tools & Materials ▸

Screwdriver
Masking tape

New thermostat
Protective equipment

A programmable thermostat allows you to significantly reduce your energy consumption by taking greater control over your heating and cooling system.

TRADITIONAL LOW-VOLTAGE THERMOSTATS

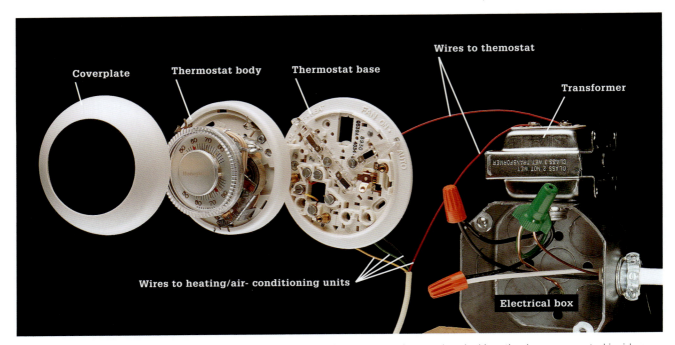

Coverplate   Thermostat body   Thermostat base   Wires to themostat   Transformer

Wires to heating/air- conditioning units

Electrical box

Low-voltage thermostat system has a transformer that is either connected to an electrical junction box or mounted inside a furnace access panel. Very thin wires (18 to 22 gauge) send current to the thermostat. The thermostat constantly monitors room temperatures and sends electrical signals to the heating/cooling unit through additional wires. The number of wires connected to the thermostat varies from two to six, depending on the type of heating/air-conditioning system. In the common four-wire system shown above, power is supplied to the thermostat through a single wire attached to screw terminal R. Wires attached to other screw terminals relay signals to the furnace heating unit, the air-conditioning unit, and the blower unit. Before removing a thermostat, make sure to label each wire to identify its screw terminal location.

PROGRAMMABLE THERMOSTATS

Programmable thermostats contain sophisticated circuitry that allows you to set the heating and cooling systems in your house to adjust automatically at set times of the day. Replacing a manual thermostat with a programmable model is a relatively simple job that can have big payback on heating and cooling energy savings.

HOW TO UPGRADE TO A PROGRAMMABLE THERMOSTAT

1

Start by removing the existing thermostat. Turn off the power to the furnace at the main service panel and test for power. Then remove the thermostat cover.

2

The body of the thermostat is held to a wall plate with screws. Remove these screws and pull the body away from the wall plate. Set the body aside.

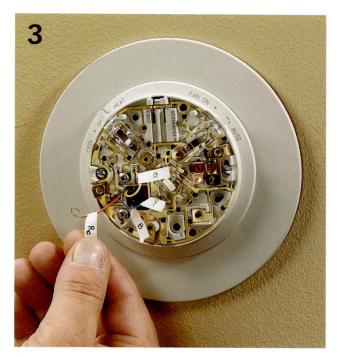

3

The low-voltage wires that power the thermostat are held by screw terminals to the mounting plate. Do not remove the wires until you label them with tape according to the letter printed on the terminal to which each wire is attached.

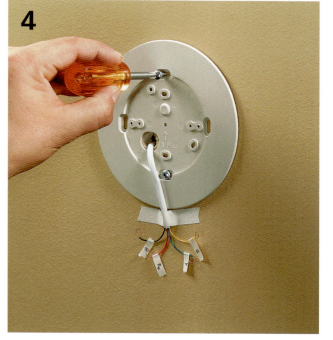

4

Once all the wires are labeled and removed from the mounting plate, tape the cable that holds these wires to the wall to keep it from falling back into the wall. Then unscrew the mounting plate and set it aside.

(continued)

5

Position the new thermostat base on the wall and guide the wires through the central opening. Screw the base to the wall using wall anchors if necessary.

6

Check the manufacturer's instructions to establish the correct terminal for each low-voltage wire. Then connect the wires to these terminals, making sure each screw is secure.

7

Programmable thermostats require batteries to store the programs so they won't disappear if the power goes out in a storm. Make sure to install batteries before you snap the thermostat cover in place. Program the new unit to fit your needs, and then turn on the power to the furnace.

Mercury Thermostats ▸

Older model thermostats (and even a few still being made today) often contained one or more small vials of mercury totaling 3 to 4 grams in weight. Because mercury is a highly toxic metal that can cause nerve damage in humans, along with other environmental problems, DO NOT dispose of an old mercury thermostat with your household waste. Instead, bring it to a hazardous waste disposal site or a mercury recycling site if your area has one (check with your local solid waste disposal agency). The best way to determine if your old thermostat contains mercury is simply to remove the cover and look for the small glass vials or ampules containing the silverish mercury substance. If you are unsure, it is always better to be safe and keep the device in question out of the normal waste stream.

TILE: CUTTING

Careful planning will help you eliminate unnecessary cuts, but most tile jobs require cutting at least a few tiles and some jobs require cutting a large number of tiles, no matter how carefully you plan. For a few straight cuts on light- to medium-weight tile, use a snap cutter. If you're working with heavy tile or a large number of cuts on any kind of tile, a wet saw greatly simplifies the job. When using a wet saw, wear safety glasses and hearing protection. Make sure the blade is in good condition and the water container is full. Never use the saw without water, even for a few seconds.

Other cutting tools include nippers, hand-held tile cutters, and rod saws. Nippers can be used on most types of tile, but a rod saw is most effective with wall tile, which is generally fairly soft.

A note of caution: hand-held tile cutters and tile nippers can create razor-sharp edges. Handle freshly cut tile carefully, and immediately round over the edges with a tile stone.

Before beginning a project, practice making straight and curved cuts on scrap tile.

HOW TO USE A SNAP CUTTER

Mark a cutting line on the tile with a pencil, then place the tile in the cutter so the cutting wheel is directly over the line. While pressing down firmly on the wheel handle, run the wheel across the tile to score the surface. For a clean cut, score the tile only once.

Snap the tile along the scored line, as directed by the tool manufacturer. Usually, snapping the tile is accomplished by depressing a lever on the tile cutter.

HOW TO USE A WET SAW

Individual saws vary, so read the manufacturer's directions for use and make sure you understand them. Refer any questions to the rental center. Wear safety glasses and hearing protection; make sure water is reaching the blade at all times.

Place the tile on the sliding table and lock the fence to hold the tile in place, then press down on the tile as you slide it past the blade.

HOW TO MARK SQUARE NOTCHES

Place the tile to be notched over the last full tile on one side of the corner. Set another full tile against the ½" spacer along the wall and trace along the opposite edge onto the second tile.

Move the top two tiles and spacer to the adjoining wall, making sure not to turn the tile that is being marked. Make a second mark on the tile as in step 1. Cut the tile and install.

HOW TO CUT SQUARE NOTCHES

Cut along the marked line on one side of the notch. Turn the tile and cut along the other line to complete the notch. To keep the tile from breaking before you're through, slow down as you get close to the intersection with the first cut.

To cut square notches in a small number of wall tiles, clamp the tile down on a worktable, then use a jigsaw with a tungsten carbide blade to make the cuts. If you need to notch quite a few tiles, a wet saw is more efficient.

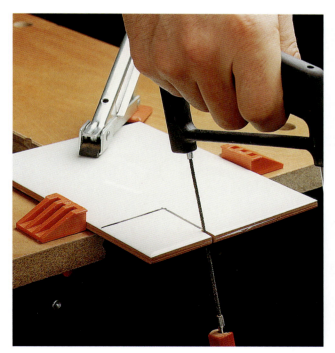

To make a small number of cuts in wall tile, you can use a rod saw. Fit a tungsten carbide rod saw into a hacksaw body. Firmly support the tile and use a sawing motion to cut the tile.

To make a very small notch, use tile nippers. Score the lines and then nibble up to the lines, biting very small pieces at a time.

HOW TO MARK & CUT IRREGULAR NOTCHES

Make a paper template of the contour or use a contour gauge. To use a contour gauge, press the gauge onto the profile and trace it onto the tile.

Use a wet saw to make a series of closely spaced, parallel cuts, then nip away the waste.

HOW TO CUT TILE WITH TILE NIPPERS

Tile nippers have sharp carbide tipped jaws that are used to firmly grip the leading edge of a tile and snap off small fragments of unwanted material. They are primarily used to make irregular cuts in tile.

To avoid breaking the tile, use the tile nippers to take very small bites out of the cut. Afterwards, use a rubbing stone to smooth the sharp edges of exposed cuts.

HOW TO MARK TILE FOR CUTTING HOLES

1

Align the tile to be cut with the last full row of tile and butt it against the pipe. Mark the center of the pipe onto the front edge of the tile.

2

Place a ¼" spacer against the wall and butt the tile against it. Mark the pipe center on the side edge of the tile. Using a combination square, draw a line through each mark to the edges of the tile.

3

Starting from the intersection of the lines at the center, draw a circle slightly larger than the pipe or protrusion.

Cutting Mosaic Tile ▸

Score cuts on mosaic tiles with a tile cutter in the row where the cut will occur. Cut away excess strips of mosaics from the sheet, using a utility knife, then use a handheld tile cutter to snap tiles one at a time. *Note: Use tile nippers to cut narrow portions of tiles after scoring.*

(continued)

OPTIONS FOR CUTTING HOLES IN TILE

Drill around the edges of the hole using a ceramic tile bit. Gently knock out the waste material with a hammer. The rough edges of the hole will be covered by a protective plate (called an escutcheon).

Variation: Score and cut the tile so the hole is divided in half, using the straight-cut method, then use the curved-cut method to remove waste material from each half of the circle.

HOW TO CUT A HOLE WITH A HOLE SAW

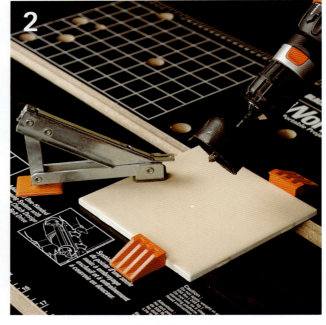

Make a dimple with a center punch to break through the glaze, to keep the drill bit from wandering.

Select a tungsten carbide hole saw in the appropriate size and attach it to a power drill. Place the tip at the marked center and drill the hole.

TILE: REGROUTING

The process of removing old grout and filling the cleaned joints with new grout is the same for most ceramic and porcelain tile installations (including floors, walls, and countertops). For improved adhesion and waterproofing, use a polymer-modified grout mix.

It's important to note that regrouting is an appropriate repair only for tile that is securely bonded to its substrate. Several loose tiles in one area indicate that the mortar has failed or there are problems (usually moisture-related) with the substrate. If multiple tiles are loose, retiling the floor may be your only option. If a tile job is generally in good shape and you can find a perfect color match with your old grout, you can regrout only the affected areas. Otherwise, it will look best to replace all of the grout within an area.

Carbide-blade grout saws are used to remove failing grout.

Before

After

Failed grout allows water underneath tiles, which causes the damage to spread rapidly. If the grout lines in your tile floor are crumbling or a few tiles are loosened, the best solution is to regrout the entire floor.

HOW TO REGROUT FLOOR TILE

1

2

Scrape out the old grout with a grout saw or other tool, being careful not to scratch the tile faces or chip the edges. You may choose to regrout only the filed grout lines for a quick fix, but for more pleasing results and to prevent color variation in the grout lines, remove the grout around all tiles and regrout the entire floor.

Wash the tiled floor with a 1:1 mix of white vinegar and water, paying special attention to the areas around the tile joints. Vacuum the floor first to get rid of all debris.

3

4

Apply new grout. Prepare grout mix according to the instructions on the package and then pack fresh grout deep into the joints using a rubber grout float. Hold the float at a 30° angle to the tiled surface.

Wipe diagonally across the tiles and grouted joints to remove excess grout and smooth the joints. Seal the grout joints with grout sealer after they've dried for a week or so. *Note: Sealing all the grout joints will help new grout lines blend with old grout if you're only doing a partial regrouting.*

TILING: BACKER BOARD

Use tile backer board as the substrate for tile walls in wet areas. Unlike drywall, tile backer won't break down and cause damage if water gets behind the tile. The three basic types of tile backer are cementboard, fiber-cementboard, and Dens-Shield.

Though water cannot damage either cementboard or fiber-cementboard, it can pass through them. To protect the framing members, install a water barrier of 4-mil plastic or 15# building paper behind the backer.

Dens-Shield has a waterproof acrylic facing that provides the water barrier. It cuts and installs much like drywall, but requires galvanized screws to prevent corrosion and must be sealed with caulk at all untaped joints and penetrations.

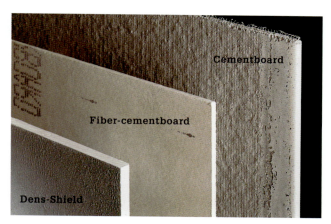

Common tile backers are cementboard, fiber-cementboard, and Dens-Shield. Cementboard is made from Portland cement and sand reinforced by an outer layer of fiberglass mesh. Fiber-cementboard is made similarly, but with a fiber reinforcement integrated throughout the panel. Dens-Shield is a water-resistant gypsum board with a waterproof acrylic facing.

Tools & Materials ▸

Work gloves	Hammer	Cementboard	Spacers
Eye protection	Jigsaw with a carbide	1¼" cementboard screws	Screwgun
Utility knife or carbide-tipped cutter	grit blade	Cementboard joint tape	Ceramic tile adhesive
T-square	Taping knives	Latex-Portland cement mortar	Paper joint tape
Small masonry bits	Stapler	15# building paper	Drywall joint compound
	4-mil plastic sheeting		

HOW TO HANG CEMENTBOARD

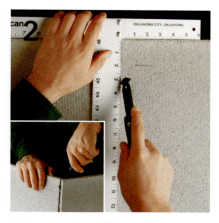

Staple a water barrier of 4-mil plastic sheeting or 15# building paper over the framing. Overlap seams by several inches, and leave the sheets long at the perimeter. *Note: Framing for cementboard must be 16" on center; steel studs must be 20-gauge.*

Cut cementboard by scoring through the mesh just below the surface with a utility knife or carbide-tipped cutter. Snap the panel back, then cut through the back-side mesh (inset). *Note: For tile applications, the rough face of the board is the front.*

Make cutouts for pipes and other penetrations by drilling a series of holes through the board, using a small masonry bit. Tap the hole out with a hammer or a scrap of pipe. Cut holes along edges with a jigsaw and carbide grit blade.

(continued)

WALLS & CEILINGS

4

5

Install the sheets horizontally. Where possible, use full pieces to avoid butted seams, which are difficult to fasten. If there are vertical seams, stagger them between rows. Leave a ⅛" gap between sheets at vertical seams and corners. Use spacers to set the bottom row of panels ¼" above the tub or shower base. Fasten the sheets with 1¼" cementboard screws, driven every 8" for walls and every 6" for ceilings. Drive the screws at least ½" from the edges to prevent crumbling. If the studs are steel, don't fasten within 1" of the top track.

Cover the joints and corners with cementboard joint tape (alkali-resistant fiberglass mesh) and latex-Portland cement mortar (thin-set). Apply a layer of mortar with a taping knife, embed the tape into the mortar, then smooth and level the mortar.

FINISHING CEMENTBOARD

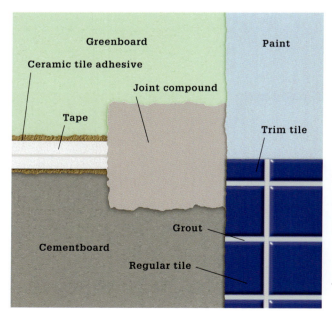

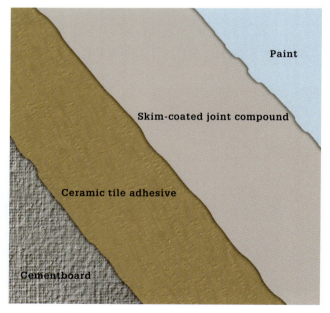

To finish a joint between cementboard and greenboard, seal the joint and exposed cementboard with ceramic tile adhesive, a mixture of four parts adhesive to one part water. Embed paper joint tape into the adhesive, smoothing the tape with a taping knife. Allow the adhesive to dry, then finish the joint with at least two coats of all-purpose drywall joint compound.

To finish small areas of cementboard that will not be tiled, seal the cementboard with ceramic tile adhesive, a mixture of four parts adhesive to one part water, then apply a skim-coat of all-purpose drywall joint compound using a 12" drywall knife. Then prime and paint the wall.

TILING: BACKSPLASH

There are few spaces in your home with as much potential for creativity and visual impact as the space between your kitchen countertop and your cupboards. A well-designed backsplash can transform the ordinary into the extraordinary. Tiles for the backsplash can be attached directly to wallboard or plaster and do not require backerboard. When purchasing the tile, order 10 percent extra to cover breakage and cutting. Remove the switch and receptacle coverplates and install box extenders to make up for the extra thickness of the tile. Protect the countertop from scratches by covering it with a drop cloth during the installation.

Tools & Materials ▸

Level	Mastic adhesive
Tape measure	Masking tape
Pencil	Grout
Tile cutter	Caulk
Notched trowel	Drop cloth
Rubber grout float	Caulk gun
Rubber mallet	Scrap 2 × 4
Sponge	Carpet scrap
Story stick	Buff cloth
Tile spacers (if needed)	Protective
Wall tile	equipment

Mosaic Backsplash ▸

Break tiles into fragments and make a mosaic backsplash. Always use sanded grout for joints wider than ⅛".

Contemporary glass mosaic sheets create a counter-to-cabinet backsplash for a waterproof, splash-proof wall with high visual impact.

HOW TO INSTALL A TILE BACKSPLASH

Make a story stick by marking a board at least half as long as the backsplash area to match the tile spacing.

Starting at the midpoint of the installation area, use the story stick to make layout marks along the wall. If an end piece is too small (less than half a tile), adjust the midpoint to give you larger, more attractive end pieces. Use a level to mark this point with a vertical reference line.

While it may appear straight, your countertop may not be level and therefore is not a reliable reference line. Run a level along the counter to find the lowest point on the countertop. Mark a point two tiles up from the low point and extend a level line across the entire work area.

Variation: Diagonal Layout. Mark vertical and horizontal reference lines, making sure the angle is 90°. To establish diagonal layout lines, measure out equal distances from the crosspoint, and then connect the points with a line. Additional layout lines can be extended from these as needed.

4

Apply mastic adhesive evenly to the area beneath the horizontal reference line using a notched trowel. Comb the adhesive horizontally with the notched edge.

5

Press tiles into the adhesive with a slight twisting motion. If the tiles are not self-spacing, use plastic spacers to maintain even grout lines. If the tiles do not hang in place, use masking tape to hold them in place until the adhesive sets.

6

Install a whole row along the reference line, checking occasionally to make sure the tiles are level. Continue installing tiles below the first row, trimming tiles that butt against the countertop as needed.

7

Install an edge border if it is needed in your layout. Mosaic sheets normally do not have bullnose tiles on the edges, so if you don't wish to see the cut edges of the outer tiles, install a vertical column of edge tiles at the end of the backsplash area.

(continued)

When the tiles are in place, make sure they are flat and firmly embedded by laying a beating block against the tile and rapping it lightly with a mallet. Remove the spacers. Allow the mastic to dry for at least 24 hours, or as directed by the manufacturer.

Mix the grout and apply it with a rubber grout float. Spread it over the tiles, keeping the float at a low 30° angle, pressing the grout deep into the joints. *Note: For grout joints ⅛" and smaller, be sure to use a non-sanded grout.*

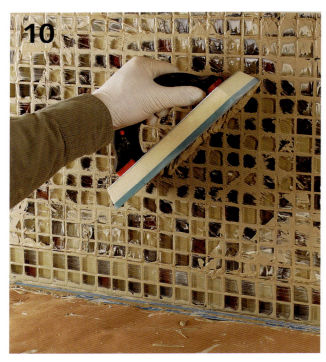

Wipe off excess grout, holding the float at a right angle to the tile, working diagonally so as not to remove grout from the joints.

Clean excess grout with a damp sponge. When the grout has dried to a haze, buff the tile clean with a soft cloth. Apply a bead of caulk between the countertop and the tiles.

TILING: COUNTERTOP

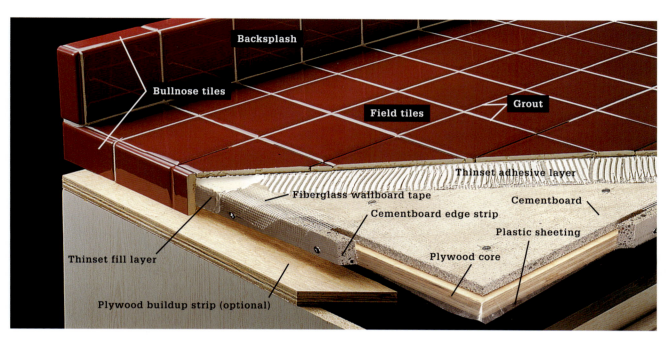

A ceramic tile countertop made with wall or floor tile starts with a core of ¾" exterior-grade plywood that's covered with a moisture barrier of 4-mil polyethylene sheeting. Half-inch cementboard is screwed to the plywood, and the edges are capped with cementboard and finished with fiberglass mesh tape and thinset mortar. Tiles for edging and backsplashes may be bullnose or trimmed from the factory edges of field tiles.

OPTIONS FOR BACKSPLASHES & COUNTERTOP EDGES

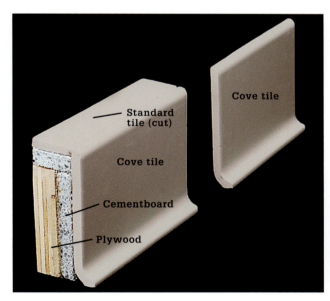

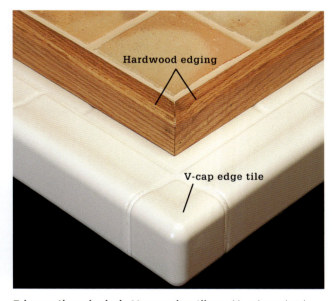

Backsplashes can be made from cove tile attached to the wall at the back of the countertop. You can use the tile alone or build a shelf-type backsplash using the same construction as for the countertop. Attach the plywood backsplash to the plywood core of the countertop. Wrap the front face and all edges of the plywood backsplash with cementboard before laying tile.

Edge options include V-cap edge tile and hardwood strip edging. V-cap tiles have raised and rounded corners that create a ridge around the countertop perimeter—good for containing spills and water. V-cap tiles must be cut with a wet saw. Hardwood strips should be prefinished with at least three coats of polyurethane finish. Attach the strips to the plywood core so the top of the wood will be flush with the faces of the tiles.

Tips for Laying Out Tile ▸

- You can lay tile over a laminate countertop that's square, level, and structurally sound. Use a belt sander with 60- or 80-grit sandpaper to rough up the surface before setting the tiles. The laminate cannot have a no-drip edge.

  If you're using a new substrate and need to remove your existing countertop, make sure the base cabinets are level front to back, side to side, and with adjoining cabinets. Unscrew a cabinet from the wall and use shims on the floor or against the wall to level it, if necessary.

- Installing battens along the front edge of the countertop helps ensure the first row of tile is perfectly straight. For V-cap tiles, fasten a 1 × 2 batten along the reference line using screws. The first row of field tile is placed against this batten. For bullnose tiles, fasten a batten that's the same thickness as the edging tile, plus ⅛" for mortar thickness, to the face of the countertop so the top is flush with the top of the counter. Bullnose tiles should be aligned with the outside edge of the batten. For wood edge trim, fasten a 1 × 2 batten to the face of the countertop so the top edge is above the top of the counter. The tiles are installed against the batten.

- Before installing any tile, lay out the tiles in a dry run using spacers. If your counter is L-shaped, start at the corner and work outward. Otherwise, start the layout at a sink to ensure equally sized cuts on both sides of the sink. If necessary, shift your starting point so you don't end up cutting tile segments that are too narrow.

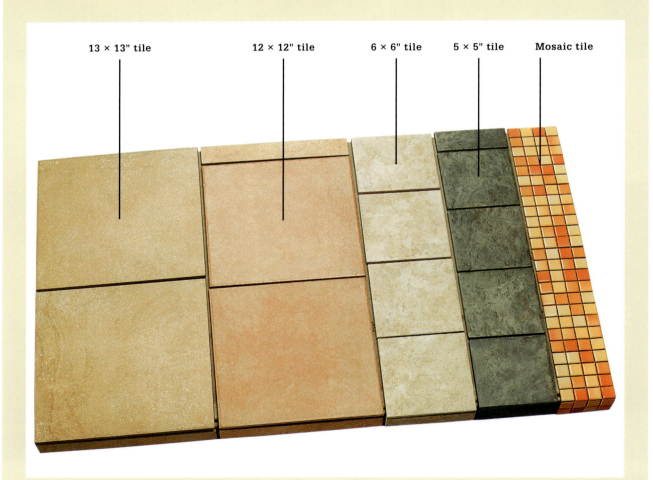

13 × 13" tile   12 × 12" tile   6 × 6" tile   5 × 5" tile   Mosaic tile

The bigger the tile the fewer the grout lines. If you want a standard 25"-deep countertop, the only way to get there without cutting tiles is to use mosaic strips or 1" tile. With 13 × 13" tile, you need to trim 1" off the back tile but have only one grout line front to back. As you decrease the size of your tiles, the number of grout lines increases.

HOW TO BUILD A TILE COUNTERTOP

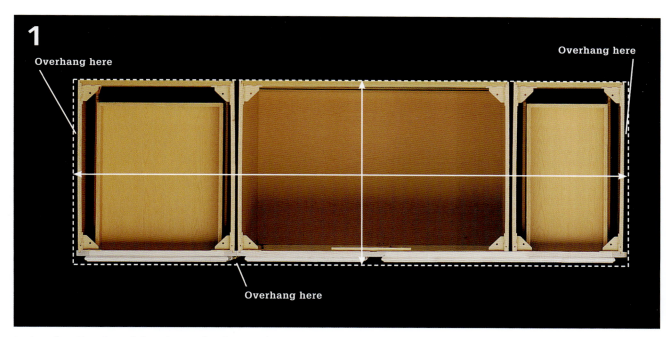

1

Overhang here

Overhang here

Overhang here

Determine the size of the plywood substrate by measuring across the top of the cabinets. The finished top should overhang the drawer fronts by at least ¼". Be sure to account for the thickness of the cementboard, adhesive, and tile when deciding how large to make the overhang. Cut the substrate to size from ¾" plywood using a circular saw. Also make any cutouts for sinks and other fixtures.

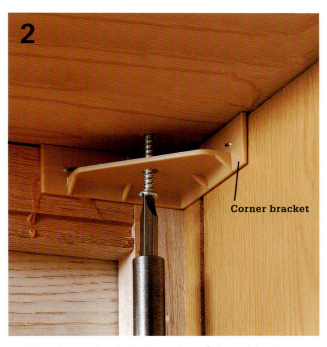

2

Corner bracket

Set the plywood substrate on top of the cabinets, and attach it with screws driven through the cabinet corner brackets. The screws should not be long enough to go through the top of the substrate.

3

Cut pieces of cementboard to size, then mark and make the cutout for the sink. Dry-fit them on the plywood core with the rough sides of the panels facing up. Leave a ⅛" gap between the cementboard sheets and a ¼" gap along the perimeter.

(continued)

Option: Cut cementboard using a straightedge and utility knife or a cementboard cutter with a carbide tip. Hold the straightedge along the cutting line, and score the board several times with the knife. Bend the piece backward to break it along the scored line. Back-cut to finish.

Lay the plastic moisture barrier over the plywood substrate, draping it over the edges. Tack it in place with a few staples. Overlap seams in the plastic by 6", and seal them with packing tape.

Lay the cementboard pieces rough-side up on top of the moisture barrier and attach them with cementboard screws driven every 6". Drill pilot holes using a masonry bit, and make sure all screw heads are flush with the surface. Wrap the countertop edges with 1¼"-wide cementboard strips, and attach them to the core with cementboard screws.

Tape all cementboard joints with fiberglass mesh tape. Apply three layers of tape along the front edge where the horizontal cementboard sheets meet the cementboard edging.

7

Fill all the gaps and cover all of the tape with a layer of thinset mortar. Feather out the mortar with a drywall knife to create a smooth, flat surface.

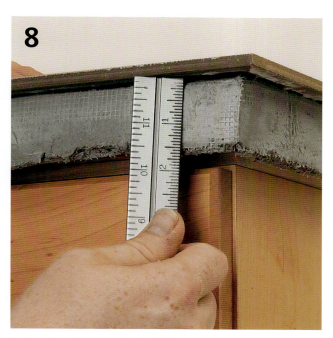

8

Determine the required width of the edge tiles. Lay a field tile onto the tile base so it overhangs the front edge by ½". Hold a metal ruler up to the underside of the tile and measure the distance from it to the bottom of the subbase. The edge tiles should be cut to this width (the gap for the grout line causes the edge tile to extend the subbase that conceals it completely).

9

Cut edge tiles to the determined width using a wet saw. It's worth renting a quality wet saw for tile if you don't own one. Floor tile is thick and difficult to cut with a hand cutter (especially porcelain tiles).

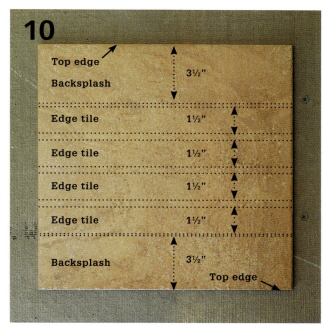

10

Cut tiles for the backsplash. The backsplash tiles (3½" wide in our project) should be cut with a factory edge on each tile that will be oriented upward when they're installed. You can make efficient use of your tiles by cutting edge tiles from the center area of the tiles you cut to make the backsplash.

(continued)

14

Sink cutout area

Dry-fit tiles on the countertop to find the layout that works best. Once the layout is established, make marks along the vertical and horizontal rows. Draw reference lines through the marks and use a framing square to make sure the lines are perpendicular.

Small Floor Tiles & Bullnose Edging ▶

Lay out tiles and spacers in a dry run. Adjust the starting lines, if necessary. If using battens, lay the field tile flush with the battens, then apply the edge tile. Otherwise, install the edging first. If the countertop has an inside corner, start there by installing a ready-made inside corner or by cutting a 45° miter in the edge tile to make your own inside corner.

Place the first row of field tile against the edge tile, separating the tile with spacers. Lay out the remaining rows of tile. Adjust the starting lines if necessary to create a layout using the smallest number of cut tiles.

12

Use a ⅜" square notched trowel to apply a layer of thinset mortar to the cementboard. Apply enough for two or three tiles, starting at one end. Hold the trowel at roughly a 30° angle and try not to overwork the mortar or remove too much.

13

Set the first tile into the mortar. Hold a piece of the edge against the countertop edge as a guide to show you exactly how much the tile should overhang the edge.

14

Cut all the back tiles for the layout to fit (you'll need to remove about 1" of a 13 × 13" tile) before you begin the actual installation. Set the back tiles into the thinset, maintaining the gap for grout lines created by the small spacer nubs cast into the tiles. If your tiles have no spacer nubs, see the option.

Option: To maintain even grout lines, some beginning tilers insert plus-sign-shaped plastic spacers at the joints. This is less likely to be useful with large tiles like those shown here, but it is effective. Many tiles today feature built-in spacing lugs, so the spacers are of no use. Make sure to remove the spacers before the thinset sets. If you leave them in place they will corrupt your grout lines.

(continued)

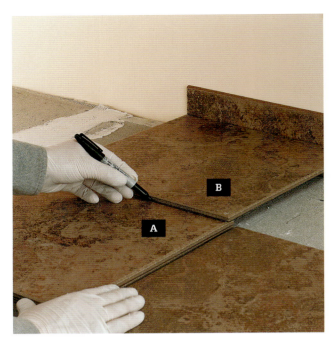

Tip: To mark border tiles for cutting, allow space for the backsplash tiles, grout, and mortar by placing a tile against the back wall. Set another tile (A) on top of the last full tile in the field, then place a third tile (B) over tile (A) and hold it against the upright tile. Mark and cut tile (A) and install it with the cut edge toward the wall. Finish filling in your field tiles.

To create a support ledge for the edge tiles, prop pieces of 2 × 4 underneath the front edge of the substrate overhang using wood scraps to prop the ledge tightly up against the substrate.

Apply a thick layer of thinset to the backside of the edge tile with your trowel. This is called "buttering" and it is easier and neater than attempting to trowel adhesive onto the countertop edge. Press the tiles into position so they are flush with the leading edges of the field tiles.

Butter each backsplash tile and press it into place, doing your best to keep all of the grout lines aligned. Allow the mortar to set according to the manufacturer's recommendations.

18

Mix a batch of grout to complement the tile (keeping in mind that darker grout won't look dirty as quickly as lighter grout). Apply the grout with a grout float.

19

Let the grout dry until a light film is created on the countertop surface, then wipe the excess grout off with a sponge and warm, clean water. See grout manufacturer's instructions on drying tiles and polishing.

20

Run a bead of clear silicone caulk along the joint between the backsplash and the wall. Install your sink and faucet after the grout has dried (and before you use the sink, if possible).

21

Wait at least one week and then seal the grout lines with a penetrating grout sealer. This is important to do. Sealing the tiles themselves is not a good idea unless you are using unglazed tiles (a poor choice for countertops, however).

TILING: FLOORS

Ceramic tile installation starts with determining the best layout. You snap perpendicular reference lines and dry-fit tiles to ensure the best placement.

When setting tiles, work in small sections so the mortar doesn't dry before the tiles are set. Use spacers between tiles to ensure consistent spacing. Plan an installation sequence to avoid kneeling on set tiles. Be careful not to kneel or walk on tiles until the designated drying period is over.

Floor tile can be laid in many decorative patterns, but for your first effort stick to a basic grid. In most cases, floor tile is combined with profiled base tile (installed after flooring).

Make sure the subfloor is smooth, level, and stable. Spread thin-set mortar on the subfloor for one sheet of cementboard. Place the cementboard on the mortar, keeping a ¼" gap along the walls.

Fasten it in place with 1¼" cementboard screws. Place fiberglass-mesh wallboard tape over the seams. Cover the remainder of the floor.

Draw reference lines and establish the tile layout (see pages 528 and 529). Mix a batch of thin-set mortar, then spread the mortar evenly against both reference lines of one quadrant, using a ¼" square-notched trowel. Use the notched edge of the trowel to create furrows in the mortar bed.

Set the first tile in the corner of the quadrant where the reference lines intersect. When setting tiles that are 8" square or larger, twist each tile slightly as you set it into position.

(continued)

T

FLOORS

Using a soft rubber mallet, gently tap the central area of each tile a few times to set it evenly into the mortar.

Variation: For large tiles or uneven stone, use a larger trowel with notches that are at least ½" deep.

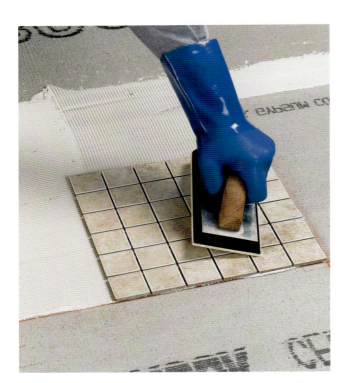

Variation: For mosaic sheets, use a ³⁄₁₆" V-notched trowel to spread the mortar and a grout float to press the sheets into the mortar. Apply pressure gently to avoid creating an uneven surface.

To ensure consistent spacing between tiles, place plastic tile spacers at the corners of the set tile. With mosaic sheets, use spacers equal to the gaps between tiles.

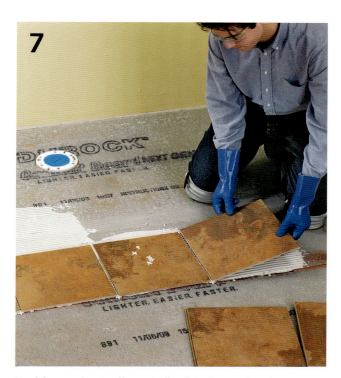

7 Position and set adjacent tiles into the mortar along the reference lines. Make sure the tiles fit neatly against the spacers.

8 To make sure the tiles are level with one another, place a straight piece of 2 × 4 across several tiles, then tap the board with a mallet.

9 Lay tile in the remaining area covered with mortar. Repeat steps 2 to 7, continuing to work in small sections, until you reach walls or fixtures.

10 Measure and mark tiles to fit against walls and into corners. Cut the tiles to fit. Apply thin-set mortar directly to the back of the cut tiles, instead of the floor, using the notched edge of the trowel to furrow the mortar.

(continued)

Set the cut pieces of tile into position. Press down on the tile until each piece is level with adjacent tiles.

Measure, cut, and install tiles that require notches or curves to fit around obstacles, such as exposed pipes or toilet drains.

Carefully remove the spacers with needlenose pliers before the mortar hardens.

Apply mortar and set tiles in the remaining quadrants, completing one quadrant before starting the next. Inspect all of the tile joints and use a utility knife or grout knife to remove any high spots of mortar that could show through the grout.

Install threshold material in doorways. If the threshold is too long for the doorway, cut it to fit with a jigsaw or circular saw and a tungsten-carbide blade. Set the threshold in thin-set mortar so the top is even with the tile. Keep the same space between the threshold as between tiles. Let the mortar set for at least 24 hours.

Prepare a small batch of floor grout to fill the tile joints. When mixing grout for porous tile, such as quarry or natural stone, use an additive with a release agent to prevent grout from bonding to the tile surfaces.

Starting in a corner, pour the grout over the tile. Use a rubber grout float to spread the grout outward from the corner, pressing firmly on the float to completely fill the joints. For best results, tilt the float at a 60° angle to the floor and use a figure eight motion.

Use the grout float to remove excess grout from the surface of the tile. Wipe diagonally across the joints, holding the float in a near-vertical position. Continue applying grout and wiping off excess until about 25 sq. ft. of the floor has been grouted.

(continued)

19

Wipe a damp grout sponge diagonally over about 2 sq. ft. of the floor at a time. Rinse the sponge in cool water between wipes. Wipe each area only once since repeated wiping can pull grout back out of joints. Repeat steps 15 to 18 to apply.

20

Allow the grout to dry for about 4 hours, then use a soft cloth to buff the tile surface and remove any remaining grout film.

21

Apply grout sealer to the grout lines, using a small sponge brush or sash brush. Avoid brushing sealer on tile surfaces. Wipe up any excess sealer immediately.

Variation: Use a tile sealer to seal porous tile, such as quarry tile or unglazed tile. Following the manufacturer's instructions, roll a thin coat of sealer over the tile and grout joints, using a paint roller and extension handle.

HOW TO INSTALL BULLNOSE BASE TRIM

1

Dry-fit the tiles to determine the best spacing. Grout lines in base tile do not always align with grout lines in the floor tile. Use rounded bullnose tiles at outside corners, and mark tiles for cutting as needed.

2

Leaving a ⅛" expansion gap between tiles at corners, mark any contour cuts necessary to allow the coved edges to fit together. Use a jigsaw with a tungsten-carbide blade to make curved cuts.

3

Begin installing base-trim tiles at an inside corner. Use a notched trowel to apply wall adhesive to the back of the tile. Place ⅛" spacers on the floor under each tile to create an expansion joint.

4

Press the tile onto the wall. Continue setting tiles, using spacers to maintain ⅛" gaps between the tiles and ⅛" expansion joints between the tiles and floor.

5

Use a double-bullnose tile on one side of outside corners to cover the edge of the adjoining tile.

6

After the adhesive dries, grout the vertical joints between tiles and apply grout along the tops of the tiles to make a continuous grout line. Once the grout hardens, fill the expansion joint between the tiles and floor with caulk.

TILING: FLOORS: REPAIRING

With a carbide-tipped grout saw, apply firm but gentle pressure across the grout until you expose the unglazed edges of the tile. Do not scratch the glazed tile surface. If the grout is stubborn, use a hammer and nail set to first tap the tile (step 2).

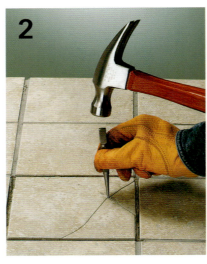

If the tile is not already cracked, use a hammer to puncture the tile by tapping a nail set or center punch into it. Alternatively, if the tile is significantly cracked, use a chisel to pry up the tile.

Insert a chisel into one of the cracks and gently tap the tile. Start at the center and chip outward so you don't damage the adjacent tiles. Be aware that cementboard looks a lot like mortar when you're chiseling. Remove and discard the broken pieces. Be sure to wear eye protection.

Use a putty knife to scrape away old thinset mortar; use a chisel for poured mortar installation. If the underlayment is covered with metal lath, you won't be able to get the area smooth; just clean it out the best you can. Once the mortar is scraped from the underlayment, smooth the rough areas with sand paper. If there are gouges in the underlayment, fill them with epoxy-based thinset mortar (for cementboard) or a floor-leveling compound (for plywood). Allow the area to dry completely.

Set a new tile into the empty spot. Use a notched trowel to apply thinset mortar to the back of the tile before setting it into place. Make sure all debris is cleaned from the floor. Rap on a carpet-covered wood block with a mallet to set the tile.

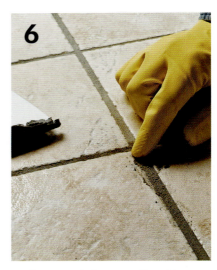

Fill in around the new tile with grout that matches the grout already on the floor. Because most grout darkens over time, choose a shade that's a bit darker than the original color.

TILING: MEMBRANES FOR

Tile membranes are thin, flexible tile underlayment materials designed to isolate tile installations from problematic substrates, provide for sound abatement, or waterproof and vapor-proof tile installations in wet areas and steam rooms. There are dozens of different types of tile membranes on the market. Please refer to the manufacturer for specific information pertaining to the limitations, benefits, and installation of the membrane selected.

Waterproofing membranes are installed in wet areas and are designed to prevent the migration of water beyond the membrane. They often provide additional benefits, including crack suppression. Tile installed in steam rooms, wet saunas, and steam showers requires the installation of a membrane that is both vapor-proof and waterproof.

Sound isolation membranes are designed to reduce the transmission of impact sounds from hard surface flooring to lower level living spaces. This type of membrane is usually installed in apartment dwellings and condominiums (and behind drywall in home theaters).

Crack isolation and anti-fracture membranes, also called crack suppression membranes, isolate tile installations from tile substrates that are susceptible to stresses that produce horizontal movement. They can absorb movement of as much as ⅛-inch to ⅜-inch. Some membranes are liquid applied to the substrate with a trowel or roller, others are sheet applied. There are even anti-fracture thinset mortars, eliminating the need in some cases, for a separate sheet or liquid applied membrane.

Uncoupling membranes isolate the finished tile installation from the substrate while allowing both to move independently. This type of membrane is typically installed over problematic sub-floors and newly installed or problematic concrete slabs.

Note: Crack suppression and uncoupling membranes are not intended to be a substitution for sound building practices. Tile installations that exceed structural recommendations may see little benefit with the installation of these types of products. Likewise, marginal installations will benefit more from structural reinforcement or repairs. Whenever possible, reinforce weak wall framing and floor joists with wood blocking and install an additional layer of plywood over wood sub-floors if needed.

Membranes used for laying tile include: Roll-on waterproofing and crack prevention membrane (A); multipurpose membrane for uncoupling, waterproofing and vapor management (B); 40-mil thick PVC shower pan liner (C); 40-mil thick (1⁄16") self-bonding membrane designed for use under floor tile requiring protection from structural movement (D); crack prevention mat (E).

HOW TO INSTALL ISOLATION MEMBRANE

Thoroughly clean the subfloor, then apply thinset mortar with a notched trowel. Start spreading the mortar along a wall in a section as wide as the membrane and 8 to 10 ft. long. *Note: For some membranes, you must use a bonding material other than mortar. Read and follow label directions.*

Roll out the membrane over the mortar. Cut the membrane to fit tightly against the walls using a straightedge and utility knife.

Starting in the center of the membrane, use a heavy flooring roller (available at rental centers) to smooth out the surface toward the edges. This frees trapped air and presses out excess bonding material.

Repeat steps 1 through 3, cutting the membrane as necessary at the walls and obstacles, until the floor is completely covered with membrane. Do not overlap the seams, but make sure they are tight. Allow the mortar to cure for two days before installing the tile.

TILING: THINSET MORTAR

Introduced in the early 1950s, thinset is an adhesive mortar consisting of Portland cement, a water retentive agent, sand or aggregate (optional), and other additives. Prior to thinset, tiles were installed with a thick paste consisting of Portland cement and water. Unless they were soaked in water prior to installation, absorbent tiles would quickly soak up the moisture in the paste and fail to bond to the substrate. Thinset mortar made it possible for installers to install tile over a variety of cementitious substrates without needing to soak the tile beforehand.

Thinset mortars have improved substantially in quality and ease of use over the years. Because no two products are exactly alike, you should always read the package label carefully to make sure the product you select is an appropriate adhesive for the tile and the substrate to which it will be applied.

The adhesive mortars used for the projects in this book include dry-set thinset mortar, polymer-modified thinset mortar, and latex-modified thinset mortar. Modified thinset, the most common adhesive used, is widely employed to adhere a variety of different types of tile to cementboard and concrete substrates. Use gray thinset for darker grout selections and white thinset for lighter grout selections.

Dry-set mortars are mixed with potable water and used as a setting bed to seat backer board panels. In special circumstances, it can also be used as an adhesive to set tile.

Thinset mortar is applied in a thick layer to make a bed for setting tile. It is sold in premixed tubs and in dry powder forms—most professionals prefer to mix their own. If the product you buy has not been modified with polymer additive, you can mix in latex additive yourself. Different thinset mortars have different ratios of additives and fortifiers for specific purposes. You will also find some color variation. Most is cement gray, but white thinset intended for use with glass tile is also available. You can also use white thinset to reduce the chance of color bleedthrough if you are applying a light-colored grout.

Polymer-modified thinset mortar contains dry-polymer additives. It also should be mixed with potable water. Latex-modified thinset is prepared by mixing dry-set thinset mortar with a liquid latex additive. Although more costly and difficult to work with than conventional modified blends, liquid latex modified mortars usually offer higher bond strengths, higher flexural values, and increased water and chemical resistance.

Small quantities of mortar can be mixed by hand to a smooth and creamy consistency using a margin trowel. Larger batches of mortar can be mixed at speeds of less than 300 rpm, using a ½-inch drill fitted with a mixing paddle.

Cementboard setting beds are applied using a ¼-inch square notch trowel. Use a ¼-inch V-notch trowel to install mosaic tiles two inches square or less. Most varieties of larger tile can be installed using a ¼-inch or ⅜-inch square or U-notch trowel. Very large tiles and certain types of stone may require larger trowel sizes.

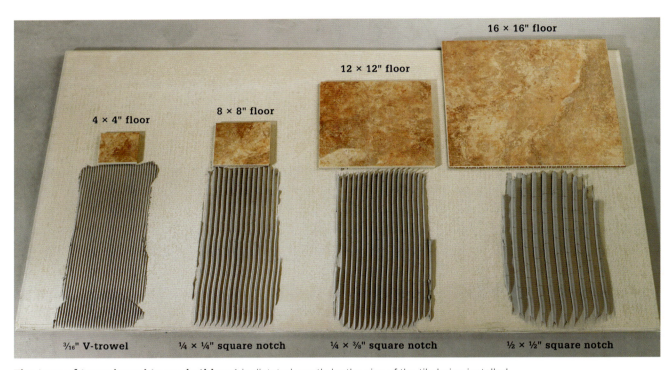

The type of trowel used to apply thinset is dictated mostly by the size of the tile being installed.

Premixed Thinset Mortar ▶

Most professionals prefer to mix their own thinset mortar because it is considerably cheaper than premixed material. But homeowners who are only tiling a small area should consider purchasing tubs of premixed thinset mortar. Not only is it a convenience, you are assured that the material contains an adequate ratio of latex additive and is blended to the proper consistency.

TILING: WALLS

Design the layout and mark the reference lines. Begin installation with the second row of tiles above the floor. If the layout requires cut tiles for this row, mark and cut the tiles for the entire row at one time.

Mix a small batch of thinset mortar containing a latex additive. (Some mortar has additive mixed in by the manufacturer and some must have additive mixed in separately.) Cover the back of the first tile with adhesive, using a ¼" notched trowel.

Variation: Spread adhesive on a small section of the wall, then set the tiles into the adhesive. Thinset adhesive sets fast, so work quickly if you choose this installation method.

Beginning near the center of the wall, apply the tile to the wall with a slight twisting motion, aligning it exactly with the horizontal and vertical reference lines. When placing cut tiles, position the cut edges where they will be least visible.

(continued)

Continue installing tiles, working from the center to the sides in a pyramid pattern. Keep the tiles aligned with the reference lines. If the tiles are not self-spacing, use plastic spacers inserted in the corner joints to maintain even grout lines. The base row should be the last row of full tiles installed. Cut tile as necessary.

As small sections of tile are completed, set the tile by laying a scrap of 2 × 4 wrapped with carpet onto the tile and rapping it lightly with a mallet. This embeds the tile solidly in the adhesive and creates a flat, even surface.

Spacers

Tile marked for cutting

To mark bottom and edge row tiles for straight cuts, begin by taping ⅛" spacers against the surfaces below and to the side of the tile. Position a tile directly over the last full tile installed, then place a third tile so the edge butts against the spacers. Trace the edge of the top tile onto the middle tile to mark it for cutting.

Install any trim tiles, such as the bullnose edge tiles shown above, at border areas. Wipe away excess mortar along the top edges of the edge tiles. Use bullnose and corner bullnose (with two adjacent bullnose edges) tiles at outside corners to cover the rough edges of the adjoining tiles.

WALLS & CEILINGS

8

Let mortar dry completely (12 to 24 hours), then mix a batch of grout containing latex additive. Apply the grout with a rubber grout float, using a sweeping motion to force it deep into the joints. Do not grout joints adjoining bathtubs, floors, or room corners. These will serve as expansion joints and will be caulked later.

9

Wipe a damp grout sponge diagonally over the tile, rinsing the sponge in cool water between wipes. Wipe each area only once; repeated wiping can pull grout from the joints. Allow the grout to dry for about 4 hours, then use a soft cloth to buff the tile surface and remove any remaining grout film.

10

When the grout has cured completely, use a small foam brush to apply grout sealer to the joints, following the manufacturer's directions. Avoid brushing sealer on the tile surfaces, and wipe up excess sealer immediately.

11

Seal expansion joints at the floor and corners with silicone caulk. After the caulk dries, buff the tile with a soft, dry cloth.

TOILET: CLEARING CLOGS

The toilet is clogged and has overflowed. Have patience. Now is the time for considered action. A second flush is a tempting but unnecessary gamble. First, do damage control. Mop up the water if there's been a spill. Next, consider the nature of the clog. Is it entirely "natural" or might a foreign object be contributing to the congestion? Push a natural blockage down the drain with a plunger. A foreign object should be removed, if possible, with a closet auger. Pushing anything more durable than toilet paper into the sewer may create a more serious blockage in your drain and waste system.

If the tub, sink, and toilet all back up at once, the branch drainline that serves all the bathroom fixtures is probably blocked and your best recourse is to call a drain clearing service.

Tools & Materials ▸

Towels
Closet auger

Plunger with foldout skirt (force cup)

A blockage in the toilet bowl leaves flush water from the tank nowhere to go but on the floor.

The trap is the most common catching spot for toilet clogs, Once the clog forms, flushing the toilet cannot generate enough water power to clear the trap, so flush water backs up. Traps on modern 1.6-gallon toilets have been redesigned to larger diameters and are less prone to clogs than the first generation of 1.6-gallon toilets.

Plunger

Force cup

Not all plungers were created equal. The standard plunger (left) is simply an inverted rubber cup and is used to plunge sinks, tubs, and showers. The flanged plunger, also called a force cup, is designed to get down into the trap of a toilet drain. You can fold the flange up into the flanged plunger cup and use it as a standard plunger.

Drain Clearers ▸

The home repair marketplace is filled with gadgets and gimmicks, as well as well-established products, that are intended to clear drains of all types. Some are caustic chemicals, some are natural enzymes, others are more mechanical in nature. Some help, some are worthless, some can even make the problem worse. Nevertheless, if you are the type of homeowner who is enamored with new products and the latest solutions, you may enjoy testing out new drain cleaners as they become available. In this photo, for example, you'll see a relatively new product that injects blasts of compressed CO_2 directly into your toilet, sink, or tub drain to dislodge clogs. It does not cause any chemicals to enter the waste stream, and the manufacturers claim the CO_2 blast is very gentle and won't damage pipes. As with any new product, use it with caution. But if a plunger or a snake isn't working, it could save you the cost of a plumber's house call.

HOW TO PLUNGE A CLOGGED TOILET

Plunging is the easiest way to remove "natural" blockages. Take time to lay towels around the base of the toilet and remove other objects to a safe, dry location, since plunging may result in splashing. Often, allowing a very full toilet to sit for 20 or 30 minutes will permit some of the water to drain to a less precarious level.

Force Cups ▶

A flanged plunger (force cup) fits into the mouth of the toilet trap and creates a tight seal so you can build up enough pressure in front of the plunger to dislodge the blockage and send it on its way.

There should be enough water in the bowl to completely cover the plunger. Fold out the skirt from inside the plunger to form a better seal with the opening at the base of the bowl. Pump the plunger vigorously half-a-dozen times, take a rest, and then repeat. Try this for four to five cycles.

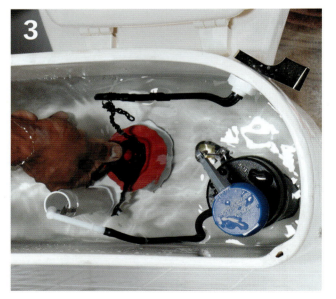

If you force enough water out of the bowl that you are unable to create suction with the plunger, put a controlled amount of water in the bowl by lifting up on the flush valve in the tank. Resume plunging. When you think the drain is clear, you can try a controlled flush, with your hand ready to close the flush valve should the water threaten to spill out of the bowl. Once the blockage has cleared, dump a five-gallon pail of water into the toilet to blast away any residual debris.

HOW TO CLEAR CLOGS WITH A CLOSET AUGER

1

Protective
rubber boot

Place the business end of the auger firmly in the bottom of the toilet bowl with the auger tip fully withdrawn. A rubber sleeve will protect the porcelain at the bottom bend of the auger. The tip will be facing back and up, which is the direction the toilet trap takes.

Closet Augers ▶

A closet auger is a semirigid cable housed in a tube. The tube has a bend at the end so it can be snaked through a toilet trap (without scratching it) to snag blockages.

2

Rotate the handle on the auger housing clockwise as you push down on the rod, advancing the rotating auger tip up into the back part of the trap. You may work the cable backward and forward as needed, but keep the rubber boot of the auger firmly in place in the bowl. When you feel resistance, indicating you've snagged the object, continue rotating the auger counterclockwise as you withdraw the cable and the object.

3

Fully retract the auger until you have recovered the object. This can be frustrating at times, but it is still a much easier task than the alternative—to remove the toilet and go fishing.

TOILET REPLACEMENT

Remove the old supply tube. First, turn off the water at the stop valve. Flush the toilet, holding the handle down for a long flush, and sponge out the tank. Use a wet/dry vac to clear any remaining water out of the tank and bowl. Unthread the coupling nut for the water supply below the tank using channel-type pliers.

Grip each tank bolt nut with a box wrench or pliers and loosen it as you stabilize each tank bolt from inside the tank with a large slotted screwdriver. If the nuts are stuck, apply penetrating oil to the nut and let it sit before trying to remove them again. You may also cut the tank bolts between the tank and the bowl with an open-ended hacksaw. Remove and discard the tank.

Remove the nuts that hold the bowl to the floor. First, pry off the bolt covers with a screwdriver. Use a socket wrench, locking pliers, or your channel-type pliers to loosen the nuts on the tank bolts. Apply penetrating oil and let it sit if the nuts are stuck, then take them off. As a last resort, cut the bolts off with a hacksaw by first cutting down through one side of the nut. Tilt the toilet bowl over and remove it.

Prying Up Wax Rings ▶

Removing an old wax ring is one of the more disgusting jobs you'll encounter in the plumbing universe (the one you see here is actually in relatively good condition). Work a stiff putty knife underneath the plastic flange of the ring (if you can) and start scraping. In many cases the wax ring will come off in chunks. Discard each chunk right away—they stick to everything. If you're left with a lot of residue, scrub with mineral spirits. Once clean, stuff a rag-in-a-bag in the drain opening to block sewer gas.

PLUMBING

T

HOW TO INSTALL A TOILET

Clean and inspect the old closet flange. Look for breaks or wear. Also inspect the flooring around the flange. If either the flange or floor is worn or damaged, repair the damage. Use a rag and mineral spirits to completely remove residue from the old wax ring. Place a rag-in-a-bag into the opening to block odors.

Installation Tip ▸

If you will be replacing your toilet flange or if your existing flange can be unscrewed and moved, orient the new flange so the slots are parallel to the wall. This allows you to insert bolts under the slotted areas, which are much stronger than the areas at the ends of the curved grooves.

Insert new tank bolts (don't reuse old ones) into the openings in the closet flange. Make sure the heads of the bolts are oriented to catch the maximum amount of flange material. To firmly hold the bolts upright, slide on the plastic washers and press them down.

Remove the wax ring and apply it to the underside of the bowl, around the horn. Remove the protective covering. Do not touch the wax ring. It is very sticky. Remove the rag-in-a-bag. If you have an older 4" flange, place the ring on the flange rather than the toilet to make sure it is centered.

(continued)

4

Lower the bowl onto the flange, taking care not to disturb the wax ring. The holes in the bowl base should align perfectly with the tank bolts. Add a washer and tighten a nut on each bolt. Hand tighten each nut and then use channel-type pliers to further tighten the nuts. Alternate back and forth between nuts until the bowl is secure. Do not overtighten.

5

Spud nut

Spud washer

Install the flush valve. Some tanks come with a flush valve and a fill valve preinstalled. For models that do not have this, insert the flush valve through the tank opening and tighten a spud nut over the threaded end of the valve. Place a foam spud washer on top of the spud nut.

6

Threaded fill valve shank

Adjust the fill valve as directed by the manufacturer to set the correct tank water level height and install the valve inside the tank. Hand tighten the nylon lock nut that secures the valve to the tank (inset photo) and then tighten it further with channel-type pliers.

7

Intermediate nut goes between tank and bowl

With the tank lying on its back, thread a rubber washer onto each tank bolt and insert it into the bolt holes from inside the tank. Then, thread a brass washer and hex nut onto the tank bolts from below and tighten them to a quarter turn past hand tight. Do not overtighten.

PLUMBING

8

Position the tank on the bowl, spud washer on the opening, and bolts through the bolt holes. Put a rubber washer, followed by a brass washer and a wing nut, on each bolt and tighten these up evenly.

Intermediate nut

9

You may stabilize the bolts with a large slotted screwdriver from inside the tank, but tighten the nuts, not the bolts. You may press down a little on a side, the front, or the rear of the tank to level it as you tighten the nuts by hand. Do not overtighten and crack the tank. The tank should be level and stable when you're done. Do not overtighten.

10

Hook up the water supply by connecting the supply tube to the threaded fill valve with the coupling nut provided. Turn on the water and test for leaks. Do not overtighten.

11

Attach the toilet seat by threading the plastic or brass bolts provided with the seat through the openings on the back of the rim and attaching nuts.

TRIM: CHAIR RAIL: INSTALLING

Chair rail molding typically runs horizontally along walls at a height of 32 to 36 inches (the rule of thumb is to install it one-third of the way up the wall). Originally installed to protect walls from chair backs, today chair rail is commonly used to divide a wall visually. Chair rail may cap wainscot, serve as a border for wallpaper, or divide two different colors on a wall. Or more interesting chair rail profiles can be effective alone on a one-color wall.

Stock chair rail moldings are available at most lumberyards and home centers. However, more intricate and elaborate chair rails can be crated by combining multiple pieces of trim.

Tools & Materials ▸

Pencil	Metal file set
Stud finder	Moldings
Tape measure	Pneumatic fasteners
Power miter saw	Painter's tape
4-ft. level	Carpenter's glue
Air compressor	Finishing putty
Finish nail gun	Finishing materials
Coping saw	Eye protection
Finish nails	

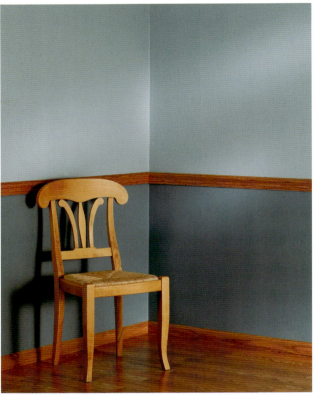

Chair rail once was installed to protect fragile walls from chair backs, but today it is mainly installed as a decorative accent that visually breaks up dull walls.

HOW TO INSTALL CHAIR RAIL

On the starting wall of your installation, measure up the desired height at which you plan to install the chair rail, minus the width of the molding. Mark a level line at this height around the room. Locate all studs along the walls and mark their locations with painter's tape below the line.

Measure, cut, and install the first piece of chair rail with the ends cut squarely, butting into both walls (in a wall run with two inside corners). Nail the molding in place with two 2" finish nails at each stud location.

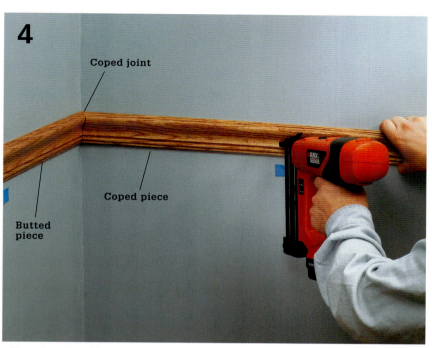

Miter-cut the second piece of molding with a power miter saw and then cope the end with a coping saw. Clean up the edge of the cope cut with a metal file to ensure a tight fit. Dry-fit the piece to check for any gaps in the joint.

When the coped joint fits tightly, measure, mark, and cut the opposing end of the second piece of trim squarely with a miter saw. Nail the second piece in place with two nails at each stud location. Follow the level line with the bottom edge of the molding.

Install the third piece of chair rail with a cope cut at one end. Use a butt joint where the molding runs into door and window casings. Fill all nail holes with putty and apply a final coat of finish to the molding.

OPTION: Apply a painted finish for a more casual appearance. White semigloss is a safe choice.

TRIM: COPING

At first glance, coping moldings appears to be difficult work that only a professional would attempt. But in actuality, coping only requires patience and the right tools. Whether a molding is installed flat against the wall or is sprung to fill an inside corner junction, as with crown molding, the concept of coping is the same. It is essentially cutting back the body of a trim piece along its profile. This cutting is done at an angle so that only the face of the molding makes direct contact with the adjoining piece.

For beginners, coping a molding requires a coping saw, a utility knife, and a set of metal files with a variety of profiles. The initial cope cut is made with the coping saw and the joint is fitted with a utility knife and files. This fitting can be a long process, especially when working with intricate crown moldings, but the results are superior to any other method.

Tools & Materials ▸

Miter saw	Pneumatic finish
Metal files or rasp set	nail gun
Utility knife	Air compressor
Pencil	Air hose
Tape measure	Molding
Coping saw	Eye protection

Coping is a tricky skill to learn, but a valuable capability to possess once you've got the process down. With very few exceptions, a coped cut can be made only with a handsaw (usually, a coping saw like the one shown above).

HOW TO MAKE COPED CUTS

Measure, cut, and install the first trim piece. Square-cut the ends, butting them tightly into the corners, and nail the workpiece at the marked stud locations.

Cut the second piece of molding at a 45° angle as if it were an inside miter. The cut edge reveals the profile of the cope cut.

WALLS & CEILINGS

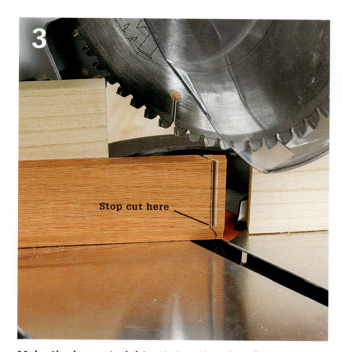

Make the long, straight cut along the edge of the molding. An easy, accurate way to do this is to use a power miter saw set at about a 2° miter. Use a spacer between the workpiece and the saw fence and cut through the workpiece, stopping just short of the profile.

The more traditional way to make this cut is to use a coping saw cutting at a 45° bevel. Finish cutting the profile with the coping saw.

Test-fit the piece (inset photo) and use a metal file to fit the joint precisely. When the joint is properly fitted, nail the coped piece in place.

TIP: Trim components such as this chair rail can be complex to cope properly. A variety of rasps or metal files with different profiles is the key to fitting these joints tightly.

TRIM: CROWN MOLDING

Simply put, crown molding is angled trim that bridges the joint between the ceiling and the wall. In order to cover this joint effectively, crown moldings are "sprung." This means that the top and bottom edges of the molding have been beveled, so when the molding is tilted away from the wall at an angle, the tops and bottoms are flush on the wall and ceiling surfaces. Some crown moldings have a 45° angle at both the top and the bottom edges; another common style ("38° crown") has a 38° angle on one edge and a 52° angle on the other edge.

Installing crown molding can be a challenging and sometimes confusing process. Joints may be difficult for you to visualize before cutting, and wall and ceiling irregularities can be hard to overcome. If you have not worked on crown molding joints before, it is recommended that your first attempt be made with paint-grade materials. Stain-grade crown is commonly made of solid hardwood stock, which makes for expensive cutting errors and difficulty concealing irregularities in joints.

Inside corner joints of crown molding should be cope-cut, not mitered, except in the case of very intricate profile crown that is virtually impossible to cope (and must therefore be mitered). While mitering inside corners may appear to save time and produce adequate results, after a few changing seasons the joints will open up and be even more difficult to conceal.

Installing crown molding in a brand-new, perfectly square room is one thing, but what happens when the walls and ceilings don't meet at perfect right angles? In most houses that have been around for more than a couple of seasons, walls have bulges caused by warped studs or improper stud placement that's causing the drywall to push out into the room. Ceilings have issues caused by warped joists or drywall that has loosened or pulled away from the ceiling joists. Corners may be best finished with extra-thick layers of joint compound that has been applied a bit heavily, causing an outside corner piece to sit further away from the corner bead. These are just a few of the issues that can work against you and cause even an experienced carpenter to become frustrated.

Tools & Materials ▸

Hammer	Coping saw
Utility knife	Finish nails
Drill	Spackling compound
Deck screws	or wood putty
Scraps of wood	Sandpaper
2× lumber	Paint or wood finish
Pencil	Caulk
Painter's tape	Nailer
Miter saw	Eye protection
Tablesaw	

Basic crown molding softens the transitions between walls and ceilings. If it is made from quality hardwood, crown molding can be quite beautiful when installed and finished with a clear top coat. But historically, it is most often painted—either the same color as the ceiling (your eye tends to see it as a ceiling molding, not a wall molding) or with highly elaborate painted and carved details.

How to Make a Gauge Block ▶

Make and use a gauge block to ensure that crown molding is installed uniformly. A gauge block is used to show where the bottom edge of the crown will sit on the wall. This is especially important for laying out inside and outside corners. To make a gauge block, place the profile of crown upside down against the fence of your saw. The top edge of the crown should lay flat against the base. The fence represents the wall and the base represents the ceiling. The crown will be situated in the same position as it would sit on the wall. Run a pencil line across the bottom edge of the crown. Tape can be placed against the fence to help see the pencil marks. Measure from the base to this line and subtract 1⁄16". Cut a block to this measurement and label it to match the profile of crown that you're installing.

Cutting compound miters is tricky. Throughout this book, crown molding is shown being mitered with the workpiece held against a fence or fence extension. This hand-held approach is quick and effective, but takes some getting used to. A practically foolproof option is to use an adjustable jig, such as the compound miter jig shown here.

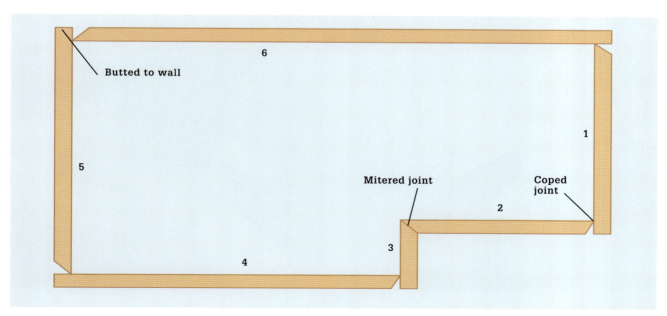

Butted to wall

6

1

5

Mitered joint

Coped joint

2

3

4

Plan the order of the installation to minimize the number of difficult joints on each piece and use the longest pieces for the most visible sections of wall. Notice that the left end of first piece is cope-cut rather than butted into the wall. Cope-cutting the first end eliminates the need to cope-cut both ends of the final piece and places the cuts in the same direction. This simplifies your installation, making the method to cut each piece similar.

HOW TO USE BACKERS TO INSTALL CROWN MOLDING

WALLS & CEILINGS

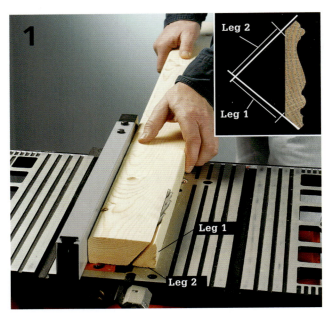

Installing crown molding is greatly simplified if you first attach triangular backers in the crotch area between the walls and ceilings. You can run the backers continuously along all walls or you can space them at regular intervals for use as nailers. To measure the required length for the triangle legs, set a piece of the crown molding in the sprung position in a square in an orientation like the inset photo above. Rip triangular backer strips from 2× stock on your tablesaw, with the blade set at 45°.

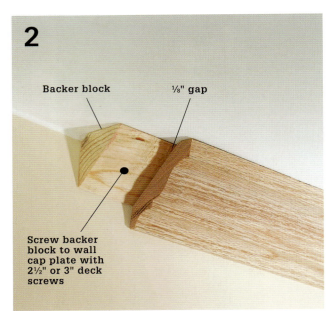

Locate the wall studs with a stud finder and mark the locations on the wall with blue painter's tape. Secure the backer block to the wall by driving 2½" or 3" deck screws at an angle through the block and into the top plate of the wall. Now, your crown molding can be attached to the backers wherever you'd like to nail it. Install crown according to the following instructions.

HOW TO INSTALL BASIC CROWN MOLDING

Test cope cuts against this profile

Cut a piece of crown molding about 1-ft. long with square ends. Temporarily install the piece in the corner of the last installation wall with two screws driven into the blocking. This piece serves as a template for the first cope cut on the first piece of molding.

Place the first piece of molding upside down and sprung against the fence of the miter saw. Mark a reference line on the fence for placement of future moldings, and cut the first coped end with an inside miter cut to reveal the profile of the piece.

3

Cope-cut the end of the first piece with a coping saw. Carefully cut along the profile, angling the saw as you cut to back-bevel the cope. Test-fit the coped cut against the temporary scrap from step 1. Fine-tune the cut with files and fine-grit sandpaper.

4

Temporary scrap

Measure, cut to length, and install the first piece of crown molding, leaving the end near the temporary scrap loose for final fitting of the last piece. Nail the molding at the top and bottom of each stud location.

5

Test pieces

Cut two test pieces to check the fit of outside corners. Start with each molding cut at 45°, adjusting the angles larger or smaller until the joints are tight. Make sure the test moldings are properly aligned and are flush with the ceiling and walls. Make a note of your saw settings once the joint fits tightly.

6

Position the actual stock so a cut end is flush against the wall at one end and, at the other end, mark the outside corner on the back edge of the molding. Miter-cut the piece at the mark, according to the angles you noted on the test pieces.

(continued)

7

Measure and cut the third piece with an outside corner miter to match the angle of your test pieces. Cut the other end squarely, butting it into the corner. Install the piece with nails driven at stud locations. Install the subsequent pieces of crown molding, coping the front end and butting the other as you work around the room.

8

Temporary spacer removed

To fit the final piece, cope the end and cut it to length. Remove the temporary scrap piece from step 3, and slide the last molding into position. Nail the last piece at the stud locations when the joints fit well, and finish nailing the first piece.

9

Fill all nail holes (use spackling compound if painting; wait until the finish is applied and fill with tinted putty for clear finishes). Use a putty knife to force spackling compound or tinted wood putty into loose joints and caulk gaps ⅛" or smaller between the molding and the wall or ceiling with flexible, paintable, latex caulk.

10

Lightly sand the filled nail holes and joint gaps with fine sandpaper. Sand the nail hole flush with the surface of the moldings and apply a final coat of paint to the entire project.

HOW TO INSTALL CROWN AT A SAGGING CEILING

Make light pencil marks on the wall to show where the bottom of the crown will sit. **TIP:** Make and use a gauge block for this (see page 515). This is especially important on outside corners.

Score the drywall slightly in the sagging portion of the ceiling. Set the crown along the lines made by the gauge block and the top of the point where the drywall is scored. Mark the edges of the sagging area in a visible spot on the walls.

Use a small wood block to drive the sagging drywall up where it meets the wall. Don't get too aggressive here.

Install the crown so the bottom edge is flush with the gauge line. The molding will conceal the damage to the drywall.

TUCK-POINT MORTAR JOINTS

Clean out loose or deteriorated mortar to a depth of ¼" to ¾". Use a mortar raking tool (top) first, then switch to a masonry chisel and a hammer (bottom) if the mortar is stubborn. Clear away all loose debris, and dampen the surface with water before applying fresh mortar.

Tuck-pointer

Mortar hawk

Mix the mortar, adding concrete fortifier; add tint if necessary. Load mortar onto a mortar hawk, then push it into the horizontal joints with a tuck-pointer. Apply mortar in ¼"-thick layers, and let each layer dry for 30 minutes before applying another. Fill the joints until the mortar is flush with the face of the brick or block.

Apply the first layer of mortar into the vertical joints by scooping mortar onto the back of a tuck-pointer, and pressing it into the joint. Work from the top downward.

After the final layer of mortar is applied, smooth the joints with a jointing tool that matches the profile of the old mortar joints. Tool the horizontal joints first. Let the mortar dry until it is crumbly, then brush off the excess mortar with a stiff-bristle brush.

VENT FAN: INSTALLING

Most vent fans are installed in the center of the bathroom ceiling or over the toilet area. A fan installed over the tub or shower area must be GFCI protected and rated for use in wet areas. You can usually wire a fan that just has a light fixture into a main bathroom electrical circuit, but units with built-in heat lamps or blowers require separate circuits.

If the fan you choose doesn't come with a mounting kit, purchase one separately. A mounting kit should include a vent hose (duct), a vent tailpiece, and an exterior vent cover.

The most common venting options are attic venting and soffit venting. Attic venting routes fan ductwork into the attic and out through the roof. Always insulate ducting in this application to keep condensation from forming and running down into the motor. And carefully install flashing around the outside vent cover to prevent roof leaks.

Soffit venting involves routing the duct to a soffit (roof overhang) instead of through the roof. Check with the vent manufacturer for instructions for soffit venting.

To prevent moisture damage, always terminate the vent outside your home—never into your attic or basement.

You can install a vent fan while the framing is exposed or as a retrofit, as shown in this project.

Tools & Materials ▸

Drill	NM cable (14/2, 14/3)
Jigsaw	Cable clamp
Screwdrivers	Hose clamps
Caulk gun	Pipe insulation
Reciprocating saw	Roofing cement
Drywall screws	Self-sealing roofing nails
Double-gang retrofit	Shingles
electrical box	Wire connectors
2 × 4 lumber	Switch and timer
Vent hose	Eye protection
Vent cover	

Check the information label attached to each vent fan unit. Choose a unit with a fan rating at least 5 CFM higher than the square footage of your bathroom. The sone rating refers to quietness rated on a scale of 1 to 7; quieter is lower.

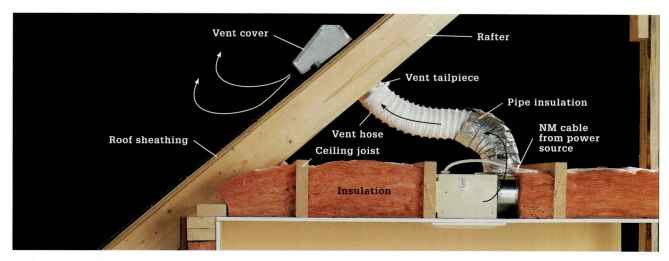

Bathroom vent fans must be exhausted to the outdoors, either through the roof or through a wall. Flexible ductwork is allowed for bath vent fans (but not for clothes dryers).

HOW TO INSTALL A BATHROOM VENT FAN

Position the vent fan unit against a ceiling joist. Outline the vent fan onto the ceiling surface. Remove the unit, then drill pilot holes at the corners of the outline and cut out the area with a jigsaw or drywall saw.

Remove the grille from the fan unit, then position the unit against the joist with the edge recessed ¼" from the finished surface of the ceiling (so the grille can be flush mounted). Attach the unit to the joist using drywall screws.

Variation: For vent fans with heaters or light fixtures, some manufacturers recommend using 2× lumber to build dams between the ceiling joists to keep the insulation at least 6" away from the fan unit.

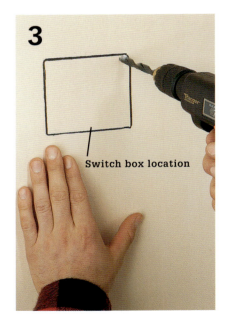

Mark and cut an opening for a double-gang box on the wall next to the latch side of the bathroom door, then run a 14/3 NM cable from the switch cutout to the fan unit. Run a 14/2 NM cable from the power source to the cutout.

Strip 10" of sheathing from the ends of the cables, then feed the cables into a double-gang retrofit switch box so at least ½" of sheathing extends into the box. Clamp the cables in place. Tighten the mounting screws until the box is secure.

Strip 10" of sheathing from the end of the cable at the vent unit, then attach a cable clamp to the cable. Insert the cable into the fan unit. From the inside of the unit, screw a locknut onto the threaded end of the clamp.

Exhaust tailpiece

Mark the exit location in the roof next to a rafter for the vent duct. Drill a pilot hole, then saw through the sheathing and roofing material with a reciprocating saw to make the cutout for the exhaust tailpiece.

Remove a section of shingles from around the cutout, leaving the roofing paper intact. Remove enough shingles to create an exposed area that is at least the size of the exhaust termination flange.

Attach a hose clamp to the rafter next to the roof cutout about 1" below the roof sheathing (top). Insert the exhaust tailpiece into the cutout and through the hose clamp, then tighten the clamp screw (bottom).

Exhaust termination flange

Slide one end of the exhaust duct over the tailpiece, and slide the other end over the outlet on the fan unit. Slip hose clamps or straps around each end of the duct, and tighten the clamps.

Wrap the exhaust duct with pipe insulation. Insulation prevents moist air inside the hose from condensing and dripping down into the fan motor.

Apply roofing cement to the bottom of the exhaust termination flange, then slide the termination over the tailpiece. Nail the termination flange in place with self-sealing roofing nails, then patch in shingles around the cover.

(continued)

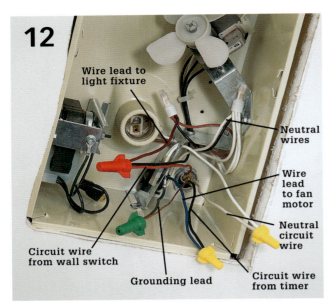

12

Wire lead to
light fixture

Neutral
wires

Wire
lead
to fan
motor

Neutral
circuit
wire

Circuit wire
from wall switch

Grounding lead

Circuit wire
from timer

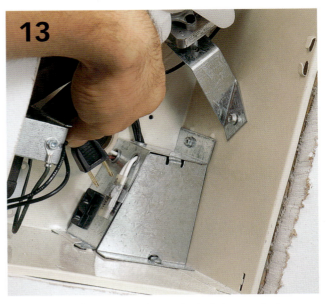

13

Ensure power is off and test for power. Make the following wire connections at the fan unit: the black circuit wire from the timer to the wire lead for the fan motor; the red circuit wire from the single-pole switch (see step 14) to the wire lead for the light fixture in the unit; the white neutral circuit wire to the neutral wire lead; the circuit grounding wire to the grounding lead on the fan unit. Make all connections with wire connectors. Attach the cover plate over the unit when the wiring is completed.

Connect the fan motor plug to the built-in receptacle on the wire connection box, and attach the fan grille to the frame using the mounting clips included with the fan kit. *Note: If you removed the wall and ceiling surfaces for the installation, install new surfaces before completing this step.*

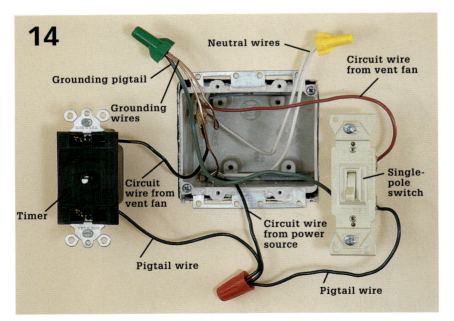

14

Neutral wires

Circuit wire
from vent fan

Grounding pigtail

Grounding
wires

Single-
pole
switch

Timer

Circuit
wire from
vent fan

Circuit wire
from power
source

Pigtail wire

Pigtail wire

15

Ensure power is off and test for power. At the switch box, add black pigtail wires to one screw terminal on the timer and to one screw terminal on the single-pole switch; add a green grounding pigtail to the groundling screw on the switch. Make the following wire connections: the black circuit wire from the power source to the black pigtail wires; the black circuit wire from the vent fan to the remaining screw on the timer; the red circuit wire from the vent fan to the remaining screw on the switch. Join the white wires with a wire connector. Join the grounding wires with a green wire connector.

Tuck the wires into the switch box, then attach the switch and timer to the box. Attach the cover plate and timer dial. Turn on the power.

VINYL PLANK FLOOR: INSTALLING

The grip strips attached to the vinyl planks are coated with an adhesive that activates as the product is warmed. If you are installing a vinyl plank floor in a room that is relatively cold, it helps to heat the seams with a heat gun or a hair dryer and roll them with a J-roller immediately after you form them. This helps activate the adhesive and creates a tighter bond between planks.

Store planks in their boxes in the room in which they'll be installed (at least 65°) for 24 to 48 hours before installation. For the flooring to acclimate properly, the room temperature and the anticipated conditions should be the same as after the flooring is installed.

Adhesive

Adhesive

Vinyl plank flooring is a two-ply product with adhesive strips that overlap in the seam areas where two planks meet. Both the underside of the top ply and the top of the bottom ply are treated with adhesive, forming a near-impervious bond that sets permanently after a very brief window of time to make adjustments.

Purchase self-leveling floor underlayment to fill in any dips in the floor being covered. Even very small low areas will telegraph through the vinyl planks because they are so thin. Levelers differ somewhat from product to product, so read the label carefully to make sure the product you buy is suitable for your application and that you have all the materials you need. The product above, for example, is specially formulated for glue-down floors and requires a primer that's purchased separately.

HOW TO INSTALL VINYL PLANK FLOORING

1

Measure the length and width of the room to determine square footage. Measure alcoves, bumpouts, and other areas separately. Add 10% to the total square footage when ordering the floor. While measuring, check that the room is square by measuring the length of the room at different points along two walls.

2

Apply floor leveler (see pages 178 to 179) to fill large cracks, deep grout lines, dips, holes, or other irregularities in the subfloor before installing planks. Use an appropriate floor leveler product for the particular subfloor material.

3

Beginning along the longest wall, lay out the first row of planks without connecting them. Mark the end plank for cutting by setting it down backwards and upside-down on the previous plank in the row. The top attachment strip should be facing away from the wall. Mark the back of the plank and cut with a utility knife and straightedge.

4

Begin laying planks using ⅛" spacers to maintain uniform expansion gaps between the row and the wall. Lay planks so that the bottom attachment strip is on the opposite side of the wall edge. Trim the top strip from the wall side before laying planks.

Attach planks in the row by rolling the top attachment strip of the new plank at a 45° angle into the bottom attachment strip of the preceding plank. Work slowly and carefully and make sure the seams are tight.

Cut planks as necessary by marking the top of the plank, scoring with a utility knife equipped with a new, sharp blade, and snapping off the waste section.

Stagger the planks. Start the second row by cutting a plank ⅔ of the length of the first plank in the starter row. Start the third row with a ⅓ length plank. Continue this pattern throughout the rows.

Roll the seams. Immediately after you finish laying the floor, use a weighted floor roller to roll all the seams between planks. The floor is ready to be walked on as soon as it has been rolled.

VINYL TILE: INSTALLING

As with any tile installation, resilient tile requires carefully positioned layout lines. Before committing to any layout and applying tile, conduct a dry run to identify potential problems.

Keep in mind the difference between reference lines (see opposite page) and layout lines. Reference lines mark the center of the room and divide it into quadrants. If the tiles don't lay out symmetrically along these lines, you'll need to adjust them slightly, creating layout lines. Once layout lines are established,

installing the tile is a fairly quick process. Be sure to keep joints between the tiles tight and lay the tiles square.

Tiles with an obvious grain pattern can be laid so the grain of each tile is oriented identically throughout the installation. You can also use the quarter-turn method, in which each tile has its pattern grain running perpendicular to that of adjacent tiles. Whichever method you choose, be sure to be consistent throughout the project.

Tools & Materials ▸

Tape measure	Heat gun	Flooring adhesive (for dry-back tile)	$\frac{1}{16}$" notched trowel
Chalk line	Resilient tile	$\frac{1}{8}$" spacer	Ceramic tile cutter
Framing square	Pencil	Threshold material (if necessary)	Protective equipment
Utility knife	Cardboard		

Resilient tiles have a pattern layer that is bonded to a vinyl base and coated with a transparent wear layer. Some come with adhesive preapplied and covered by a paper backing, others have dry backs and are designed to be set into flooring adhesive.

Check for noticeable directional features, like the grain of the vinyl particles. You can set the tiles in a running pattern so the directional feature runs in the same direction (top), or in a checkerboard pattern using the quarter-turn method (bottom).

HOW TO MAKE REFERENCE LINES FOR TILE INSTALLATION

Position a reference line (X) by measuring along opposite sides of the room and marking the center of each side. Snap a chalk line between these marks.

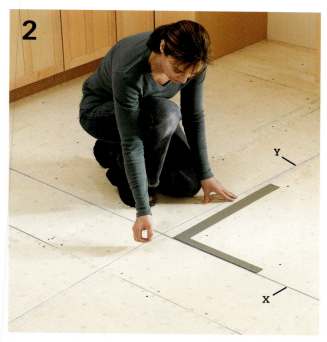

Measure and mark the centerpoint of the chalk line. From this point, use a framing square to establish a second reference line perpendicular to the first one. Snap the second line (Y) across the room.

Check the reference lines for squareness using the 3-4-5 triangle method. Measure along reference line X and make a mark 3 ft. from the centerpoint. Measure from the centerpoint along reference line Y and make a mark at 4 ft.

Measure the distance between the marks. If the reference lines are perpendicular, the distance will measure exactly 5 ft. If not, adjust the reference lines until they're exactly perpendicular to each other.

HOW TO INSTALL DRY-BACKED RESILIENT TILE

Snap perpendicular reference lines with a chalk line (see previous page). Dry-fit tiles along layout line Y so a joint falls along reference line X. If necessary, shift the layout to make the layout symmetrical or to reduce the number of tiles that need to be cut.

If you shift the tile layout, create a new line that is parallel to reference line X and runs through a tile joint near line X. The new line, X1, is the line you'll use when installing the tile. Use a different colored chalk to distinguish between lines.

Dry-fit tiles along the new line, X1. If necessary, adjust the layout line as in steps 1 and 2.

If you adjusted the layout along X1, measure and make a new layout line, Y1, that's parallel to reference line Y and runs through a tile joint. Y1 will form the second layout line you'll use during installation.

Apply adhesive around the intersection of the layout lines using a trowel with 1/16" V-shaped notches. Hold the trowel at a 45° angle and spread adhesive evenly over the surface.

Spread adhesive over most of the installation area, covering three quadrants. Allow the adhesive to set according to the manufacturer's instructions, then begin to install the tile at the intersection of the layout lines. You can kneel on installed tiles to lay additional tiles.

When the first three quadrants are completely tiled, spread adhesive over the remaining quadrant, then finish setting the tile.

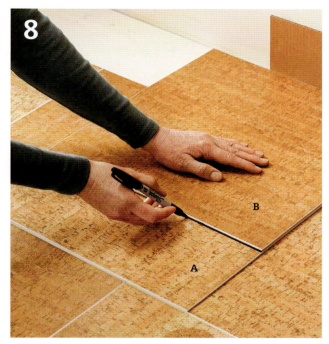

To cut tiles to fit along the walls, place the tile to be cut (A) face up on top of the last full tile you installed. Position a 1/8"-thick spacer against the wall, then set a marker tile (B) on top of the tile to be cut. Trace along the edge of the marker tile to draw a cutting line.

(continued)

Outside Corners ▸

To mark tiles for cutting around outside corners, make a cardboard template to match the space, keeping a ⅛" gap along the walls. After cutting the template, check to make sure it fits. Place the template on a tile and trace its outline.

9

Cut tile to fit using a ceramic-tile cutter to make straight cuts. You may use a straightedge guide and utility knife instead.

10

Install cut tiles next to the walls. If you're precutting all tiles before installing them, measure the distance between the wall and install tiles at various points in case the distance changes.

11

Check the entire floor. If you find loose areas, press down on the tiles to bond them to the underlayment. Install metal threshold bars at room borders where the new floor joins another floor covering.

HOW TO INSTALL SELF-ADHESIVE RESILIENT TILE

Once your reference lines are established, peel off the paper backing and install the first tile in one of the corners formed by the intersecting layout lines. Lay three or more tiles along each layout line in the quadrant.

Rub the entire surface of each tile to thoroughly bond the adhesive to the underlayment. Begin installing tiles in the interior area of the quadrant. Keep the joints tight between tiles.

Finish setting full tiles in the first quadrant, then set the full tiles in an adjacent quadrant. Set the tiles along the layout lines first, then fill in the interior tiles.

Continue installing the tile in the remaining quadrants until the room is completely covered. Check the entire floor. If you find loose areas, press down on the tiles to bond them to the underlayment. Install metal threshold bars at room borders where the new floor joins another floor covering.

VINYL TILE: REPAIRING

Repair methods for resilient sheet flooring depend on the type of floor as well as the type of damage. With sheet vinyl, you can fuse the surface or patch in new material. With linoleum, a patch is usually the only way to repair serious damage.

Small cuts and scratches can be fused permanently and nearly invisibly with liquid seam sealer, a clear compound that's available wherever vinyl flooring is sold. For tears or burns, the damaged area can be patched. If necessary, remove vinyl from a hidden area, such as under an appliance, to use as patch material. Linoleum scratches and small damage can be repaired with a paste made from wood glue and shavings of scrap linoleum.

When sheet flooring is badly worn, or the damage is widespread, the only answer is complete replacement. Although it's possible to add layers of flooring in some situations, evaluate the options carefully. Be aware that the backing of older vinyl tiles made of asphalt may contain asbestos fibers.

Tools & Materials ▸

Carpenter's square	Plywood scrap
Utility knife	Duct tape
Putty knife	Chisel
Heat gun	Flooring scraper
J-roller	Cloth or sponge
Notched trowel	Lacquer thinner
Masking tape	Applicator bottle
Scrap of	Weights
matching flooring	Protective
Mineral spirits	equipment
Floor covering	
adhesive	
Wax paper	
Liquid seam sealer	
Tape measure	

When sheet flooring is damaged, the best remedy is to slice out the damaged area and replace it with new material, carefully seaming the edges of the patch.

HOW TO PATCH SHEET VINYL

Measure the width and length of the damaged area. Place the new flooring remnant on a surface you don't mind making some cuts on—like a scrap of plywood. Use a carpenter's square for a cutting guide. Make sure your cutting size is a bit larger than the damaged area.

Lay the patch over the damaged area, matching pattern lines. Secure the patch with duct tape. Using a carpenter's square as a cutting guide, cut through the new vinyl (on top) and the old vinyl (on bottom). Press firmly with the knife to cut both layers.

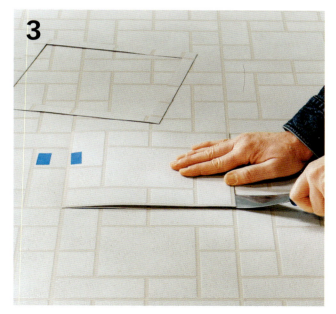

Use tape to mark one edge of the new patch with the corresponding edge of the old flooring as placement marks. Remove the tape around the perimeter of the patch and lift up.

Soften the underlying adhesive with an electric heat gun and remove the damaged section of floor. Work from edges in. When the tile is loosened, insert a putty knife and pry up the damaged area.

(continued)

Scrape off the remaining adhesive with a putty knife or chisel. Work from the edges to the center. Dab mineral spirits or spritz warm water on the floor to dissolve leftover goop, taking care not to use too much; you don't want to loosen the surrounding flooring. Use a razor-edged scraper (flooring scraper) to scrape to the bare wood underlayment.

Apply adhesive to the patch using a notched trowel (with ⅛" V-shaped notches) held at a 45° angle to the back of the new vinyl patch.

Set one edge of the patch in place. Lower the patch onto the underlayment. Press into place. Apply pressure with a J-roller or rolling pin to create a solid bond. Start at the center and work toward the edges, working out air bubbles. Wipe up adhesive that oozes out the sides with a clean, damp cloth or sponge.

Let the adhesive dry overnight. Use a soft cloth dipped in lacquer thinner to clean the area. Mix the seam sealer according to the manufacturer's directions. Use an applicator bottle to apply a thin bead of sealer onto the cutlines.

HOW TO REPLACE RESILIENT TILE

Use an electric heat gun to warm the damaged tile and soften the underlying adhesive. Keep the heat source moving so you don't melt the tile. When an edge of the tile begins to curl, insert a putty knife to pry up the loose edge until you can remove the tile. *Note: If you can clearly see the seam between tiles, first score around the tile with a utility knife. This prevents other tiles from lifting.*

Scrape away remaining adhesive with a putty knife or, for stubborn spots, a floor scraper. Work from the edges to the center so that you don't accidentally scrape up the adjacent tiles. Use mineral spirits to dissolve leftover goop. Take care not to allow the mineral spirits to soak into the floor under adjacent tiles. Vacuum up dust, dirt, and adhesive. Wipe clean.

When the floor is dry, use a notched trowel—with ⅛" V-shaped notches—held at a 45° angle to apply a thin, even layer of vinyl tile adhesive onto the underlayment. *Note: Only follow this step if you have dry-back tiles.*

Set one edge of the tile in place. Lower the tile onto the underlayment and then press it into place. Apply pressure with a J-roller to create a solid bond, starting at the center and working toward the edge to work out air bubbles. If adhesive oozes out the sides, wipe it up with a damp cloth or sponge. Cover the tile with wax paper and some books, and let the adhesive dry for 24 hours.

WAINSCOTING

Snap a level line at the top rail height. Because the rails and stiles are the same thickness, the backer panel should run all the way from the floor to just shy of the top of the top rail. Cut the backers so the grain will run vertically when installed. Attach them to the walls with panel adhesive, notching to fit around obstructions such as this window opening.

Install the baseboard and top rail directly over the backer panels, using a finish nailer or by hand-nailing with 6d finish nails. The top edge of the top rail pieces should be slightly higher then the backer panels. Use your reference line as a guide for the top rail, but double check with a level.

Attach the cap rail pieces with a finish nailer. The caps should butt flush against the wall, concealing the top edges of the backer panels. Also butt the cap rails against the window and door casings.

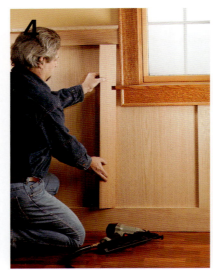

Cut the stiles to fit between the top rail and the baseboard and install them. It's okay to vary the spacing slightly from wall to wall, but try to keep them evenly spaced on each wall. Where the wainscot meets door or window casing, butt the edges of the stiles against the casing. This can mean notching around window aprons or horns as well as door plinth blocks.

Add decorative touches, such as the corbels we cut for this installation. The corbels provide some support for the cap rail but their function is primarily decorative. We glued and nailed one corbel at each end of each cap rail piece and above each stile, and then added an intermediate one between each pair of stiles.

WALLS & CEILINGS

WATER HAMMER ARRESTOR: INSTALLING

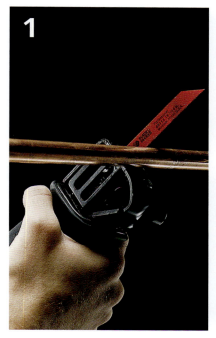

1

Shut off the water supply and drain the pipes. Use a tubing cutter or reciprocating saw to cut out a section of horizontal pipe long enough for a T-fitting.

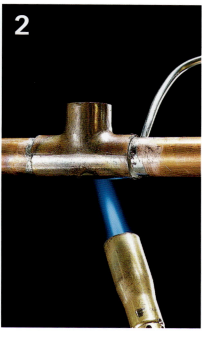

2

Install a T-fitting as close to the valve as possible.

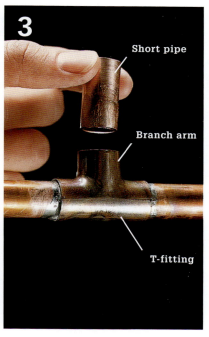

3

Short pipe

Branch arm

T-fitting

Install a short piece of pipe in the branch arm of the T-fitting. This short pipe will be used to attach a threaded fitting.

4

Install a threaded fitting. Use a fitting recommended by the manufacturer of your arrester.

5

Wrap the threads of the arrester in Teflon tape. Thread the arrester onto the fitting by hand. Tighten by holding the fitting with one adjustable wrench and turning the arrester with the other. Do not overtighten. Turn the water on and check for leaks.

WATER HEATER: INSTALLING

Shut off the gas supply at the stopcock installed in the gas line closest to the water heater. The handle of the stopcock should be perpendicular to the gas supply pipe. Also shut off the water supply.

Drain the water from the old heater by hooking a garden hose up to the sillcock drain and running it to a floor drain. If you don't have a floor drain, drain the water into buckets. For your personal safety, wait until the water heater has been shut off for a couple of hours before draining it.

Disconnect the gas supply from the water heater. To do so, loosen the flare fitting with two wrenches or pliers in a soft copper supply line or loosen the union fitting with two pipe wrenches for black pipe supply lines (inset photo).

Disconnect the vent pipe from the draft hood by withdrawing the sheet metal screws connecting the parts. Also remove vent pipes up to and including the elbow so you may inspect them for corrosion buildup and replace if needed.

PLUMBING

5

Image showing cutting the water supply lines.

Cut the water supply lines. Prior to cutting, shut off the cold water supply either at the stop valve near the heater or at the water meter. Inspect the shutoff valve. If it is not a ball-type valve in new condition, replace it with a ball valve.

Install a Relief Valve ▸

Prepare the new water heater for installation. Before you put the water heater in place, add a T & P (temperature and pressure) relief valve at the valve opening. Make sure to read the manufacturer's instructions and purchase the recommended valve type. Lubricate the threads and tighten the valve into the valve opening with a pipe wrench. *Note: The water heater shown in this sequence came with a T & P relief valve that's preinstalled.*

6

Remove the old water heater and dispose of it properly. Most trash collection companies will haul it away for $20 or $30. Don't simply leave it out at the curb unless you know that is allowed by your municipal waste collection department. A two-wheel truck or appliance dolly is a big help here. Water heaters usually weigh around 150 pounds.

7

Drip pan

Hose bib

Position the new unit in the installation area. If you have flooring you wish to protect from leaks, set the unit on a drip pan (available where water heater accessories are sold). The shallow pans feature a hose bib so you can run a drain line from the pan to a floor drain. If the water heater is not level, level it by shimming under the bottom with a metal or composite shim. Note that you'll need to shift the unit around a bit to have clearance for installing the water supply connectors (step 10).

(continued)

Attach a discharge tube to the T & P relief valve. You may use either copper pipe or CPVC drain pipe. Cut the tube so the free end is 6" above the floor (some locales may allow 3" above the floor). If you have floorcoverings you wish to protect, add a 90° elbow and a copper drain tube that leads from the discharge tube to a floor drain.

Fabricate water connectors from lengths of copper tubing, threaded copper adaptors, and plastic-lined galvanized threaded nipples. Plastic-lined nipples (inset photo) reduce the corrosion that can occur when you join two dissimilar metals. Size the connector assemblies so they will end up just short of the cut copper supply tubing when the connectors are inserted into the water heater ports.

Install the connectors in the cold water inlet port (make sure you use the blue-coded lined nipple) and the hot outlet port (red-coded nipple) on top of the water heater. Lubricate the nipple threads and tighten with channel-type pliers. Slip a copper tubing repair coupling over each connector and reposition the unit so the supply pipes and connector tops align.

Join the connectors to the supply tubes with slip-fitting copper repair couplings. Be sure to clean and prime the parts first.

Reassemble the vent with a new elbow fitting (if your old one needed replacement, see step 4, page 540). Cut the duct that drops down from the elbow so it will fit neatly over the top flange of the draft hood.

Draft hood

Follow the manufacturer's instructions for configuring the vent; this varies from model to model. Attach the vertical leg of the vent line to the draft hood with ⅜" sheet metal screws. Drive at least three screws into each joint.

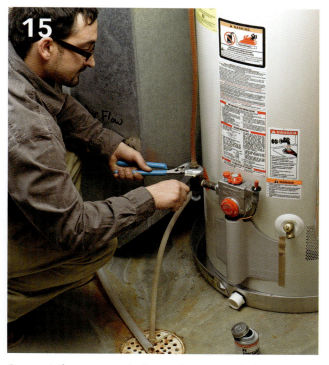

Air Flow

Install the parts for the black pipe gas connector assembly (see photo page 540). Use pipe dope to lubricate all joints. Attach a T-fitting to one end of a 3" nipple first and attach the other end of the nipple into the female-threaded regulator port. Attach a cap to another 6" nipple and then thread the other end into the bottom opening of the T-fitting to form a drip leg. Install a third nipple in the top opening of the T-fitting.

Connect the gas supply line to the open end of the gas connector. Use a union fitting for black gas pipe connections and a flare fitting for copper supply connections. See page 540 for more information on making these connections.

(continued)

PLUMBING

16

17

Test the connections. Turn on the gas supply and test the gas connections with testing solution. Before turning on the water supply, make sure the tank drain valve is closed. Allow the tank to fill with water and then turn on a hot water faucet until water comes out (the water won't be hot yet, of course). Visually check all plumbing joints for leaks.

Light the pilot. This is usually a multistep process that varies among manufacturers, but all new water heaters will have pilot-lighting instructions printed on a label near the water heater controls. Adjust the water temperature setting.

Tip: Hooking Up Electric Water Heaters ▸

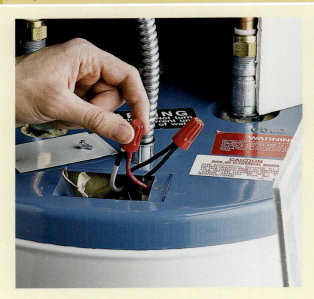

The fuel supply connection is the only part of installing an electric water heater that differs from installing a gas heater, except that electric heaters do not require a vent. The feeder wires (240 volts) are twisted together with mating wires in the access panel located at the top of the unit.

Temperature adjustments on electric water heaters are made by tightening or loosening a thermostat adjustment screw located near the heating element. Always shut off power to the unit before making adjustment. In this photo you can see how close the live terminals for the heating element are to the thermostat.

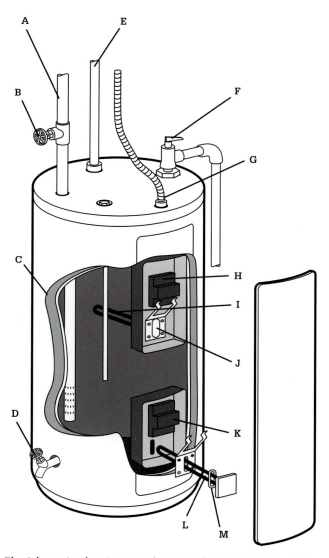

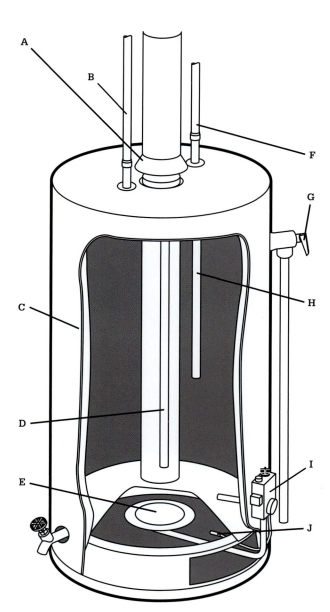

GAS WATER HEATER

Gas water heater parts include:
(A) Flue
(B) Hot water outlet
(C) Tank
(D) Anode rod
(E) Gas burner
(F) Cold water inlet pipe
(G) Pressure-relief valve
(H) Dip tube
(I) Thermostat
(J) Thermocouple

ELECTRIC WATER HEATER

Electric water heater parts can include:
(A) Cold water inlet pipe
(B) Cold water inlet valve
(C) Insulation
(D) Draincock
(E) Hot water outlet pipe
(F) Pressure-relief valve
(G) Power cable
(H) High temperature thermostat
(I) Upper heating element
(J) Bracket
(K) Lower heating thermostat
(L) Lower heating element
(M) Gasket

Gas water heaters operate on either propane or natural gas and are generally very economical to run. They do cost a bit more than electric heaters up front. The following installation features a gas water heater. Check with your local building department to find out if homeowners are allowed to install gas appliances in your municipality.

Electric water heaters require 240-volt service, which might overload your service panel if you are replacing a gas heater with an electric model. Their primary advantage is that they are cheaper to purchase (but not to operate) and they do not require that you make gas connections.

WATER HEATER: FIXING

Standard tank water heaters are designed so that repairs are simple. All water heaters have convenient access panels that make it easy to replace worn-out parts. When buying new water heater parts, make sure the replacements match the specifications of your water heater. Most water heaters have a nameplate that lists the information needed, including the pressure rating of the tank and the voltage and wattage ratings of the electric heating elements.

Many water heater problems can be avoided with routine yearly maintenance. Flush the water heater and test the pressure-relief valve once a year. Set the thermostat at a lower water temperature to prevent heat damage to the tank. (*Note: Water temperature may affect the efficiency of automatic dishwashers. Check manufacturer's directions for recommended water temperature.*) Water heaters last about 10 years on average, but with regular maintenance, a water heater can last 20 years or more.

Do not install an insulating jacket around a gas water heater. Insulation can block air supply and prevent the water heater from ventilating properly. Many water heater manufacturers prohibit the use of insulating jackets. To save energy, insulate the hot water pipes instead, using tube insulation sleeves available at home improvement centers.

The pressure-relief valve is an important safety device that should be checked at least once each year and replaced, if needed. When replacing the pressure-relief valve, shut off the water and drain several gallons of water from the tank.

Replacing a water heater is not a difficult project, but check with local codes for installation restrictions. Your community may require that a licensed plumber make gas hookups, for example, or that electrical water heaters be connected by an electrician.

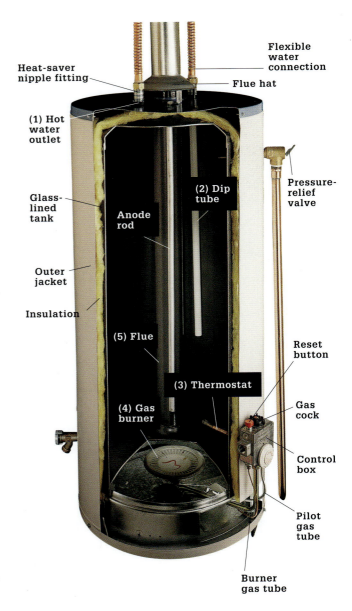

Heat-saver nipple fitting

Flexible water connection

Flue hat

(1) Hot water outlet

Glass-lined tank

Anode rod

Outer jacket

Insulation

(2) Dip tube

Pressure-relief valve

(5) Flue

Reset button

(3) Thermostat

Gas cock

(4) Gas burner

Control box

Pilot gas tube

Burner gas tube

How a gas water heater works: Hot water leaves tank through the hot water outlet (1) as fresh, cold water enters the water heater through the dip tube (2). As the water temperature drops, the thermostat (3) opens the gas valve, and the gas burner (4) is lighted by pilot flame. Exhaust gases are vented through flue (5). When water temperature reaches preset temperature, the thermostat closes gas valve, extinguishing burner. The thermocouple protects against gas leaks by automatically shutting off gas if pilot flame goes out. Anode rod protects tank lining from rust by attracting corrosive elements in the water. Pressure-relief valve guards against ruptures caused by steam buildup in tank.

Problems	Repairs
No hot water, or not enough hot water.	1. Gas heater: Make sure gas is on, then relight pilot flame (page 544). Electric heater: Make sure power is on, then reset thermostat (page 544). 2. Flush water heater to remove sediment in tank (photo, below). 3. Insulate hot water pipes to reduce heat loss. 4. Gas heater: Clean gas burner & replace thermocouple (pages 548 to 549). Electric heater: Replace heating element or thermostat (pages 550 to 551). 5. Raise temperature setting of thermostat.
Pressure-relief valve leaks.	1. Lower the temperature setting (photo, below). 2. Install a new pressure-relief valve (page 541). 3. Install a water hammer arrester (page 539).
Pilot flame will not stay lighted.	Clean gas burner & replace the thermocouple (pages 548 to 549).
Water heater leaks around base of tank.	Replace the water heater immediately (pages 540 to 544).

Tips for Maintaining a Water Heater ▸

Flush the water heater once a year by draining several gallons of water from the tank. Flushing removes sediment buildup that causes corrosion and reduces heating efficiency.

Lower the temperature setting on thermostat to 120° F. Lower temperature setting reduces damage to tank caused by overheating and also reduces energy use.

WATER HEATER: FIXING: GAS

If a gas water heater does not heat water, first remove the outer and inner access panels and make sure the pilot is lighted. During operation, the outer and inner access panels must be in place. Operating the water heater without the access panels may allow air drafts to blow out the pilot flame.

If the pilot will not light, it is probably because the thermocouple is worn out. The thermocouple is a safety device designed to shut off the gas automatically if the pilot flame goes out. The thermocouple is a thin copper wire that runs from the control box to the gas burner. New thermocouples are inexpensive and can be installed in a few minutes.

If the gas burner does not light, even though the pilot flame is working, or if the gas burns with a yellow, smoky flame, the burner and the pilot gas tube should be cleaned. Clean the burner and gas tube annually to improve energy efficiency and extend the life of the water heater.

A gas water heater must be well ventilated. If you smell smoke or fumes coming from a water heater, shut off the water heater and make sure the exhaust duct is not clogged with soot. A rusted duct must be replaced.

Remember to shut off the gas before beginning work.

Tools & Materials ▸

Adjustable wrench   Thin wires
Vacuum cleaner   Replacement
Needlenose pliers   thermocouple

HOW TO CLEAN A GAS BURNER & REPLACE A THERMOCOUPLE

Shut off gas by turning the gas cock on top of the control box to the OFF position. Wait 10 minutes for gas to dissipate.

Disconnect the pilot gas tube, the burner gas tube, and the thermocouple from the bottom of the control box, using an adjustable wrench.

Remove the outer and inner access panels covering the burner chamber.

Pull down slightly on the pilot gas tube, the burner gas tube, and thermocouple wire to free them from the control box. Tilt the burner unit slightly and remove it from the burner chamber.

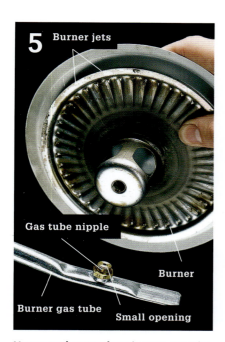

5 Burner jets

Gas tube nipple

Burner

Burner gas tube   Small opening

Unscrew burner from burner gas tube nipple. Clean small opening in nipple, using a piece of thin wire. Vacuum out burner jets and the burner chamber.

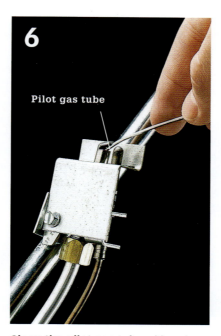

6 Pilot gas tube

Clean the pilot gas tube with a piece of wire. Vacuum out any loose particles. Screw burner onto gas tube nipple.

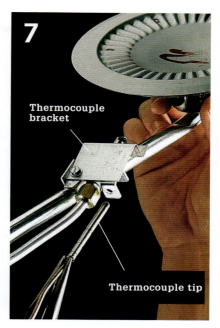

7 Thermocouple bracket

Thermocouple tip

Pull the old thermocouple from bracket. Install new thermocouple by pushing the tip into the bracket until it snaps into place.

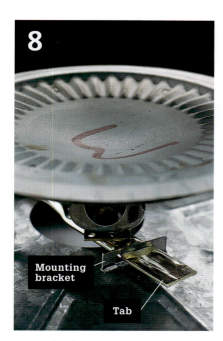

8 Mounting bracket

Tab

Insert the burner unit into the chamber. Flat tab at end of burner should fit into slotted opening in mounting bracket at the bottom of the chamber.

9

Burner gas tube

Thermocouple

Pilot gas tube

Reconnect the gas tubes and the thermocouple to the control box. Turn on the gas and test for leaks. Light the pilot.

10 Pilot flame

Thermocouple tip

Make sure pilot flame wraps around tip of thermocouple. If needed, adjust thermocouple with needlenose pliers until tip is in flame. Replace the inner and outer access panels.

WATER HEATER: FIXING: ELECTRIC

The most common problem with an electric water heater is a burned-out heating element. To determine which element has failed, turn on a hot water faucet and test the temperature. If the water heater produces water that is warm, but not hot, replace the top heating element. If the heater produces a small amount of very hot water, followed by cold water, replace the bottom heating element.

If replacing the heating element does not solve the problem, then replace the thermostat, found under convenient access panels on the side of the heater.

Remember to turn off the power and test for current before touching wires.

Tools & Materials ▸

Screwdriver
Gloves
Neon circuit tester
Channel-type pliers
Masking tape
Replacement heating element or thermostat
Replacement gasket
Pipe joint compound

HOW TO REPLACE AN ELECTRIC THERMOSTAT

Turn off power at main service panel. Remove access panel on side of heater, and test for current.

Disconnect thermostat wires, and label connections with masking tape. Pull old thermostat out of mounting clips. Snap new thermostat into place, and reconnect wires.

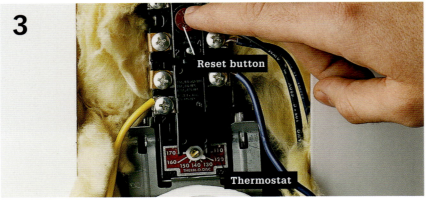

Press thermostat reset button, then use a screwdriver to set thermostat to desired temperature. Replace insulation and access panel. Turn on power.

PLUMBING

HOW TO REPLACE AN ELECTRIC HEATING ELEMENT

Remove access panel on side of water heater. Shut off power to water heater (page 390, step 1). Close the shutoff valves, then drain tank (page 540, step 2).

Wearing protective gloves, carefully move insulation aside. Caution: Test for current, then disconnect wires on heating element. Remove protective collar.

Unscrew the heating element with channel-type pliers. Remove old gasket from around water heater opening. Coat both sides of new gasket with pipe joint compound.

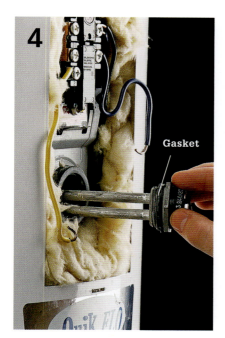

Slide new gasket over heating element, and screw element into the tank. Tighten element with channel-type pliers.

Replace protective collar, and reconnect all wires. Turn on hot water faucets throughout house, then turn on water heater shutoff valves. When tap water runs steadily, close faucets.

Use a screwdriver to set thermostat to desired temperature. Press thermostat reset buttons. Fold insulation over thermostat, and replace the access panel. Turn on power.

WHIRLPOOL TUB: INSTALLING

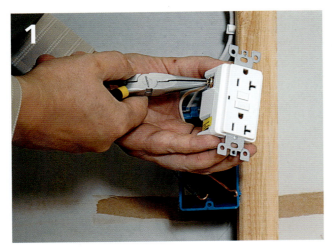

Prepare the site for the installation. Remove wall coverings in the installation area to expose bare studs. Provide a dedicated electrical circuit or circuits to the tub area according to the specifications in your installation manual (hire an electrician if you are not comfortable with wiring). This model plugs into a GFCI-protected receptacle on a dedicated 120-volt, 20-amp circuit.

Make framing improvements such as adding 1 × 4 bracing at supply risers and the faucet body location. For drop-in tubs that do not have nailing flanges, you may need to add short stub walls to provide a stable resting point. Here, a short stub wall was installed at one end to serve as the tub wet wall.

Requirements for Making Electrical Hookups ▸

The electrical service for a whirlpool should be a dedicated 115- to 120-volt, 20-amp circuit. The pump motor should be grounded separately, normally to a metal cold water supply pipe. Most whirlpool motors are wired with 12/2 NM cable, but some local codes require the use of conduit. Remote timer switches (inset), located at least 5 ft. from the tub, are required by some codes, even for a tub with a built-in timer.

A GFCI circuit breaker at the main service panel is required with whirlpool installations. Hire an electrician to connect new circuits at your service panel if you are uncomfortable installing circuit cables on your own.

Cut the drain tailpiece to length depending on the distance you'll need to span to the trap. Use a hacksaw or tubing cutter to make the cut.

Floor leveler compound

Prepare the floor or subfloor. Check with a level and fill any dips with floor leveling compound or mortar. If there is a joint in the subfloor in the installation area, make sure the sides are level. (The floor has to be level in order to support the weight of the tub, the water, and bathers.) Also make sure there is no rot or weakness in the structural elements.

Test the tub fit. First, cut a piece of the shipping carton to fit inside the tub and protect its surface. Have someone help you slide the tub into the installation area, flush against the wall studs, so you can check the fit. *Tip: Lay a pair of 1 × 4s perpendicular to the tub opening and use them as skids to make it easier to slide the tub in. Remove the skids and lower the tub on the floor.*

Set a 4-ft. level across the rim of the tub and check it for level. If it is not level, place shims under the tub until it is.

(continued)

7

Mark the top of the tub's rim or nailing flange at each stud as a reference for installing additional supports or ledgers. Remove the tub from the alcove.

8

Add support frames or ledgers as directed by the manufacturer and secure them in the installation area so the top of the tub or nailing flange will be at the height you scribed in Step 7.

9

Assemble the drain-waste-overflow kit to fit the drain and overflow openings, following the tub manufacturer's directions. Install the DWO kit (it is virtually impossible to attach it once the tub is in place).

10

Fasten the threaded parts of the drain assembly. A ring of plumber's putty between the drain coverplate and the tub will help create a good seal. If you will be installing a pop-up drain, install it now as well.

Attach the overflow coverplate so it conceals the overflow opening. Adjust the pop-up drain plug linkage as directed by the manufacturer.

Begin the actual installation. For some tubs, it is recommended that you trowel a layer of thinset mortar in the installation area. But read your instructions carefully. Many tubs feature integral feet that are meant to rest directly on the floor.

Slide the tub back into the opening. Remove the skids, if you are using them. Press down evenly on the tub rims until they make solid contact with the ledgers or frames.

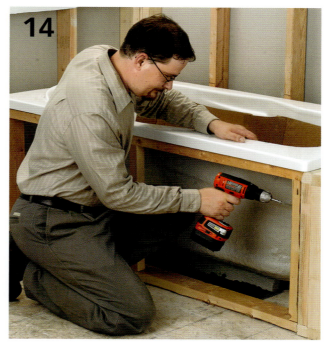

Provide support for the tub on the open side if it does not have a structural skirt. Here, a 2 × 4 stub wall is built to the exact height of the underside of the rim and then attached in place. Screw it to both end walls and to the floor.

(continued)

Drain Hookups ▸

Overflow pipe · T-fitting · Branch drain · Tailpiece · Slip nut · P-trap · Cutaway view

Make the plumbing drain connections before you proceed further. To connect the drain tailpiece to the trap you will need access either from below or from an access panel. The photo above shows a typical tub drain configuration seen cutaway through the floor.

15

Cover the gaps in the wallcoverings around the tub. Here, cementboard is installed in preparation for a tile backsplash. If your tub has nailing flanges, attach strips of metal flashing to the wall so they extend down to within about ¼" of the tub rim. If your tub has a removable apron, install it.

16

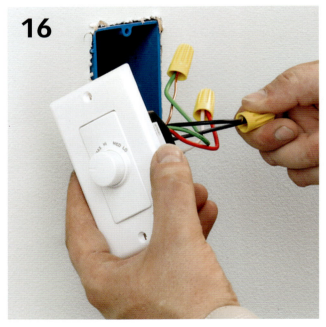

Make wiring connections according to the tub manufacturer's instructions. The requirements vary greatly among jetted spas. Some municipalities may require that a licensed professional do this work. Here, the airflow regulator is being wired. Note that most codes have a safety requirement that the on/off switch must be located so it cannot be reached by a bather in the tub.

17

Test the operation of the jetted spa before you finish the walls or deck in case there is a hidden problem. Fill it with a hose if you have not installed the faucet (the faucet normally is installed after the wall surfaces, unless you are deck-mounting the faucet on the tub rim). Run the spa. If it works, go ahead and drain the water.

WINDOWS: INSTALLING

Preventing water from getting in is one of the most important considerations when installing a window. The key is to seal all joints around the window and block anyplace the water could wick in. Although caulking can be effective, it's also easy to miss small spots, and caulking will deteriorate over time. That's why builders in wetter parts of the country install plenty of flashing around the window with waterproof membrane. If you want extra protection against water infiltration, start from the bottom, cut strips of self-adhesive waterproof membrane, and apply them under the window, up the sides, and then on top of the window. All seams should face down and the top and bottom strips should run out 6 inches on either side of the window. Repeat the procedure over the nailing flanges.

Tools & Materials ▸

Hammer
Tape measure
Level
Utility knife
Handsaw
Caulk gun
Window
Self-adhesive flashing
Exterior-grade
    silicone caulk
Shims
Flashing

Brickmold
Roofing nails
Minimal expanding
    foam insulation
Vinyl or latex gloves
Metal drip edge
Protective
    equipment

Mullion post

New windows can be installed after the wall framing and sheathing is done. Many builders sheath over the window openings, then cut them out as they install each window, to keep weather and wildlife out.

HOW TO INSTALL A WINDOW

Flash the rough sill. Apply 9"-wide self-adhesive flashing tape to the rough sill to prevent moisture infiltration below the window. Install the flashing tape so it wraps completely over the sill and extends 10 to 12" up the jack studs. Fold the rest of the tape over the housewrap to create a 3" overlap. Peel off the backing and press the tape firmly in place. Install tape on the side jambs butting up to the header, and then flash the header.

Caulk the opening. Apply a ½"-wide bead of caulk around the outside edges of the jack studs and header to seal the window flange in the opening. Leave the rough sill uncaulked to allow any water that may penetrate the flashing to drain out.

Green Window Choices ▶

Installing the right windows for your home and region can instantly trim your energy usage. That's why, when choosing windows for an addition, you should always look for the Energy Star label. A designation given by the U.S. Department of Energy, the Energy Star label ensures a window meets or exceeds federal guidelines for home energy efficiency. An even more important gauge than simply looking for an Energy Star label is to read the NFRC label on the window. Specifically, note the U-factor and Solar Heat Gain Coefficient (SHGC) ratings for the window. If you live in a fairly cold region of the country, you want the lowest U-factor you can find, with a moderate to high SHGC. If your home is located in a temperate area with consistently warm temperatures, the SHGC number is the most important one to you, and it should be as low as possible.

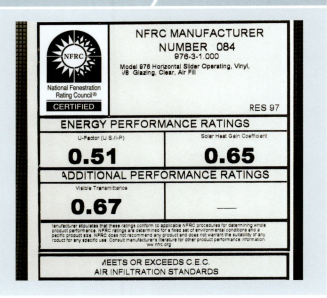

Position the window. Set the window unit into the rough opening, and center it side to side. Check the sill for level.

Tack the top corners. Drive a roofing nail through each top corner hole of the top window flange to tack it in place. Do not drive the rest of the nails into the top flange yet.

Plumb the window. Have a helper hold the window in place from outside while you work inside. Check the window jamb for square by measuring from corner to corner. If the measurements are the same, the jamb is square. Insert shims between the side jambs and rough opening near the top corners to hold the jambs in position. Use additional shims as needed to bring the jamb into square. Recheck the diagonals after shimming.

Nail the flanges. Drive 2" roofing nails through the flange nailing holes and into the rough sill to secure it. Handnail this flange, being careful not to damage the flange or window cladding.

(continued)

Flash the side flanges. Seal the side flanges with flashing tape, starting 4 to 6" below the sill flashing and ending 4 to 6" above the top flange. Press the tape firmly in place.

Install the drip cap. Cut a piece of metal drip edge to fit over the top window jamb. This is particularly important if your new window has an unclad wooden jamb with preinstalled brickmold. Set the drip edge in place on the top jamb, and secure the flange with a strip of wide flashing tape. Do not nail it. Overlap the side flashing tape by 6". *Note: If you plan to trim the window with wood brickmold or other moldings, install the drip edge above that trim instead.*

Finish the installation. Cut the shim ends so they are flush with the inside of the wall using a utility knife or handsaw.

Spray minimal expanding foam insulation for windows and doors around the perimeter of the window on the interior side.

WINDOWS: INSTALLING: EGRESS

If your home has an unfinished or partially finished basement, it's an enticing and sensible place to expand your practical living space. Another bedroom or two, a game room, or maybe a spacious home office are all possibilities. However, unless your basement has a walk-out doorway, you'll need to add an egress window to make your new living space meet most building codes. That's because the International Residential Code (IRC) requires two forms of escape for every living space—an exit door and a window large enough for you to climb out of or for an emergency responder to enter.

Code mandates that a below-ground egress window will have a minimum opening area of at least 5.7 square feet. There are stipulations about how this open area can be proportioned: The window must be at least 20 inches wide and 24 inches high when open. Additionally, the installed window's sill height must be within 44 inches of the basement floor to permit easy escape. Typical basement windows do not meet these requirements. A large egress window requires an oversized window well. The well must be at least 36 inches wide and project 36 inches or more from the foundation. If the window well is deeper than 44 inches, it must have a fixed ladder for escape.

What does this all mean for the ambitious do-it-yourselfer? The good news is that if you've got the nerve to cut an oversized opening in your home's foundation, and you don't mind spending some quality time with a shovel, installing a basement egress window is a manageable project. Here's a case where careful planning, a building permit, and some help can save you considerable money over hiring a contractor to do the work. To see a complete step-by-step egress window and well installation, see pages 562 to 566. Contact your local building department to learn more about specific egress requirements that apply to your area.

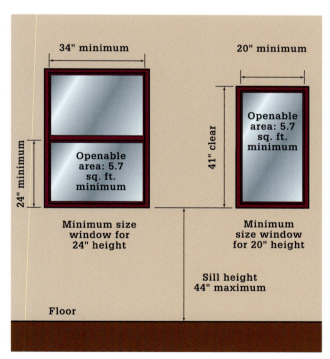

In order to satisfy building codes for egress, a basement window must have a minimum opening of 5.7 sq. ft. through one sash, with at least 20" of clear width and 24" of clear height. Casement, double-hung, and sliding window styles can be used, as long as their dimensions for width and height meet these minimum requirements.

Egress window wells must be at least 36" wide and project 36" from the foundation. Those deeper than 44" must have a means of escape, such as a tiered design that forms steps or an attached ladder. Drainage at the bottom of the well should extend down to the foundation footing drain, with pea gravel used as the drainage material.

HOW TO INSTALL AN EGRESS WINDOW & WINDOW WELL

1

Lay out the border of the window well area with stakes and string. Plan the length and width of the excavation to be several feet larger than the window well's overall size to provide extra room for installation and adjustment.

2

Excavate the well to a depth 6 to 12" deeper than the well's overall height to allow room for drainage gravel. Make sure to have your local public utilities company inspect the well excavation area and okay it for digging before you start.

3

Measure and mark the foundation wall with brightly colored masking tape to establish the overall size of the window's rough opening (here, we're replacing an existing window). Be sure to take into account the window's rough opening dimensions, the thickness of the rough framing (usually 2x stock), and the width of the structural header you may need to build. Remember also that sill height must be within 44" of the floor. Remove existing wall coverings inside the layout area.

4

If the floor joists run perpendicular to your project wall, build a temporary support wall parallel to the foundation wall and 6 to 8 ft. from it. Staple sheet plastic to the wall and floor joists to form a work tent that will help control concrete dust.

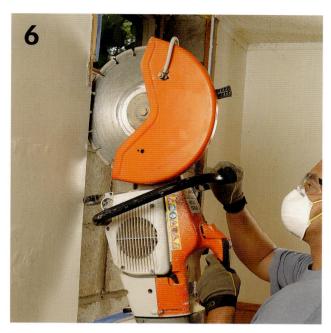

Drill reference holes at each bottom corner with a hammer drill and long masonry bit. These holes will provide reference points for cutting from both sides, ensuring clean breaks.

Equip a masonry cutting saw (or large angle grinder) with a diamond blade and set it for a ½" cut to score the blocks first. Then reset the saw to full depth and make the final bottom and side cuts through the blocks. Wear a tight-fitting particle mask, ear and eye protection, and gloves for all of this cutting work; the saw will generate a tremendous amount of thick dust. Feed the saw slowly and steadily. Stop and rest periodically so the dust can settle.

On the outside foundation wall, score the cuts, then make full-depth cuts.

Strike the blocks with a hand maul to break or loosen the block sections. When all the blocks are removed, carefully chip away remaining debris with a cold chisel to create flat surfaces.

(continued)

WINDOWS & DOORS

Fill the hollow voids in concrete block walls, with broken pieces of block, then level and smooth the voids by trowelling on a fresh layer of quick-curing concrete. Flatten the surfaces, and allow the concrete to dry overnight.

If your project requires a new header above the new window, build it from pieces of 2× lumber sandwiching ½" plywood and fastened together with construction adhesive and 10d nails. Slip it into place and tack it temporarily to the mudsill with 3½" deck screws driven toenail style.

Cut the sill plate for the window's rough frame from 2× treated lumber that's the same width as the thickness of the foundation wall. Fasten the sill to the foundation with ³⁄₁₆ × 3¼" countersunk masonry screws. Drill pilot holes for the screws first with a hammer drill.

Cut two pieces of treated lumber just slightly longer than the opening so they'll fit tightly between the new header and sill. Tap them into place with a maul. Adjust them for plumb and fasten them to the foundation with countersunk masonry screws or powder-actuated fasteners.

13

Apply a thick bead of silicone caulk around the outside edges of the rough frame and set the window in its opening, seating the nailing flanges into the caulk. Shim the window so the frame is level and plumb. Test the action of the window to make sure the shims aren't bowing the frame.

14

Attach the window's nailing flanges to the rough frame with screws or nails, as specified by the manufacturer. Check the window action periodically as you fasten it to ensure that it still operates smoothly.

15

Seal gaps between the rough frame and the foundation with a bead of exterior silicone or polyurethane caulk. If the gaps are wider than ¼", insert a piece of backer rod first, then cover it with caulk. On the interior, fill gaps around the window shims with strips of foam backer rod, fiberglass insulation, or a bead of minimally expanding spray foam. Do not distort the window frame.

16

Fill the well excavation with 6 to 12" of pea gravel. This will serve as the window's drain system. Follow the egress well kit instructions to determine the exact depth required; you may need to add more gravel so the top of the well will be above the new window. *Note: We added a drain down to the foundation's perimeter tile for improved drainage as well.*

(continued)

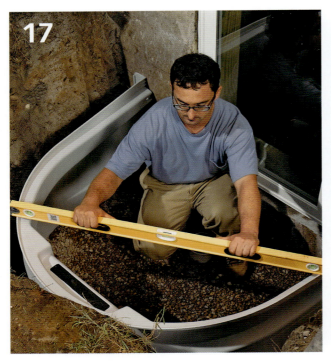

Set the bottom section of the well into the hole, and position it evenly from left to right relative to the window. Adjust the gravel surface to level the well section carefully.

Stack the second well section on top of the first, and connect the two with the appropriate fasteners.

Fasten the window well sections to the foundation wall with concrete sleeve anchors driven into prebored pilot holes. You could also use masonry nails driven with a powder-actuated tool.

When all the well sections are assembled and secured, nail pieces of trim around the window frame to hide the nailing flange. Complete the well installation by using excavated dirt to backfill around the outside of the well. Pack the soil with a tamper, creating a slope for good drainage. If you are installing a window well cover, set it in place and fasten it according to the manufacturer's instructions. The cover must be removable.

WINDOWS: SASH CORDS

1 Cut any paint seal between the window frame and stops with a utility knife or paint zipper. Pry the stops away from the frame, or remove the molding screws.

2 Bend the stops out from the center to remove them from the frame. Remove any weatherstripping that's in the way.

3 Slide out the lower window sash. Pull knotted or nailed cords from holes in the sides of the sash (see step 9).

4 Pry out or unscrew the weight pocket cover in the lower end of the window channel. Pull the weight from the pocket, and cut the old sash cord from the weight.

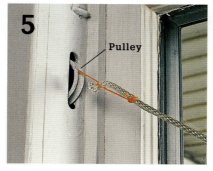

5 Tie one end of a piece of string to a nail and the other end to the new sash cord. Run the nail over the pulley and let it drop into the weight pocket. Retrieve the nail and string through the pocket.

6 Pull on the string to run the new sash cord over the pulley and through the weight pocket. Make sure the new cord runs smoothly over the pulley.

7 Attach the end of the sash cord to the weight using a tight double knot. Set the weight in the pocket. Pull on the cord until the weight touches the pulley.

8 Rest the bottom sash on the sill. Hold the sash cord against the side of the sash, and cut enough cord to reach 3" past the hole in the side of the sash.

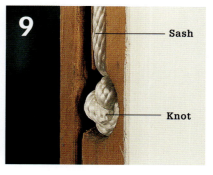

9 Knot the sash cord and wedge the knot into the hole in the sash. Replace the pocket cover. Slide the window and any weatherstripping into the frame, then attach the stops in the original positions.

WINDOWS: STOOL & APRON

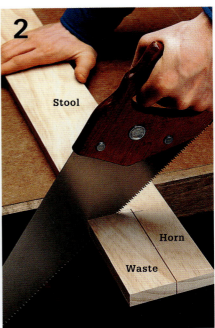

Cut the board for the stool to length, with several extra inches at each end for the horns. Temporarily position the stool in the window opening, pressed against the wall and centered on the window. Use a combination square to measure the setback distance from the window frame to the near edge of the stool. Mark the setback onto the stool at each edge of the window rough opening (if the measurements are different, use the greater setback distance for each end). Then use a compass and pencil to scribe the profile of the wall onto the stool to complete the cutting line for the horn (inset photo).

Cut out the notches to create the stool horns. For straight lines, you can use a large handsaw, but for the scribed line use a more maneuverable saw like the jigsaw or a coping saw. Test-fit the stool, making any minor adjustments with a plane or a rasp so it fits tightly to the window frame and flush against the walls.

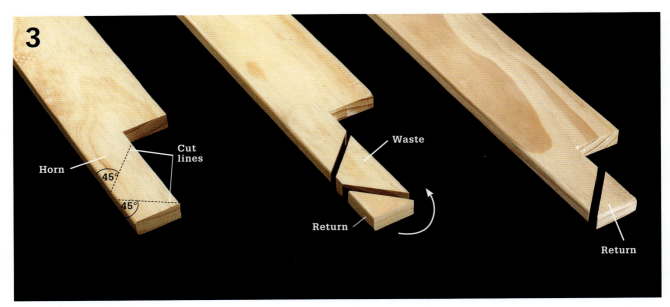

To create a return at the horn of the stool, miter-cut the return pieces at 45° angles. Mark the stool at its overall length and cut it to size with 45° miter cuts. Glue the return to the mitered end of the horn so the grain wraps around the corner. **NOTE:** Use this same technique to create the returns on the apron, but make the cuts with the apron held on edge, rather than flat.

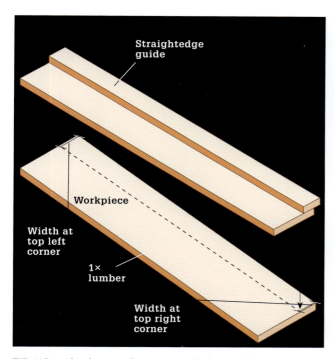

TIP: Where jamb extensions are needed, cut the head extension to its finished length—the distance between the window side jambs plus the thickness of both side extensions (typically 1× stock). For the width, measure the distance between the window jamb and the finished wall at each corner; then mark the measurements on the ends of the extension. Use a straightedge to draw a reference line connecting the points. Build a simple cutting jig, as shown.

Clamp the jig on the reference line, and rip the extension to width. Using a circular saw; keep the baseplate tight against the jig and move the saw smoothly through the board. Reposition the clamp when you near the end of the cut. Cut both side extensions to length and width, using the same technique as for the head extension (see TIP at left).

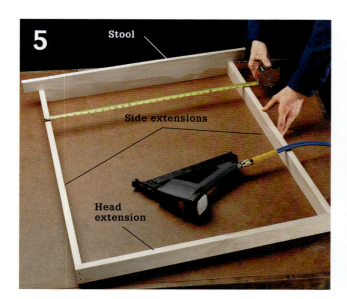

Build a box frame with the extensions and stool, using 6d finish nails and a pneumatic nailer. Measure to make sure the box has the same dimensions as the window jambs. Drive nails through the top of the head extension into the side extensions and through the bottom of the stool into side extensions.

Apply wood glue to the back edge of the frame, and position it against the front edge of the window jambs. Use wood shims to adjust the frame, making sure the pieces are flush with the window jambs. Fasten the frame at each shim location, using 8d finish nails driven through pilot holes. Loosely pack insulation between the studs and the jambs, or use minimal-expanding spray foam.

(continued)

7

Reveal mark

Reveal

On the edge of each jamb or jamb extension, mark a ³⁄₁₆" to ¼" reveal. Place a length of casing along the head extension, aligned with the reveal marks at the corners. Mark where the reveal marks intersect; then make 45° miter cuts at each point. Reposition the casing at the head extension and attach, using 4d finish nails at the extensions and 6d finish nails at the framing members.

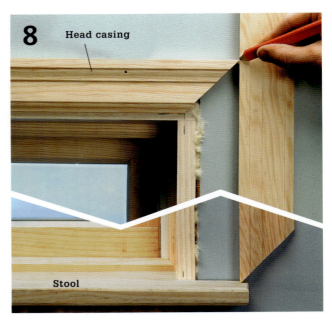

8

Head casing

Stool

Cut the side casings to rough length, leaving the ends slightly long for final trimming. Miter one end at 45°. With the pointed end on the stool, mark the height of the side casing at the top edge of the head casing.

9

To get a tight fit for side casings, align one side of a T-bevel with the reveal, mark the side extension and position the other side flush against the horn. Transfer the angle from the T-bevel to the end of the casing, and cut the casing to length.

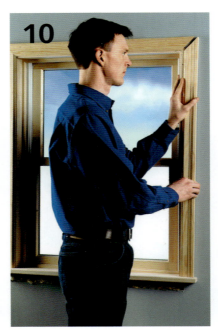

10

Test-fit the casings, making any final adjustments with a plane or rasp. Fasten the casing with 4d finish nails at the extensions and 6d finish nails at the framing members.

11

Cut the apron to length, leaving a few inches at each end for creating the returns (step 3). Position the apron tight against the bottom edge of the stool, and then attach it, using 6d finish nails driven every 12".

WIRES & CABLE

Wires are made of copper, aluminum, or aluminum covered with a thin layer of copper. Solid copper wires are the best conductors of electricity and are the most widely used. Aluminum and copper-covered aluminum wires require special installation techniques.

A group of two or more wires enclosed in a metal, rubber, or plastic sheath is called a cable. The sheath protects the wires from damage. Metal conduit also protects wires, but it is not considered a cable.

Individual wires are covered with rubber or plastic vinyl insulation. An exception is a bare copper grounding wire, which does not need an insulation cover. The insulation is color coded (chart, below) to identify the wire as a hot wire, a neutral wire, or a grounding wire.

In most wiring systems installed after 1965, the wires and cables are insulated with plastic vinyl. This type of insulation is very durable and can last as long as the house itself.

Before 1965, wires and cables were insulated with rubber. Rubber insulation has a life expectancy of about 25 years. Old insulation that is cracked or damaged can be reinforced temporarily by wrapping the wire with plastic electrical tape. However, old wiring with cracked or damaged insulation should be inspected by a qualified electrician to make sure it is safe.

Wires must be large enough for the amperage rating of the circuit (chart, right). A wire that is too small can become dangerously hot. Wire sizes are categorized according to the American Wire Gauge (AWG) system. To check the size of a wire, use the wire stripper openings of a combination tool (page 325) as a guide.

Wire Color Chart ▸

Wire color		Function
	White	Neutral wire carrying current at zero voltage.
	Black	Hot wire carrying current at full voltage.
	Red	Hot wire carrying current at full voltage.
	White, black markings	Hot wire carrying current at full voltage.
	Green	Serves as a grounding pathway.
	Bare copper	Serves as a grounding pathway.

Individual wires are color-coded to identify their function. In some circuit installations, the white wire serves as a hot wire that carries voltage. If so, this white wire may be labeled with black tape or paint to identify it as a hot wire.

Wire Size Chart ▸

Wire gauge		Wire capacity & use
	#6	60 amps, 240 volts; central air conditioner, electric furnace.
	#8	40 amps, 240 volts; electric range, central air conditioner.
	#10	30 amps, 240 volts; window air conditioner, clothes dryer.
	#12	20 amps, 120 volts; light fixtures, receptacles, microwave oven.
	#14	15 amps, 120 volts; light fixtures, receptacles.
	#16	Light-duty extension cords.
	#18 to 22	Thermostats, doorbells, security systems.

Wire sizes (shown actual size) are categorized by the American Wire Gauge system. The larger the wire size, the smaller the AWG number.

WIRES & CABLE: CONNECTING

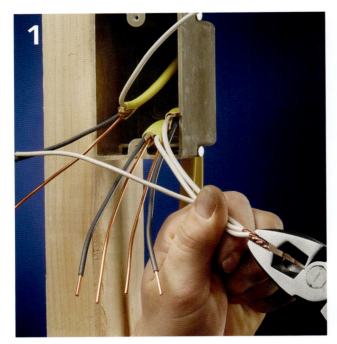

Ensure power is off and test for power. Grasp the wires to be joined in the jaws of a pair of linesman's pliers. The ends of the wires should be flush and they should be parallel and touching. Rotate the pliers clockwise two or three turns to twist the wire ends together.

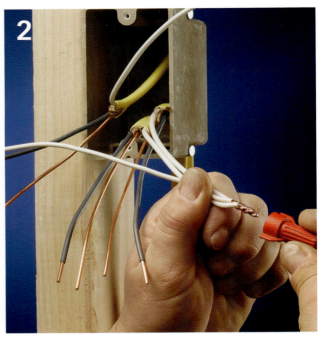

Twist a wire connector over the ends of the wires. Make sure the connector is the right size (see page 571). Hand-twist the connector as far onto the wires as you can. There should be no bare wire exposed beneath the collar of the connector.

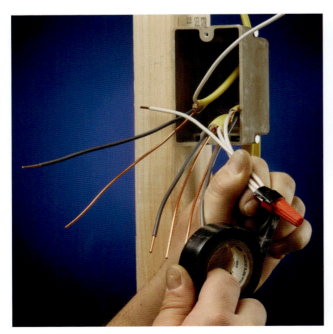

Option: Reinforce the joint by wrapping it with electrician's tape. By code, you cannot bind the wire joint with tape only, but it can be used as insurance. Few professional electricians use tape for purposes other than tagging wires for identification.

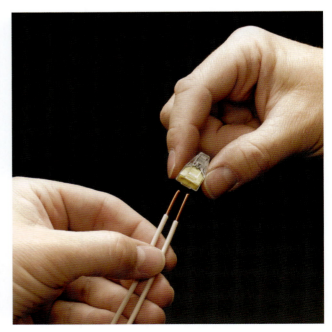

Option: Strip ¾" of insulation off the ends of the wires to be joined, and insert each wire into a push-in connector. Gently tug on each wire to make sure it is secure.

HOW TO PIGTAIL WIRES

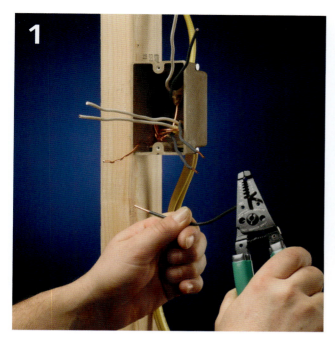

Cut a 6" length from a piece of insulated wire the same gauge and color as the wires it will be joining. Strip ¾" of insulation from each end of the insulated wire. *Note: Pigtailing is done mainly to avoid connecting multiple wires to one terminal, which is a code violation.*

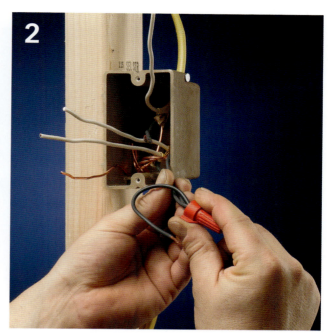

Join one end of the pigtail to the wires that will share the connection using a wire nut (see previous page).

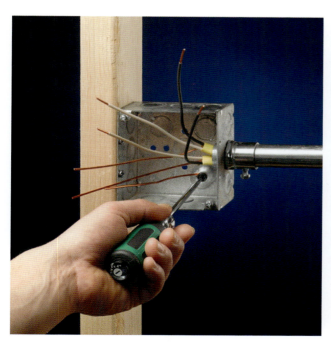

Alternative: If you are pigtailing to a grounding screw or grounding clip in a metal box, you may find it easier to attach one end of the wire to the grounding screw before you attach the other end to the other wires.

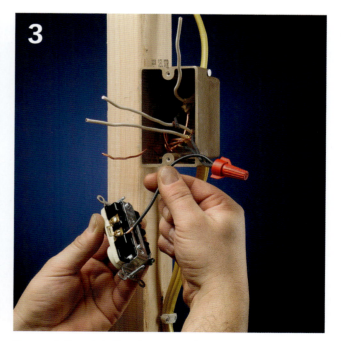

Connect the pigtail to the appropriate terminal on the receptacle or switch. Fold the wires neatly and press the fitting into the box.

WIRES & CABLE: INSTALLING IN WALLS

From the unfinished space below the finished wall, look for a reference point, like a soil stack, plumbing pipes, or electrical cables, that indicates the location of the wall above. Choose a location for the new cable that does not interfere with existing utilities. Drill a 1" hole up into the stud cavity.

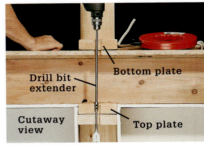

From the unfinished space above the finished wall, find the top of the stud cavity by measuring from the same fixed reference point used in step 1. Drill a 1" hole down through the top plate and into the stud cavity using a drill bit extender.

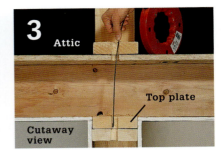

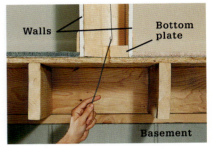

Extend a fish tape down through the top plate, twisting the tape until it reaches the bottom of the stud cavity. From the unfinished space below the wall, use a piece of stiff wire with a hook on one end to retrieve the fish tape through the drilled hole in the bottom plate.

Trim back 2" of sheathing from the end of the NM cable, then insert the wires through the loop at the tip of the fish tape.

Bend the wires against the cable, then use electrical tape to bind them tightly. Apply cable-pulling lubricant to the taped end of the fish tape.

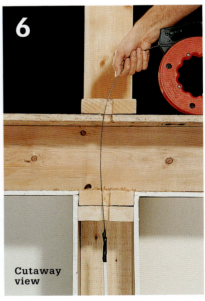

From above the finished wall, pull steadily on the fish tape to draw the cable up through the stud cavity. This job will be easier if you have a helper feed the cable from below as you pull.

WIRING

RUNNING CABLE INSIDE FINISHED WALLS

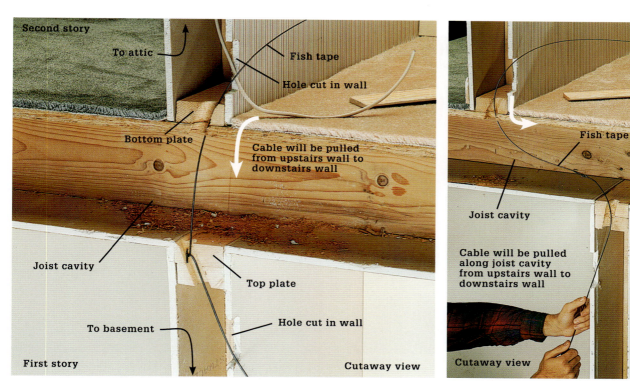

If there is no access space above and below a wall, cut openings in the finished walls to run a cable. This often occurs in two-story homes when a cable is extended from an upstairs wall to a downstairs wall. Cut small openings in the wall near the top and bottom plates, then drill an angled 1" hole through each plate. Extend a fish tape into the joist cavity between the walls and use it to pull the cable from one wall to the next. If the walls line up one over the other (left), you can retrieve the fish tape using a piece of stiff wire. If walls do not line up (right), use a second fish tape. After running the cable, repair the holes in the walls with patching plaster or wallboard scraps and taping compound.

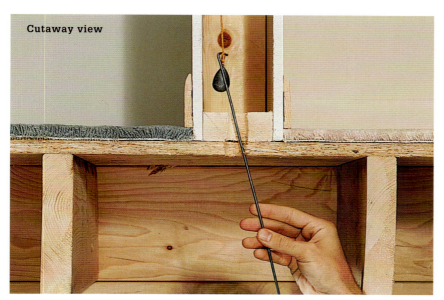

If you don't have a fish tape, use a length of sturdy string and a lead weight or heavy washer. Drop the line into the stud cavity from above, then use a piece of stiff wire to hook the line from below.

Use a flexible drill bit, also called a bell-hanger's bit, to bore holes through framing in finished walls.

WOOD FINISH: APPLYING

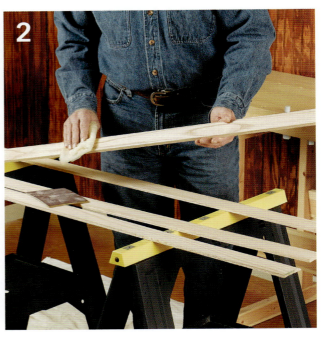

Set up the work station area with two sawhorses and a drop cloth or sheet of cardboard on the floor. Place the trim pieces to be finished on the horses. Inspect each piece for large blemishes or flaws, repairing any large splinters.

Sand each piece as necessary, finishing with a fine-grit paper. Wipe the moldings with a clean, dry cloth to remove any leftover dust.

If desired, apply a coat of stain to the moldings with a foam or bristle brush. For more even coverage of the stain, apply a pre-stain wood conditioner. Follow the manufacturer's instructions for stain drying time, and remove the excess with a clean rag.

Let the stain dry sufficiently and apply the first thin coat of polyurethane with a brush. Stir the polyurethane frequently before you begin, between coats, and during application. Let the finish dry for four to six hours.

After the finish has dried, lightly sand the entire surface with 220-grit sandpaper. This will ensure a smooth finish with a strong bond between layers. If the sandpaper gums up quickly, the moldings need more time to dry.

Wipe the moldings with a clean, dry rag to remove any dust. Apply a second layer of polyurethane. Check each piece for skipped areas and heavy drips of urethane. These areas need to be corrected as soon as possible or they may show through the final coat.

Let the moldings dry for four to six hours and lightly sand the entire surface with 220-grit sandpaper.

Apply a third and final coat of polyurethane to the moldings. Keep the third coat very thin, using only the tip of the brush to apply it. Lightly drag the tip across the molding on the flat areas. If the moldings have deep grooves or intricate details, skip these areas; two coats will be sufficient. Try to maintain constant pressure and avoid smashing the brush as this will create air bubbles in your finish. Allow the moldings to dry for a minimum of 12 hours (check the manufacturer's recommended drying times).

CLEAR-COAT FINISHING TIPS

Seal brushes in a plastic bag to avoid the necessity of cleaning the brush between coats. Wear latex gloves to protect your hands, especially when working with oil-based products.

Choose a brush that's well-suited for the application. If applying finish to round trim pieces with irregular surfaces, like the Victorian fretwork above, select a brush that's roughly the same width as the diameter of the workpieces.

Always stir urethane products to properly mix them. Never shake them. Shaking creates tiny air bubbles in the product that will follow to your project. Before opening the can, roll it gently upside down a few times to loosen the settled material from the bottom.

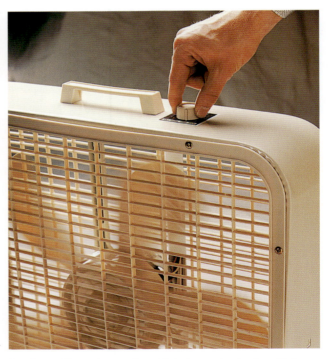

Apply urethane in a well-ventilated area. Lack of ventilation or heavily applied product will result in longer drying times. If you use a fan to increase ventilation, aim it away from the project: do not blow air directly on the project or dust and other contaminants will adhere to your finish.

WOOD SHAKES & SHINGLES

Double-course installation offers a greater look of depth between rows. Each course of shingles is installed ½" lower than an undercourse that's placed beneath it. A lower-grade, less-expensive shingle is typically used for the undercourse.

Staggered butt–course installation features a random, three-dimensional look. The application starts with a double starter row, and shingles in overlapping courses are staggered by up to 1".

VARIATIONS FOR CORNER INSTALLATIONS

Woven corners have shingles that overlap at the corners for a weave effect. This overlap alternates between walls with each successive course.

Mitered corners are made by cutting corner shingles at a 45° angle and butting them together. This method is very time-consuming.

HOW TO INSTALL SINGLE-COURSE WOOD SHAKES & SHINGLES

Cover the exterior sheathing with felt paper. Starting at the bottom of a wall, install the paper horizontally using staples. Wrap corners a minimum of 4". Overlap vertical seams 6" and horizontal seams 2". Cut out openings around doors and windows.

Starting at the lowest corner of the house, snap a level chalk line at the bottom of each wall where the siding will start. Measure the height of the wall from the chalk line to the soffits.

To determine the exposure of the shingles—the amount of wood revealed beneath the overlap—divide the wall height by the number of proposed rows. The goal is to find an exposure measurement that can be multiplied by a whole number to equal the wall height—a 120" wall can have twelve rows with a 10" exposure, for example. Create a story pole on a straight 1 × 3 by making a series of marks equal to the exposure. *Tip: It's best for rows to align with the tops and bottoms of doors and windows.*

Place the story pole at a corner, aligning the bottom with the chalk line. Transfer the marks onto the wall. Do this at each corner, door, and window location.

Place a 1 × 3 board at an outside corner, aligning it with the chalk line at the bottom. Keep the outside edge flush with the adjacent wall. Nail it in place. Overlap the edge of the board with a 1 × 4, align it with the chalk line, and nail in place. If more than one trim board is needed to span the length of the wall, miter the ends at 45° and place them together. Do this for all outside corners. *Tip: As soon as you cut a shingle or piece of trim, apply sealer to the cut edge.*

Fasten a 2 × 2 in an inside corner flush with the chalk line at the bottom. If more than one board is needed to span the height of the wall, miter the adjoining ends at 45° and butt them together.

If the chalk line is hard to see, run a string from the bottom of the corner trim pieces. Starting at a corner, install the starter row of shingles ½" above the chalk line. Keep the manufacturer's recommended distance between shingles and between shingles and trim, usually a ⅛ to ¼" gap. Keep nails ¾" from edges and 1" above the line of exposure.

Place the first course of shingles over the starter row flush with the chalk line at the bottom. Overlap the seams in the starter course by at least 1½".

(continued)

EXTERIOR

Snap a chalk line across the shingles to mark the exposure using the reference lines from step 4. Install a course of shingles at the chalk line, offsetting the seams. Install remaining rows the same way.

Option: To ensure straight lines, tack a 1 × 4 flush with your reference lines. Nail the board through gaps between shingles. Use the board as a guide for installing the shingles.

Cut shingles to fit around doors, windows, and protrusions in the walls using a coping saw or handsaw. Make sure gaps between shingles aren't aligned with the edges of doors and windows. *Tip: Whenever possible, plan your layout so you can install full shingles next to doors and windows rather than cutting shingles to fit.*

Cut and install the tops of shingles over windows and doors. Align the tops with adjacent shingles on either side of the door or window.

When applying shingles on a dormer or above a roof line, keep the bottom edge of the shingles ½" above the roof shingles. Cut shingles with a handsaw or circular saw.

Measure and cut the last row of shingles to fit under the horizontal eaves. Leave the recommended gap between shingles and soffits. Nail the shingles in place.

Use a T-bevel to determine the roof angle on the gable end of the house. Cut shingles at this angle for each row at the gable end using a handsaw or circular saw. Install shingles up to the peak. *Tip: As you near the top of a wall, measure from the soffits to the shingles on each side of the wall. If the measurements aren't equal, make small adjustments in successive rows until the distance is the same.*

Caulk around all doors, windows, protrusions, and corner trim. Apply your choice of stain or primer and paint (see Painting: Exteriors, starting on page 298).

KEYWORDS

INDEX

A

abrasive pads
  paint preparation, 296, 297
  refinishing floors, 234
ABS pipes
  cutting, 94–95
  solvent gluing, 96–97
abuse-resistant drywall, 133
acoustic tiles, 62–63
aerators, 161
AFCI circuits, smoke detectors and, 419
alarms
  CO, 419
  heat, 419
  smoke, 419–420
aluminum siding
  patching, 392
  replacing end caps, 392
American Wire Gauge sizes, 571
angle grinders, 563
anti-scald valves, 176
appliances
  dishwashers, 76–79
  in electric circuits, 138–139
  food disposers, 192–195
  high-efficiency, 12
  high-voltage receptacles, 342
  icemakers
    about, 243–244
    connecting, 244–245
    installation of new, 246–248
  range hoods, 339–340
  water heaters
    gas vs. electric, 545
    installation, 540–544
    maintaining, 547
    repairing electric, 546–547, 550–551
    repairing gas, 546–549
asphalt shingles
  about, 364
  buckled/cupped, 352, 354
  damaged, 352
  installing, 365–371
  obstructions and, 366–368
  reattaching loose, 354
  removing old, 346
  replacing, 355
  surface area and, 345
attics
  insulation, 13
  leak evaluation and, 353
  skylight shafts and, 415–418
  vent fans and, 521
  ventilation
    continuous soffit vents, 357
    ridge vents, 357
    roof vents, 359
augers, 407
aviation snips
  aluminum fascia and, 147–148
  drip edge and, 348
  metal cornerbead and, 98
  steel framing, 440
  suspended ceilings, 451

B

back blockers, installation, 119
backsplashes, 474–476
balancing valves, 176
balusters, 438
baseboard heaters
  end-cap thermostats, 240
  installation, 239–240
  multiple heaters, 240
  planning, 238
basements
  egress windows
    building codes, 561
    installation, 562–566
  exterior aprons, 14–15
  floors
    concrete, 8–11
    cracks in, 10
    finishing, 8
    leveling, 8–9
    patching, 10–11
    subfloor panels, 8
  furnace ducts, 13
  moisture and, 18–19
    preventing, 21
  rim joists
    insulating, 16–17
  sump pump installation, 448–449
  walls
    cracks, 20
    dry walls, 13
    exterior, 14–15
    framing, 202–203
    insulating, 12–16
    interior insulation, 16
  See also suspended ceilings
basin wrenches
  bathroom faucet installation and, 149–150
bathrooms
  bathtubs
    installation, 28–31
    sliding doors for, 33
  faucets
    ball-type, 167
    common problems, 160
    compression, 162–163
    disc-type, 168
    indentifying type, 159–161
    installing, 149–151
    one-handle cartridge, 165–166
    single-body, 152
    washerless two-handle, 164
  grab bars
    backing/blocking, 217
    installation, 218
  medicine cabinets
    recessed, 286
    surface-mounted, 285
  National Electrical Code and, 144
  showers
    door installation, 384–385
    enclosure installation, 386–390
  sink
    clogs in, 406
    drop-in installation, 27
    integral installation, 267
    pop-up drains, 404–405
  toilets
    clogs in, 502–505
    replacing, 506–509
  vanity cabinet installation, 24–25
  wall tile installation, 499–501
  whirlpool tubs, 552–556

bathtubs
  adjusting temperature, 176
  faucets
    deep-set valve removal, 173
    indentifying type, 169
    replacing tub spouts, 173
    scald control, 176
    single-handle, 174–176
    three-handle, 170–171
    two-handle, 172–173
  flexible shower adapters, 169
  grab bars, 217–218
  installation of, 28–31
  removal of deep-set faucet valves, 173
  sliding door installation, 31–35
  tub spouts
    replacing, 173
  whirlpool tub installation, 552–556
batt insulation, fiberglass
  about, 249
  installation, 250
beadboard, 13
beating blocks, 476
bedrooms, codes for, 144
bell-hanger's bit, 575
blanket insulation, 249
blueboard, 133
board and batten siding
  painting, 301
  replacing, 393
boilers, draining, 337
bracket-mounted fans, 60
brushes (paint)
  loading/distributing paint, 299
  polyurethane and, 578
  selecting, 299
  using, 300, 303
building codes
  cross-linked polyethylene (PEX) pipe, 313
  egress windows, 561
  stairways and, 430–435
  See also electrical codes

C

cabinets
  kitchen
    base installation, 256–257
    European hinge adjustment, 259
    face-frame, 258
    hanging installation, 253–255
    island installation, 260
    sink installation, 261
  medicine
    recessed, 286
    surface-mounted, 285
  undercabinet lights, 278–280
cables
  about, 571
  connecting, 572
  installing in walls, 574–575
  National Electrical Code and, 143
  pigtailing, 573
  sizes, 571
carbide grit blades, 471
carbon monoxide detectors, 419
carpet
  about installing, 36
  carpet square installation, 52–55